A History of Henry County Virginia

WITH

BIOGRAPHICAL SKETCHES
OF ITS MOST PROMINENT
MEN AND WOMEN

AND

GENEALOGICAL HISTORIES
OF HALF A HUNDRED OF ITS
OLDEST FAMILIES

Judith Parks America Hill

HERITAGE BOOKS
2008

HERITAGE BOOKS
AN IMPRINT OF HERITAGE BOOKS, INC.

Books, CDs, and more—Worldwide

For our listing of thousands of titles see our website
at
www.HeritageBooks.com

A Facsimile Reprint
Published 2008 by
HERITAGE BOOKS, INC.
Publishing Division
100 Railroad Ave. #104
Westminster, Maryland 21157

Originally published
Martinsville, Virginia
1925

Copyright © 2003 Heritage Books, Inc.

— Publisher's Notice —
In reprints such as this, it is often not possible to remove blemishes from the original. We feel the contents of this book warrant its reissue despite these blemishes and hope you will agree and read it with pleasure.

International Standard Book Numbers
Paperbound: 978-0-7884-2302-4
Clothbound: 978-0-7884-7184-1

	Page
CHAPTER I	7
(Location, Geography and Original Inhabitants)	
CHAPTER II	15
(The Revolution to the Civil War)	
CHAPTER III	25
(From the War between the States to the present time)	
CHAPTER IV	28
(Courts, Musters and Plantation Life)	
CHAPTER V	40
(The High Schools of Henry County)	
CHAPTER VI	46
(The Churches of Henry County)	
CHAPTER VII	52
(Towns and Societies)	
CHAPTER VIII	61
(Biographies)	
CHAPTER IX	110
(Family Histories)	
APPENDIX	293
(Abstracts of Henry County Legislative Petitions and other Henry County Data)	

THIS book is affectionately inscribed to my dearly beloved pupils of fifty-two YEARS of teaching.

      Lovingly,

   "Miss Judie," (J. P. A. HILL).

MISS J. P. A. HILL

Preface

This History was not begun with the intention of writing a book for the public but merely to produce a family booklet. As time wore on and I found myself connected with so many of the families of the County, I determined that I would use my best endeavors to get as much information about the facts and families as I could. History is an important study. It has been said that if history were taken away the world would go back into savagery. While I am merely compiling information obtained from others, I feel most deeply the many imperfections in my part of this work. I hope all will read this book with an impartial mind as it is most assuredly a labor of love in preserving the memory of our forefathers. I have been compelled to leave out my reminiscences in order to make room for contributed matter of more interest to the general reader.

This book is too small to relate many of the glowing incidents that have transpired in the County and it is with genuine regret and through no lack of appreciation that the long roll of World War Soldiers is left out of this book through want of space. Henry County has been represented in every war we have had. She has sent out her citizens to every State. We are told by Mrs. Julian C. Lane, who is writing a history of the early settlers of Georgia, that nearly one-half of these early settlers were from Henry County, Virginia. This County is represented from Ocean to Ocean and from the Lakes to the Gulf. Her sons have given their life-blood to uphold what they believed to be right and her daughters have never failed to do their part.

Many important matters have been omitted from this History because data was not at my disposal. I am greatly indebted to the writings of Col. C. B. Bryant. Many have unearthed old Bible facts and family histories. To all such I extend my most heartfelt thanks. To Judge

Whittle for his contribution on Patrick Henry Academy; Rev. J. B. Allen fo rhis encouraging words, his canvassing work, his subscriptions obtained and his offer of pecuniary aid to tide the work over; Miss E. R. Traylor for encouraging words, her extreme kindness in research work, her subscriptions and pictures furnished; Rev. Marshall Wingfield for his most valuable research work; Asst. Librarian of William & Mary College; and last, but not least, to Dr. J. B. Deshazo for his untiring labor in condensing my data, for his many trips to and fro and visits to homes in search of data and also for his contributed articles.

I also extend my warmest thanks to the subscribers. I trust all will feel repaid for time and money expended.

JUDITH P. A. HILL.

Martinsville, Virginia,
July 4, 1925.

CHAPTER I

LOCATION, GEOGRAPHY AND ORIGINAL INHABITANTS

HENRY COUNTY is in Piedmont, Virginia, bordering on the North Carolina line and lies south of the 37th parallel of latitude, and just east of the 80th degree of longitude. It is hilly or rolling with plains and bottom land, each in great plently and variety. Two peaks, the Nance Mountain and Chestnut Knob, are greater than the hills and from the summit of the latter, a beautiful view of the five largest valleys of Smith and Mayo rivers, Marrowbone, Leatherwood and Horsepasture creeks, as well as the other chief towns and most noted residences, is the delight of every tourist here and on each it leaves everlasting memories.

The county was formed in 1776 from Pittsylvania county. The latter was cut out from Halifax in 1767, while Lunenburg gave origin to Halifax in 1752. In 1748, Brunswick was divided to form Lunenburg. Two counties, Isle of Wight and Surry, contributed to make Brunswick in 1720. The county of Surry was taken from James City county in 1652, and here we cease the division for Isle of Wight and James City counties were original shires, there being only eight in Virginia.

FIRST INHABITANTS

The Indians peopled the river and creek valleys in large numbers. These, here located, belonged to the great Algonquin family and this was the lower border of the tribe. The Cherokees were their neighbors on the south, in Carolina. The men engaged in hunting, fishing and fighting, while the women raised corn, beans and tobacco and reared the children. Only legends tell of the fierce combats of the warriors along the banks of Smith's river and the Marrowbone. Throughout the county flints and Indian axes have been found, and large pieces of pottery also, that prove they were artists of no mean order in their handiwork. Near Ridgeway, on the north side, is a large soapstone hill literally covered with broken pieces of crockery showing that they were made here for a long period. One large pot, that would hold three gallons, was found almost complete near this hill but the slaves in ante-bellum days broke most of these pieces of crockery, however, many are preserved as relics of this departed race.

The easiest way to travel, being up stream, it is not a wonder that Smith and Mayo rivers and the two largest creeks in the eastern part of the county were first inhabited. These settlements were scattered many times a mile or more apart and the land was granted often in large tracts for a small consideration. Unfortunately we can not name the original white inhabitants for no volume preceded this on the subject, and traditions, and notes with old letters give what is really authentic.

The first to come were just the overflow that backed up from Dan and Smith rivers, together with the typical backwoodsmen that loved adventure and moved again to the wilds whenever crowded by neighbors. They never were the victims of an Indian Massacre, but the dread of one, hovered over the county for a hundred years.

A distinguished British writer and traveller traversed the county in 1774 and described the appearance of the central section when the people were in a panic over a report that the Indians had taken up the hatchet. He wrote, "There were several large plantations on the rich low grounds of Leatherwood and Beaver creeks deserted, not a single inhabitant to be seen. The cattle and horses, etc., were wandering about their masters' habitations conveying the most mournful melancholy and dismal ideas that can be easily conceived." He told of finding a mill on Beaver creek with the hopper half full of corn, the miller left in such haste; and finally finding the entire populace in the fort (Fort Trial) on Smith river all huddled together in the most woeful and unsanitary condition. It was only by searching the community for miles around, without finding an Indian, that he could allay the alarm of the inhabitants.

The same writer reported traveling a long distance prior to reaching the Lower Saura Town settlements on Dan river opposite Leaksville's present site, without seeing a habitation. He followed a "blazed" path on the east side of Smith river till he reached Leatherwood creek and saw no houses, just a few friendly Indians.

Since the earliest grants of the county now on record at Lunenburg Court-house which was made a county in

THE COURT HOUSE AND SOLDIERS MONUMENT
Martinsville, Va.

1748, showing Smith river and Marrowbone valleys, then a part of that county, few, indeed must have been the genuine settlers here at that date, if any, and most likely, as late as 1746 when this county became a part of Brunswick, there were not many hundred bona fide homes, but from 1750 to 1775 there was a great influx.

In 1770, George Hairston, the father of "Old Rusty," came and bought 30,000 acres of land. A little later John Dillard came from Amherst county, and three years later in 1773, Joseph Martin arrived and settled in the north-eastern part of the county at "Belle Monte," and in 1779, Patrick Henry came in the summer and built a home, "Leatherwood," on a tract of 10,000 acres he had previously been granted and purchased. The site of this old house is marked by a monument erected by the D. A. R's. About this time there was a great rush for thousand acre farms and soon most of the valuable land, especially on the streams, was appropriated.

From 1750 till the end of this period, agriculture was rapidly developing under the stimulus of slavery and the plantation system. About this period, tradition, undoubtedly true, tells us that one of the early settlers, George King, learned the use of plow-lines, and how to make furrows horizontal instead of going up and down hill, and strange to relate before this demonstration, two men always attended, one to lead the horse and the other to hold the plow. At a much later period another citizen of Leatherwood claimed to have built the first rockflue in a tobacco barn to cure the leaf.

The "Telegraph Apparatus" to bring water from the spring to the farmers' houses, came later and if not invented in the county, certainly was popularized in this part of the State. These things show that the people of the county have not only been inventors themselves but always have been boosters of inventions that improved farming operations. (This does not mean to include the churn of Cartwright.)

In 1728, during the month of October, Col. William Byrd wrote of locating the State line between Henry County, Va., and North Carolina, that they crossed the river Irvin, so christened in honor of the Professor with his party, and surveyed six miles during the day, and camped on the west side of Matrimony creek "So called by an unfortunate marry'd man because it was exceedingly noisy and impetuous."

From here looking to the northwest about four miles, he saw a round point that he named "Wart" mountain. This was evidently the Holt Knob, the last spur of the Chestnut Knob highlands. He made no note of any inhabitants along here, nor at any place to the Stokes line. The following day they traversed five miles killed a turkey and a bear and camped next about where Price is to-day.

After describing the rough hills at the junction of North and South Mayo, named for one of the engineers, he stated that they brought into camp six bears; he said, "They pitched their camp on the west side for the purpose of being lulled to sleep by the cataract." Let us pause a moment: think of this eternal song of the waters here, through sunshine and shadows of two centuries, which was just as soothing and fascinating to them as to the living of this day!

FORT TRIAL

The General Assembly in March 1756, ordered a chain of forts to be built along the frontier, the last, of course, to be near the State line. George Washington left Winchester Sept. 29th, 1756, to visit the forts and wrote later that he visited Fort Trial on Smith river. He then had the opportunity to see the county in October, its mast, chestnuts, and forests teeming with wild game —the golden foliage and glorious sunsets.

About 18 years later, the latter part of May, 1774, Capt. J. F. D. Smythe, formerly an army officer of England, visited the fort on his tour through Virginia and gives a good description of the location two or three miles above the mouth of Beaver creek, on the bank of the river. His notes say: "The fort is situated on an eminence that commands a very fine view of Smith river for several miles and of the confluence of Beaver creek, but it is only the low grounds of the river and creek up the northeast side that can be perceived, the lofty timber on the opposite bank of the river effectually prevents any greater distance being seen."

The fort was built in the form of a square. The walls were made of split trees planted in the earth four feet close together and sixteen feet high above the ground with holes cut the proper height to use firearms. There was a bastion at each corner, and a log house, musket proof, at each side of the gate. Within the area of the fort near the center was a common framed house and between the outer and inner walls it was filled with stones and earth to the height of six feet as an additional defense.

The fort was not used alone by the soldiers in protecting the frontier, but in time of alarm to this the whole population scurried for protection. Later on the Indians were driven back and this no longer being needed, the fortification was abandoned with the other fourteen of its era. As this site is across the creek from the National Highway, it is destined to be a stopping place of historic interest to tourists.

This county was pitched upon the pages of history amid the stirring days of 1776, just after the Declaration of Independence, consequently it was christened in a baptism of fire, for just now the Revolutionary War was spreading in its greatest fury and the hearts of the patriots were throbbing for freedom.

By an act of the Assembly of October that year, the first county court was held at the home of John Rowland, on the third Monday in January, 1777. The records show that 630 took the oath of allegiance to the United States, and around forty refused to renounce theirs to Great Britain. Many had joined the army under Washington, as may be seen in the biographical chapter in this volume, besides many were away hunting or trading at this time, for there was certainly a much larger male citizenry in the entire county.

In her youth and from her scattered homes, the county furnished only one organized body of troops to the nation. This was under Col. Abram Penn and began the march from Beaver creek March 11th, 1781, crossed Rowland's ford just below Fontaine followed the old road, deep cuts now showing its location, up the Marrowbone valley crossing the creek west of where Ridgeway now stands, thence along the ridge two miles, then crossed Matrimony creek half a mile, to the State line (only one mile of this from the Marrowbone home of "Old Rusty" Hairston to the National Highway is now used for a public road). From the line south their route is not known, however, they marched so rapidly they soon reached General Green and took part in the battle of Guilford Court House on March 25th, 1781. This battle was not decisive and was followed by a lull. Again we hear of them at Eutaw Springs, and finally Yorktown crowned their glory on Oct. 19th, 1781.

It should be remembered that in the following list of those with Col. Penn and his Adjutant, Major George Waller, many prominent names do not appear, but the reason is they were in the Northern army under Washington, or had served their terms of enlistment and had been honorably discharged.

SOLDIERS WHO LEFT FROM HENRY COUNTY FOR THE REVOLUTIONARY ARMY

The county was formed while the Revolutionary War was going on and many joined other commands before the first and only body of organized troops left the county to join the warring Army under General Green.

Of those who had been in service before this body of troops left in March, 1781, we have collected the names of some from the county, viz: Maj. Thomas Cooper, William DeShazo, George Dyer, Peter France, Col. John Fontaine, James Johnson, Dr. Benjamin Jones, John King, Jacob Koger, Jacob McCraw, David Mullins, John Salmons, James Shelton, George King, Daniel Burchel, Thomas Fleuman, William Hopper, Moses Spencer, Griffin Griffith, Elisha Arnold, Michael Burns, Lewis Franklin, Newsum Pace, Charles Philpott, John Price, Wm. Shackleford, Benjamin Stratton, Samuel Shumate, Axton Whitecotton and Maj. John Redd.

NAMES OF MILITIAMEN WHO MARCHED TO THE ASSISTANCE OF GEN. GREEN AT GUILFORD COURT HOUSE, MARCH 11, 1781

Abram Penn, Col. Commanding, Maj. George Waller, Adjutant, First Captain, Jonathan Hamby, Second Captain, David Lanier, Third Captain, George Hairston. Lieutenants: 1st, Edward Tatum, 2nd, Isaac Cloud, Josiah Shaw, Joshua Rentfro. First Sergeant, Robt. Watson, Second Sergeant, John Smith. Ensigns: James Prathey, Jesse Corn.

Hamon Critz's Company: Charles Dotson, Patrick Ewel, Thomas Lockhart, William Dotson, Deverix Gilliam, Patterson Childers, S. William Going, William Smith, S. Daniel Swilwant.

John Cunningham's Company: Joseph Cunningham, Thomas Hollinsworth, Nathan Beal, Josiah Turner, Mumford Perryman, Samuel Packwood, William Turner, Daniel Smith, Reuben Webster.

HISTORY OF HENRY COUNTY, VIRGINIA

James Cowdin's Company: John Robertson, Stephen Herd, Jesse Hall, Dudley Mileham, William Hodges, Thomas Watson, William Cheek, Joseph Channel, Charles Summerdale, John Arthur, Jordan Mileham.

S. Tarrant's Company: John Carrol, Phillip Brashears, Humphrey Scroggins, Thomas Scroggins, Richard Gilley, John Wilson, Sr., John Wilson, Jr., William Moore, Archie Murphey, John Farris, Thomas Edwards, John Gray, John Rea, John Davis, William Cox, Jacob Stalings.

Thomas Smith's Company: William Stewart, John Hurd, James Strange, Henry Smith, Francis Tillston, Jesse Burnett, Thomas Hurd, George Stewart, David Atkins, Jonathan Pratt, George Bowles, Henry Law.

Peter Hairston's Company: Joseph Perregoy, Joseph Pearson, William Bowling, Jarratt Martin, John Aragan, Nathan Jones, William Brown, John Nance, Joseph Bowling.

James Tarrant's Company: Joseph Gravely, Robert Tate, James Bryant, son of Warren, Henry Warren, John Burch, Charles Dickerson, Edward Smith, John Doyal, Samuel Wane, William Elkins, James Cox.

Thomas Henderson's Company: Richard Reynolds, Samuel Hoof, Michael Barker, Alexander Jones, Thomas Small, James Crawley, Joseph Hurt, William Bramham, John Branham, Barnabas Branham, John Edwards, John Gibson, Joel Barbour, George Folly, Moses Arms, William Brainbridge.

Elephaz Shelton's Company: Francis Barrat, James Barrat, Matthew Sims, Jacob Adams, William McGhee, Thomas Harrisby, Jacob Arnols, Thomas Hudson, Shadrack Barrett, Hezekiah Harris, John Carrol.

John Hanby's Company: Dudley Stephens, Ben Hensley, John Bowman, Joshua Stephens, John Cartwell, John Howell, Nelson Donothan, John Chandler, Henry Hensley, Hickman Hensley.

James Poteet's Company: Peter Bays, Ninon Prater, Ben Hubbard, John Ratford, John Sneed, Joseph Street, Stephen Watkins, Thomas Tinson, George Nevil, Peter Tittle, Charles Hibbert, Joseph Perregoy, Richard Potson, William Elliott, John Mullins, Ambrose Mullins, Joseph Waldin, Acquilla Black.

Brice Martin's Company: John Rea, John Cox, Nathaniel Tate, James Barker, Archibald Hatcher, Thomas Jones, Abraham Moore, James Billings, John Prytle, Joseph Piper, Peleg Rogers, John Pursell, Michael Rowland, Henry Tate, Peter Mitchell.

John Rentfro's Company: Robert English, John Kelly, Thomas Welch, Thomas Harris, Thomas Bell, Ebenezer Pryatt, Abraham Jones, William Dunn, Isaac Jones, James Grier, John Miles, Samuel Fox.

Owen Ruble's Company: Robert Grimmet, Phillip Massey, John Atkins, David Atkins, Richard Copeland, William Mullins, John Stanley, William Bohanan, Joseph Davis, John Brammer.

Swinfield Hill's Company: Soloman Davis, George Fargason, Ambrose Warren, William Stewart, Anderson McGuire, John Holloday, Doziar Grinnet, Josiah Woods, John Woods. Jeremiah Holloday, William Dellingham, William Thompson, William Bartee, David Peake, Obediah Graves, John Graham.

Lanier's Company: William Hays, Noble Johnson, John Alexander, Fisher Allen, Alexander Joyce, David Mays, John Richardson, Sadwick Kiziah, John East, Charles Denham, Joseph Anglin, Howell, Ivey, John Bowling, James Pratley, Ham McCain, Hans Hambleton.

George Hairston's Company: Richard Parsley, Joseph Brackley, Samuel Jamerson, Arristophus Baughn, John Kitchen, John Jamerson, John Rivers, John Crouch, John Jones, Lewis Bradberry, Thomas Finch, Jesse Elkins, James Davis.

James Dillard's Company: William Fee, Jesse Witt, James Roberts, John Atkins, John Taylor, William Roberts, Augustin Sims, Bartlett Reynolds, Morris Humphreys, Joseph Sewell, Josiah Smith, John DePriest, Thomas Hambleton.

Tully Choice's Company: Samuel Luttrel, Moses Broos, Joel Estes, William Bennet, Isaac Skidmore, William Long, Elisha Estes, John Wilkes, James Prunty, David Pruit, Noah Atkins, Daniel Richardson, Nathan Davis, Nathan Ryan.

Thomas Haile's Company: Jesse Cook, Jesse Coats, Joseph Haile, Peter Anderson, Joseph Richards.

John Fontaine's Company: James Rea, Thomas Doolings, George Pool,, John Willingham, Thomas Leak Thomas Parsley, Samuel Weaver, Stephen King, Alexander Barnes, Henry Mannings, Abraham Payne, William Graves, Joseph Rice, William Bledsoe.

CHAPTER II

THE REVOLUTION TO THE CIVIL WAR

THE British yoke had been thrown off and the country was independent but the county of Henry was much in evidence when the new Constitution of the United States was being ratified, for the head of the opposition to its strong central government was no other than Patrick Henry now a citizen of the county. No other question aroused the people so much, especially this county, since the struggle over Independence. The South feared that the great North would outweigh the influence of the South and the rights of States would be at the mercy of those who wanted a strong central government. Here was the beginning of the division of sentiment on the question, that was destined to be settled in fratricidal strife in a sea of brother's blood. But in 1788 Virginia ratified the Constitution, and soon thereafter amendments were adopted pacifying the opposition by guaranteeing certain rights heretofore in dispute, and the whole country entered upon the growing of the nation till it was destined before the end of this era to be a continent full of peace and prosperity with country homes; the primary unit of the very foundation of the structure.

The smoke of battles of the Revolution dissipated, showed the people of Henry county housed chiefly in hewed log buildings and no roadways worthy of the name; however, the rich virgin soil under the quickening touch of slave labor, produced the finest tobacco in the world, commanding the highest price and soon brought the reward of a golden harvest.

TOBACCO AND SLAVES

No other combination ever brought such rewards, such prosperity to the county, as tobacco and slavery. The use of barn flues, to cure the weed imparting to it a most delightful odor an unsurpassed flavor made the manufactured article from the county noted far abroad for its "Sweet Chew." The planters made, and they saved, and with the rapid rise in real estate values soon many splendid fortunes, for the day, were accumulated.

Here it should be recorded that for several generations, tobacco was packed in hogsheads with a large pole protruding through the center and out several inches at the ends, to which shafts were attached and otherwise rigged up. To these a shaft horse was hooked, and in this manner the 90 to 100 miles trip to the James river, at Lynchburg, was made by rolling up hill and down through streams and mud to that point, the nearest market.

Several generations after, the covered wagons became popular, the master driving and his dog attending under the hind axletree, but ere long these luxuries of bygone days pass their zenith and are relegated to second place. It is indeed a far cry from the days of rolling tobacco in the crude manner described to this day when the descendants of those hardy souls spin along in their benzine buggies, and three-ton trucks laden with the same popular cargo.

The county had not reached its fifteenth year when it was divided in 1791, and the western part to the mountains, took the name of Patrick after the Christian name of Virginia's greatest orator. A part of it was restored to this county in 1858, which has often been called New Henry when in reality it was, of course, a part of the old.

The poor transportation facilities and very limited number of newspapers, and slow mail services for a long time, resulted in the slow dissemination of news. A long period often elapsed before news of important events reached the county, however, when the tocsin of war sounded, her sons were ever in the front of the battles. The War of 1812, and the Mexican war of 1845 and 46 found the county well represented and their deeds will long be read of and gloried in by their successors and descendants. As the most of this history is noted in the chapters of personal sketches and family histories, it will not be here presented.

Such questions as tariff or no tariff disturbed this section but little for most of their requirements were met at home, made there. So long as the people's rights were not restricted and they added wealth to their families, government was of very great interest to but few. By the very nature of things they were too far

The county elections were run in a simple manner for four generations and were always held at the county seat. The head of a barrel of whisky was knocked out, the name of the candidate, nearly always of some prominent family, was announced, drinks were distributed and the voting began. Every eligible voter (for several generations 20 acres of land were to be possessed to be a qualified voter) "Cried his vote," and after his preference was announced and recorded, the next came to declare his favorite and so on, there being no deception. Every candidate knew his friends. How much have we improved on this satisfactory primitive method?

Each census showed the population increasing regularly and the slaves keeping pace. This was a constant source of trouble through this entire period. A great number of slave-holders, down in their hearts knew the great wrong of it but how was it to be abolished without a revolution in the whole labor and social world was a question never answered.

The slaves were mostly inherited, were very valuable and were such an important part of every prominent gentleman's prosperity, the very mention of disturbing the status of affairs aroused every fiber of his being. They did the labor, attended to the personal wants of every member of the family, till labor was thought his special sphere in life and not the white man's at all, especially in the higher class of society.

Why wonder at this custom that was inherited, for under the slave system, sons and daughters could be highly educated—the heads of families could read the papers and discuss politics and entertain with such genuine hospitality that was never before seen in all the world. If the father aspired to the political field he had the means and the time and if the son aspired to oratory, in which field, this county excelled, he was encouraged to the limit, for did not the heart of every Virginian rebound to the charms of oratory, and despite the snarls of critics, forever will. Of such was the life of the people for 80 years of elegance and happy ease under the plantation system, and nowhere else did they enjoy their lives more than in this section of the State.

Mills operated by water power increased in number, roads built by slaves were constructed, finer dwellings were erected, and many tobacco factories were operated and some very successfully, but agriculture was the greatest industry when the eternal question of States Rights came up for final solution and war jeopardized the nation.

The brick for the fine mansions were made on the farms, and the lumber for framed houses was sawed with the old up-and down saws till the latter half of this period. The earliest and finest brick buildings were often covered with slate, but tin of the very finest, never equaled now, came into more general use. The mansions were well heated and beautifully furnished, with heavy furniture, and with plenty for table, books for the library, stables full of fine horses and carriages and servants galore, the country homes of Henry county had every attraction that heart could desire,—why move to town?

Our villages were small this entire epoch, and it may appear unreasonable that during one decade when slavery was in its zenith, Ridgeway was the most important trading place in the county.

These plentiful years exhibited the perfected turnpike system and the rapid spread of the postal service, put the whole county up to date on public questions as never before. The railroads came at the very climax of slavery and when it reached Danville business increased by leaps and bounds and the whole world got closer together apparently.

Higher education was acquired at the University of Virginia or later on at the Virginia Military Institute, and at William and Mary College, and the girls attended Salem in great numbers. However, the greatest learning for the multitude was acquired from private tutors or neighborhood schools and every pupil paid tuition. The noted teachers were Dennis Marshall, Joe P. Godfrey and Joshua Smith.

One of these schools most noted and patronized by the greatest number of our antebellum boys was conducted by one Joshua Smith whose school was located at Ridgeway, the pupils boarding in the best private families. English, Latin and Higher Mathematics were taught. The last resting place of this distinguished educator is unknown. It were far better could a monument be erected to his memory.

Here were the descendants of the best blood of Europe, educated, and commanding highest influence in the State and Nation, enjoying heretofore the greatest privileges and prosperity, altogether producing the highest type of the Virginia patriot. Can any one wonder

HISTORY OF HENRY COUNTY, VIRGINIA

when the very foundation of everything near and dear to them, was threatened, that they rushed to arms and fought the bloodiest war in all history. Thanks be to the great God of Hosts that the great principles founded on rights for which they fought and died can never be reconstructed.

The incomplete list of the followers of the Stars and Bars is now added:

Allen, Joseph; Allen, James; Allen, O. M.; Austin, Charles F.; Adams, Josiah; Armstrong, John R.

Barbour, Dick; Barbour, Frank; Barbour, Criss, Barrow, Ferdinand; Barrow, Flournoy; Bowles, G.R.; Beal, Sam; Beal, William; Beal, John; Belton, Wm.; Boaz, S. P.; Burge, Lakin; Burge, Wm.; Brock, T. F.; Billings, P. W.: Booker, E. H.; Bryant, Col. C. B.; Bondurant, J. S.; Burgess, Wm. G.; Barrow, A. F.; Booker, E. M.; Beale, John M.; Beck, James; Barrow, Capt. Orrin W.; Beale, Marcus W.; Burton, J. W.; Byrd, S. W.; Barrow, B. F.; Bocock, T. M.; Burton, W. T.; Barrow, B. F., Sr.; Burch, J. B.; Burch, J. G.; Bowen, David; Belcher, Thos.; Belcher, Jabe; Belcher, John; Bell, James; Bell, G. M.; Burch, J. W,; Burch, Richard; Bock, R. J.

Craig, Thomas; Clanton, George; Crews, Jack; Campbell, Wm.; Carter, Mat; Creasey, Ben; Cox, Darvin; Carter, James H.; Carter, T. J.; Cahill, Thomas; Cahill, Perry; Cox, J. H.; Cox, Wm.; Cheshire, John W.; Clark, N. C.; Cahill, B. M.; Clark, W. A.; Cahill, Z. T.; Cheatham, John C.; Campell, J. H.; Cheatham, John D.; Clark, T. J.; Carter, E. H.; Corbin, Benj.; Cobbs, Capt. Thomas E.; Clark, R. A.; Champton, James; Goggin; Cook, Thomas; Carter, Carey; Carter, Joseph; Cole, Abner; Cole, James; Cooper, Austin; Cooper, Guss; Cooper, Sterling; Carter, E. H.

Dillon, Jack; Dillon, Thad; Dillon, Henry; Dillon, Wm.; Dillon, James; Davis, Robt.; Draper, E. H.; Davis, Geo. W.; Doyle, S. M.; Dunavant, G. W.; Dalton, Sam C.; Dodson, B. F.; Dunavant, T. W.; Draper, P. D.; Doss, E. H.; Dillon, H. H.; Draper, John H.; Draper, Thomas J.; Davis, James W.; DeShazo, William T.; DeShazo, Larkin; DeShazo, Nathaniel C.; DeShazo, George Reid; DeShazo, Richard T.; Davis, Eli M.; Dyer, Thomas; Dillon Elijah; Dillon, Henry H.

East, Martin; Eanes, B. H.; Eggleton, John; Eggleton, Newson; Eggleton, Geo. R.; Edwards, Robt.; Edwards, R. W.; Estes, E. H.; Edwards, J. L.; Eanes, James A.; Eggleston, M. J.; Eggleton, Logan.

HISTORY OF HENRY COUNTY, VIRGINIA

Franklin, J. L.; Franklin, G. T.; Frazier, P. F.; Frye, Jesse; Floyd, W. H.; Fair, C. W.; Ford, Sam C.; Franklin, W. H.; Fountaine, N. C.; Freeman, Jess; Fontaine, W. Hale; Fontaine, Sam.

Grogan, J. J.; Grogan, Wm.; Grogan, Frank; Grogan, J. W.; Grogan, Geo.; Grogan, Joseph; Griggs, William; Gunnell, Wm.; Giles, P. H.; Gravely, Wm. A.; Gravely, P. B.; Gravely, Thomas; Gravely, George; Gravely, Joseph H.; Gilbert, James; Giles, S. S.; Griggs, J. W.; Gravely, W. Frank; Gilbert, J. H.; Gravely, Geo. W.; Gravely, J. E.; Gibson, H.; Gravely, Goggin; Gravely, Fount; Gravely, Jabes; Gregory, R. Lindsey; Gregory, Joseph; Griffin, Thomas.

Horsely, G. W.; Hundley, J. W.; Hundley, H. B.; Hundley, J. L.; Hatcher, W. H.; Hatcher, Robt.; Hodges, H. K.; Hollandsworth, James; Hollandsworth, John; Hollandsworth, William; Hollandsworth, Fount; Hardie, Thrashley; Hardie, Joe; Hill, W. D.; Harris, John; Hairfield, John; Hereford, Bullard; Hereford, Fell; Hancock, Peter; Haislip, Frank; Huddlestone, Wm.; Hefferfinger, John; Helm, Geo. T.; Harris, G. L.; Hurd, H. C.; Hairston, J. T. W.; Hairston, Col. Peter; Harris, Paul; Horsley, J. W.; Henderson, W. A.; Hall, J. H.; Harris, H. H.; Hawkins, A. W.; Hodges, J. F.; Haley, James, R.; Hunter, James; Harris, Peter; Harris, Paul; Harris, Henry; Hollinsworth, Bart; Hardie, Elijah; Hobson, Monroe; Hairfield, Joseph; Hairfield, James; Hereford, Joseph.

Ingram, J. D.; Ingram, C. W.; Ingram, J. L.; Ingram, J. T.

Jarrett, A. L.; Jarrett, H. F.; Jarrett, J. H.; Jarrett, A. J.; Jarrett, Peter; Jones, David; Jones, Chas. W.; Jones, W. L.; Jones, Green; Joyce, Alfred; Jones, A. M.; Johnson, David; Jamerson, Thomas J.; Jones, John G.; Jones, Benjamin Seward; Jones, George Osborne; Jenkins, John.

Kindrick, John; Koger, J. L.; Koger, Wm.; Koger, W. L.; Koger, Pink; King, Joe B.; King Thomas J.; King, Capt. Thomas H.; King, Joseph Bolin; King, Tyler, C.; King, D. F.

Law, Green; Leake, J. B.; Leake, P. F.; Lester, John C.; Lester, M. J.; Lester, Wm. A.; Land, Wm.; Land, Joseph; Lovelace, J. W.; Lee, Harden W.; Lamkin, Jos.; Lawrence, Peter F.; Lee, W. P.; Lavinder, J. P.; Lavinder, Jesse Ben; Lester, Osborne; Lyle, J. H.; Lyle, Bartlett.

HISTORY OF HENRY COUNTY, VIRGINIA

Mason, James; Mason, Lee; Matheley, G. W.; Minter, James; Mills, Rich; Mills, Francis; McMellon, Joseph; McMellon, Thomas; Merryman, James; Merryman, J. L.; Martin, Thomas J.; Morrison, Bushrod; Minter, Silas; Minter, Joseph; Morris, Wm.; Matthews, David; Moore, Thomas; Marshall, James; Meeks, Thomas; Meeks, J. T.; Mitchell, E. R.; Morris, John T.; Morris, Dr. W. W.; Minter, William S.; Merryman, J. B.; Meadows, D. T.; Moore, A. L.; Miles, S. J.; Metts, John A.; Mills, J. P.; McBryde, Robt.; McMellon, S. H.; McLaray, J. G.; Martin, Oregon; Manning, Samuel.

Odell, George, Oliver, N. G.

Parcell, Robert; Purcell, C. R.; Pettit, Robt.; Philpott, C. W.; Philpott, B. W. L.; Philpott, Nat; Philpott, Thomas; Pannill, William; Pannill, Jack; Philpott, John; Payne, Green B.; Prunty, William; Pratt, Richard; Pratt, Thomas; Purdy, Joseph; Pace, H. C.; Peay, Sam; Prilliman, F. M.; Patterson, Giles; Patterson, D. M.; Patterson, John; Patterson, Thomas; Patterson, George W.; Patterson, Jarratt; Penn, Capt. Edmund; Penn, Joseph G.; Payne, R. C.; Powell, Ben. F.; Perry, M. F.; Parcell, Peter; Purdy, James; Purdy, General.

Richardson, Henry; Riley, Ben F.; Rangeley, John; Richardson, Sam; Richardson, Thomas G.; Ross, Thomas J.; Redd, Capt. W. S.; Richardson, George L.; Ramsey, John H.; Richardson, John; Richardson, Frank; Richardson, Joseph; Rice, Leroy.

Stultz, Thomas; Stone, James; Stone, J. L.; Stone, J. D.; Stone, Reid; Stultz, Silas; Shumate, Sam; Stob, Jarrett; Shelton, George; Shelton, James; Shelton, P. H., Sr.; Shelton, A. N.; Shelton, Henderson; Scruggs, Riley; Scruggs, Lee; Stovall, W. T.; Stovall, J. T.; Stokes, Benton H.; Smith, W. S.; Smith, David; Smith, John; Smith, James R.; Stone, A. J.; Self, Silas M.; Stultz, J. W.; Stultz, Johnson W.; Smith, Dr. James M.; Smith, O. C.; Smith, Frank; Stultz, Peyton W.; Stultz, B. L.; Stanley, Burwell; Stone, J. O.; Seay, B. H.; Self, W. J.; Stultz, O. M.; Stultz, V. L.; Stultz, A. M.; Stultz, G. H.; Stultz, T. C.; Stultz, Ben; Stegall, William.

Taylor, Alfred; Taylor, L. C.; Taylor, J. F., Jr.; Trent, J. D.; Turner, Nat; Thomasson, Mike; Terry, Jake; Turner, C. M.; Thomasson, S. G.; Thomasson, R. W.; Thomasson, W. O.; Thomasson, J. R.; Thomasson, M.; Turner, John W.; Thomasson, John S.; Trent, Thomas F.; Turner, Wm.; Turner, Wm. H.H.; Turner, H. C.; Turner, J. H.; Trent, George W.

Wells, W. B.; Wells, James; Wells, John; Wells, Wm;
Wells, W. H.; Wray, Coan, Watkins, Wesley; Watkins,
Wm.; Watkins, Horsley; Wilson, Albert; Wilson, W. C.;
Wyatt, W. T.; Wyatt, Silas; Wyatt, V. E.; Wingfield,
Capt. H.; Wade, Henry; Winn, T. L.; Wilson, W. W.;
Wiggington, C. N.; Watkins, H. S.; Winn, Henry J.;
Waller, George E.; Warren, J. S.; Wray, Pinkey C.;
Wray, H. L.; Warren, Columbus S.; Wade, James A.;
Walker, J. A.; Winn, Andrew.

STONEMAN'S RAID IN SIXTY-FIVE

Three hundred Federal troops passed through the county in April 1865 under General Stoneman, who was on his way to reinforce General Sherman in North Carolina. They camped at Rough and Ready Mills north of Martinsville, near Rev. Anderson Wade's residence. A few Confederates were in the county at the time and hearing of the appearance of the Union troops, three of them, Joe King of Ridgeway, Sam Martin of Magna Vista and Hairston Watkins of Shawnee, wishing to know their strength, proposed to reconnoiter. On their way up Smith River, beyond Martinsville, they met a negro man on an army horse, who told them there were no Yankees near. Not long afterwards this same man returned, at a swinging gallop, going towards the Mills. King called out "Hairston shoot him, he is going to betray us." The negro was soon out of range of Hairston's gun and the reconnoiters found themselves near the Federal camp. The picket called out "Halt" but they preferred to retreat. Watkins dropped his cap and while recovering it was almost captured. In fact, they were so closely pursued that they took to the woods.

The negro not only reported them, but informed the Federals of Wheeler's little band encamped on Jones's creek. Next morning while the latter was at breakfast, they were attacked by Stoneman and knowing that they could not defeat the Federals, they defended themselves valiantly before scattering for protection and safety.

Five Federals were killed and two mortally wounded, and only one Confederate was killed and then only after surrendering. The former buried their dead in the Episcopal Churchyard, but left the murdered man on the ground unburied. Marshall and Robert Hairston made a box and interred him on the spot, but later the body was taken to the Episcopal Graveyard and buried as far as possible from the Federals. These were finally carried to the National Cemetery at Danville.

As the Federal troops went through the county, they took horses, provisions, silverware, and in fact everything valuable they could take along. Occasionally, a kind hearted soldier would leave a horse for the women folks when they would plead their helplessness and poverty.

Upon reaching Martinsville, Gen. Stoneman took up his abode at the home of Mrs. Ruth Redd, although he was told that he was an unwelcome visitor. Tents were pitched in any yard that attracted their attention and the place was in fact captured, in every phase of its meaning.

Mrs. Ballard Preston of Montgomery county had sent her family plate to Preston quarters for safe keeping by burying it. One of the negroes betrayed its hiding place for twenty-five cents. The soldiers made an unusual appearance with their valuable booty as they rode through the remainder of the county with silver pitchers and fruit stands tied to their saddles, mugs and cups strung on their bridle-reins, and spoons, knives and forks sticking out of their pockets.

In the last days of the Civil War, both the cradle and the grave were robbed to supply the places of those left dead on the many battlefields of the Old Dominion. Only old, feeble and otherwise incompetent men for active service, were left as "Home Guards." While Virginia was one of the great battlefields, Henry county was off the regular line of march and therefore not subjected to many raids.

While the ladies were not called upon to go to the front as nurses, they did their part at home. They helped grow the cotton for their dresses, gathered it from the fields, picked the seeds out with their fingers, carded it, spun it, wove it, cut the garments and with their fingers fashioned tasty garments using thread spun by themselves. Their hats, though common were made from braided straws of wheat, rye and oats and trimming made from same material. The tops for shoes were home woven, often using wooden soles that the Boys at the front might have the leather. Thorns were used for pins, pine knots for light to spin by; sorghum took the place of sugar. Cattle needed salt, smokehouse floors were dug up to get the salt leaked out of the meat barrels; corncobs were burned for soda; shucks and sassafras leaves were made into soap, rabbit fur took the place of 'kid" for gloves; rags were woven into rugs that the soldiers might have the blankets, carpets, even were turned into blankets. Many families cooked on open hearths, but the iron vessels used, burned out. What must be done' Bread must be had. So hearths were swept free from ashes, and corn dough was dropped upon the hot rocks, covered with hot cinders and then a heavy coat of ashes, while the heat from the burning logs finished the cooking; when thoroughly baked, this bread was drawn out, washed and dried and eaten while warm with milk and butter and you may be assured it was food fit for the gods.

HISTORY OF HENRY COUNTY, VIRGINIA 25

CHAPTER III

FROM THE WAR BETWEEN THE STATES TO THE PRESENT TIME

DISASTER was never more complete than when the Confederate cause was committed to the ages. The fields were destitute of cattle, the homes mourning their dead, the larder empty and the stoutest hearts saw no dawn of a better day from out the gloom. The plantation system of over a hundred years' construction was gone, and the farms must be cultivated by the owners' hands or by the hired help of former slaves.

But undaunted the planters returned to work and soon a silver cloud appeared. Tobacco sold high for nearly a decade and the thriftiest citizens, from nothing to begin with, accumulated enough to repay their debts and buy homes. The manufacture of tobacco, which was a source of prosperity, increased, and soon thereafter most of these manufacturers moved to the county seat carrying much of the colored population.

Education was boosted by the establishment in 1870 of the free school system, and from then to this day, better buildings and higher grade teachers, have brought about unthought of changes. Now it is rare to find children ten years old unable to read and write. Half a dozen high schools dot the county, and more recently, while it has been done at the expense of the whites, mostly, these great blessings have been extended to the colored population.

The war with Spain in 1893 was fought by the regular army but volunteers from this county contributed towards carrying the flag of the U. S. to victory as always, against every foreign foe.

In 1901 a beautiful monument to the Confederate soldier was erected on the public square at Martinsville by the U. D. C. Society and there it will stand through long, long ages to speak in granite the undying fame of Henry county's sons who went to glory or the grave.

The narrow-guage railroad was built through the county in 1883, and a standard guage road at right angles to it north and south, in 1889, and these together have contributed more to the general prosperity of the whole county than all other public improvements together in its history. Along the lines of each, new buildings, better homes and farms and more villages have sprung into being, resulting in a very great increase in wealth and population. It paved the way for the manufacture of all varieties of wood-work, brick, furniture and cotton, all together transforming the county into a great manufacturing community, as well as agricultural with the former in the ascendency.

The introduction of the internal-combustion engine which has resulted in the general use of the automobile and now admitted the parent of good roads, has transformed education, houses of worship, homes, and every grade of society beyond the wildest conception. Trucks for towns and tractors for the farm, followed along as night follows day, till rush! go! do! is the spirit of the day, think of it, all founded on oil!

Every phase of living and every line of business reacts to the present source of energy. Cities must no longer be built on streams and depend upon waterpower, for now by wires the alternating currents of electricity can be carried any distance, wherever available in the county; and other places, the gas engines supplement, till nearly all the hard labor done by work animals, can be shifted and these poor creatures rested from their greatest burdens.

The old decanter of Colonial days and many generations thereafter, gradually took a more retired place in the social life of our people as the evils of drink became more marked and more destructive to life, until in 1915, the great blessing of national prohibition covered the land and ere long after the older drinking fraternities pass away intoxicating liquors, as a beverage will be no more and the vile poison will be used for medicinal purposes exclusively.

The great world war is too recent to be fully written in any history especially of a county, but the horrors of the years of 1917 and '18 will be memorable in our annals. The drafting of all our unmarried men was complete and while many were never called to the firing line, the great number that went to France, included a son from nearly every home in the county.

The mounting up of taxes, during this era while entirely local, yet is worthy of recording. At the beginning of this period real estate soon brought about large incomes, which declined for thirty years, but in two decades taxes began to go up and with every decade they almost doubled till now, real estate, as a whole, is taxed three and often four times what it formerly was, still the income from the same has declined gradually, except two years of world war inflation, with untold changes in our population. The higher prices for labor on public works and in the factories, which the farmers can not pay, have drained the farm of manual labor as never before, and is destined, without a change, to materially revolutionize our agricultural life unfavorably unless tractors and mechanical means can supply the deficiency.

While the general burdens borne, and the collection of the crimes of the world by wires displayed in daily papers, give the pessimist opportunity to declare that the world is getting worse, in reality our county has improved in morals each generation from the first, and with modern homes, with every comfort and manifold blessings, there is enough to silence the grouchers, and each individual should be grateful from the very depths of the heart, to the Great Creator, that he has been privileged to live in these days of peace, plenty and a future all tinted in golden hues.

CHAPTER IV

COURTS, MUSTERS AND PLANTATION LIFE

THE County Courts under the old system during almost a century, were made up of five magistrates who headed the judicial proceedings in law. These Courts were held monthly like those discontinued in 1904.

After the Civil War, beginning in 1870 and ending as above stated, the Court was held by a County Judge. Judge John Lea Dillard was the first and most popular and died in the middle of his term.

The County Judges and terms in years were as follows: J. L. Dillard, 2; S. J. Mullins, 6; N. H. Hairston, 8; H. G. Mullins, 12; Geo. L. Dillard, 3; and N. Emory Smith, 3 and the last under the Constitution.

It was claimed that it would lessen expense and litigation to have a Circuit Court only, by those responsible for its abolition: however taxes have gone steadily upward, and those people who wish, continue to carry their cases to court with the usual cost of a lawsuit.

In the County Court era, the second Monday was the most important day of the month. It was generally attended because nearly every business man went knowing he would most likely meet those he had business with and thus save a special trip across the county to attend to it. The news, special, published and unpublished, and political affairs not in shape for the public, as well as, the regular meeting and exchange of greetings made the people more compact in thought and action.

The most popular of all Courts was August Court for by this time the crops were laid by and the biggest political speakers harangued the big crowd while the great loads of delicious watermelons were sold to the thirsty auditors. A "Cheap John," or a "Patent Medicine Man," often helped to entertain according to belief or fancy. Jockey street was in dress parade and the eternal, "How will you swap," filled the dusty air mingled with the clatter of horsefeet and the neighing of the mother animals for their fleet-footed babies.

Some of these horse-jockeys frequently made remarkable gains, in a small way, in a few Court Days. Beginning with a poor animal by fattening till next Court, exchange getting "boot," and repeating till they went into liquidation, it was easy to compute the exact profit. On one occasion a noted follower of the trail was rehearsing how he made $150.00 in three different Courts in trading. He was asked if he always did it—this was Peter Frazier—"No," he said "I have ridden a fine horse to Court, and gone home with my bridle in my hand and tears in my eyes."

COUNTY MUSTERS

From soon after the War of 1812, to May 1861, about 50 years, the musters were regular occurances in the county, but like the County Courts, tournaments and the negro corn-shuckings, are things we see no more.

In many different localities, they took place twice a year or oftener. At these the young men participating, elected their officers who taught them, without guns, to go through the evolutions of the soldier, to come to "Attention," "Right Dress," "Front," "March," in single file, or in columns, "Column Right," or "Column Left," and so on according to regular military tactics. Many a time the day was almost over before they ceased their maneuvers.

Once a year, at Martinsville, there was a general muster of the men from all over the county, and the officers of the highest rank were in command, wore gaudy uniforms, mounted on horseback, and made an imposing parade. At these, too, there were the fife and kettle drum to make music, and the whole affair had a splendor and fascination that aroused the military spirit in those beholding, as well as those taking part in the great pageant.

Frequently noted speakers expounded their political creeds and added interest to the occasion. It was at these, too, that old Mrs. William Draper made her great reputation supplying to the crowds ginger-cakes and sweet cider said to be unequaled in all the earth. Add to this a large assembly of ladies with their youth and charming beauty then no one ever wonders any more that these great days were considered some of the most notable of that wonderful era.

Major Harden H. Dyer was the last in the county to hold that rank, but Maj. John Price of Ridgeway was a Major some years before. The last surviving Captain of the county musters was Capt. John H. Cox of the State Militia.

It is proper to record Patrick Eggleton as the "Fifer," and his Brother George, the "Drummer," for these two made the martial music for years at all the great county musters.

In the spring of 1861, the last of these went into history and the loyal sons of Henry marched with guns to the front and proved their valor on a hundred fields by following the path of glory that led too often to the grave.

THE PLANTATION

From the first settlements in Virginia till the Mountains were approached, the tendency was to take up, or buy, large boundaries of land. The plantation usually embraced hundreds, and often thousands, of acres. Under the slave system they were cultivated and made profitable. In this county the middle class had from one to five hundred acres, and the well-to-do thought nothing of owning 1,000 acre tracts. The doings and social customs of those days must be registered and preserved.

The landlord generally had an overseer who superintended the slaves in the fields, and the good landlady surrounded by the brightest female servants, supervised the household and reared her sons and daughters like her ancesters, many of whom were of royal blood.

Besides the animals of every description and the usual agricultural equipment, since there was no coummunity center to fully serve the public, being so widely separated, each plantation had its own sawyers, carpenters, blacksmiths, brick and rock masons, a few owned stores, and last but not least, a distiller to make the purest of liquors.

In the mansion there was usually found the "Black Mammy" who did the most sacred duties to the little ones and was adored next to the real mother herself; and skilled artists with the needle were ever present, and many had "Weavers" who could make the ancient brilliant blankets seen these days on the yard fences still doing service for this generation.

Being separated such distances, the visits of casual strangers were encouraged, and the coming of the kinfolks, especially an uncle's family, was the great event of this happy life. They came in great heavy carriages surrounded by servants all in gala attire, and made occasions of joy, only exceeded by the festivities of the Christmas holidays. On these large estates with sideboards ornamented with filled decanters, old Virginia hospitality grew to world wide fame and the sons and daughters developed into men and women that added luster to their family traditions and developed statesmen that led the nation to victory and to renown.

But the War of Emancipation ended the great plantation system and on its ruins small farms have been built and the State again marches in her accustomed place in the great constellation of States.

NEGRO CORN SHUCKING

Since the War between the States and the end of slavery, the hitherto great annual period in autumn, when corn was shucked by the slaves, has grown of less and less importance. For many years after the Emancipation the customs, songs, dances, and fun galore, held on, but gradually the cutting off of public drinking, and the migration of much of the colored population from the farm, these old celebrations of mingled work, fun, and frolic gradually passed into history. Two years ago on Marrowbone creek, these people staged the last of these festivities of song and story. Peter Wade, one of the old colored "Uncles," lead the singing.

Language fails to picture accurately the delight in ante-bellum days with which the black men, women, and largest children, came from neighboring plantations, many of them singing as they came to the corn-husking. Just permission to go, and where it was to be, even if four or five miles away, was all that was necessary to get them together.

The corn was in two large heaps as near equal as possible, each on arriving began pulling as rapidly as possible, the shucks from the corn, men and women both engaged, keeping time with their whole bodies to the singing. A prize was given to the first to finish his pile of corn.

Freedom was in the air and every soul was happy for the masters allowed them to do, say, and sing as they pleased, so long as the work was done rapidly and satisfactorily. The jokes, the stories, and general news of slavedom were told, and amidst the intervals of singing, the loudest peals of laughter shook the air evidencing the perfect happiness of all.

The leader of the singing, generally stood on the cornpile, and led the song which was responded to by everybody large and small in the loudest possible voices. Some crowds of singers have been heard miles and miles away in the still nights in the late fall of the year.

Of the songs, "Dan, dan, who is the dandy" was very popular, but the words are not recalled. Another very old one had for its response to the leader was, "Cur de Corn," and was nearly always sung during the evening. Some of the old leaders had powerful voices, and could cut the most comical didoes imaginable for amusement, and, to fit the lines of their weird wording.

The slaves often gave animals special distinction in their songs, like in this old low-pitched one referring to the terrapin as a boatman.

The words were as follows:

"De cooter is de boatman,
Jump Jim crow.
De red bird de soger,
Jump Jim crow.
De mocking-bird de lawyer,
Jump Jim crow.
De alligator de sawyer,
Jump Jim crow.

Not all their songs were comical, the following had a plaintive air:

"Johnny come down the hollow.
Oh hollow!
De nigger-trader got me.
Oh hollow!
De speculator bought me.
Oh hollow!
I'm sold for silver dollars.
Oh hollow!
Boys go catche the pony.
Oh hollow!
Bring him around the corner.
Oh hollow!
I'm goin' away to Georgia.
Oh hollow!
Boys, good-by forever.
Oh hollow."

After the work was finished, supper over, dancing was the regular order. It was marvelous the number of steps that could be cut of the clog variety, the wonderful agility exhibited, and the length of time they could continue after the days' labor and long walk to be present.

The only thing they had to mark time was the clapping of their hands on their knees, or the drumming of sticks on the floor; yet they enjoyed it more than if going along with an orchestra, for they could hear their feet in perfect harmony.

Military drills in imitation of the "Musters" of their masters, often furnished much merriment, especially when sticks were used for guns and the most outlandish caricatures of military commands were given.

Speeches, too, were frequent and delivered in the most formal manner. The orator would dwell on the importance of "De Issue of De Day." the "Dignitee of De State," and etc.

It was frequently mid-night when these jollifications ended and the trip to their own homes at other plantations had to be made, then a little sleep and a deep slumber made them ready and eager for the next.

THE TOURNAMENT

The advent of the automobile marked the passing of the horse as the most popular method of local traveling and with it the graceful art of riding in the saddle, the beautiful and noblest of animals. It appears, also, to have relegated almost to oblivion, the tournament, the most popular sport on horseback in by-gone years, a pleasure worthy of a place in history.

The chief actors were a Marshal, and the Knights, who usually bore the name of the place, home, or stream from which they came. They wore gorgeous sashes, or other regalia, and mounted on their finest and fleetest decorated steeds, made a brilliant and imposing spectacle. Each carried a long pointed lance to catch the rings hung about shoulder high to the riders, as they made the course at great speed.

The Marshal, all being ready would call in the loudest voice possible, the Knights in regular order, as "Knight of Shawnee," Knight of Red Plains," or "Knight of the Marrowbone," etc. In response to the call, each would do his best to make the fastest time and catch the most rings for the day.

Music by stringed instruments accompanied every

rider, and contributed to the jolly spirit of the great crowds that always gathered to witness the spectacular contests. When equal skill entered and the scores were close, the interest in this remnant of Knight-errantry would be aroused to the very limit.

The one making the highest score won the crown which was given to his sweet-heart, thus making her the "Queen of Love and Beauty." This was done at the dance that followed in the evening of the tournament. This was a great feature of the occasion, and often scores of couples enjoyed the old Virginia reel, and similar innocent dances—if any are innocent—for a certainty they were on a much higher plane than later ones.

The game of base-ball draws its crowds, and the automobile races, theirs, with the long string of fatalities attached, but the exhibition of horseback riding in the tournaments of other days brought fourth thrills that nothing else ever can. It is regrettable that they are no more, for truly they were gala days in Henry county and furnished sport for the young men participating as well as a real pleasure for the multitude.

It was at one of these happy affairs that the spirit of chivalry was recalled, surrounded by youth and beauty when Dr. P. R. Reamey delivered his "Charge to The Knights" a speech that for charming beauty of language has never been surpassed in this county since the world famous Patrick Henry spoke when living on Leatherwood.

RECOLLECTIONS OF EDWARD BOOKER, RIDGEWAY,
HENRY COUNTY, VIRGINIA, APRIL, 1881.

I was born in Cumberland county, Va., on the 8th of April, 1794. My father, after whom I was named, was a soldier of the Revolution, and was at the siege of Yorktown. He was a Lieutenant and his brother, Samuel Booker, was a Captain. I served in the War of 1812. I volunteered at Cumberland Court House in September 1813 in the Cumberland Troops. Our officers were John Miller, Captain; Daniel A. Wilson, first Lieutenant, and Maurice Langhorne, second; George Horsly, Orderly Sergeant; and Dr. John Trent, Surgeon. The battalion was first under the command of Major Robinson and when attached to a regiment, it was commanded by Colonel Thomas Mann Randolph. I was stationed at Hampton the, most of the time that I was in service. I was at Yorktown on detached service when the news was received of Perry's victory on Lake Erie.

I recollect when a school-boy in 1806, when returning home, meeting Col. Aaron Burr, a prisoner under guard on his way to Richmond. He was traveling in a "Shick-gig." I well remember his appearance. He was a small man with uncommonly bright eyes and rather sharp features.

I also remember seeing Lorenzo Dow and hearing him preach at Smith's Chapel in Cumberland. He was very uncouth in his appearance, rather repulsive, and walked on foot through the country. His wife, Peggy Dow, accompanied him, riding on a flea-bitten gray mare. She was an ordinary looking woman, with auburn hair and freckles. As soon as he finished his sermon, he opened the window near the pulpit and jumped out and went his way. His oddities and eccentricities attracted large crowds to hear him.

I also heard Mr. Jefferson give in his evidence in a trial of a will case at Buckingham Court House in 1817. He was dressed remarkably plain and his language was simple and to the point. He was a tall, rawboned man, according to my recollection of him. Profound silence was observed while he was in court.

I have seen Peter Francisco many times. He was a large muscular man, though I think some exaggerated stories have been told about his strength. His son, James Francisco, was in the Army with me. Peter Francisco, was a remarkably good-natured man and very peaceably inclined.

I well remember the canvass between Randolph and Eppes. Party excitement was higher than I ever knew it. A friend of Randolph, who lived in Cumberland near Farmville, loaned a neighbor a horse to ride to Cumberland Court House to vote, as he expected, for his favorite, but when he went to the polls, the neighbor voted for Eppes. This so enraged the friend of Randolph that he said to the man that he should not ride his horse home. A friend of Eppes who was present told the man if he would go with him home he would give him a horse. I heard Mr. Randolph make the best speech he ever made, at Buckingham Court House. It was, I think, in 1835. He was without doubt the greatest orator I ever heard.

On one occasion an important law suit was sent from Amelia to Cumberland for trial. Amongst the lawyers engaged in it and whom I heard were John Wickham, William West, and William S. Archer.

In 1817, I made a trip to Tennessee and Alabama on horseback. I was in Nashville when the first hogshead of tobacco was inspected there. It was then only a small town comparatively speaking.

I removed to the County of Patrick in 1819 and have lived in that county and this ever since. I am the only survivor of a family of four sons and two daughters and have lived to a greater age than any of them.

I have been remarkably healthy and am now able to ride on horseback and to work on the farm. I can write a legible hand. If I am able and living, I wish to attend the celebration at Yorktown in October.

I am, perhaps, the only survivor of the Cumberland Troop with whom I served in the War of 1812. If there is any other living, I hope that he will inform me through the mail.

NOTE. In one more summer's suns and another winter's nights, he passed from the finite to the infinite.

FIRST THINGS

Ranseleer Trent was the first postmaster at Martinsville after the Civil War. The post office at Ridgeway was established in 1850 and John C. Jones was the first postmaster.

Henry G. Lavinder, son of J. B. Lavinder, owned the first bicycle.

Watt Hairston, son of Major Watt Hairston, owned the first automobile.

At the death of her husband, Mrs. Maggie Lavinder Ford turned her love for flowers and her talent for growing them into business and became the first Florist in town.

Dr. C. P. Kearfott installed the first telephone in his home. He also brought the first phonograph to Martinsville and gave an entertainment in the Baptist Church and altho it was inaudible to half of the audience it was considered wonderful.

Ernest Kelly was the owner of the first Moving Picture business. He also established the first bakery and fresh fruit stand and brought the first grape fruit to town, which was quite a curiosity.

In 1915 J. W. Hamilton built, in front of the Hotel Hamilton, adjoining the Masonic Hall, the first Moving picture building. This old Hamilton Theatre was the first public building in Martinsville to fly the National flag when "Uncle Sam" announced his entrance into the World War.

The Local Red Cross Chapter realized its first money through benefit pictures given at the Hamilton theater. The Home Guards, organized during the war, were recruited at this theater and thousands of dollars of Liberty Bonds were sold between pictures during the war.

George H. Jamerson was the first Brigadier General born in Henry County, Va.

Gus Ashworth son of Mr. and Mrs. J. H. Ashworth, courteously offered to assist Mrs. C. W. Green aboard the N. & W. train and while waiting, with her baby George in his arms saw Mr. John Wells a man bent with the infirmities of old age trying to cross the track before the incoming train, with a bound across the track he hurled the old man to safety. Mr. Wells and the baby were unhurt and Gus only received minor bruises. For his bravery and quickness of action he received the Carnegie Hero Medal.

In 1906, Thomas A. Edison and his son Charles passed through Martinsville for the first time. Mr. Edison was given an ovation in front of the Hamilton on the lot now occupied by the Masonic Temple and the Old Hamilton Theater. Pictures were taken of Mr. Edison, surrounded by admiring friends on the porch of Hotel Hamilton. Those in the group were Mr. Edison dressed in Motor cap and linen duster; Messrs R. B. Semple, Will Peyton, W. W. Hamilton, Dr. John Anderson, Mrs. Starling Thomas, Mrs. Allie Edwards, Mrs. W. W. Hamilton, Miss Janie Lavinder, Miss Mary Lavinder, Miss Bettie Hill and little Overton Gregory.

Mrs. Lottie Turner Dodson, of Bachelor's Hall, was the first woman delegate to be sent to the Annual Va. Conference of the Methodist Church from Danville District, and Mrs. R. B. Semple from the Martinsville Church.

In 1923 New Hamilton Theater was built. This theater was the first business house to install an electric flashing light sign.

J. W. Hamilton had the first radio for commercial purposes.

Mr. Akers Brown bought the first phonograph brought into town for sale.

The American Furniture Company built the first furniture Factory.

Schottland Bros. own the only Mirror Factory.

The family of George King, the pioneer, introduced the method of ploughing alone with a horse and ploughlines about the time of the Revolution.

Feb. 14, 1922 one of the heaviest sleets, for many years swept the county, doing much damage to fruit trees and forest, also to electric wires.

Feb. 15, John H. Pharis, an able electrician of Martinsville, while in discharge of his duties, instead of sending one of his men into danger, climbed to the top of an ice covered pole and accidentally touched a high powered live wire which had become crossed with a phone wire; Jesse R. Chappel, tho small in stature, was brave in spirit, threw his body beneath his falling chief and thus broke the fall and saved his life.

THE SONG OF THE CHURN

About forty years ago one Cartwright, arrived in Martinsville, Va., the county seat of Henry, then a village, and introduced a churn that was reputed to get the butter out of the milk in three minutes.

It churned water so beautifully no one doubted it doing the milk the same way, and our best business men, old and young, bought State and County rights to the patent precipitately. The said Cartwright gathered up the cash and departed before the churn was proven just good to look at, and not adapted to churning milk at all.

The fake was published in the following poem soon thereafter.

The whole affair was so rich in humor, it is no disrespect to those who have gone to the other shore, to reproduce it here.

"SONG OF THE CHURN"
BY W. W. MORRIS, M. D.

Wish I'd had the smallpox,
  And the fever in its turn;
The day I met young Cartwright,
  In the buggy with the Churn!

Go it, Cartwright! Go it,
  You are the coming man
You soaked well Henry Lester—
  Please tell us, Who else can?

And Hamilton—friend Charlie,
  Has learned his lesson well;
That the way to make most money,
  Is to run a live Hotel.

One more name, next in order,
  Whom young Cartwright did not miss;
He made a haul among the Barkers,
  And lifted "Big Man Chris."

Other names would deck my story,
  If the names could be rhymed with;
Among the Joneses quite a number,
  If I mistake not, J. Moss Smith.

Yes, all these took to nibbling.
  Nor could ever be kept straight;
All the "small fry" bought by Counties,
  But Henry Lester swallowed State

"I, too, want a County,"
  Said a lawyer, with a snarl;
"And because old Massey's in it"
  You may give me Albermarle."

Come on, Big Fool Killer,
  For Henry never waits;
Hereafter, if one doubts it,
  I'll tell of St. John's Gate.

Now, when they write from Nashville,
  To know just what is said,
Write them plainly, Cartwright,
  The Fools are not all dead.

All my nearest neighbors,
  To Cartwright paid their bill;
Hodges and Woodson Bassett,
  And Miss Judith P. A. Hill.

To these I send greeting,
  Whom no humbug ever sells;
But my poem is too late coming,
  To Bill Hill and Tom P. Wells.

CHAPTER V

THE HIGH SCHOOLS OF HENRY COUNTY

IN the days before the Free-School system was established, education was acquired by private tutors or community schools. Thee names stand high above all others as teachers of High-Schools of the county and to one or the other practically every young man went for higher education. Dennis Marshall, Joe P. Godfrey and Joshua Smith were the teachers of the schools most noted in Henry. Another school that taught common studies as well as high-school subjects at a more recent date will first be considered.

SYLVAN RETREAT

This school was located between Rangeley and Mt. Bethel and was built by the Rev. W. W Hill for the benefit of his own, and neighbor's children. It was located in a pleasant grove and was patronized by boys and girls far and near. The boys often rode horseback quite a distance and fed these animals in boxes nailed to trees. At the head of this school was placed a young man who loved humanity, was of fine attainments, and of the highest moral character.

DR. G. W. G. ESTES

Left an orphan at an early age, he was placed in the care of W. A. Taylor, as his guardian, and as long as he wished, the Taylor home was his though he at times boarded out. After the latter home was broken up by death and marriages, he made Mr. Hill's his home while he taught the school.

He was educated at Hollins when both sexes attended, and at Jefferson Medical College, Philadelphia, where he was graduated. He did not enter the practice of medicine but loved the work of teaching. The pupils at his school loved him for he was a man who won the esteem of all those who came in contact with him. He was quiet but possessed a sympathetic nature and no one was too lowly to elicit his kind heart and willing help. He was generous to a fault, and from the time he began to teach till his death, there was always some special boy or girl he was trying to train up for an honorable place in life.

When called to the Civil War, he recommended Miss Hill, the founder's daughter to fill his chair at Sylvan Retreat. His recommendation was eminently satisfactory.

As a nurse on the battle-field or in the hospital, he performed every act of kindness as gentle as a woman, as thousands of soldiers will assert. After the War, he took up railroad work and was located at Drake's Branch till his health gave down, and he retired and spent his declining hours with his brother at Danbury, N. C. where he died Jan. 28, 1882.

His pupils and descendants of his old patrons will always hold his name in tender remembrance.

DENNIS MARSHALL

The oldest school for higher learning in the county was conducted by Dennis Marshall, who tradition locally states, was a relative of the great Chief Justice John Marshall. His parents, Sam Marshall and Cassandra Alfriend his wife, came from Mecklenburg county and settled on the head-waters of Leatherwood creek. Here they lived and died, and on the hill north of the Wesley Griggs home, they lie in an unmarked grave.

Dennis Marshall was born in 1768 and was the oldest of seven children. He was highly educated, and spent about forty years teaching. This was between 1790 and 1840. He built his home near Nance Mountain in 1813. His school building was near his residence. The latter was converted into a tobacco factory in 1843.

To him for miles around came the ambitious youths from every prominent family to acquire the education so hard to get in those days, and in which he was so gifted in imparting. Not yet have the old people near ceased to talk of him and his school, though long years have passed, but the good he did lives on and on unto succeeding generations.

He was 5 ft. and 11 inches in height. He had blue eyes, a fair complexion, and was almost completely bald, but with all, he possessed a personality that was strong and impressive. While with a relative near Shady Grove in Franklin county, he died in 1843, but his remains were returned to the old home on Leatherwood where they sleep by the side of his parents.

PATRICK HENRY ACADEMY

The site of the Academy is imposing. It is in the western part of the county on the road from Mt. Bethel to Spencer on the Anthony place at the crest of a plateau, sufficiently elevated to afford an unobstructed view of the surrounding landscape and the picturesque Blue Ridge Mountains. A few bricks are all that is left of this once proud seat of learning.

It is not known just what year the first rude building was constructed, but it was built two stories on account of rough settlers and roving bands of Indians in those days. It was not considered safe to leave the school belongings in the room below, so access was had to the upper story by means of a ladder which was drawn up at night. Later on a brick building with two rooms replaced the old log structure.

In 1770 Francis Asbury was sent by John Wesley from England to America as a missionary. In 1784 he was made the first Bishop of the Methodist Church in America, and Virginia was in his diocesan jurisdiction where he died in 1816.

In 1813, the Bishop sent Rev. J. C. Traylor as a circuit rider to Henry county with instructions to build a Methodist church, a school from which to feed a college in the western part of the State, and another to feed Patrick Henry Academy.

Mt. Bethel was the church he built, Patrick Henry Academy was the school, and a smaller one in his dooryard for his and his neighbor's children was the feeder. The reference was to Emory and Henry College beyond the mountains that stands like a great monument to its builders.

JOSEPH P. GODFREY

Joseph P. Godfrey, the Principal placed at the head of the Academy, was a classical scholar of attainment whose fame extended beyond the bounds of Virginia.

The neighbors felt it incumbent upon them to board boys coming from a distance, either with or without renumeration. A great number came on horseback and a pasture was added to the grounds for the stock to graze in till time for returning home.

Many of the early settlers after moving West and building new homes, brought their children back here to be educated. In the Thirties, three of the Whittles, uncles of S. G. Whittle, our distinguished jurist, rode from Mecklenburg county on horseback to enter the Academy.

Among the students of local distinction we note, the Mullins, Hills, Traylors, and Dr Peter R. Reamey. Sorry indeed that this list can not be extended of our own who have gone forth into the world not only an ornament to the county but to the State and Nation.

Among the long list of Alumni of the School distinguished in after years, we note Samuel and Waller Staples, the latter of the Supreme Court of the State; Judge Henry Pedigo of Texas; Col. Lewis Neale Whittle, a leader at the bar and member of the Legislature from Macon, Ga.; Stephen Decatur Whittle, a lawyer, and Clerk of the House of Delegates of Virginia, and member of the Convention of 1849-50; Francis McNiece Whittle, D. D., L. L. D., the fifth Bishop of the Protestant Episcopal Diocese of Virginia; Alexander Stuart, brother of Gen. J. E. B. Stuart and most likely the latter; Gen. Jubal Early, the noted Confederate, and scores of others lost in the sands of time.

JOSHUA SMITH

Another High School, at a much later period, was taught by Joshua Smith near Ridgeway. Few men distinguished after the Civil War reared in the south side of the county, failed to attend when boys, this noted seat of learning. It was on the western border of the corporation limits of the town, but the grading of the railroad at the long rock-cut has removed most of the site of the building.

Prof. Smith was highly educated, and knew how to control as well as teach the young. He managed them by the honor system and was very successful. Many of the young ladies sought his instruction and to every pupil he was patient, and withal a model master of the school-room.

Besides the usual high school studies, he taught Latin and other languages, and after a student finished in his school, he was fitted to begin law or medicine as subsequent time showed clearly.

The pupils from a distance boarded in the neighborhood and quite a few at Squire King Jones' about a quarter of a mile to the south.

His roll included the most important leaders in the county in many walks of life: We note Dr. John R. Dillard of Spencer, Judge Peter H. Dillard of Rocky

Mount, Judge N. H. Hairston of Roanoke at one time County Judge of this county, Dr. Poet G. Trent of Roanoke, Ala. Locally we enumerate Cabell Hairston of Red Plains, the Jones brothers, Ben, John and George; Price brothers, J. M. and R. P., J. W. Griggs, Len Sheffield and scores of others who rose to distinction in the county. If judged by the fruits of his labors as a teacher, his was eminently a successful career.

To the heroes of war great monuments have been erected to perpetuate their memory, but to the great heroes of the school-room on the hill whose life work is greater by far than that of the soldier, few are remembered for three generations, and so with Joshua Smith. How cruel is fate! When we attempt to appraise him in history, not one can tell when he died or where, nor on what spot his ashes lie buried! But his fame and his name are revered by the descendants of those he taught, and let his memory be kept ever green and properly cherished by those who inherited his merits.

NOTED TEACHERS IN HENRY COUNTY

Charles Hibberts was a Revolutionary soldier but after the war he worked for the county as teacher, so did Woodson Morris.

Hon. Geo. W. Booker, who later became Congressman taught in the "Old Field" schools when a young man.

Miss Hattie Williams taught a young ladies' school in Martinsville in its earliest days.

Miss Sarah Meade was a private teacher for many years, her first school was taught at the old Academy, near the site of the late Miss Ann Marshall's residence. J. M. Darlington taught a session in the same building. Mr. Darlington finally located in Washington, D. C. and accepted a Chair in the Georgetown University.

Wythe Peyton, a lawyer of Martinsville, was both teacher and principal of the first graded school in the county. He later was appointed Supt. of Schools in the county.

Miss Mary Wade, daughter of Dr. Anderson Wade, taught a private school for years and then went in as first assistant in the 1st graded school. Miss Electra Smith was second assistant in the same school. Mr. Parrott came to the county as principal and teacher of Ruffner. After leaving Ruffner he built and taught a private school in the town. He was not only a fine teacher but a most worthy man as well.

W. B. Gates, who is now and has been for some time Supt. of Schools, came to the county as teacher and principal of Martinsville High School until appointed Superintendent. He has been untiring in his work.

Miss Gillie N. Koger is another of the noted teachers of public schools in the county. She has served both as principal and assistant.

Miss Sallie Reamey has taught long enough to retire on a pension. Dr. Reamey, her father and Daniel Reamey, her grand-father, before her, were prominent teachers in the county.

Miss Virginia Pedigo has not only taught here acceptably but has won a name as a teacher in Kansas City.

Mrs. J. W. Booker has retired, but was one of Henry's most popular teachers.

Greenberry T. Griggs was first Supt. of Public Schools after 1870. Dr. J. M. Smith was also Superintendent for a term of years. J. R. Gregory and W. G. Shackleford served the county faithfully in this capacity.

Miss Janie Ford was a popular teacher for many years in the Martinsville High School.

The Misses Terrys were eminently popular and successful teachers for many years.

Mrs. John R. Dillard came to Henry County from Lunenburg when she was "Miss Lee," and began teaching in private families. As time passed on she joined the corps of public school teachers and taught out the necessary number of years and is now one of the pensioned teachers.

Miss Kate Merrimac Mosby of Christianburg, Montgomery County, Va. first came to Martinsville, in the spring of 1894 and taught a kindergarten in the home of Mrs. A. D. Witten. She was elected to teach the primary grades at Ruffner Institute in 1900 and taught continuously through 1919 in the public school of Martinsville.

Charles F. Myers, who assisted in the M. M. A., is now pastor of First Presbyterian Church in Greensboro.

Mrs. Jessie Aaron was a successful teacher in the public schools for years, as was Mrs. E. J. Pannill, daughter of Dr. P. R. Reamey, who served as principal and assistant.

Miss Pocahontas Wray is now one of the leading teachers in the Martinsville High School, and is noted for her work in mathematics.

CHAPTER VI

THE CHURCHES OF HENRY COUNTY

LEATHERWOOD being the first settled region, the earliest churches were built in that part of the county. From old letters and church data collected, apparently, the Leatherwood church was built just before or after the Revolution. John King was pastor for a long time, and died when still serving this congregation in 1821. Reed Creek was built perhaps about 1825, old Center later, Ridgeway near 1850, Good Will a little later. Horsepasture was built as a free church in the twenties.

The Methodist church at Ridgeway was erected 1893. Geo. O. Jones gave the site and most of the funds to erect the edifice. Soon thereafter, Mrs. Sue Garrett was the prime factor in building the Baptist church in the same town, and she truly spent the remainder of her life supporting and nurturing its congregation.

Prior to 1806, the Methodists worshipped in private houses, schoolhouses and court houses, but in that year, John Travis deeded, for five shillings, an acre of land to the trustees, John French, John Abington, James Patterson, and W. F. Mills. On this was a building, which was called Travis's Meeting-House, 18 years later Rev. J. C. Traylor deeded 2 more acres to the old plot and built a church which was named Mt. Bethel. The Trustees, French and Patterson, were succeeded by W. A. Taylor and Thomas I, Wootton.

In that day the men and women sat on opposite sides of the aisles and the colored people in the rear. Among the old leading members what you might call the backbone of the church were the Schoolfields, Baileys, Hunters, Mills, Hills, Bakers, Bouldins, Wells, Pannills. Few empty benches in those days. Among the pastors were Pines Allen, Alfred Norman, James Moore, Bibb, Betts, Phillips, Hodges, Joyner, Rowzie, Rich, Crider, Crowder, Hendren, etc. Class meetings were held every Sunday and its leaders almost always got happy before the meeting was over and often you might hear shouts of joy issuing from that church not only from the leaders but

MOUNT BETHEL CHURCH
Henry County

the members joined their leaders and many times sinners were converted. Obediah Bouldin, Geo. Baker and Franklin Mitchell are three of the leaders that the compiler remembers well.

In 1858 the present Mt. Bethel church was built. The present pastor, G. E. Powell is a native of Franklin county and is untiring in his zeal and is reawakening this old church. Rev. Geo. Pannill, W. W. Hill, W. M. Schoolfield and Jack Fontaine were among the local preachers, each one continuing his work in this field until sickness prevented. Then the families took up the work and kept it up till they too moved to other points. W. W. Hill was for years Superintendent of S. School and taught a Bible class both summer and winter and acted as Steward and general worker. His daughters Bettie, Lucy and Ella assisted him as teachers and singers and then Miss Ella assisted in the Superintendency of Sunday Schools when her father's illness and death removed him from the scene. His son-in-law O. R. Gregory filled the Superintendent's place for a time and became one of its most efficient workers in various ways. At the present writing Mr. Willis Clark is one of the leading members of Mt. Bethel church. He is a man blessed with common sense, one of the finest traits given to man.

The Methodist church of Martinsville was erected 1838 on a site deeded by Geo. Hairston (Rusty), to the following trustees: Anthony Dupuy, Wm. Martin, J. C. Traylor, John G. Redd, James Smith, Sr. Some of the old leading families were the Smiths, Hamiltons, Lavinders, Reameys, Penns, Graveleys, Wallers, Sanders, Putzels, Tuggles, Pharis and many others.

This church from 1838 to 1882 belonged to the Henry Circuit when it became a station. The Presiding Elders are as follows:

Rev. O. Littleton, 1882-1884
J. H. Amiss, 1888-1892
W. P. Wright, 1896-1900
J. C. Reed, 1901-1902
W. H. Atwell, 1905-1909
M. S. Colonna, 1913-1915
C. E. Watts, 1885-1888
J. E. DeShazo, 1892-1898
W. H. Edwards, 1900-1901
J. H. Amiss, 1902-1905
B. M. Beckham, 1909-1913
S. J. Browne, 1915-1919
J. A. Thomas, 1919-1920 and a part of 1921
B. M. Beckham, part of 1921
S. J. Battin, 1921-1924

PASTORS

C. F. Comer, 1882-1885   Wilbur Davis, 1885-1889
J. W. Howell, 1889-1891   T. O. Edwards, 1891-1892
During Rev. Howell's pastorate, Rev. John W. Carroll assisted in a big revival.

W. H. Christian,   J. W. Shackford,
1892-1894   1894-1896

Under Mr. Christian the church was remodeled and a new parsonage built.

Under Mr. Shackford, W. G. Burch was licensed to preach. Epworth League organized in 1896 with 42 members enrolled and Miss Mattie Reamey president. In 1895 James E. Schoolfield of Danville, Va., held an evangelistical meeting in the Lester tabernacle in which the church was greatly revived, back-sliders reclaimed and many sinners converted.

W. H. Gregory, 1896-1897   J. W. S. Robins,
W. W. Royal, 1900-1902   1902-1904
M. S. Colonna, 1904-1906   L. T. Williams, 1906-1908
W. G. Bates, 1908-1909   S. J. Battin, 1909-1911
Bascom Dey, 1911-1913   Geo. F. Green, 1913-1914
J. R. Laughton, 1914-1916   W. R. Proctor 1916-1919
J. R. Sanders, part of 1920   and part of 1920
J. G. Unruh, 1920-1921   W. B. Jett, 1921-22-23-24
H. C. Cheatham,   and 25
1897-1900

Rev. Wilbur Davis was the first preacher to remain four years. Rev. W. R. Proctor was the second. Mr. Proctor was the first pastor lost by death. Mr. Proctor was greatly loved by the whole town.

Mr. Jett the pastor at the present writing is true to the principles he professes. He reaches all classes, boys and girls, young men and maidens, middle aged and the old. He goes out among the people and is gradually building up the spirituality of the church.

The building of the present church was proposed during the administration of Mr. Proctor and completed under that of W. B. Jett. The corner-stone was laid July 4, 1922. Building was finished, May 1923 and cost $65,000. Committee: Dr. C. T. Womack, Chairman,

REV. AND MRS. W. B. JETT
Pastor of M. E. Church, South
Martinsville, Va.

THE METHODIST EPISCOPAL CHURCH
Martinsville, Va.

R. P. Graveley, Treasurer, Miss Bessie Tuggle, Secretary, J. R. Smith, Hugh Dyer, H. S. Teague, I. M. Groves and A. D. Beckner.

SUNDAY SCHOOL SUPERINTENDENTS

L. S. Thomas, J. B. Lavinder, Wm. Riley Nunn and I. M. Groves. The latter was appointed Superintendent in 1907 and has served to this time. His pastor, Rev. W. B. Jett, says of him: "He is the most efficient Superintendent that has ever served under me." H. S. Teague was made Superintendent in 1907 and steward in 1904 and has served faithfully in both capacities till now.

J. B. Lavinder joined the church in 1879 and conducted a Bible class in the Sunday School. In 1890 he was elected Superintendent, which position, with that of church secretary and treasurer, he retained until his death. From the time he joined the church until the end, Aug. 18, 1903, he was a true, loyal, faithful and consistent member, putting God and his church first always.

Jno. H. Pharis was assistant secretary for many years. In 1904 he became secretary and has been punctual and prompt to this present time.

Dr. Womack, a direct descendant of Robt. Carter (King), was born 1875, came to Henry Co., 1899, married 1904, Lena Robins, daughter of Rev. J. W. S. Robins. Mrs. Womack is one of the sweetest singers in Virginia and has for years been the leading soloist in the choir. Dr. Womack was made treasurer 1902, and is now holding this office with those of steward and trustee. He, like Dr. Pomp Smith, has served without a break since his first appointment. Dr. Smith was appointed 1897. Dr. Womack 1901.

Mrs. Mary Lavinder Semple, since 1904, has led the choir and has been the efficient teacher of the Primary class of the Sunday School almost as long a period.

Mrs. Champe Penn, Miss Dora Hamilton (now Mrs. C. E. Crist) and Mrs. Nellie Lightly have filled the office of organist most satisfactorily.

The Epworth League has been reorganized by Rev. W. B. Jett with Overton Hill Gregory as president. It has grown rapidly and is doing a good work.

The Rose-bud Society for years was under the leadership of Miss Susie Thomas and Miss Janie Lavinder. In

1920 the Rose-buds merged into the W. F. Missionary Society. At present there are several Missionary societies and two Ladies' Aids working for the upbuilding of the church.

The Missionary Baptist Church was orginized in Martinsville, 1884, in the home of Dr. C. P. Kearfott, on Graveley street. There were fifteen charter members among them, Dr. Kearfott and wife, Mr. and Mrs. J. C. Ambrose, Mrs. Magdalene Shelton, Mrs. Griggs. Miss Matilda Penn was the first to offer for baptism and admission to the church. Having no church nor Sunday School rooms, and believing the Sunday School to be a great feeder for the church they asked permission to hold their Sunday School in Ruffner Institute. Here they held a flourishing school till they built the Broad St. Church in 1890. Many useful men were sent out from this Sunday school. Mr. Haymore was one of its first pastors. Mr. Hugh Smith filled the pulpit for a number of years and did a glorious work, loved by all his members and many of the townspeople. Rev. F. Fuller was another eminent minister in this church, leaving behind him many evidences of his work.

Beginning in 1923, they are building a new and imposing edifice near the old site on the corner of Broad and Church. Dr. J. P. McCabe, of Bedford County, is its present pastor. He is above reproach.

Among the earliest Baptist Churches in Henry County, Va., was Hall Church on Marrowbone Creek. For a long time Nathaniel Hall was the pastor of this church, hence the name "Hall." The Hall land adjoined the Gilmore property. Mr. Hall moved away to Missouri and his descendants still live in their adopted home.

The Episcopal Church was erected on West Church street in 1847, on a lot donated by Marshall Hairston.

Trustees: Anderson Wade, Wm. Clark, Hughes Dillard, Jesse Wootton and George Hairston. The latter's wife was the first one confirmed in this church. In 1900 the new Episcopal building was built on East Church street and soon thereafter the Primitive Baptists purchased the old building.

Rev. Alfred Anson for twenty-eight years served acceptably in this church as rector, and when ill health caused him to resign it was with the genuine regret of his people whom he had served so well. At the present writing Rev, W. E. Roach is the popular rector.

The Christian Church of the town was built 1883-4. It has had a number of pastors but the present minister in charge, is Rev. C. M. Wales. Dr. Chester Bullard was among the first evangelists who introduced this denomination in Henry County. Rev. Stone, Abel, Spencer are some of the prominent ministers.

Horsepasture was for a long time the leading church of this denomination in the county. Then Old Well was built, and next Pleasant Grove. Large Sunday schools are flourishing at each church.

Bassetts, Sheffields, Bullards, Browns, Matthews, Spencers, Dillards, Morris, Fry, etc., are some of its leading families.

CHAPTER VII

TOWNS AND SOCIETIES
MARTINSVILLE

MARTINSVILLE nestling at the foot of the Blue Ridge, protected thereby from the devastating storms and cooled in summer by the pure mountain breezes, is the county-seat. It is built on a rolling plateau having an elevation of 1,100 feet above sea level, two miles from Smith river which supplies water power for furnishing the town with electricity.

The present government has a council of eight men, a mayor and a sergeant all elected by the people. The council appoints a clerk, assessor, health officer, superintendent (or manager of utilities and streets) and also a board of managers of three councilmen subject to the approval of the board of managers and confirmation by the council. The superintendent appoints the other town employees.

In April of 1924, the question was agitated and a vote taken as to whether the town should change the present form of government to what is known as "The Town Manager form." (Carried, not to change the form).

In a speech, prior to the 26 of April, Mr. Geo. L. Graveley, a well known lawyer and ex-mayor, said in regard to his memory of Martinsville before it was incorporated into a town in 1875: "I wish to say I knew Martinsville when it was an insignificant country village of less than 300 people, with only two one-horse village stores, about a dozen residences, large and small, mostly small, four or five grogshops, two ten-pin alleys, at which gambling was openly indulged in, and two so-called hotels with only three or four spare rooms each. It had no sidewalks, mud in the streets a foot deep, hogs wallowed in mud holes in every street. There were no industries of any kind in the town. This is not an exaggerated picture of the town of Martinsville, when practically, the present form of government went into operation.

"I have seen the village above described transformed into the present town of Martinsville, with a busy and hustling population of 5,000, with its comfortable if not palatial homes, with its six white churches and commodious school buildings, with large and varied manufacturing industries, with its numerous, and up-to-date Mercantile establishments, with its smoothly paved streets, with its municipally owned telephone, water, sewerage system, electric lights and power plant sufficient for all municipal purposes for the town, including the lighting of our homes and business buildings and many other improvements and advantages."

At present there are four hotels—The new "Henry," a splendid and commodious building completed August, 1921; The "Hamilton," remodeled and under new management in 1924; The "Mountain View" and the "Lewis." There are three banks—The People's National, The First National and the Piedmont Trust.

There are two hospitals—Shackelford and Lucy Lester.

Woman's Clubs:

The Woman's Club. President, Mrs. J. C. Kearfott.
The Literary Club. President, Mrs. Richard Taylor.
The Current Events Club. President, Mrs. D. H. Pannill.
The Round Dozen Club. President, Mrs. Jno. W. Hamilton.
The Professional and Business Woman's Club. President, Miss Lula Carter.
The Garden Club. President, Mrs. J. D. Glenn.
The Auxiliary of the American Legion. President. Mrs. K. C. Whittle.
The Red Cross. President, Miss Bessie Tuggle.
The Duplicate Bridge Club. President Miss Virginia Pedigo.
The W. C. T. U. President, Mrs. Faith Parrott.
The Patrick Henry Chapter, (D. A. R.) Regent, Mrs. Faith Parrott.
The Joseph Martin Chapter (D. A. R.) Regent, Mrs. H. S. Kearfott.

Men's Clubs:

Patrick Henry Lodge, No. 82 (K. of P.) meets every Friday night.

Piedmont Lodge, No. 152 (A. F. & A. M.) meets every second Monday night.

Pannell Post No. 42 (American Legion, Department of Virginia) C. S. Turner, Post Commander—I. M. Groves, Jr., Post Adjutant.

Kiwanis Club.

FIELDALE

In 1916, the Marshall Field Corporation bought up a large area of land, about 4 miles west of Martinsville, consisting of farming land and primitive forests, involving an investment of $10,000,000. To-day, it is a thriving town with its textile mills and 2,028 inhabitants, according to census of 1920.

BASSETT

Bassett, ten miles from the county-seat, named for the late owner, John H. Bassett. His sons have made it a progressive "Furniture Town." They have good schools, churches of several denominations and one bank —The First National.

SPENCER

Spencer, a small village noted for the Colonial home of Mrs. M. S. Buchanan—"The Homestead."

The village has one church "Old Well," one store and railway station. In its palmy days it was a great tobacco center.

PRESTON

Preston began in 1883 with the building of the D. & W. Railway station with O. R. Gregory as agent. A store room and post office were added with S. R. Hill as postmaster.

These two men formed a partnership in the three Departments: railroading, store and post office, and were the founders of Preston. O. R. Gregory, in time, moved to Martinsville. S. R. Hill remained till his death and was called the "Father of Preston." Ballard Preston owned a large boundary of the land now called Preston, then known as "Preston's Quarters," because he had so many slaves quartered there (See Stoneman's Raid.) O. R. Gregory bought the Preston land, divided it into small tracts and sold it to the present owners. This town has three stores, and a graded school.

RIDGEWAY

Ridgeway is one of the oldest towns in the county. The N. & W. Railroad passes through it. It has one bank, several churches, both graded and high school, with library attached. It has a W. T. C. U. and an active Red Cross organization.

AXTON

Axton, on the D. & W. Railroad, has a good school with an agricultural school attached. Her bank was organized 1923. She also has several churches and stores.

KOEHLER

Koehler was named for the Lumber Company which was established by Mr. Koehler about 1898 under the management of Frank E. Proctor. The Union Station of the D. & W. and N. & W. railways were built several years later. The village has a public garage and a store.

The Patrick Henry Cold Storage Company has an apple storage of 60,000 barrels; its ice capacity being 25 tons daily; its authorized capital $80,000. The plant is located 8 miles west of Martinsville. The N. & W. and D. & W. railways having access to its facilities of transportation. Koehler is the depot.

PATRICK HENRY CHAPTER, D. A. R.

This Chapter was organized June 15, 1905. Mrs. Kizzie Carter, Mrs. Cabell Smith and Mrs. Faith Parrott took the initial steps. Mrs. Smith was appointed the organizing Regent. Mrs. Faith Thomas Parrott has since, with the exception of one year when the office was held by Mrs. Albert Graveley, been Regent. The Chapter has a record of influence, for patriotic and selfsacrificing work. The two outstanding tasks being the "Marker" of North Carolina granite, with bronze tablet, with suitable inscription placed at the entrace of the home and estate of Patrick Henry, seven miles from Martinsville, Va. Mr. Henry lived at this place from 1779 to 1874. The marker was unveiled Nov. 2, 1922. Dr. Waller Barrett, State Regent, made responses to the formal presentation to the Virginia Society by the local Regent, Mrs. Faith Parrott. An oil portrait of the Chapter's namesake, after Sully, by Edward Rosenthal of

Philadelphia, was presented by the Chapter's Regent to the Continental Hall during the thirty-third annual Congress in Washington. D. C. Mrs. Anthony Wayne Cooke accepting it.

OFFICERS PATRICK HENRY CHAPTER

Regent— Mrs. Faith Thomas Parrott, Martinsville.
First Vice Regent—Mrs. Olivia Simmons Keesee.
Second Vice Regent—Mrs. Sarah H. Glenn.
Recording Secretary—Mrs. Minnie Martin Mullins.
Corresponding Secretary—Mrs. Eliza Reamey Pannill.
Treasurer—Mrs. Laura Hairston Penn.
Historian—Miss Virginia Pedigo.
Custodian—Miss Woods Stephens.
Registrar—Mrs. Mary Martin Lester.
Chaplain—Mrs. Elizabeth Morgan Simmons.

UNITED DAUGHTERS OF THE CONFEDERACY

On April 3, 1896, the Confederate Monument Association which had been organized the previous year, was merged into a chapter of the "Daughter of the Confederacy," having for their special work, the building of a monument in Martinsville, in honor of the Confederate Soldiers of Henry County.

The following names were enrolled as charter members of Mildred Lee Chapter U. D. C:—Mrs. N. H. Hairston, President, Mrs. H. C. Smith, Vice-President, Mrs. M. M. Mullins, Secretary, Mrs. S. L. Waller, Treasurer, Mrs. M. L. Zentmeyer, Mrs. O. C. Smith, Mrs. Peter Hairston, Mrs. T. A. Ranson, Mrs. H. S. Williams, Mrs. C. P. Kearfott, Mrs. H. G. Mullins, Mrs. L. L. Graveley, Mrs. B. H. Ingles, Mrs. P. R. Preston.

Other names were added later and then followed continued efforts to raise money for the monument, often with meager returns and many discouragements, for the active membership began to grow smaller and smaller until it was finally reduced to seven, but these seven women with spirits undaunted, inspired by a leader who knew no such word as fail, kept steadily on until after six years of untiring effort on June 3, 1901 in the presence of an immense throng the Confederate Monument in the Court House square, Martinsville, was unveiled by four little girls, Misses Roy Smith, Mary Lu Kearfott, Ivey Smith and Elizabeth Hairston.

A short while after the completion of the monu-

Monument Erected to the Memory of the
Soldiers of the Confederacy by
U. D. C.
Martinsville, Va.

ment, Mrs. N. H. Hairston, who had been president of the Chapter for seven years, having seen the dearest hope of her life realized, decided to remove to a neighboring city and tendered her resignation as president.

Mrs. O. C. Smith succeeded to the presidency and for eighteen years has been the faithful leader of the Chapter. Mrs. J. T. Marshall and Mrs. John W. Carter each having for a short while filled with loyal hearts, this responsible office.

The chapter has grown wonderfully and its members are unfailing in their 'labor of love." The graves of Confederate soldiers in Oakwood Cemetery are marked with marble slabs giving regiment and company of each. Every year the Chapter decorates these graves with flags and flowers. No Confederate veteran is ever laid to rest unnoticed by Mildred Lee Chapter, while the sick and needy veterans and their families are not forgotten; the annual dinner given the Stuart Hairston Camp when they meet to reorganize making the 30th April a red letter day with them.

Gifts of books and pictures to the public school and medals and other rewards for essays on Southern history, attest the interest of the chapter in the training of the youth of Henry County.

HENRY COUNTY RED CROSS CHAPTER

The Henry County Red Cross Chapter was organized in June 1917 with the following officers: W. B. Gates, President, Miss Jane H. Lavinder, Vice-President, Miss Bessie Tuggle, Secretary, and Jno. R. Smith, Treasurer. During the period of the World War the Chapter was very active in the different phases of war work alloted to the Red Cross, it holding the record of achievement for small Chapters in the Potomac Division, with Headquarters at Washington, D. C. Miss Virginia Michael of Roanoke, Va. served as Home Service Secretary from the fall of 1918 until June 1919, which office has been held by Mrs. R. B. Semple since that time. This department looks after the ex-service man and his family, adjusting compensation claims, etc., a large number having been handled by this Chapter. After the close of the war. the Red Cross recognized the health work as the greatest community need, in which the local Chapter is still most actively engaged. The first step in fighting disease and educating our people in health work was to engage the interest of the State Health Department, having a representative visit our Chapter with a view to establishing a permanent Health Unit. This was done in the fall of 1919, the start being made with a Sanitary Demonstrator, who is still actively in the field being sustained by the County and State. The next important step was to put in a Public Health Nurse, Mrs. F. W. Drewry having filled this position with great credit since its installment. The Health Statistics will show what this work has meant to Henry County, as every year beside the inspection of school children, etc., clinics are held in our County for Crippled children, Tuberculosis, Baby Welfare and others, these clinics being in charge of such noted physicians as Dr. W. T. Graham of Richmond, Dr. Samuel Newman of Danville and Dr. Edwards of New York, assisted by the local physicians.

The Henry County Chapter considers that next to winning the war against the Germans, is the winning of the war against disease in Henry County, to which end its members are most actively at work, giving of their time and means with no thought of reward other than the good health of our people. The officers of the Chapter at this time are as follows: Miss Bessie Tuggle, President, Mrs. E. G. Penn, Vice-President, Mrs. O. D. Ford, Secretary, Mrs. J. R. Taylor, Treasurer, Mrs. R. B. Semple, Secretary Home Service and Miss George Griggs of Ridgeway, Virginia, Chairman Junior Red Cross.

COUNTY COURT CLERKS

John Cox, 1777-1808.
Waller Redd, 1808-1825.
Sanford Reamey, 1825-1831.
A. M. Dupuy, 1831-1845.
Jerry Griggs, 1845-1864.
George D. Gravely, 1870-1875.
T. E. Donegan, 1869-1870.
Geoge D. Gravely, 1870-1875.
J. H. Matthews, 1875-1911.
T. C. Matthews, 1911—term not expired.

NEGROES OF TOWN AND COUNTY

As the county is made of both white and colored inhabitants, its history would not be complete without telling something of the latter class.

In 1924 the negro population of Martinsville was 1900.

HISTORY OF HENRY COUNTY, VIRGINIA

The compiler does not know of any race situated as the negroes were, who behaved as well as they did during the Civil War. In this county, they were true and faithful to their masters and their families. For the most part the descendants of these worthy slaves have made good citizens and are progressing along all lines. Good schools are scattered all over the county, taught by their own race. Preston, Spencer and other places have graded schools of two and three teachers.

Every settlement has its churches. Many of the people have long owned their little homes and as the years go by, they are improving their houses as well as their grounds, building gardens, planting orchards, raising poultry, cattle and hogs.

Some of them of small means go to West Virginia and work in the mines and bring their wages home to help their families and improve their little farms.

Jimmy Mullins, at the death of Peter Griggs (white), bought "Snow Bird Mill' one of the curiosities of the county, on account of its size, the original being not over 6 feet by 8 feet and built at the cost of $4.75 by original owners Mr. Griggs (white) and Winston Mullins (colored). This Winston Mullins was the grandfather of Jimmy, the present owner.

This mill is situated on the D. & W. Railroad between Fieldale and Preston and makes as good meal as any in the State.

Mack Baker, a renter of the compiler's mother in her old age, took pride in surpassing the other renters in raising corn in the lowland by keeping the creek banks well cleaned up and the low places fortified against washouts.

Jim Dodson, another renter of Mrs. Hill, is kindness itself to all sick people, both white and black. In fact, kindheartedness is one of the characteristics of this race.

There are many small settlements throughout the county, Cherry Town, east of Martinsville, being the largest.

The colored citizens of Martinsville have the most beautifully located residential section of the town. They have as many churches as the white people, good public schools with two large, new commodious buildings well equipped and the "Piedmont Christian Institute," a mission school for training both boys and girls. James H. Thomas, principal.

Two physicians and one dentist—Dr. E. O. Woodward, Dr. D. O. Baldwin. Dr. Baldwin was the first physician of Martinsville to volunteer in the World War. There is a business block and theater in his town called by his name. Dr. W. A. Fears is the dentist.

There is a sufficiency of hotels, cafes and restaurants, a barbers' shop, pressing club, etc., etc.

Dossie Hoyle's and Madame King's Beauty Parlors are well patronized by the white ladies.

The colored people have as many lodges and clubs as the white people.

CHAPTER VIII

BIOGRAPHIES

REV. ROBERT C. ANDERSON

Robert Campbell Anderson was born in Campbell county, Virginia, March 16, 1823. He graduated in 1843 with first honors from Hampden Sidney College, and in 1847 from Union Theological Seminary, New York, also licensed the same year by the Presbytery of Hanover. Staying a short time at Appomatox Court House Church, he moved to Henry county, and in 1854 organized the first Presbyterian church in the county, now the Martinsville Anderson Memorial church, with three members. He was connected with this church for forty years. He built Cedar Chapel near his home and about the Civil War period, he erected another at Ridgeway, but all later became centered in the Martinsville organization.

In March 1895, the people of Martinsville held a union meeting of prayer at the Christian church. Mr. Anderson was to close his pastorate of his church (the Presbyterian) the first of April, and had been so faithful, and had lived such an exemplary life, and so full of faith in God's abiding love that it touched the hearts of all members of the churches and every one united in paying him due respect. Many tributes were paid him and at the close of the services the entire congregation united in singing: "Blessed be the tie that binds."

He was a man of good natural capacity, highly educated and a great theologian, and his sermons were imbued with the evangelistic spirit.

Faith was his favorite subject. No man more fully exemplified the power of that faith, "That works by love purified the heart and overcomes the world." Many were believed to have been restored to health through his prayers. In answer to his prayer for feed for his animals, a neighbor drove up with a load for him. "Ah! brother," he exclaimed, "God has sent that in answer to my prayer, and I thank him for it."

On another occasion a fire was sweeping through

the heart of the town and every one was aroused to the very highest pitch, but he just went home and begged for aid and Lo! the wind changed, and the town was saved!

In this age of commercialism, when the ministers generally know the amount of their yearly income in advance, it is wonderful to think of the years of services given without money and without price by this man to the people of Henry county. Few hearts equaled this great soul who spoke the word of God for real love, and always appealed to his congregation. "To keep yourselves unspotted from the world."

On Nov. 8, 1899 his spirit took its flight to rest with the God he served so faithfully and trusted so implicitly.

MISS KATE ANDERSON

Miss Katherine Virginia Anderson was born Jan. 9, 1857 in this county where she spent her useful and happy life. When nine years of age she joined the Presbyterian church and announced that she would give one tenth of what she made to the Lord's cause, and this she always did.

Nature endowed her with rare gifts of heart and mind. She had a beautiful christian character, and her life was filled with the fruits of the Spirit and abounded in a great variety of good works. She was an artist of acknowledged ability, and painted hundreds of portraits and miniatures that are treasures of the highest works of art.

The income from her labors was contributed to the welfare of those she loved in a most beautiful and beneficial method and the success attained by her people in the professions rightly belongs to her in a great meausure. There is no parallel to her life in this sphere of sisterly affection and accomplishment in all the great history of Virginia.

The great service rendered to her family is almost equaled in her great work in her community for the Church and the sunday schools she loved so well and cared for so devotedly. She was an active leader in the Woman's Auxiliary as well as the Young People's work. There was nothing closer to her heart than the Mission Cotton Mill Sunday School which she conducted for years at the expense of her health and strength.

She was loyal and faithful to her church and pastor, untiring and unlimited in her devotion to her family and

HON. J. M. BARKER, SR.
Axton, Va.

friends, and freely gave her life, her strength, and her means that others might be happy in the homes that her labors blessed.

This county has developed many grand women, thousands of the best of God's creation, but it pleased Him to make her a character that ought to be remembered as the highest type of womanhood, Miss Kate Anderson. She died at Orando, Florida, March 8, 1922.

HON. J. M. BARKER

The history of the county offers no parallel to Hon. J. M. Barker of Axton who was born about 1840 and who lived in this county all his active life. He belongs to the order of self-made men.

He was not given the opportunity for an education, but he learned to work with his hands and use his head to the best purpose.

The Civil War ended to find him possessed of just two things brains and energy. He studied how to grow crops and improve his land at the same time and made money growing tobacco all along. He invested his savings in more land and continued this process till he was one of the largest land owners in the county and one of the biggest growers of tobacco in the state. He made it fine and sold it well and here was the secret of his prosperity.

He was elected Supervisor of his district and soon made Chairman of the Board and this position he held for many years. He and W. G. Burgess, the Supervisor from the Ridgeway District, were two of the ablest members that ever graced that body, and during their administrations, the finances of the county were conducted on a business and satisfactory method for the whole county.

Gov. J. Hoge Tyler appointed him a member of the State Board of Agriculture and his acts were so satisfactory that Gov. A. J. Montague appointed him a second time. His whole services were of a high order and redounded to the welfare of the entire state.

He was hospitable, big hearted, appreciative, and a great citizen and at home he was an ambitious father that gloried in the achievements of his family and friends. When he died the county lost one of its big men by nature, made great by human endeavor.

J. R. BROWN

John R. Brown of Martinsville, Va., was born Jan. 14, 1842, in Franklin Co., Va. His family is American in all its branches. He is a descendant of the distinguished families of Rives and Spotswood of Colonial and Revolutionary fame.

Frederick Brown, the founder of the branch in America, of which he is a descendant, reached here from Eng, and in 1745. He was a gallant soldier in the War of the Revolution. The subject of this sketch, at the age of nineteen, entered the Confederate Army, Company D, 24th Virginia Volunteers. He was married in 1862 to Miss Anne Eliza Vial. Of this union there were ten children.

He came too Martinsville, with his father Frederick Rives Brown in 1882, both having previously built their homes, and at once erected a large place for the manufacture of tobacco under the old firm name of J. R. & F. R. Brown. They also built a splendid and commodious warehouse for the sale of leaf tobacco.

He organized the first bank in Martinsville, known as the Henry County Bank and was engaged in the mercantile business for several years. At that time Martinsville had only two or three stores: Messrs. J. B. Lavinder, Thomas Green Penn and C. A. Hamilton.

He was elected Mayor of Martinsville in 1884. He is a prominent Mason, having been an active member of this order over sixty years and Master of the Lodge soon after moving to Martinsville. He is public-spirited and exceedingly popular, easily making friends, always ready to lend a helping hand in any movement to advance the interest of the town. He became an active leader in politics and a lifelong republican. He was elected to the 50th Congress from the 5th Virginia District, receiving 12,773 votes against 9,614 for Col. George C. Cabell, democrat.

He is now one of Martinsville's oldest and most honored citizens—celebrated his 82nd birthday January 14th, 1924. He has always been a great reader and still takes a lively interest in current events and political news of the day. We predict that he will live to see Martinsville the greatest city in this section of Virginia.

MRS. JOHN S. BROWN
McDonough, Ga.

MRS. KATE BRADFIELD BROWN

Mrs. Kate Bradfield Brown is a lineal descendant of Mrs. Susan Traylor Bradfield, daughter of J. C. Traylor. She is the daughter of William Robert Bradfield and Willie Florence Pitman. Her father is the youngest son of Mrs. Susan Traylor Bradfield.

Mrs. Brown was educated at La Grange College, La Grange, Ga., the oldest organized, although not the first chartered college for women in the world. Later she received a certificate from the University of Tenn. After teaching three years, she married John S. Brown of Locust Grove, Henry county, Ga., and with her husband she has traveled extensively in the United States and Canada.

Later, she taught for a number of years, holding some of the most responsible positions in Henry and Butts counties, Ga.

For eight years she served as assistant postmaster at Locust Grove, Ga.; was president of Locust Grove Woman's Club, and was the first president of Henry County Federation of Women's Clubs.

She has been very active in church, Sunday school and missionary work, having taught in Sunday school for more than twenty years, served as an officer in the Methodist Church and president of the Missionary Society.

She also was Chairman of some of the Liberty Loan Drives in Henry County, and under her leadership the county went well over the top in subscriptions; also, District Chairman for War Savings Stamp Drive, and worked strenuously in the Red Cross during the World War. receiving a Certificate of Honor signed by Woodrow Wilson for service rendered in the Red Cross.

June 1924, she was elected Superintendent of Henry County schools.

CHARLES BENJAMIN BRYANT

Col. C. B. Bryant was born in 1842, the son of Rowland Bryant who came from Rockbridge county. He had no college advantages, but was an apt and close student of men. He married, Malinda, the daughter of George Waller, in 1865. No issue.

He studied civil engineering and later law. He was admitted to the bar and was fond of chancery practice.

He delighted in military and was made a Colonel of the Virginia Militia.

During the Civil War, he was in the Quartermaster Department, being an adjutant in this army before he was elected Clerk of Henry county and Circuit Courts. He held this office during the remainder of the Confederacy.

He was an expert penman and the Clerk's office shows his beautiful writing covering a long period. Later he was made Commissioner of Accounts and added to his reputation as a pen artist as well as public accountant.

For a short time he did civil engineering, but was elected Mayor in 1881. He was a very efficient officer, and the town never had a more enthusiastic booster and promoter of expansion. Not possessed of much means himself, he could make plans so plain and plausible to others, that he easily elicited capital in many enterprises that meant for the town's prosperity. There are not many public utilities of his day, you can mention that he did not formulate, project, or boost in some helpful way. No man who knew his work and influence would deny him to have been one of the most useful citizens the town ever had. So accustomed was everybody to demand and accept his services for the public, he was not properly rated during his career.

He was a great advocate of power, inventions, and transportation for the entire county. No one excelled his work in promoting both of the railroads that traverse the county and projected its permanent prosperity.

He was the engineer and diplomatic negotiator of the town's water-rights and system, secretary of the Phospho-Lithia Springs Company, and had time to fill the position of Secretary of the Henry County Historical Society.

He was a man of erect carriage, mentally alert, cordial in greeting, censervative in advising, calm in temperament, and a pleasant companion. He was a true patriot, a faithful friend, a good neighbor, and bore an air that was impressive and a wit that rarely failed him. The county as a whole will never have a more loyal and devoted son to labor for the general welfare than Col. Bryant.

He died on Nov. 30, 1915, and was buried in Martinsville, which is, in many of its developments, a monument to his energy and sagacity, among the friends and neighbors he loved so well.

COLONEL JOHN DILLARD

Colonel John Dillard, the first of the family to settle in this county, was born in Amherst county, Virginia, in 1751. His father was James Dillard who was born in the same county in 1727, married Mary Hunt of Essex (1734—1748), and died in 1794.

James Dillard was an officer in the Colonial Militia. (See Statutes of Henning 1758) ; a King's Magistrate (See Va. Mag. page 254, 1909) ; High Sheriff of Amherst county (See Deed Book C. Rec. 1771) ; besides other positions of honor and trust.

Naturally, he inherited the love of military from his father, and so he early enlisted in the Continental Army in the early years of the Revolution (See War Department Records). He was wounded at the battle of Princeton and sent home to recuperate. As soon as able physically, he was commissioned Captain of the Committee of Safety of Pittsylvania when this county was included, and was also appointed to gather supplies for the army. This is about the date of his arrival, for the records show that he had a tract of land surveyed in 1778.

We can review his career during this period from Pittsylvania Accounts as follows: Committee of Safety, 1775-6-120, H. D. May 1777-75. Audits Accounts 1779-141. War 23-1777, also from volume 15 of the North Carolina State Records, page 123, is seen where at the Abraham Cresons Camp, Oct. 19, 1780, Virginia officers were asked to join in a council to determine upon measures to be put in execution against insurgents. In response to this we read the records showing the officers that attended this council; viz.

From North Carolina: Martin Armstrong, C. C.; Joseph Williams, Lieut. Col.; William Meridith, Capt. (Surry) ; Samuel Henderson, Capt. (Guilford).

From Henry County, Virginia: Abraham Penn, Col.; Peter Hairston, Capt.; John Dillard, Col.; James Poteat, Capt.; James Torrents, Capt.; Samuel Hairston, Capt.; Thomas Bush, Capt.

This discussion by the officers resulted in the issuing of a proclamation urging the tories to join the patriots and promising to use their influence with the general assembly of North Carolina, to obtain a pardon to those who availed themselves under this opportunity.

In the sketch of Col. George Hairston is found the Fletcher tragedy and the marriage of his widow to Col. Hairston, depicted from the Hairston standpoint. Here is presented the same incident, from the Dillard information, claiming in addition to the family tradition that a lady now living at Mt. Airy, N. C., corroborates the facts, her grandfather being at the time one of Capt. Dillard's soldiers.

Captain Letcher, of Patrick county, a man of wealth and high character, who belonged to General Steven's brigade of those Virginia troops then serving under General Greene, was at home with his wife, whose condition required his presence. One evening after dark, he was called to the door, and shot down while his wife looked on from her bed with her three year old girl. A Tory named John Nickolds was the assassin, and had a camp near by collecting cattle, horses, etc., for the British. William Carter, a soldier on furlough, notified Captain Dillard, and the latter with his company and such volunteers as he could get, overtook Nickolds with his gang of thieves, routed them, and scattered the gang, killing the leader and sent the booty to General Stevens, who wrote a letter, now in the family, thanking him for the supplies for the army, and complimenting him for "bagging that abominable scoundrel, Nickolds." This Nickolds did not belong to the Va. family but perhaps to the N. C. family. There was only one Nickolds of Henry Co. family of military age and he was a patriot.

On the spot where he lies buried we read: In memory of William Letcher who was assassinated in his own house in the bosom of his family by a Tory of the revolution on the 2nd day of August, 1780, age, 30 years. May the tears of sympathy fall on the tomb of the brave".

The grave evidently was in the yard, or near it, as part of the foundation of the house, is still standing. Letcher's widow married George Hairston, and the little baby girl, Bethenia, when grown, married David Pannill, and in the course of time became the great grandmother of Gen. J. E. B. Stuart. On a near by hill is the grave of Capt. Archibald Stuart, the father of the latter, and a revolutionary soldier. Captain Stuart conducted a law school in the neighborhood which several Henry county lawyers attended.

Not alone as a warrior did Col. Dillard serve his

country, but in other fields as well. He was a member of the legislature from Henry county the session of 1785-86, and later served as magistrate, besides other offices, showing the esteem in which he was held by his fellowman.

He was a patriot, brave and true to his country, schooled in the pioneer days to hardship that developed leaders that lead, and accomplished something for country, as well as for his own family, and left a record of achievements worthy of preserving to posterity. He died in 1882.

GENERAL JOHN DILLARD

General John Dillard was born in this county in 1783, surrounded by the usual blessings of a plantation in those days. He had no peculiar advantages of education, or a large patrimony, but he had energy and a will that combined with his judgment soon laid the foundation of a competency. Font Hill, his home was six miles east of Martinsville.

He was early honored by the almost unanimous vote of his countymen to a seat in the House of Delegates of Virginia. This was repeated to the entire satisfaction of his constituency, and his official acts were ever in the interest of the State, till the call to arms in the war of 1812. In this he was one of the first to volunteer at the head of a gallant body of men from this county.

It was in the campaign around Norfolk he showed the qualities of leader, by his display of military tactics in the field of action, as well as in caring for his men taken from the hills to the miasmatic country around that besieged city by the sea.

When this strife was over, he returned to his home to care for his neglected private affairs. Then, at the first vacancy, the legislature conferred upon him the rank and office of Brigadier General of militia, and this, too, with almost a unanimous vote of that august body.

As a magistrate, often his advice was followed that led to compromise instead of litigation restoration of friendships instead of feuds.

He was at one time sheriff of the county, filling it as carefully, and painstakingly as he did the office of Brigadier General of militia, and at the time of his death, he was a member of the old county court, which adjourned at their January term, when the sad tidings came in testimony of their regard for their deceased brother.

A Richmond paper, when it announced his death said:

"He died as he had lived, without fear and without reproach. A soldier and a philosopher through life, he met death unflinchingly, as the portion of all."

He died January 9, 1847, as he said: "Death, by far the most important hour of life." This when urging his family to meet him in Heaven.

COL. JEREMIAH GRIGGS

Jeremiah Griggs, the oldest son of Jeremiah Michael Griggs by his first wife, was born in Henry county, Sept. 25, 1800, and died May 6th, 1871.

He early in life took great interest in public affairs and was prominently identified with every movement for the advancement of the county's welfare.

He had only the local advantages of education usual in those days, and never entered college. However, he was a great student of nature and of men. He was quiet and modest in demeanor, but acquired much learning, and had great abilities as displayed in his every undertaking. So unassuming was he that scarcely no one knew he possessed a library however it was learned that after his death he possessed many rare old volumes of English classics.

The public trusted him implicitly and soon called him into public life. In 1841-42, he was a member of the legislature of Virginia from Henry county. Here he demonstrated his abilities as a legislator.

For many years he was a colonel of the Virginia Militia, and although past sixty years of age when the Civil war broke out, he gave generously his worldly goods and his time and talents to the Confederacy. A good portion of his ready cash went for flannel to make shirts for the soldiers. He was at first opposed to leaving the union, but when his native State withdrew, he followed wholeheartedly in the cause. He made many expeditions to the army, helping the soldiers, and his widow, Mrs. Alzira Griggs, has told interestingly of many of these trips to the front and on his return of his having to be disrobed and "deloused" at the gate in order not to spread infection within doors of his home.

He was Clerk of the County Court of Henry for years and held the office till his death. His official acts are recorded for all time in his own handwriting here, which were eminently satisfactory to his countrymen.

MRS. M. W. HAMILTON
Martinsville, Va.

He was a member of the Baptist church, and a Blue Lodge mason, and served his lodge at Martinsville many years as chaplain. His dying words give a good character sketch of the man,— "I have always done the right as I saw the right, and I die at peace with God and Man."

MARTHA WOODSON HAMILTON
(Written By Her Daughters)

July 14, 1845, in the home of Rev. and Mrs. W. W. Hill, in Henry Co. Va., a little daughter was born and named Martha Woodson for a sister and a brother of Mrs. Hill.

She grew as any normal child, among her brothers and sisters. Thru the days of her childhood and youth the attributes, courage, fortitude and strength, coupled with an every-day sunshiny disposition, were apparent. An incident of her school day life suggests the development of these sterling qualities. While playing in a creek near the little school-house she stepped into a bed of quicksand. When help arrived she was down to her armpits in the treacherous suckhole. With calmness the little heroine watched her rescuers and smiled thru the moments of peril. Courage was ever one of the distinguishing marks of her after life.

As a girl and in her young womanhood she was much sought after socially: an excellent conversationalist; brilliant in repartee, handsome in person; cheerful in disposition, and with a happy laugh that all liked to hear. Public spirited, she never failed to lend a hand to every worthy cause.

At the age of 25, she was married to Samuel Henry Lavinder, in 1870, and to them were born two children Mary Catherine, who died at the age of 22 months, and Jane Hickey.

After a few years of happy wedded life her husband became ill and the physicians told her the trouble was tubercular, advising her to go at once to Florida with him.

By the time they had reached the end of the railroad on their journey she was ill with pneumonia, and for several days hovered between life and death. At last the physicians told her husband that there were no hopes for her recovery, and that she would be dead by the time he could get a message to their people in Virginia. Over hearing the conversation and so weak that the nurses had to bend to catch the words, she whispered: "Mr. Lavinder may cry all he wants to, and he may send the message but I am not going to die".

When speaking of the occurrence later she said: "I went to nurse Mr. Lavinder; not to die".

As soon as she was able they went to a secluded spot on Miami Bay, far from friends and neighbors. Here and later, up and down the St. John's River, they camped, hoping in roughing it in an out-door life to cure her husband.

Many and varied were their experiences, and in after years nothing delighted her children more than to gather around the fireside and hear her tell of them. One of the most thrilling adventures was with a man-eating shark. She was in the bay one day, when Mr. Lavinder saw a sudden flash of white. He called with a frenzied cry of warning to her, and she swam quickly to shallow water.

A short while later they were lost on the bay in a small row boat, and night coming on they lost all sense of direction. Her husband decided to run close to shore which he could see faintly outlined, and then wade to land. Leaving her in the boat when they had reached shallow water he went ashore. Huge porpoises played about the boat, blowing and leaping out of the water, leaving long streaks of light on the water, until finally it seemed as if she were adrift in a lake of fire. Mr. Lavinder got his bearings and called to her directions, which she followed.

Their stay in Florida had reduced their savings until she had barely enough for their return home, which they reached to find deeply involved in debt, and her husband a confirmed invalid.

She had received excellent training in all house-keeping arts from her mother; knowing how to cook and serve with true Southern hospitality. Nature had endowed her with the tact of good management and circumstances had taught her economy; and now both served her well, for she was face to face with a great problem. She faced the situation with a brave resolution. Taking advantage of her training she kept table boarders.

In 1876 her husband passed away leaving his wife and little daughter to win or lose in the battle of life. She opened her house to roomers, and with the help of her father she paid off the indebtedness on her house and land.

Her 2nd marriage was to Charles Atley Hamilton in 1879, and to them four children were born (See Hamilton family). The home, a large brick structure, was added to and transients invited and a hotel opened which was destined to become known farther than nation wide, and it was said of Mrs. Hamilton as she lay in her last sleep in her beautiful new home: "She has been a blessing to Martinsville, and she is known from Ocean to Ocean and from the Lakes to the Gulf".

While her husband had assisted her in building "Hotel Hamilton". in the year 18—he felt called to enter the ministry as an evangelist, and managing the affairs of the Hotel and other business was left entirely to her.

Soon the reputation of "The Hamilton " reached beyond Martinsville; traveling men from near towns and cities made it a point to spend their Sundays and off days there, stating that they found it more of a home than anywhere in their travels.

As the name and fame of the hotel spread more rooms were added and more help secured to give the service that won praise from every one who visited Martinsville and found rest and enjoyment in the real home life felt wherever Mrs. Hamilton's presence ruled. While being firm with her negro servants she was never unjust. At times she would administer ringing rebukes, but was always considerate of them, and they loved her with an ardent affection. Thirty years of service proved this love of her servants. "Mammy" Sally Joyner, who was indeed mammy to Mrs. Hamilton as well as to the family, remained with her even after she retired from the hotel over thirty years in all, and is still with the family of her youngest son. Laura Smith was cook for over twenty-five years; Jim Preston, porter for about the same time. Mort Smith, head waiter, was allowed to remain and draw full wages long after his days of usefulness were over. He was incapacitated by blindness and old age after serving faithfully for over thirty-five years. These trusty old servants proved their faith and love by their works.

Visitors from all parts of Virginia and from other States paid Mrs. Hamilton high tribute in telling their friends that she was the greatest factor in putting Martinsville on the map with Hotel Hamilton.

The following incident took place in England. Mr.

and Mrs. Keesee, prominent in the business and social life of Martinsville, were at the home of Shakespeare, in Stratford, Eng. Mrs. Keesee had been chatting with an elderly Englishman, and when she registered as from Virginia., U.S. A., this Englishman said to her: "From what part of Virginia"? She replied, "Martinsville". He said: "Oh! I've been there; such a nice hotel you have". "She interposed: "Owned by Mrs. Hamilton". "Yes, Hamilton Hotel. They had the best fried chicken in the world or rather the best I've ever eaten". After Mrs. Hamilton's death the hotel property was sold out of the family and was burned Sept. 5, 1925.

While constantly busy with the cares of life she never lost sight of her children and their welfare. She always knew where they were, and took time for their best interests in the home, school, and society; and on Sunday mornings, she saw them ready for the Sabbath school and church. She was a member of all the societies of the church and responded to all calls generously.

Her hotel sample rooms, chairs, tables were always at the disposal of the young people for their church teas, candy-stews, and suppers; the parlors opened to their social gatherings. Her home was ever open to the preachers, and she made it a home for them whenever they wished.

One of her great characteristics was her laugh: its music, its sweetness, and its infection. One lady remarked: "Her laugh is like a tonic". The world about her was made better and happier by it.

She did not have opportunity to go out among her friends and mix socially to a great extent outside her own home, but her acquaintances came to her. In these social intercourses she seemed possessed with a dual personality. She would not lose a word of the conversation; no interruption marred its pleasure, tho at the same time she would be directing the work of her house, giving directions to her servants, etc., her mind taking note of each without interference. She could write a letter without interruption, at the same time conscious of the work going on about her and directing its course: this dual nature of her mind being of great value in her busy life.

When at last her health gave way she retired to a private home accompanied by her daughter, Miss Janie, who was her mainstay until the angel of death "called the weary one to rest". After a lingering illness she died at her home in Martinsville, Va., at 7:15 P. M. Nov. 10, 1916.

HAMLETT

Wm. Jesse Hamlett, born in Prince Edward county, Va., son of Wm. J. Hamlett. Wm. Jesse Hamlett's mother was a sister of Frank Taylor Wootton, of Prince Edward Co., Va. Issue: John Thomas Mar. Miss Puckett, of Wythe Co. Addie md. John Booker, Julia C. md. W. C. Philips, Cornelia M. md. W. H. Schroder. Annie d. Young, so did Geo. T. J. C. md. Miss Brankley, of N. C. Kit's children; James, Roy, Wootton, Henon, Starling, Winnie, Annie, Julian. Col. Hamlett was a merchant, deputy sheriff, teacher and soldier in Civil War.

PATRICK HENRY

Patrick Henry was born in Hanover county May 29th, 1736, and came to this county in 1779 and settled on Leatherwood. He inherited from his mother's people, the Winstons, the gift of oratory, but his mother's wit came from a long line of ancestors. She was Sarah Winston, and was a fine specimen of Welsh womanhood, vivacious, dramatic in turn, and eloquent in speech.

He was not a studious boy, but loved sports more than books. However, he acquired in some way a great command of English and also Latin by a method hard to explain. By association he formed the habit of pronouncing these words, yearth, naiteral and larning, not according to the standard authorities, therefore Mr. Jefferson critically styled him uneducated. It was a fact, however, that he really acquired much practical learning.

He was anything but a success till he began the study of law, which he learned after beginning the practice of it. His examiners granted him license because of his special ability of arguing his side of a question. He was a far better student of human nature, and on this element he built his everlasting fame. Assemblies fell under the spell of the music and charm of his voice and he swayed them like the March wind the treetops.

At eighteen, he married Sarah Shelton, a poor girl, and reared a family. She died in 1777, and he married Dorothea Dandridge, granddaughter of Governor Spotswood, who was much his junior. At his death the baby in his house was four years old, and during his life he never slept at home beyond the sound of the cradle. The music he was accustomed to make on the violin was never as sweet to his ears as the peals of childhood laughter around his fireside.

He was deeply religious, being a member of the Episcopal church and opposed to strong drink. He tried to substitute home made beer for alcohol, and had it served on his table on great occasions. However, he was far ahead of his times, and the people could not be easily changed in habit.

Having bought ten thousand acres of land lying on the eastern and north-eastern part of the county on Leatherwood creek, he built his house on a ridge a few miles east of Henry courthouse, and began the practice of law. In the public records here may be seen his papers and one may learn his methods which show the great amount of work done and how neat and finished each was executed by his hands.

The next year, Henry county, in 1780, sent him to the General Assembly where he was the leading spirit not only in State affairs, but those affecting the nation.

His position and speeches on the adoption of the Constitution by Virginia is a part of the history of the United States, and it is beyond the scope of this volume to present them here. Suffice it to say, he was ever fearful that his native state would lose her rights under the plan proposed, and he opposed ratification. However, after the amendments were adopted, he became satisfied, and embraced the Constitution.

At Leatherwood he could rest from the strife of the world and live in ease on his great estate. Here he wrote to Washington, and other great figures in National affairs, that he wanted to live his life out free from public care. However, the people would not allow it.

He had served three terms as Governor during the Colonial period, but no sooner than Virginia became free, he was elected the first Governor of the first State of a free people, and he left for the State capital at Williamsburg in 1784.

He left his daughter on Leatherwood, so called from a tough species of willow that grows on the banks of that stream, and after spending his time as Governor of the State, located in Charlotte county, where he had a beautiful home, and here he died June 6th, 1799.

He left a large family and a still larger estate, and now his descendants number hundreds scattered throughout the United States, but his fame as an orator is worldwide, and his name is among the immortals.

MRS. MARY CATHERINE HILL
(BY HER DAUGHTER, ELLA HILL)

In eighteen and twenty four there came to the home of Alexander Hunter Bassett and his wife, Mary Koger Bassett, a bright little girl who was given the name of her mother and aunt (Mary C. Bassett). She became the idol of the home and her parents and was subject to them: her education was limited on account of scarcity of schools. One of her teachers, Miss Charlotte Grimes was an all round teacher and the good influence she exerted upon her continued with her throughout life.

She was united in marriage to W. W. Hill in eighteen and forty. The young couple commenced housekeeping at once, and she was the home maker. Their means were limited but nothing seemed to discourage her, always saying "It is better further on". She was aided much in the training and educating of her children by Dr. G. W. G. Estes, a teacher in the family. When he was called to another field this duty devolved upon her eldest daughter.

The Civil War found her with nine living children and one dead. These, indeed, were trying days but she was equal to the task. She raised her cotton, picked out the seed with her fingers, carded, spun and wove it into cloth and then made the garments with her fingers with thread spun at home. Of course she had the help of her children in this work.

The soldiers in returning from the war, found in her a friend, that would deprive herself of food in order to help them.

She had some knowledge of medicine and gave her friends and neighbors the benefit of it, cheering and brightening many homes in this way.

She united with the Methodist Church when she was ten years old. Many years afterwards her parents united with the Church having been, to some extent, awakened by her bright Christian living.

The famous campmeetings held at old Mt. Bethel Church had in her a great worker for she kept a tent and the poor and needy as well as many others were her guests. At one of these meetings an infant daughter was very ill, she did not abandon her post but pressed on and the little infant became the famous Hotel Keeper of Martinsville, Va. Mrs. Hill's home was the home of the Methodist itinerant and many of them have been heard to say what a blessing she had been to them.

She had a musical voice and lead the singing in her younger days. Her husband preceded her to the Better Land 31 yrs.

Two children were the only ones of the family left in the homestead and one of them was called higher nineteen years later. The remaining daughter and her mother lived alone for twelve years. This good woman seemed to have for her motto. "Press Onward", for she not only toiled with her hands but, was the guiding spirit of the farm life and it was only when she was compelled by physical infirmities to lay aside work that she did so. Even then she kept her fingers busy knitting for children and grand children until loss of sight denied her even this pleasure. How she missed the reading of the New Testament and Psalms? It was the greatest privation she had. Her hearing was bad also so she rested in bed much of her time and employed her time by singing, praying, quoting Scripture and reciting hymns, often saying "I have had a good time".

Her eldest daughter prevailed upon her to move to Martinsville in the fall of 1921 where she was received with open arms by her son-in-law, O. R. Gregory and his wife. They built her a comfortable home in their yard and rendered her every comfort that love could think of. Three of her daughters were near to help her in every way they could. Rev. W. B. Jett of the Martinsville Church, greatly comforted and cheered her while she was waiting for the summons. "It is enough. "Come Home".

Her Christian Spirit continued to develop during her dark hours and every particle of dross seemed to be burned and the gold refined. Her one thought was to help others in life.

After the death of her husband she leaned upon her eldest son S. R. Hill till he was summoned to the Better Land. She never ceased to feel this deprivation but was submissive to the Divine will.

On July 9, 1922, just at sunset her pure spirit took

its flight so quietly that the dear ones watching could scarcely tell when it left. Her body was taken to the family Cemetery attended by relatives and friends. Rev. W. B. Jett and Rev. G. E. Powell officiated. The floral offerings were beautiful and they were offered by loving and tender hearts.

She awaits her dearly loved ones over there and they know where to find her.

REV. WILLIAM WIRT HILL
(BY HIS DAUGHTER, ELLA HILL)

The subject of this sketch was born in 1822 in Henry county, the son of John Waddy and Judith Parks Hill. His educational advantages were very meagre, acquiring nothing of English grammar, but became very well versed in Latin. This was learned at the Patrick Henry Academy.

His father died when he was fourteen years of age. His mother survived her husband forty-four years, and was cared for by him all this time. "Mother" was a most sacred name to him.

He sowed some wild oats in youth, but after his marriage to Miss Mary C. Bassett, he was converted and joined the Methodist Episcopal Church, South, and in time became a local preacher.

He was an enthusiast on the "Temperance Question", and did his first work on this subject at Temperance Hall, near Mt. Bethel church. "The Cold Water Band" was the society he most delighted in.

He cherished the Sunday School and was very successful in this work. In his younger days, he had regular appointments for preaching and he is remembered by his friends as a good earnest preacher. He spent much time visiting the sick, the lonely, and the distressed, cheering and comforting them.

Both he and his wife had great ambition to have their children become men and women of culture and refinement. Each lived to watch over them and had the pleasure of seeing them all attain maturity and filling their little "niches" in the world.

In his latter years he devoted his labors mostly to the farm, and took the greatest interest in dairy products.

He never desired political office but was interested in the politics of his better days. Clay, Webster, and Calhoun, were familiar names in the household, but when politics became corrupt he ceased his work in it. He had many tried and true friends in the ministry. Among them we recall the Rev. A. D. Betts and Rev. Charles Phillips of the N. C. Conference, and the Revs. D. F. Hodges and J. L. Pribble of the Va. Conference.

He was never robust, but aged fast, and while he was only sixty-nine when he passed away, he appeared very much older.

His last illness continued three years and he suffered much without anodynes, paregoric being given at first, then fluid opium. One day he called a daughter and said: "I have preached temperance all my life and I do not want to go to heaven with a perfumed breath. I am going to quit taking it. Don't let me hurt any one tie me to a tree if necessary, but I must quit it." He did quit by leaving off one drop at a time. He had an unusual strong mind and resolution that served him well at this time.

He was tenderly cared for throughout his last illness by his wife and two of his daughters, and many, many friends. One day just before the end, he called one of his daughters and said to her: "I am ready." "Ready for what father?" He replied, "To meet my Savior, Lucy, Johnny, and all the dear ones."

On July, 22, 1891, his spirit took its fllight to the mansion in the skies.

COL. GEORGE HAIRSTON

George Hairston was of Scotch descent on his father's side, while his mother came of English stock. He was born in Franklin county, Virginia in 1750, and came to Henry county 20 years later, and bought the Beaver Creek home with 20,000 acres of land. Martinsville stands on a part of this purchase which tradition says was made at ten cents per acre. It was by this investment he laid the permanent foundation of great wealth that stayed with him and his descendants for over a century.

He was brave, patriotic, and farsighted to the limit. When the Revolutionary war raged we find his name enrolled in the list that went to death or glory. His deeds are a part of the history of this great struggle, and will not be repeated here. He was Captain of a company that marched from Beaver Creek in March 1781 and hurried to General Greene's assistance, and during that month covered themselves with glory at the battle of Guilford Court House, where the patriot army fought Lord Cornwallis to a standstill.

When the war was over he returned to his plantation and by careful attention gathered great wealth rapidly from his vast estate. However, he responded again to to his country's call. In the war of 1812 he was acting Brigadier General in command of the 3rd, 4th, 5th, and 6th, Virginia and 35th North Carolina regiments, with the rank of colonel. He saw much service, and was in the engagement that repulsed General Ross who burned Washington and was killed at Bladensburg.

For the second time he left the field of battle after peace was declared, and resumed the quiet life of a planter, but soon the public called him again, and he served his county as sheriff, and later still, he was elected a member of the legislature from the county.

This closed his long public career, and from this period he dwelt in peace by his own fireside, which he had most assuredly earned.

He was unmarried when in the war of Independence. A tragedy enacted during this war, changed the whole tenor of his life. Captain Letcher, a friend in the army, came home on a furlough to see his sick wife He entered his home and had barely put his gun on the rack when he was shot down in the presence of his wife and a 3 year old girl, by a band of Tories lying in wait. George Hairston gathered his band of men pursued and caught the Tories and convicted them before a drumhead court martial, and hanged every one of them. This spot, in Patrick county, is still called "Drumhead".

This baby, in the course of time, became the grandmother of Gen. J. E. B. Stuart, the great Confederate leader. The widow Letcher, in five months after the death of her husband became the wife of the avenger of her first husband's death, and presided over the great hospitable home on Beaver creek, with true Virginia grace. (This marriage was hastened by the difficulties surrounding Mrs. Letcher, and fear of Tories.) She came from distinguished families herself, for she was a Perkins, a daughter of the pioneer, and her grandmother was a Harden, of the celebrated House of Buccleugh.

Col. Geo. Hairston died at this home on the 5th of

March, 1827, and not many years later his good wife followed him; and now, side by side, on Beaver creek, in their narrow home of clay, they wait the Brighter Day.

GEORGE OSBORNE JONES

Geo. O. Jones was born in 1846, at Ridgeway, where he spent his life. He attended the Joshua Smith School there and became proficient in mathematics. He was 1st Sergeant during the Civil War in a 16 year old company. He early entered the tobacco business. He married Mary Churchill in 1873 and reared eight children to maturity.

Besides manufacturing tobacco thirty years, he was in the mercantile business with Geo. I. Griggs, and when the latter died, the firm of Jones & Griggs was the oldest business house in the county. He also owned a large quantity of land, and did extensive farming on a paying basis.

He bought the old mineral springs property, later known as the Phospho-Lithia Springs, two miles north of Ridgeway, and developed this popular watering place. In fact, he was the builder of the greater part of his town. Besides scores of dwellings, he built a large tobacco factory, a drug store, warehouse, was the largest contributor to the building of the Methodist church and Ridgeway Institute when organized, as well as a large stock-holder in the Bank of Ridgeway. He was president of the latter for many years.

He was a great believer in the Methodist Church, and supported its institutions liberally. He was active in the Sunday School, and attended whenever possible. His home was always ready for the ministers where they were hospitably entertained.

It was not his nature to refuse aid to his friends, and the needy, and his expenditures this way would have crippled the finances of most business men in the county; but he was, with all his losses, a good financier, and accumulated much property.

He was a model neighbor, a patriotic citizen, and the most indulgent of fathers. In his home he extended a wholesouled welcome that few men knew how to bestow on visitors. In his office he offered every help reasonable to his fellowman, and in his private life he presented to the world a kind heart, and did his best to

GEORGE O. JONES
Ridgeway, Va.

HISTORY OF HENRY COUNTY, VIRGINIA

walk in the way of his Master. He died in Nov. 1922, and was buried at the Ridgeway Cemetery.

AMBROSE JEFFERSON JONES

The family claim their descent from Welsh stock although it comes through England with Lord Bacon in their line. The Progenitor of the Henry county family, Ambrose J. Jones, came from beyond the Blue Ridge where he was born in 1770. He settled on Beaver creek about 1790, where he married Mary Le Seau, a descendant of French nobility. Here he lived reared a large family and died in 1859. Children of this union were as follows: Joseph Mosby, William, Green, Jackson, Mary, Dolly, Pitsy, and Winnie.

FIRST GENERATION

Mary Jones married Thomas West; Dolly Jones married Leftridge Baker, Pitsy married Seth Barber; Martha married John Burgess; Winnie married Carter Barber.

William Jones married Elizabeth Hardy. Issue: Mary who married Silas N. Self, Abram died during the War Between the States, William Jones married Elizabeth Jones, and John Green married Nannie Wells.

Jackson Jones married Nellie Barber: Issue; James, Charles, and Ruth who married Geo. Dyer.

Joseph Mosby Jones was born in 1812, married Margeret C. Davis, daughter of Peter Davis and a descendant of Lord Baltimore. They settled on Reed Creek and reared a large family where both died, Mr. Jones, in 1886. Their children were: Alonza Thomas, Benjamin Tazwell, Lucy Ann, Sallie, Charles W., Margaret Elizabeth, Joseph P., and Mary Lou.

SECOND GENERATION

Mary Lou Jones married John Peter Lavinder. No issue.

Joseph P. Jones was killed at Drury's Bluff in the Civil War in 1865.

Margaret Elizabeth Jones married her cousin, Wm. Joseph Jones.

Sallie Jones never married.

Lucy Ann Jones married Pinkey G. Davis and reared a large family.

The following three brothers were good business men as evidenced by the Jones Building on the Public Square in Martinsville:

Alonza Thomas Jones was born in 1857. He was called "Babe" until he was old enough to name himself, a distinction worth recording in history. He was devoted to business, but never married.

Benjamin Tazewell Jones was born in 1855, located in Martinsville, and married Sallie L. Pedigo. He was elected Commissioner of the Revenue for the North side of the county, and also, Circuit Court Clerk, and was the Republican nominee for Congress in a Democratic District.

The children of this union were as follows: Mary Baldwin Jones, and Ruth Tazewell Jones, neither married; Cornelia, and Bessie Gray.

Cornelia Jones married A Watts of Jefferson City, Mo.

(Bessie Gray Jones married Edwin M. Shultz, of Greenville, Va.

Charlie W. Jones was the eldest son, of Joseph Mosby, born in 1845, and never married. He entered business at Martinsville when it was a village and grew prosperous with each year of its growth. He was in the Civil War in the 24th Virginia Cavalry, and saw much service till captured with his cousin, William Joseph Jones, and taken to Point Lookout, Md. His terrible experience here, like thousands of others, is told by him in his, "In Prison At Point Lookout." He was a public spirited and popular citizen, several times Post Master of Martinsville, and nominated for Congress once by his party in convention, but declined. He died in 1919.

DR. BENJAMIN JONES

Benjamin Jones the great grandson of David Jones, who was the first actual settler of Baltimore ,Md., was born April 25th, 1752, in Culpeper County, Virginia When he was nine years of age his father died and the responsibility of the family soon fell upon him, developing those manly qualities that distinguished his after life.

In July 1776, he enlisted as a Culpeper Minute Man His first service was on the Potomac with troops of third regiment under Colonel Taylor. "To watch movement of British fleet under Lord Dunmore." (Howe's History of Virginia, page 443.) The war department record reads: "Soldier in Continental Establishment, Benjamin Jones, Infantry, Received pay December 21st, 1786." He assisted during the War, Dr. White, a surgeon, and by close observation and practical experience laid the foundation for the practice of medicine, and became a fine physician and surgeon.

Benjamin Jones married Elizabeth de Remi (Reamey) September 7th, 1776, in Prince William County. They were Episcopalians and were married by Devereau Jarrett. She was great grandaughter of a Huguenot refugee, Jean de Remi, of Picardy, France, who came to Charleston, 1690—his son Pierre later moving to Virginia.

After living two years in Rockingham County, North Carolina, rebuilding the forge and operating Troublesome Iron Works for a company, he moved to this County in 1792, where his wife's brothers, Daniel and Samuel de Remi had previously located. As there were few roads, and no bridges the trip was made on pack horses. Mrs. Jones carried her baby in her arms, and guided her horse.

He purchased a large tract of land from Mr. Whitesides, and lodged his family in a cabin, North of Martinsville on Jones Creek. He later built one of the first weatherboarded, papered, and painted houses in the county. In a park he kept over a hundred deer to amuse his children and grandchildren. A little bell used on a pet deer is owned by descendants.

He was active in politics, and several times represented Henry County in the state legislature. He was a large man physically, measuring six feel eight inches in height, and usually weighed 225 pounds. His feet were on the same liberal scale, and he was familiarly known as "Poplar Foot Jones." He was a friend of the poor and needy, the suffering in every walk of life, a high toned Virginia gentleman of the old school, a patriot proven on the field of battle, and an honor to Henry county.

He died in 1843, aged 91. His remains, with those of his wife and son Remi, rest in Oakwood Cemetery, Martinsville.

Elizabeth Jones his wife was a woman of unusual mind and wonderful constitution. In 1846 when ninety years old she told her grandson, Beverly Jones, of General Washington's taking breakfast with them at Troublesome Iron Works. She said: "In company with General Washington was one Jackson, detestable to all for his pride." This family tradition was corroborated in 1921 by publication of Washington's Diary by Hoskins, of North Carolina. (See Diary page 9. "In this tour I was accompanied by Major Jackson," page 44. "We breakfasted at Troublesome Iron Works.") Soon after this Mrs. Jones named her infant "George Washington Jones."

She reared six sons and two daughters, lived to see numerous descendants, and enjoyed perfect health through her entire life On her last day on earth in 1856, having lived two months over a century, she but wrapped the drapery of her couch about her and lay down to pleasant dreams.

JESSE CRITZ KING

Of the descendants of the Rev. John King, the pioneer, Jesse C. King was to attain fame and the greatest fortune so quietly that the world took little notice till he passed to yonder world ere the noon-day sun scarcely marked half the measure of the skies in an ordinary life.

He was born in Henry County Jan. 22, 1872. He had only common school advantages and a term at Lexington Ky., but did not graduate there at the College. Business demands were greater than college.

He was at an early age attracted to the chemistry of the manufacture of Carbide, and was with Wilson at Spray, N. C. when Acetylene gas was discovered. He made other discoveries himself along this line and for one he received sixty-thousand dollars. He was enlisted for his talents by the Canadian Carbide Companies in their furnace developments at Meriton, and Shawinigan Falls, Canada, where he spent 27 years. Before his health gave way under the Northern climate, he was considered the greatest authority in America on electrical furnaces and allied subjects.

There was a rich field in Acetylene illumination, and it was in this one he accumulated a quarter of a million of dollars. It was just at this juncture that disease fell upon him and blighted his valuable and distinguished career.

History offers not many parallels to the generosity of this quiet young soul. There was no gift too good for parents, brothers, or sisters, and his contributions to

JESSE CRITZ KING

other numerous causes that had claim on him were freely and liberally made. Only a few heard of these gifts because they were made so unostentatiously.

He early joined the Methodist Church, and freely supported its cause and institutions. He not only gave to the Lord's works, but he walked in a Godly way in business as well as in private life. Among his friends he was indeed a Prince, with his fellowman a true Christian, and with all a high example of a blameless life. There was no truer, manlier, or better hearted son ever born in Henry county. He died Feb. 1, 1920, in Flowers' Hospital, N. Y., and was buried in Leaksville, N. C., with those he loved so faithfully.

DOCTOR FRANKLIN KING

D. F. King was born in 1843. He was a grandson of Rev. John King, and the youngest son of Joseph Seward King and Elizabeth (Lester) King. The mother was a woman of sterling character. Though widowed and moderately circumstanced, she did well for her children, and this youngest son's devotion to her was marked. He grew up a steady boy, a manly youth, a choice young man.

He and his six brothers volunteered for the Confederate service in the Civil War. He served as Second Lieutenant in the Forty-Second Virginia Regiment, his brother Jesse O. King was Captain in the Tenth Va. Cavalry. Three of his brothers were killed, two others were wounded, but he, having served bravely and faithfully, came back unhurt to take up the battle of life.

Except health and character and the stained uniform he wore, he had nothing with which to begin his career, but with energy and cheerfulness he and his brothers rented a farm and began raising tobacco. Later he moved to Leaksville, N. C., where he made his home until his death in October, 1922. For twenty five years he was engaged in buying and manufacturing tobacco. Later he established the first banking business in the vicinity. He seemed to prosper in everything he undertook, until he became the best known and most influential citizen of the place.

Forty five years he served as deacon in his church, twenty five years as moderator of Pilot Mt. Association.

He was a liberal contributor to religious causes, and with enlarging prosperity he gave in increasing sums. He was a devout believer in the inerrancy of the Bible; therefore ardently opposed the theory of evolution as being contrary to the Scripture account of creation. He was a man of strong convictions, never evaded any issue, and never left any one to doubt where he stood. He was an ardent foe of every form of unrighteousness, and the friend of morality and progress in civil and religious life. He was a devoted husband and father, a kind neighbor, a patriotic citizen, and one who never turned a deaf ear to the cry of the poor and needy. He lived a glorious life and died a true Christian gentleman.

CLARENCE P. KEARFOTT

Dr. C. P. Kearfott was born in St. Joseph, Mo., in 1856, but his parents soon moved to Martinsburg W. Va., where he grew up and attended school. He was a pupil of a distinguished educator, John Sellers. He soon took up pharmacy under his kinsman, Dr. J. B. Gorrell, of Culpeper, Va. In 1881 he was graduated from the National College of Pharmacy.

After spending a short time in Danville, he rode into Martinsville on the first passenger train to enter the corporation limits. Here he commenced the drug business under the firm name of Kearfott, Haile, & Co. In less than five years he bought the interest of the other members of the firm, and from this time to his death, he continued a very successful career as an up-to-date druggist.

After a short stay in his new home, he married Rebecca Kratz, and they had six children; viz, Clarence B., J. Conrad, Mary Lucretia, Robert Ryland, Rebecca, and Hugh Smith.

He was the first to begin the use of the telephone, and nurtured the exchange in the rear of his store for several years. It was here the first long line from Ridgeway was connected up, built by two business men of the latter place. Soon it was strong enough to be housed separately in another building.

From the first day of his appearance in the town as a citizen, he took an active and leading part in the upbuilding of the community. By his energy and ability he contributed much to the rapid growth of the place.

He was an active and leading member of the Baptist Church, and his great work here can not be fully estimated in a brief notice in this biographical sketch. However, he gave much of his time and means to further church and religious activities.

He was honored by members of his profession, and appointed by the Governor a member of the Pharmacy Board of Virginia, a position he held perhaps longer than any other druggist in the state.

His high character, and capacity as a business man soon attracted the best people in the business sphere he moved in, and he was early called to assume important positions of trust. For a long term of years he was president of the Peoples Bank, and under his wise management, this institution grew in importance, held the confidence of the business public, and greatly increased in power and wealth.

In the year 1915, his health began to decline, and he sought other climates in search of better health. He made a gallant fight with the great Reaper, but the end came too soon, for on Oct. 19, 1920, he passed away. The town and county mourned together; for a good man, a most valuable citizen, and a Christian gentleman, had gone to the farther shore.

DR. WILLIAM W. MORRIS

Dr. Morris was born Mar. 2, 1836, and reared in the Mt. Bethel Section of the county, his lifelong home. He graduated from Jefferson Medical College and entered the practice of medicine amidst the rumblings of the approaching struggle to settle the States Rights question.

He was Capt. of the second Company that volunteered from this county and J. T. Morris was Orderly Sergeant of the same and was assigned to the 42 Virginia regiment. He participated in all the glorious history made by this regiment until he was severely wounded at Kearnstown. He had before this married Mary Emeline, the daughter of Rev. Wm. M. Schoolfield, an eminent minister in the western part of Henry.

After the Civil War, he resumed the practice of medicine in which he was continually successful. He was elected School Supt. for twelve years and also sent to the legislature of Virginia in 1883, being a prominent member of the House of Delegates.

During an interval from visiting the sick, when humor, ever present in his jolly nature was at its zenith, he wrote a poem, "The New Song of the Churn", that will always be appreciated by his county people. It was published extensively, and one of the largest papers in the South offered him a salary and a position on its staff of writers to continue his poetical effusions; but as it took some especial excitant for him to successfully woo the Muses, he declined the offer with thanks.

He attended the poor and needy as carefully as those blessed with a large share of worldly possessions.

In the language of his admiring friend, Judge S. G. Whittle together when basking in the sunshine of autumn's golden foliage, "He has worthily worn the White Flower of a blameless life, and in the evening of his days, he enjoys in full measure, the love, confidence, and approbation of his fellowmen".

JOHN HILL MATTHEWS

J. H. Matthews was born on Meadow Creek in the western part of this county Dec. 7, 1837. His father died when he was seven years old, and his boyhood was spent at his grand-father's, Henry G. Mullins. When old enough to enter high school, he studied at Germanton, N. C. staying with his uncle Robert Matthews, till he finished his education.

When about grown, he returned to live in the place of his nativity and spent the remainder of his life in the county. He married three times (see Matthews and Mullins families).

During the Civil War, he saw some active service, but was awarded a contract to carry the mail, and also assigned the duty of transferring troops between Martinsville and Danville the remainder of the great national tragedy.

For five years he was deputy sheriff and soon elected Commissioner of the Revenue for a term. In May 1875, he was elected County Court Clerk, and held the office till 1911, giving 36 and a half years of uninterrupted service, not including ten years as a deputy in the same office. His majorities grew at the polls with the years of duty.

J. H. MATTHEWS
Martinsville, Va.

He was the most popular official of the county during its history. His hold on the affections of the people was so strong that it descended a generation, and his son Thomas C. easily obtained the succession, and has held the same trust for many years.

He had a smile for every caller requesting his official assistance, and willing hands ever ready to serve them promptly and satisfactorily. The whole county mourned sincerely when he died May 5, 1912. His burial was at Martinsville, with the tributes of a Mason by his Lodge of which he had been long a member.

In his public functions of fifty-eight years, it was wonderful how he entwined himself in the hearts of his countrymen, and their devotion marked the highest tribute to his characted and the most enduring monument to his memory.

GENERAL JOSEPH MARTIN

Joseph Martin was born near Charlottsville, Va., in 1740. He was of English descent. He early evinced a strong will as demonstrated by his running away from school. He acquired but a limited education from books but was a great student of nature and of men.

He married, Sarah Lucas, but this did not settle him. This was in Orange county. His besetting sin was gambling, which soon involved him in debt. About the close of the French and Indian war, he spent over six years hunting and trading with the Indians and with valuable furs and the money he made from gambling, he paid off his debts. One of his companions on these trips was Ben Cleveland, a hero of King's Mountain.

Betting and horse-racing were common in those days and some of the best people followed such callings, and it did not attract special attention then. No sketch of Martin would be complete without knowing his record in this field.

In 1763, he went beyond the Mountains and settled Powels Valley. The place is now known as Martin's Station. Three years as overseer for a relative netted him enough to buy "Scuffle Hill' farm on Smith's river below Martinsville, and in 1773, he moved with his family to this plantation.

The following year Dunmore commissioned him Capt. of Militia, however, he served as a Lieut. in Capt. Abram

Penn's company against the Shawnee Indians. At New River he was in command of scouts and Col. Preston held Culbertson Bottom with his troops, therefore they were not in the battle of Point Pleasant Oct. 10th, 1774. After being defeated here, the Shawnees agreed to give up their lands south of the Ohio and Martin returned home.

In 1775, he was made Captain of the Committee of Safety for Virginia. Now the English planned to divide the South with the help of the Indians they incited to war. The Cherokees began atrocities along the whole frontier. Mr. Martin had formed an association with Betsy Ward, daughter of Nancy Ward, a half-breed, and closely allied to some of the Indian chiefs. By this medium he was able to gain valuable information.

Eight hundred warriors under Dragon Canoe, attacked Watauga, and were defeated by 176 men, mostly Virginians. Here, the first move to crush or divide the South by the British came to naught.

Martin hurried home and collected 50 men and joined Col. Christian, who was the commander of the Virginia troops. He was put in front, and all Indian towns that refused to surrender were destroyed and the British agents expelled and a treaty of peace was made. (It was when crossing the French Broad river two of Martin's men were too ill to go into the water and he carried them across on his back).

For 12 years, beginning in 1777, he was Superintendent of Cherokee affairs having, been appointed by Patrick Henry, then Governor, and he moved into that Indian nation to counteract the British influence and keep the peace. His pay was 20 shillings a day while among the Indians, and half that when at Williamsburg, the capital.

Against the encroaching whites, the Cherokees rose again, and this time North Carolina raised 400 militia, and Martin was appointed major of the battallion; and his successes in this series of engagements raised him into national prominence, and placed him among the heroes of the American Revolution.

The position he occupied for a long term of years was full of danger. However, his association with the Wards always stood him in hand when fighting the

Indians, and was a great factor in his escaping unharmed. Whenever he reached this family and their friends he felt safe. Finally in 1783, he was commissioned to treat with the Creeks, Cherokees, and Chickamaugas, and by presents of various colored shirts, powder, lead, and "Dawlas", the warfare was ended. When the attempt was made to establish a new State to be known as Franklin, the proposed encroachment on the Indians threatened to precipitate another conflict, but at this time Congress, in 1788, forbade all such intrusions. Through the wisdom and good management of Martin the bad feeling between North Carolina and the premature state of "Franklin" was adjusted satisfactorily and the matter died a natural death.

Fifteen years of public service completed, he returned to private life on his farm. His first wife died in 1782, and he next married Susanna, daughter of Thomas Graves, who lived just across the river above the Double Branches; but not long afterwards, he was called to Georgia to fight against the Indians again, and very soon was elected to the Legislature of that state. His stay South was brief. In 1791, and for 9 years in succession, he was sent to the legislature of Virginia from this county. In this body he was a great supporter of Madison and the resolutions of 1797.

In 1793 he was made a Brigadier General of the 12th Virginia Militia, and thus became the first soldier from Henry county to attain this distinction. The town of Martinsville, previously known as Henry Courthouse, was named in his honor.

He was physically a lrage man with prepossessing appearance, bland and courteous in manners with not a lazy bone in him. He had an instinct that drove him to the wild life of the forest and fitted him for that domain in which he was eminently successful.

He was bald for many years, but wore chin whiskers that he plaited and wore beneath his shirt. He was fond of fine clothing but stuck to the old style of short trousers, knee-buckles and so on. He, however, was never drunk, lost a tooth, or bled by a lancet.

He sold his Smith river home in 1804, on which he had resided for 30 years, and bought a plantation from Randolph Harrison on Leatherwood, where he spent his declining years. It was here he died in 1808, and was buried near his home with all the honors of a soldier and a mason.

COL. ABRAM PENN

Abram Penn was born in Amherst county Dec. 27th, 1743, married Ruth, the daughter of James Stovall, of Amherst county. He was a nephew of John Penn, a signer of the Declaration of Independence.

He was in the campaign against the Shawnee Indians, and was in command of a company in the battle at Point Pleasant, which resulted in the defeat of the Indians, Oct. 10th, 1774.

Three years later, he enlisted as a Captain in the Continental army from Amherst county. In 1779, after two years of distinguished service he was promoted to Colonel. Soon after this he was granted a furlough and moved to Henry county, settling on Beaver creek, three miles north of Martinsville's present site, which was his home thereafter.

On his return to the army, he was commissioned a Colonel of Militia and sent back to organize a regiment in this sparcely settled region out of which all of Henry and Patrick and a part of Franklin counties were subsequently carved.

During the winter of 1780 and 1781 he organized the first and only organized body of troops that went from this and the adjoining counties. He was in command of this regiment when it marched to General Greene's assistance, and took part in the battles of Guilford Court House and Eutah Springs, etc., and finally was at the Surrender at Yorktown in Oct. 1781.

He was a man of resolute purpose, magnetic, with a vigorous intellect and a commanding presence. When one considers how he gathered up men from this section drilled them into soldiers, and fought them like veterans against the British, he is in a class by himself, and should be forever honored as the highest type of patriot in the wilds of the forest primeval.

He died in 1801, and was buried at Poplar Grove in Patrick. To his descendants, he left his sword brought back from Yorktown, and a name that will be cherished by his countrymen through the ages.

CAPTAIN PETER R. REAMEY

Capt. Peter R. Reamey was born in Henry County Jan. 12th, 1829. He first married Sallie Waller, and his second marriage was to Bettie Kezee, of Richmond. He reared a large family in Martinsville, where he died, June 3rd, 1891.

He began his education in his father's school, and was so unusually bright in his studies, that a diary was kept of his rapid progress. This record is still to be observed in a descendant's library. From this diary we learn that at four years of age he had read a "Life of Franklin". At five was studying English and Latin grammar, besides his other school branches.

At seven, he entered Patrick Henry Academy under the late Joe. P. Godfrey, the principal. Here he added Greek, Sacred History and took examination on Caesar and Sallust.

Before he was twelve years old he had finished practically all Latin and most of the Greek offered in the Colleges. After this he was a student at Sullivan's College, at Columbus, Ohio.

He took up medicine and graduated at the Medical College of Virginia in 1850, and immediately began to practice his profession in this county, which he continued through life, with only one interruption.

He trained the first company that went from Henry county to join the Confederate army "The Henry Guards". He was the Capt. of this proud company that left June 3rd, 1861. It was assigned to the 24th Va. Regiment under Jubal Early. It fought the battles of Bull Run, and Manassas, and many, many others, too numerous to record in this small volume.

After peace was declared he returned to Martinsville, and resumed the practice of medicine, and wrote much from a memory that was rich in learning and of great depth.

His address to the "Knight's" tournament at Martinsville Va., will always be rated as the most beautiful piece of word painting that ever came from any brain on such an occasion in the South.

He had charming manners, a splendid physique, and a great vocabulary to display a brilliant intellect that soared beyond the heights of average men.

MAJOR JOHN REDD

Major John Redd was born Oct. 25th, 1755, in Albermale county and came to this county in early youth, and from the very first appearance, he became a great actor in his adopted county's affairs. Think of a boy reared by a widowed mother in humble circumstances by pluck brains and persistency becoming an early defender of his county against the Indians, later rising by real merit to the rank of Major and you say immediately there was an unusual leader of men; and in after life, as he became next to the richest man in these new wilds, you will also admit that he was an emminently successful business man.

It is true he ran away from his home and mother, but when you recall that he left poverty for wealth and renown, you at once pardon his youthful indiscretion.

In his new location he took an humble position on a farm two miles from the county seat and worked at the usual labor on a plantation. He evidently gave satisfaction or else he would not so soo nhave been able to buy a home for himself. To this he added till he became a great owner of wide acres and attained great power in his community.

He very early responded to the call to war against the Indians and with Joseph Martin, then Col., he made several campaigns against them in Wataugua and Holstein counties out in the frontier.

Before long the War of the Revolution against England aroused his patriotism and he went again on the firing line, but his doings in this arena are a part of the history of the nation and need not be repeated here. He was at Yorktown in that great halo of glory when Lord Cornwallis bowed to the right and might of American victory.

He was elected to the legislature of Virginia and voted on every important question before that body shunning nothing. Here, too, he was a champion of the famous resolutions of 1798 and 1799.

He married Mary the daughter of Col. George Waller of Henry county. Her mother's mother, Elizabeth Winston, was Patrick Henry's cousin. After his marriage he finally settled in the Marrowbone valley in Henry county at "Belleview", and reared a large family of boys and girls. Here he managed his affairs, responded to his country's calls, educated his children and dispensed during the remainder of his days, a period of over 50 years, that rare hospitality that distinguished Virginia from the rest of the world.

Like every great soul, he was in sympathy with the pitiful lot of his slaves and provided in his will for families to be kept together and gave, to his servant Issac, the right to select his own master. When Len Anderson was chosen, both master and servant deserve to be remembered in history. Take these two items together, or just one of them, it proves to the world that he had a kind heart and an admirable character.

After three-quarters of a century of his country's history was finished and life in its fullness came to an end, his ashes were committed to the mother of all on the hill north of the home he loved so well, and there through summer's green, autumn's tints, and winter's snows, the breezes will blow on and on and sing forever his requiem.

MAJOR JESSE MARTIN RICHARDSON

Maj. Richardson was born in the eastern part of the county May 5, 1837, and grew up like the average boy on the farm without fortune or the prospect of fame; but he inherited from his great grandfather, Gen. Joseph Martin, the love of military and the total absence of fear.

It is easy then to understand what his nature was and his ready response to the call of 1861, to go forth to battle for the right, the sacred cause that appealed to every patriotic heart.

He was a lieutenant in one of the first companies that left the county under Capt. S. J. Mullins, and was mustered into the 42nd Virginia Regiment. To rehearse his career would but tell the story of much of the hardest fighting of the War Between the States, too much for this small volume; but his deeds of valor have been told by his comrades around thousands of firesides, and at every reunion in this broad land.

He was four times wounded, but went steadily on to the cannon's mouth as the conflict thickened, was soon promoted to Captain, then to Major, till he fell with his face to the enemy at the great battle of Gettysburg, and died from the wound, at Petersburg, May 5, 1863.

The county has furnished great men that have fittingly filled every office in the Commonwealth, but not one more loyal, brave, or patriotic than Maj. Jesse Richardson.

At the first peal of the bugle's call he answered, "Here",
When battle call though danger greatest, he was there,
Then for duty, love, glory, not for fear not for gain,
"Fed his country's sacred dust with floods of crimson rain."

WILLIAM DAVIS STULTZ

Davis Stultz, as he was called by his friends, was born in this county on Leatherwood April 22nd, 1822. He was reared on a farm, and married Frances Harper Marshall, who tradition says was a great, grand-niece of Chief Justice John Marshall of the United States Supreme Court, Jan. 22nd, 1852.

He was one of the builders of the great reputation of the chewing tobacco of the county. His manufacturing plant was at the foot of Nance Mountain, and he conducted it here from 1848 till 1874. He commenced the enterprise in the old school house built by Dennis Marshall, his wife's grand-father. He lived in the house built by the great teacher in 1813, and here all his children were born.

He was a self-made man, and accumulated wealth easily. He built the mill on Smith's river south of Martinsville at a cost of 30,000 dollars, and operated it for several years successfully.

In 1875, he moved to the old homestead of Patrick Henry, on Leatherwood, and the next year, on June 16th, he died, and was buried in what was at a former date Mr. Henry's garden.

His wife was born Oct. 22, 1827, and should be recorded in history. She had a remarkable memory, and it was by her that the traditions of her family, as well as other history of that section, were preserved to posterity. She died Oct. 14th, 1902.

N. EMORY SMITH

Judge N. E. Smith was born Mar. 3. 1868, on the Virginia and North Carolina line, on the side of the latter, but he was reared in this state. He attended school at Oak Ridge Institute, N. C., in addition to his freeschool instruction under Mrs. M. M. Mullins previously. He married in 1889, Kettie Poole, of Madison, N. C. There was no issue.

After a brief career in the goods business, he studied law. After his home reading, he attended the law school of Washington & Lee University, one session, and graduated.

He was admitted to the bar and practiced some at Rocky Mount, but settled at Ridgeway, looking after his practice that grew at rapid strides.

He was elected Henry County judge by the legislature of Virginia in 19—' and filled this office with distinction until the office was abolished under our new state constitution.

Judge Smith was endowed with a wonderful memory. Besides his knowledge of law, he carried the political affairs of the congressional district in his head as easily as the alphabet. While others could scarcely name the candidates at previous conventions of the Democratic party, he often recalled the vote each received at many of these conventions.

He was a large man of the blond type, handsome, and intellectual. He was dignified in bearing and slow in making friends, but never lost one. He was a pastmaster in preventing difficulties between people. It was his pleasure to straighten misunderstandings before they grew into hostile words, or unfriendly acts. He did not carry malice, and labored to restore good feelings between men. He applied this rule in his legal labors, and often effected compromises.

He was a selfmade man from first to last, accumulated his earthly possessions honestly, and grew in the estimation of his friends continually. He made mistakes, but they grew out of the tenderness of his heart because of the great kindness there was in it for those he loved. He died Nov. 14, 1911.

JOHN HUMPHREY TRAYLOR

For the first seventeen years of my life my home was Traylorsville, Henry county, Virginia. I was the youngest of the four children of the Rev. John Cousins Traylor, and Tabitha Churchill Baily his wife. I have every reason to be grateful for my home life, and also for the civilization under which I was brought up.

There never was a country where courtesy and right-doing in every day life, where culture and honor and high purpose were more constantly instilled into the minds of growing children, than in Henry county, Virginia.

When I first remember, Miss Charlotte Grimes lived with us, a teacher of primary grades, who flourished more than quarter of a century in that capacity. I spelled, read, calculated, and printed, when I was only five years old. In allowing me to be precocious, my parents did not exceed the precedent set by Susannah Wesley in the training of her five illustrous sons. Miss Charlotte left us to go and live at Beaver Creek. I am confident I never had a better instructor.

Professor Schoolfield, who was my next tutor, was impressed with our collection of dried flora, and our ability to classify, and our general knowledge of out of door life. He was widely read, and was well posted as to county and state affairs, and was an agreeable companion, though often taciturn.

By this time my proud handsome sister, Sarah, was married and lived away from us. My sister Susan was a pretty girl, with an angelic disposition. I most assuredly had a model brother. He gave me hoops to roll, balls to bounce, and tops to spin. He taught me to climb, drive, ride, swim, hunt, and fish in Smith's river. Ever so often he made a trip to a city and always brought me a present which delighted me. When the time came, he took me to Patrick Henry Academy, introduced me to the teachers and many of the boys, then saw me comfortably placed before saying goodby. After hours of school, what was my joy to find him on the grounds at recess. I may say here that throughout a long life he was ever my friend, a clean strong-souled, highminded man, one of nature's noblemen, a credit to his worthy forbears.

Throughout my childhood, one of the homes I most delighted to visit was that of my mother's sister, Susan Mills. It was at once the home of affluence and of delightful and noble influence. I also remember my beautiful Aunt Frances Abingdon, and her attractive son, Tom. My sister Susan was two years at a girls' school at Greensborough, N. C. While there she boarded in the home of the Dandridges, dear friends of ours.

HON. JOHN HUMPHREY TRAYLOR
LaGrange, Ga.

My brother, who had been baptized by Bishop Ashbury, had fired me with enthusiasm to take a course in Emory and Henry College, for which our father had given his most earnest endeavor since his appointment to the work by Bishop Ashbury, in 1815. In 1838, the school had achieved the dignity of a college, and my brother took me there the autumn of the following year. Mr. Black, a member of the faculty, for whom Blacksburg was named, donated the last thousand dollars which enabled Emory and Henry to take rank as a College. Alfred, a member of this family, was already a student, and the first Christmas, he, Preston, and I, took a cross country hike to Traylorsville. Enroute, we accepted bountiful hospitality, yet we steadily refused the offer of horses. We reached Traylorsville in hilarious humor, had a great holiday, and were willingly driven in a carriage back to school.

At Patrick Henry Academy, Archibald Stuart's son, Alexander, brother to J. E. B. Stuart, was the leader. At Emory and Henry, Milton French was considered the ablest student.

In 1841, I completed the course at Emory and Henry and moved with my parents to Georgia. Susan had been there a year and physicians declared it unwise for her to return to the rigorous climate of Virginia.

The slaves drove us to Georgia in a carriage with high heavy wheels, with wagons and out riders. Much of the way, I rode horseback. All were well and enjoyed the trip. We took immediate possession of our improved lands near LaGrange.

In two years I married Mary Elizabeth Bailey. I say truthfully and barring none, that through half a century, she has been the most faithful and purest minded person I have ever known, just as my mother was the most intellectual, and my father, the most tranquil and the most courageous.

*Col. Traylor's memoirs are typical of him. He was known as a progressive farmer, Worthy Master of Masons, inspiring Bible Class Leader, wise State Senator, distinguished in appearance, courtly in manners, and charming in conversation. Wherever he went the land was all the better that he lived in it He was of that phase of humanity which Virginia has sent at all eras to brighten and ennoble the earth.

(The comments above are from published articles and letters from John Temple Graves; J. K. Hines, Judge of the Supreme Court, Atlanta; Pres. Carter of the State Senate; and from the book, "Men of Mark in Ga." E. R. Traylor.)

MRS. J. H. TRAYLOR NEE MARY ELIZABETH BAILEY

My native home was "Elmwood" Henry county Va., where I was the youngest child of Charles Cabaniss and Martha Rowland Bailey. There occurred my christening party, at which the Rev. J. C. Traylor officiated. There were elaborate refreshments and innumerable gifts, the costliest from my grandfather Parks Bailey, and from inmates of Beaver Creek, presided over by my mother's foster sister and first cousin, Mrs. Marshall Hairston. Soon after this my parents having lost three children, emmigrated to Georgia in a carriage, outriders, and covered wagons.

In after years my parents, my aunt Elizabeth Hampton Rowland, my two brothers, and the retinue of trained servants, fascinated me with stories of the journey, the hospitality they met with, not the least being that of an Indian chief whose log house looked down upon the Chattahoochie river. We reached the village of Forsythe Georgia, in Oct. 1827.

In a few days my father left, taking with him carpenters and brick-masons he had brought from Va. They went in covered wagons, my father in the saddle with attendant rider, and made their way to this forest where they labored two years before bringing us from Forsythe.

Five houses had been built each two stories as roofing was rather difficult to obtain, and there were so many wild animals it was safer to sleep upstairs; only the brute beasts were housed on the ground. The dwelling floors were well supplied with skins of bears, etc.

The first ladder steps built in 1827, are now used in this colonial house to connect the second story with the attic. The original residence was kept 14 years after we began living in this.

At a tender age I learned to say Henry county, Virginia, and to realize that we were living as near as possible as we had lived there. Much that was most desirable in the F. F. V's was to be found in those who lavished unceasing care for my pleasure and advancement.

Dr. Porteus Browne, an alumnus of Oxford, England, was establishing a school for girls near Lagrange. My parents and Aunt, Elizabeth Rowland, worked in the interest of this school, frequently entertaining Dr. Browne, who directed my studies for several years before I entered Brown, and where I was enrolled as a pupil for five years. There were pupils from several States, and we all learned to love England.

For a short time my two brothers were at school at LaGrange, but for several years they were students at Oxford Academy, and one year at Emory College, Ignitius Few, President. They were greatly attached to Dr. Alexander Means, head of the Academy, and while at Emory College walked the two miles back to Oxford for divine service.

At Emory my brother Parks died, which was my first great sorrow. The previous year we had been at the closing exercises, had listened to his speech, and had witnessed an enthusiastic conferring of the medal on his effort.

A year previous to this we had visited Pulaski, Tenn., home of my grandfather Parks Bailey. It was a large brick house of many rooms. Here for an entire month we were delightfully entertained, eighteen first cousins with several uncles and aunts. We were seriously taught family history, and the superiority of Henry county, Virginia, by Sarah Lewis, the daughter of Charles, for whom the eldest of the party was named, Sarah Lewis Bailey, whose daughter married Henry Washington and whose son, General Samuel Bailey, was Quartermaster of the 11th, Va. Reg., at the age of 57 years. He had been, in his 20's and 30's, several times a commissioned officer in the French and Indian Wars. His son, Parks Bailey, at whose house we were being entertained had taken part in the battle of Yorktown at 18 years of age. The Huguenot Cabaniss family, who intermarried with the Helderness of the English Gentry, would have us know that Henry county, Virginia, was a section of rare natural beauty and resource, populated by noble, admirable, trust-worthy people, who called upon the youths to emulate Patrick Henry, a man so noted for sobriety and faith in God, as to give him vision and courage to take often a step in advance of his colleagues. They called him the "Morning Star of the Revolution."

My husband's nephew, Col. John H. Traylor, of Dallas, highly prized a copy of "The Life of Patrick Henry" by Wirt, presented to his father by Granville

Waller, in 1830. Tradition has it that very many of the youths of Henry Co. received a copy of the same from the time it was issued until the middle of the 19th. Century.

Patrick Henry was the first to declare Gen., then Col., Washington was the greatest American, an opinion in which he was followed by the rest of the worth-while world. The proper example is a mighty great force in character building.

Mother and Aunt Elizabeth spoke often of their father, Baldwin Rowland, that he was intelligent, cultured, noble, and wholly charming: that he was eloquent in praise of his mother nee Ruth Norman, she was a tall blond, qeenly in bearing, daughter of a Baldwin, descendants of the Counts of Flanders. One of them was the Crusader King of Jerusalem.

The family in America is widely known for its Judges and in its work for higher education. It was a Baldwin who founded the University of Ga., and a considerable number of select schools in the United States as a result of their efforts. This Rowland family descended from an English Duke. A Ducal Coronet is the chief Charge in their Crest. In England, they intermarried with the Stuarts, and very many occupied places close to the crown.

My mother was handsome rather than pretty, brought up never to touch the back of her chair. She was erect and active at seventy years. Her features were noble in design and expression, violet eyes, and a most exquisite complexion. Blessed with a high order of mind, well educated, she had also inherited from her mother a Celtic intuition, which often seemed wisdom from above. I am quite sure her spirit was the loveliest that ever blessed humanity.

Devotedly inscribed,
Elizabeth Rowland Traylor.

SUSAN E. TRAYLOR
(BY GRANDAUGHTER PATTERSON)

My grandmother, Susan E. Traylor, was born in Henry county, Va. in 1820. At the age of thirteen years she was brought by her father to Georgia because it was thought the climate would suit her better.

After attending school in Greensboro, N. C., she married my grandfather, James Bradfield. In after years she lived with my father, and many and interesting are the accounts she gave us of her life as a child. I have heard her speak of her teacher, Miss Charlotte Grimes, of the frolics in the Virginia snows, and of her experience when boarding at Greensboro and her school life there.

My grandfather was a very religious man, and believed that God was on the side of the South in the War between the States, and sold, as much of his property as possible for Confederate money. I remember distinctly a small hair trunk full of this. In after years my grandmother, in answer to advertisement, sent a large package of these bills, but of course, never realized anything from it. The remainder of it was gradually given away and destroyed.

For six months after the Surrender she heard nothing of my grandfather and thought he was among the unknown dead, but one day when looking up the road, she saw him approaching in a very emaciated condition. He had suffered an attack of brain fever and on convalescing found that he had been cared for in the home of a relative.

While he was away in the Army, my grandmother acted as Sunday School Superintendent for the Methodists. I do not suppose it looked so strange in those fiery days as it would now to have a woman in that capacity.

My grandfather and one of his brothers were partners in business and by some unfortunate business transaction of the brother, the business failed. Rather than protect himself by a bankrupt law, he sold everything he possessed and cleared the business. In this my grandmother fully agreed, and was willing to undergo the hardships which such an action would entail rather than dodge behind a law which seemed to them dishonest.

My grandfather died in a few years, and just before the end came he told my father, William Robert Bradfield, then fourteen years old, that he was leaving his mother and two daughters in his care. "Care for them like a man". Never was a trust more faithfully filled, and her later years were spent in comfort and happiness.

I remember an account she gave of a trip from Texas to Georgia by stage coach. This was in the pioneer days of the West. When they camped for the night, fires were made around the camp to keep the wolves away, and during the night they came up close, barked and howled, their eyes looking very fierce and their teeth showing.

On one occasion we were invited to a party and my father objected very strenuously to our going on account of our youth and the distance. It was at one of my grandmother's friends she called "Sister Hicks". Her sympathy was immediately enlisted in our cause, and she went to my father in our behalf. "No mother", he said, "they can not go, I don't want them away at night anyway". "Willie" said grandmother, "Sister Hicks is a dear friend of mine, the children will be safe in her house, and you are my baby; and I shall slap you if I choose and order you to send the children to the party". My father laughingly consented and let her have her way after receiving a playful slap in his face.

Her affection for her sister-in-law, Mrs. Mary Bailey Traylor, was beautiful and amusing. She made, sometimes, long visits to this sister-in-law, and each would look after the pleasure of the other. For instance on Sunday mornings the family attended Sunday School. They usually stopped by to get some member of a cousin's family to ride with them in the carriage. Aunt Mary was lame on account of a fall, and my grandmother would go in the house for one of the children. She would say to the cousin, "Mattie you go out to the carriage and talk to Sister. You know we must make her happy since she is afflicted this way". And after staying a few minutes with her aunt, Mary would say, "Mattie, you go back and stay with Susan, she might be sensitive about your leaving her." This conversation was repeated on every Sunday as long as the visit lasted.

A preacher once said of her "Just give me my wife and Aunt Susan Bradfield to pray in my meetings, and I will defy the devil."

She was small of statue, very active, and loved to be well dressed. As long as she lived, she wore white dresses on many occasions. When we would drive up to the church on Sundays some of the men would very gallantly lift her from her buggy and help her up the steps. The whole community took great pleasure and pride in showing "Aunt Susan," as she was lovingly called, every courtesy.

She cared for her mother, Tabitha Traylor, for many

years during a very trying period. Her mother was almost blind and rather exacting, but the members of the family say that never an impatient word was spoken by my grandmother. This beautiful attention, I think, accounted for the very tender love which was evidenced by her two brothers, John H., and Robert Traylor.

There were many disappointments, sorrows, and even tragedies in her family, but nothing ever embittered her or shook her faith in the enduring goodness of the Lord. She was the essence of all, it seemed, that was good. On account of an unusually brilliant mind and personal magnetism, with this same piety, she shed a halo of blessings on those lives whom she touched.

She died on Easter Sunday in 1900.

(Signed) M. Bradfield Patterson.

MAJOR GEORGE WALLER

Maj. George Waller was born in 1734, and settled in this county years before the Revolutionary War. He married Ann Winston Carr in 1760. His plantation was on Smith's river between Beaver creek and Fieldale, and contained several hundred acres.

He was one of the early noted men of this section of the state. He was a great lover of sport, as well as of country, and tradition that is true as written history, relates that on one occasion he and his neighbor Purdle who owned a farm on the river just above his, ran a horserace for a mile up to the latter's farm, on the river when it was frozen solid and covered with a fall of snow, the wager being one barrel of brandy! Who won? The answer was the friends that witnessed the race for they drank the liquor: (Horse-racing, and fighting in the ring were as common those days as Church Dinners for funds are now).

Another time that called out the populace at that period was the Muster Days when the exercises and drills of the local would be soldiers occurred. He was then Major of the Militia and, of course, one of the star performers for the occasions. These drills were the stepping stones to lead to real action when the time came, and that was not so very long for the Revolutionary War soon raged and Maj. Waller heard the call.

To him the order was given by Col. Abram Penn to assemble the only organized body of troops from the then young county of Henry, to go to the assistance of

General Green at Guilford Court House. They assembled on March 11th, 1781 at Beaver Creek and hurried to battle field in time to aid in turning Lord Cornwallis back to the South. From this time the Companies of which he was Adjutant merged into the army under Gen. Green where they served till the final victory at Yorktown in Oct. 1781.

He returned from the field of battle and spent the remainder of his life quietly at his home near Waller's Ford. Here he dispensed hospitality reared his family, and lived to see his country on safe footing before he died on March 18, 1814. There his ashes lie in the land he loved so well.

HON. C. Y. THOMAS.

Christopher Y Thomas was born in 183— and married Mary Ann Reamey in 1858, the daughter of Col. Daniel and Susan Starling Reamey. Issue: Lyne Starling, Mrs. (Hope) H. C. Graveley, Mrs. Faith Parrott, Kate, and Susie, and Frank W. Thomas, of Topeka Kansas. He died in 18—. His wife survived him almost two generations.

He was Treasurer of the county of Henry without financial delinquency, commonwealth's attorney at a later date, during the civil war, and before this was a member of the Virginia senate.

It was while a member of the senate, his brother-in-law, Peyton Gravely being a member of the lower House, that he opposed the secession ordinance. He was designated by the confederate government to distribute supplies to needy families in the county.

After the war was over he was appointed military governor of the state of Virginia. However, he could not take conscientiously the "Iron-Clad Oath". Later on he was a member of the constitutional convention that framed that historic document that served the state for 33 years as its fundamental law. It was due to his labors that the free school system was made a prerequisite for readmission to the union.

He was a member of the commission that defined the boundary between Tenn. and Virginia before the civil war.

He represented the fifth District of Virginia in the national congress for a term.

MRS. A. G. WEEMS
(Daisy Williams)
Meridian, Miss.

He was an intimate friend of Gen. Grant, and in many ways, was the most trusted man by his administration in the State.

He was a man of splendid intellectual attainments, and had a most perfect control of himself. Neither mob, nor emergency, nor raging wave of public sentiment could influence him in the least; but he kept his balance and acted on his most matured judgment in every circumstance and position through life.

MRS. DAISY W. WEEMS

Mrs. Daisy W. Weems, illustrated in this volume, is a lineal descendant of Parks Bailey, youngest son of Sam Bailey, and his wife Augusta Parks. She is the dau. of C. C. Williams and Ardena Pullen. The latter is the dau. of Sarah Lewis Bailey Pullen, oldest dau. of Parks Bailey.

Mrs. Weems is a highly cultured woman, and has filled many responsible positions in various lines of women's activities in Meridian, Miss. She is a graduate of Wards Seminary, Nashville, Tenn., and has added much to her culture by travel. Not only has she traveled over the states of the union, but has taken Cuba in her route. She has visited Europe, and thus broadened herself mentally.

Mrs. Weems is well known as President of the "Winnie Davis Chapter", U. D. C., of Miss. She organized the Daughters of the Confederacy, and was president of the Miss. Federation of Women's Clubs for 2 yrs. She is an officer in the Chapter "Pushmataha", D. A. R.

CHAPTER IX

FAMILY HISTORIES

AARON FAMILY

Jacob Aaron and his wife, Juda, were the first known in Virginia. They reared three children. A daughter married a Mr. Oakes, and lived in an adjoining county. One of the boys, when eight years old was kidnapped by a relative and taken to Missouri never to be returned. The other boy, John B., located in this county.

John Burwell Aaron was born in 1826, married in 1855, Sarah Jane Oakes. Her family came from England, and her immediate family lived in Guilford county, N. C. Her grandfather served in the War of 1812, and her father, Capt. James K. Oakes, earned his title by gallant conduct in the War Between the States. Mr. Aaron died in Feb. 1900, and his wife died at the age of seventy-five, in 1907.

He was a quiet solid citizen of Martinsville who attended to business, reared his family properly, did his full duty to his country and everybody agreed that the world was better for his having lived in it. The children of this union were as follows: James, F., C. C., J. D., J. R., Talitha J., Alice L., Malina C., Lucy L., Nicholas C.

SECOND GENERATION

Jesse Fillmore Aaron married Sallie Giles; Christopher Columbus Aaron married Loula Giles; Jacob Davis Aaron never married; John Reid Aaron married Jessie Roberta Stanley; Talitha Jane Aaron married John Carter; Alice Laura Aaron married James Smith; Malinda Carr Aaron married Frank King; Lucy Evelyn Aaron married Frank B. Powell; Nicholas Aaron.

ALLEN FAMILY—2

William Allen, the founder of the Allen family in Henry Co., Va. was born, 1725, married 3 times, and died 1788.

His 1st wife was Mary Lewis, of Campbell Co., Va. She had 13 children. Among them were Reuben. Meredith, Pleasant. Darling, William, James, Mrs. Mary Morgan of Ala., Mrs. Thurman, and Mrs. Jarred, of N. C.

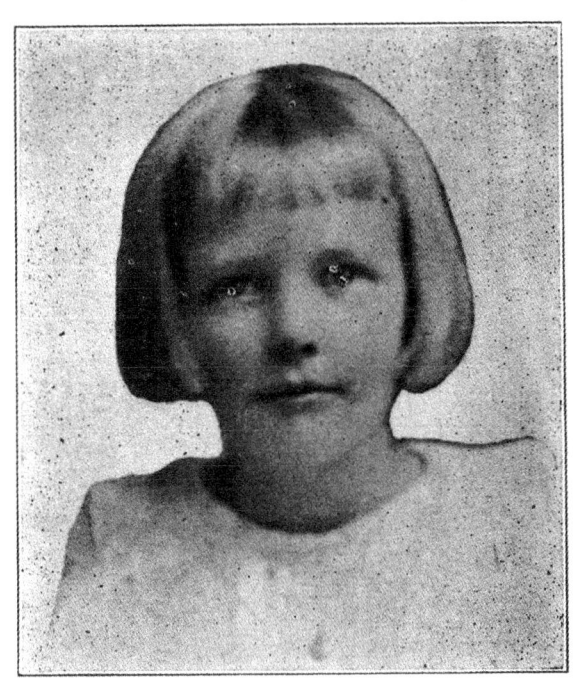

JESSIE READ AARON
Martinsville, Va.

His 2nd, wife, Miss Beverley, of Essex Co., Va., lived one year and left a son, Beverley, who won some distinction, and from whom many have descended.

His 3d wife was Sarah Ann Smith, of Prince Geo. Co. Va. and daughter of Lawyer Harry Smith and his wife Tabitha Churchill. Mr. Allen died, 1788, and left his widow with six children, Robert, Joseph Smith, Pines, Susan, Ellen, and Fannie.

The home of the Allens, in Henry, was Lewiston, said to resemble a town from its store, shops, post office and so on. Here also the stage coach stopped which added to the prosperity of the place.

This home was left to his widow and here in 1790 she married John Bailey, a bachelor of forty years, but very near her own age. Mr. Bailey built a home for her within a mile of the present Mt. Bethel Church. She gave him one daughter, Tabitha, who married Rev. J. C. Taylor. She died in 1836.

SECOND GENERATION

Robert Allen married Celia Mullins, daughter of David Mullins of Revolutionary fame. Issue: Joseph S. William, Logan, Eliza Dabney, and David Mullins Allen.

Joseph Smith Allen married 1st., Sarah Wade, 2d, Rachel May. Pines Allen married 1st., Charlotte Bailey, daughter of Parks Bailey, 2d., Nancy Hughes.

Susan Allen married Wm. F. Mills called the "Good Billy Mills," no issue. Ellen Allen married Edward Carter of Pittsylvania Co. Fannie, the youngest daughter of Wm. Allen and his wife Sarah Ann Smith, married 1st., James Shelton, a veteran of both Revolutionary War and that of 1812. Their children were Pines Henderson, Nancy, Polly, and James. Mr. Shelton died at Norfolk during war of 1812, and his widow married William Abingdon.

Meredith Allen, next to the oldest child of Wm. Allen, and his 1st. wife reared several children. Among them were Coleman, Jones, William, Darling, and a daughter.

THIRD GENERATION

David Allen, son of Robert Allen and Celia Mullins, married Sallie Ann Spencer, daughter of Billy Spencer and Sally Parks Hill. They had 12 children—8 sons and 4 daughters. Among them were Spencer, James, John Mills, Brooks, Eliza Dabney, Forest, and America.

Eliza Dabney Allen married James Matthews, of N. C. They reared a large family of children and lived and died at the old home place, Lewiston, now called the "Dr. Brengle Place".

Coleman Allen, son of Meredith, married Fannie DeShazo, daughter of William DeShazo, of Leatherwood, a Revolutionary soldier, and soon moved to Mo. The mother died leaving one child the father returned to Henry County, Va. This child became the mother of Coleman, Lethridge, and Rev. Minter.

William and Darling left no issue. Jones Allen, another son of Meredith Allen, married Nancy Cooper, and had two children, Nancy, and Obediah Allen. His descendants are all of the family, by the name of Allen, left in the county. The others having moved away from the county about 1830.

John Parks Bailey Allen, son of Pines Allen, was born in 1815, in Henry Co., Va. He moved to St. Charles Co., Mo., in 1832. At the age of seventeen, he enlisted in Capt. Nathan Boone's company. The latter was a son of Daniel Boone. Mr. Allen was made a lieut, of the company, and years after drew a pension from the U. S. Government as a Black Hawk Veteran.

Joseph Benson Allen, son of Robert Buxton Allen, and grandson of Pines Allen, was born Dec. 12, 1841 in Truxton, Mo. He made a successful lawyer of Troy, Mo., also Sec. of Christian Benevolent Association. He is a Methodist local preacher, and although a local minister, he is a much travelled preacher, carrying the gospel free to many. He has occupied pulpits in mud-daubed school houses and in the largest city churches; wherever he could tell people of the Everlasting Gospel. He married Kate M. Baker, daughter of Judge David Baker, a woman noted for goodness and beauty. One half of his family is in the "Great Beyond". A son and a daughter are still left to him, also some sweet grandchildren and great grandchildren. He has ever been much interested in the genealogy of his family, and was editor and publisher of the Troy Record, of Mo. He is also a great lover of humanity.

REV. J. B. ALLEN
Troy, Mo.

HISTORY OF HENRY COUNTY, VIRGINIA   113

FOURTH GENERATION

James Pines Allen son of John Parks Bailey Allen, and grandson of Panes Allen, was born August 12, 1850 in St. Charles county, Mo. He received his education at the Central College, Fayette, Mo., and Vanderbilt University, of Nashville, Tenn. He is a lawyer, and was once city attorney of Windsor, Mo. He was the founder and vice-president of the Citizens' Bank of Windsor, Mo., is also its largest stockholder. He married Miss Boys, and their daughter married Spencer F. Harris. The compiler wishes to thank Mrs. Harris for the gift of the Allen chart, and to say she fully realizes and appreciates the labor expended in the making of this chart.

Martha Allen, daughter of Pines Allen, married her cousin Dr. John Pines Allen, son of Joseph Smith Allen. After Mr. Bailey's death she was companion for her grandmother Mrs. Bailey, till her marriage, when Mrs. Bailey gave up her home and lived with her daughter Mrs. J. C. Traylor, till her death in 1836.

Spencer Allen, son of David Allen and his wife Sally Ann Spencer, was severely wounded in Civil War, but lingered some years. James Allen also fought in the Civil War and was seriously wounded about the head. After long suffering he recovered and lived to be one of the finest cotton merchants in the South. He was a man of fine character devoted to his Church (Christian), and attended regularly his Sunday School classes.

John Mills Allen another son of David Allen went through the Civil War, but was never wounded. He remained a "Private". After the War he was running for office, and while canvassing the State he and his opponent met at a certain point to speak. Each in his own behalf. The opponent had been an officer in the War and asked the people for their votes. John Allen rose when his turn came and said: "Gentlemen, I was a Private in the same war with my opponent. I will only say now, gentlemen, that the officers may vote for my opponent, but I will ask the privates to vote for me." Thundering applause: He won the election and was ever afterwards called "Private John Allen". He was a member of Congress for years and was considered one of five of the smartest men we ever hand in Congress. From his mother he inherited a kind of humour that carried him through many a difficult position.

Forest, the youngest daughter of David Allen, married a lawyer, Will Cox. He is now Judge Cox, and they live at the old Allen home, Baldwyn, Miss. Eliza Dabny, the oldest daughter of David Allen lived to be an octogenarian. She was a fine woman, and worked for her church as long as she lived. She has a daughter in Florida, a fine business woman, and of fine character.

ANDERSON FAMILY

The Andersons of the county are of Scotch-Irish descent. Leonard Anderson was born early in the 19th, century, and married in his native county, Prince Edward, Mary Morton, granddaughter of Capt. Hezekiah Morton, of the Revolutionary Army. There were five children from this union; viz, John, Leonard, Robert Campbell, Virginia, and Mary.

Robert Campbell Anderson (See Biography Chapter) married Justina, daughter of Rev. Samuel Armistead, a Presbyterian minister, and Mary Madison Armistead, of Campbell county, Va. From this union there were ten children. All reached maturity and united with the Presbyterian church; viz, Samuel Armisted, Mary Morton, Nannie Madison, Katherine Virginia, John Rice, Leonard W., and James Lewis, twins, Robert Campbell, Jr., Henrietta Alice, and Lucy Frances.

Samuel Anderson is a lawyer of distinction, and has practiced many years in Richmond, Va. He was one of the three appointed by the Governor of the State to revise the Virginia Code. He married Miss Pauline Daniel, of Virginia, and they have four children, as follows: Pauline, Samuel, Lavillon, and Elizabeth.

Mary Morton Anderson was a talented artist, graduated with honors at a College in Rome, Ga., and married Samuel Cole Fontaine. (See Fontaine Family).

Nannie Madison Anderson married Emmett Williamson. For several years resided out of the county, but returned to Martinsville, where they are noted for their good works, hospitality, and fine Christian character. Mr. Williamson is Elder in the Presbyterian church, and also, President of the First National Bank.

Katherine Virginia Anderson lived all her life in the county. (See Biography Chapter).

John R. Anderson graduated from a medical school in Baltimore, and became a physician of more than ordinary skill. Notwithstanding his poor health, he has practiced in the county for many years.

Leonard W. Anderson became a lawyer of ability, and for a number of years, though his health was impaired, he practiced in Rocky Mount, Va. He was an Elder in the Presbyterian church, and noted for his intellect, and fine Christian character. He died at the age of 54.

James Lewis Anderson received his degree at the University of Virginia, and practiced law in Richmond, Va. from 1884 almost to the time of his death at Saranac Lake, N. Y., Jan. 31, 1921. He was a member of the State Bar Association from its organization till the time of his death. He was a member of the Hermitage, Country, and Westmoreland clubs, and president of the former. He was chairman of the board of deacons in the 2nd Presbyterian church, Vice-President of the Y. M. C. A. of Richmond, and a director for the "Richmond Home for Ladies."

Robert Campbell Anderson graduated at Hampden-Sidney College, and Union Theological Seminary. After serving as pastor in San Antonio, Tex., Second Pres. church of Roanoke Va., Presbyterian church of Shelbyville, Tenn., and in Gastonia, N. C. He was elected by the General Assembly of the Southern Presbyterian church, president of the Montreat Association, where for the last sixteen years he has rendered the church a great service. The beautiful Auditorium is named for him.

His first wife was Kate Walker of Virginia. Later he married Sadie Gaither, of Charlotte, N. C.

Henrietta Alice Anderson married Eugene Richardson, an elder in the Presbyterian church at Farmville, Va. They have seven children: Eugene, Katherine Virginia, Robert Anderson, Horace Leonard, Hettie, Lowery, and Louise.

Lucy Frances Anderson married Daniel M. McIntosh, of N. C. He is a deacon in the Presbyterian church, of high character, and good business qualifications. Both he and Mrs. McIntosh use their talents and gifts as the Lord's stewards in the First Presbyterian church at Wilmington, N. C., where they reside.

Mrs. Justina Anderson, the mother of this family, was of English descent, and was related to four presidents of the United States.

She became a Christian in early life, and was a conspicuous example of that love which is the "Fulfilling of the Law."

She was kind, loving, patient, self-denying, charitable in judgment, forgiving in spirit, and her memory is as an ointment poured forth in this community.

She was in her ninetieth year when she died, Feb. 29, 1916.

BROWN FAMILY

Frederick Brown, the progenitor of the family in Virginia, was born in England in 1745. He stopped in York county after landing at Yorktown, and came in time to fight in the Revolutionary War. He had four sons, Frederick, Ruben, John (Jack), and Tarleton.

Ruben Brown settled in Bedford county where his large progeny lived. Tarleton settled in Franklin county.

John, called Jack, was born in 1750, and married Sarah Rives. He was a skilled brick mason and helped to build the old capitol at Richmond. He lived most of his life on Pig river in Franklin county, raised his family, and died there in 1840. The children of this union were: John Spottswood, Reuben Skelton, Frederick Rives, William Alexander, Nancy, who married Armstead Gorman, Mary who married Andrew Brooks, and Sarah who married a Jefferson.

Frederick Rives Brown was born Jan. 1, 1813, married in 1837 Jane Prunty (1819-1848), the daughter of Jesse Prunty, and Mary Finney. Issue: Eliza Jane, who married Joseph Rucker, John R., and Nancy who died unmarried. By his second marriage to Elizabeth E. Brown, there were the following: James William, Lucy, who married Henry C. Lester, Tarleton, and Millard. He was a good business man and took great interest in public affairs. He was elected Sheriff of Franklin county one term, and made a good officer. He also represented that county in the Virginia legislature.

In 1882, he and his son, J. R., moved to Martinsville in this county, and from that date the town grew by leaps and bounds. Here they manufactured tobacco for 16 years and added very much to the growth of the community. He was fond of boys as long as he lived, and was a great favorite with them, urging them to strive to attain the highest standards in life, always. He died in 1896, and was buried in the town of his adoption.

Col. William Alexander Brown was born in Franklin county in 1815, married Sarah Preston. After her death, he married in 1860, Susan, the daughter of Amos Finney and Betsy Prunty. All these were of the same county. Issue of last marriage: Sarah, William, Walter and Lula, twins and George Akers.

He manufactured tobacco for 43 years, and estabished "Brown's Log Cabin", and many other celebrated brands of plug tobacco. He was a successful business man, and took great interest in political affairs, was a staunch Democrat, and was elected to the House of Delegates, as well as the Senate of Virginia from Franklin county. He was a man of polished manners, diplomatic, and entertained with old Virginia ease and elegance. He died, in 1885.

SECOND GENERATION

Of the children of Frederick R. Brown we record as follows: John R. Brown came to Henry in 1882. (See Biography Chapter). James William, and Millard Brown both died unmarried. Lucy Brown married Henry C. Lester. (See Biography Chapter. No issue. She was given over the fortune of her husband after his death, was a distinguished business lady of Martinsville for a few years, and endowed the Lucy Lester Hospital liberally. She died in March, 1920

Tarleton F. Brown was born Sept. 16, 1861, married Annie Eliza Brown, his cousin, Feb. 8, 1862, moved to Martinsville with his father, and spent the remainder of his life in business there. The children of this union were: Elizabeth, who died in infancy, Mattie who married G. M. Andes, Lucy, who married Dr. M. E. Hundley, and Rives Brown, who married Cornelia Gregory.

Of Col. William A. Brown's family we note as follows: William B. Brown, the eldest, married Lula Dudley, and reared a daughter, Doris. He inherited the popularity of his father so completely that he was elected to the state Senate to fill out the unexpired term of his deceased parent when he was yet a very young man. He met a premature death in an accident a few years later.

Walter Spottswood Brown was born in June 1868, married Virginia Williams, grandaughter of U. S. Senator, R. E. Withers, of Virginia. He was a good business man, and one of the most popular that ever came to the county. He died in 1907, before reaching middle life.

Sarah Brown married Gustave B. Dudley and came to Martinsville in 1881. She was a devoted mother, and knew and loved all her kin, and her name will always be revered by every one of them. The children of this union were as follows:

Dr. William Brown Dudley, who married Marion McCrary Moir; Dr. Gustave B. Dudley who married Priscilla Flint Humbert; Ruby Dudley, who married J. Earnest Howard; Virginia Spottswood Dudley, who married Samuel S. Walker; Loula Brown, the youngest daughter of Col. W. A., married George William, a son of John O. Coan, a former Mayor of Ridgeway, Va., and Mary Jones, his wife. Billie Coan, as he was usually called, was Secretary and Treasurer of the R. J. R. Tobacco Company, of Winston-Salem, N. C.

George Akers Brown was born in 1872, married Minnie Mathews, and reared a family in Martinsville. (See Mathews Family). He is Mayor of this thriving city, giving eminent satisfaction.

John R. Brown, the eldest son of F. R., married Ann Eliza Vial, Oct. 26, 1862, who died Mar. 30, 1915. Their children are: Nannie Jane Brown, married Dr. Charles P. Smith, a physician of Martinsville; Alice Brown, married Edward Gaines, died in 1921, and left a large family; Frederick R. Brown married Etta Burge; Willie and Rosa, died in infancy; May Brown married George M. Finley; Annie Brown married Lewis C. Claybrook; Kate Brown is unmarried.

John Andrew Brown, the eldest, was born n 1863, married Pattie, the daughter of Dr. J. M. Smith in 1888. He was of distinguished appearance, handsome, enjoyed life, and delighted to serve his friends at any time. He was the father of the banking business in the county, and was the efficient cashier of the Henry County Bank as long as he lived. His untimely death in June, 1893, was a great sorrow to the people of the entire section he had served so faithfully. His widow died a few years after she had married E. M. Dickerson, leaving her children by her first husband as follows: John Andrew, the cashier of People's National Bank for years, Corinne, **Pattie**, and Moss Brown.

FOURTH GENERATION

John Andrew Brown, Jr., married Mary Elizabeth Jones; Corinne Brown married Pete S. Barrow; Pattie Brown married A. N. Hodgson; Moss Brown unmarried.

BOULDIN

The Bouldins are of English descent. Thomas Bouldin settled in Henry County, Va. between 1760 and 1770, on a large tract of land lying between Horsepasture and Smith River. A part of this land has never been deeded out of the Bouldin family.

Thomas C. Bouldin and 3 sisters, Misses Annie G. and Mary E. and Mrs. W. D. Wells, of Martinsville, Va., are now in possession of this old home place.

The founder of the Henry Co. Va., family, with his wife, some of his children, grandchildren, great-grandchildren, and great- great- grandchildren are buried at this place.

There are many descendants of this old pioneer scattered in various parts of the United States.

BOOKER FAMILY

The Booker family trace their ancestors to Edward Booker, of London, England, who flourished in the 17th., century. He was a large dealer in tobacco. His son, Capt. Richard, was the first to settle in Virginia. He obtained large grants of land in Gloucester county in 1685,-1695, and 1704. He married Rebecca Leake, and they reared one son, Richard.

Richard Booker, Jr., married Margaret Lowry, daughter of William Lowry, and Frances Purefoy, his wife. In 1732, a patent of 970 acres of land in Prince George (now Amelia) county was granted to "Richard Booker, of James City county, Gentleman". He was a Justice of the Court of James City county, in 1730, and died in York in 1743. There was a son, William. William Booker was born in 1714, and died in 1755. He had a son, Lowry. Lowry Booker married Phoebe Cox of Charlotte county, Va. One of his sons, Edward, settled in Franklin county, near the Henry line, at Shady Grove.

Edward Booker was born about 1810, married Martha Sheffield, sister of Col. William A. Sheffield, of Ridgeway, Va., and reared the following children: John, married Julia Hamlet; Leonard, died in the Civil War; Edward, married Judith Carter, sister of John W. Carter, Sr. Lowry never married. Mary married W. E. Haynes of W. Va.; Martha married John O. King, of Henry; and Jesse Wooton Booker married Sallie Cook of Franklin county: Issue: Samuel Edward Booker, Ella Cook Booker, Lowry Sheffield, Jesse Wootton, Fletcher Clement, Mildred Ann, Mary Catherine.

Edward Booker, a cousin of the father of the last named family, was born in Cumberland county, Va., in 1794. (See "Memories of an Old Man" in Memorial Chapter). He moved to Patrick county when 25 years of age after his services in the War of 1812, and married Elizabeth Anglin, and they reared the following children all of whom lived in Henry county: George W., Richard A., Thomas J., John A., Marshall E., and Elizabeth.

He was a highly educated farmer who spent his days in Patrick and Henry county, and died in 1882.

SECOND GENERATION

George W. Booker was born in 1822, married Maria Philpott, daughter of David Philpott, of Henry county, studied law, and followed the practice of this profession till his death in 1884.

He represented Henry county in the Legislature just after the War Between the States, and in 1868, was elected to the Congress of the United States from the Fifth District of Va. Issue: George W., John Minor Botts, Sallie, and Ruth.

Thomas Booker, a brother of the latter, was noted for his play with words; viz, "Poverty just makes many a sober man", etc., and also for his wonderful long beard. When he stood erect and unrolled it from his bosom, it almost reached the toe of his shoe. He did not accumulate property but died an honest man at his mountain home in Henry, near Price, N. C., in 1895.

BASSETT FAMILY

Bassett, the extra "t" was not added until the 15th century, is a name found on Battle Abbey roll. William the Conquerors grand falconer, who accompanied him from Normandy, was Thurstine deBassett and from him are descended all who now bear the name.

Ralph, son of Thurstine de Bassett "Justice of all Eng" at the beginning of the 12th Century, was the illustrious founder of the family's greatness, a statesman, law giver and an unsullied Judge. From him descended the Lords Bassett of Oraython-Sipote, Umberlegh and Tehidy. Many of the Bassetts were lords of the manors.

In the time of Henry 1st. Osmond Bassett was the

judge of all Britain. Sir Ralph Bassett attended Edward 1st. to the Welsh Wars. The Castele or pile of Bassett at Tehidy Wales was Sir Ralphs estate. Sir Francis Bassett was the Vice-Admiral in time of Charles 1st., and another Sir Francis in time of Geo. 3d. was Baron Bassett, as well as baron of Dunstonville.

Allan Bassett's name appeared in Magna Charta among those of the King's counselors; also his brother Thomas's name. Peter Bassett, was biographer of Henry 5th and his chamberlain and intimate friend. Fulk Bassett, Bishop of London, is remembered in the records of St. Paul's Cathedral on account of his gifts to that church.

Cornwall and Devonshire have always been strongholds of the family and the mines of Cornwall gave them princely incomes.

The first of the name in America was William Bassett who came over in the Fortune in 1621. The story is that he intended coming in the Mayflower but his bride's trousseau was not ready. He was an educated man, and brought his box of books with him, a large library for those days. His name is on the list of freemen made in 1633. He was for 6 yrs. a representative to the old colony court: was in the Pequod War; truly a man of affairs. A son, grandson and great grandson were named William, a favorite name in the family. Thomas F. Bayard's mother was a Bassett, a grand daughter of Richard Bassett, Governor of Delaware, and member of the convention of 1787 which framed the U. S. Constitution and was the first to cast a vote for the removal of the capital from Philadelphia to Washington.

One of our Revolutionary heroes was Abraham Bassett who was in the battles of Long Island and White Plains. Over 150 Bassetts from Mass. alone were in the Revolution.

In 1897 a Bassett Association was formed. It was the first reunion of the family for 600 yrs. They meet annually, usually at Boston, and William is always given a prominent place upon family charts. Among the many anecdotes told at these meetings is that of a forefather who so appreciated his wife's skill in the culinary line that he inscribed on her tombstone: "Marthy, my wife's picked up dinners were a perfect success".

VIRGINIA BASSETTS

The first known of the Va. Bassetts was Wm., of Isle of Wight, Eng. His son Wm. was a Capt. in the King's army, and after the defeat of Dunkirk, he came to America and was given a contract, at Jamestown, Va. to build a fort.

He married Bridget Cary, dau. of Col. Miles Cary, of Southampton, Eng. When his first and only son was about a year old this Capt. died, and in his will left his son to the care of Nathaniel Bacon, cousin of N. B., the Rebel. Mr. Bacon was then Gov. of Va. He reared this boy and built a brick mansion in New Kent County, Va. and named it Eltham for the name of the Bassett family residence in Eng. This son rose to the distinction of Col., hence he is designated as Col. Wm. Bassett, or Wm. (2). Col. Wm. Bassett md. Joanna Burwell, dau. of Lewis Burwell (2) and had 5 sons and 7 daughters. The oldest son Wm. died and the 2d son was named Wm. and from this Wm. has descended a large number of Bassetts. He married Elizabeth Churchill and lived at Eltham. His son Burwell next inherited the Eltham property and married Annie Maria Dandridge, sister of Martha Washington, and had 3 children, Burwell (2), Frances who md. Geo. Augustine Washington, son of Charles Washington, Bro. of Geo. Washington.

John, 3d child of Burwell (2) fell heir to Eltham, and was a member of congress for thirty years and died in 1841, left no heirs, so that Geo. Washington Bassett, oldest son of John Bassett and his wife Bettie Carter Brown, fell heir to Eltham, and carried his wife there as bride. The oldest son of this couple, also named Geo. Washington, never married, but taught school in Richmond before the Civil War. He died in Hanover Co. Va.

Eltham was burned after the Civil War, and William (4) moved the remains of Wm. (2) and his wife to Hollywood, Richmond, Va. On this tomb are inscribed the Bassett Arms, "Or, 3 bars, wavy gules, and the motto, "Pro rege et populo."

Col. Burwell Bassett and Geo. Washington rode in a carriage from Eltham to Williamsburg to hear the 1st English Troupe in America. In Wm. and Mary College will be found a portrait of Judith Walker Browne, grandmother of Judith Frances Carter Bassett. Virginia

Bassett, dau. of G. W. Bassett md. John Hughes Claiborne, of Richmond, Va., who was a Major in the C. S. Army, and their dau. Delia, md. Col. Wm. Roscoe. Ranseller Bassett was half borther to Millard Fillmore.

Elizabeth dau. of Wm. (2) and his wife Joanna Burwell, md. Benjamin Harrison (signer), and became the ancestor of two Presidents of U. S. viz: Wm. Henry Harrison, and Benjamin Harison. The Bassetts of Va., were among its most prominent people, and did good service for their country for many yrs.

In the Clerk's Office of Henry Co. Va. may be found a record of Burwell Bassett buying a tract of land from Col. Geo Hairston of Rev. fame. This particular land was the bounty land given to Peter Francisco for valiant service in Rev. It is now owned by W. J. Bassett, a great grandson of Burwell Bassett who bought it in 1790.

The said Burwell Bassett md. Mary Hunter, (called Polly) in 1794. Issue 4 sons and 2 daughters. viz: Alexander Hunter who md. Mary Koger, dau. of Henry Koger and his wife Mary King Koger, 2. Wm. Nathaniel md. Jane O. Staples dau. of Sam Staples, and moved to Monroe Co., Mo.

Third Geo. Hairston md. Columbia Staples, dau. of Sam Staples and moved to Randolph Co. Mo., 1842.

Fourth Burwell Bassett, Jr., md. Malinda Waller, dau. of Edmund Waller and his wife Maria Duncan, and moved to Monroe Co. Mo This couple left 2 children, Pocahontas who md. John L. Yager, and Maria Jane, who md. Thomas J. Teaford.

Fifth Martha Hairston Bassett, dau. of Mary Hunter and Burwell Bassett md. her cousin Burwell W. Bassett, and moved to Hawkins Co., Tenn.

Sixth Mary Dorsey Bassett, (called Polly), 1st md. Charles Philpott, 2nd. Woodson Morris, who also moved to Mo. Polly Bassett, the mother of the above children followed her children to Mo. leaving her oldest son Alexander Hunter Bassett as the only representative of her family in the county.

This Alexander Hunter Bassett was born 1795, and finally settled in the home built by his father. He married Mary Koger, dau. of Henry Koger and Mary King. Issue: Martha A., md. John Dyer, son of David Dalton Dyer, and moved to Lincoln Co., Mo., and raised a large family. Woodson Bassett b. July 25, 1820, md. 1st, Julia

Prunty, dau. of John Prunty, Feb. 14, 1850. She d. May 2. 1857, 2nd Jan. 7, 1858, Mary Price dau. of Major John Price, She d. Nov. 12, 1913. Issue: by 1st wife John, d. in infancy, and Pocahontas md. P. R. Wray, and left a large and interesting family. Second wife Mary Price had 3 sons and 5 daughters. Everett and Medora died in infancy.

W. W. Bassett md. Addie Price dau. of John A. Price. Issue: 13 children W. J. Bassett md. Alice Taylor, and has 2 girls. Anna md. James Hopper, and has a son and daughter. Mamie md. Moran Hopper, and is left a childless widow. Mattie never married. Ada md. N. M. White, he died and left 4 living children; one son, and 3 daughters.

The Henry Bassetts, like those of Eastern Va., always answered their country's call Alexander Hunter B. served in 1812 war, and his son Woodson served in Mexican War. He entered the U. S. Army from Mo. July 15, 1846, was a corporal in Company A., 2d Regiment Missouri Volunteers. Said Co. commanded by Capt. Nap. B. Giddings, Reg. Commanded by Col. Sterling Price at Santa Fe. He was discharged April 5, 1847 by reason of sickness incurred in service. Mr. Bassett also offered his services to the Confederacy but was, on account of age and health, placed on the Home Guards.

John Bassett, 2d son of Alexander Hunter Bassett md. Nancy Spencer. He was a hardworking and honorable man. His wife was one of the best business women in the county. Her children inherited this qualification, and have amassed considerable property. Issue: J. D., md. Pocahontas Hundley. C. C. Md. Roxie Hundley. Joseph md. Sallie Coleman and is a Baptist preacher. Samuel md. Miss Joyce, and died some years ago. Mary md. J. W. Ramsey, who served 2 terms in legislature. Nancy (called Dink) md. Reid Stone, and has a promising family.

Eliza Bassett, 2d dau. of Alexander Bassett, md. Allen Hopper, died childless.

Third dau., Mary Catherine md. W. W. Hill, and raised ten children—2 sons and 8 daughters, her oldest son dying at 4 yrs. of age.

Fourth Harden, the youngest child of Mr. Bassett, d. of fever contracted in army of Confederacy, Unmarried.

HISTORY OF HENRY COUNTY, VIRGINIA

Alexander Bassett was noted for his sterling character and industry. His wife, Mary Koger, was of an unusually bright intellect, and noted for untiring industry and good management. She preceded her husband to the grave several yrs. His 2d. wife was Miss Ann Hardy, who outlived him.

BARROW FAMILY

The first of the family to come to the county was William Barrow. He settled on Leatherwood creek, and soon married Susan, the daughter of Dennis Marshall. Issue: Benjamin, William, Cassandra, Mary, Julia, Ann, and Susan.

SECOND GENERATION

William Barrow about 1840 married Elizabeth, the daughter of Columbus King (1770-1836), and Maria Cahill (1809-1832). Their children were: George, Columbus, Ferdinand, Tippey, and Jennie.

Cassandra Barrow married Armistead Jones. He and the children died, and she married again, Gresham Choice, and there is recorded one child, John Choice; and the family went to Texas.

Mary Barrow married Charles Stockton. Issue: Peter, Virginia, John, Edward and Molly.

Julia Barrow married her cousin, James Arnold, and they located in St. Clair county Mo. Issue: William, who was a practitioner of medicine, Eliza, Susan, Sam, Marshall and Edd.

Ann Barrow married Willis Gravely, a brother of Peyton and a partner in the tobacco manufacturing business, establishers of "Gravely Tobacco." Issue: Ten children (See Gravely family).

Susan Barrow married William Stockton. All their children died in infancy.

Benjamin Barrow married about 1835, Susan Watkins, daughter of John Watkins. She was the last of the generation of this name of French Huguenots, the male members becoming extinct; however, the French characteristics, jolly disposition, and graceful manners at all times, descended. There were of this union: Robert, Orrin, John A., Watt, Pete Tom, Benjamin F. (Nib), Mary, Nannie, and Cassandra.

THIRD GENERATION

Robert Barrow never married, and he died comparatively early in life.

Orin W. Barrow never married. He was a patriotic son of Henry, and was a Captain of Volunteers that went from the county to fight for the South. He was a gallant officer, and was severely wounded twice. At one time against the advice of his Surgeon, he returned to his command and led them to victory while suffering from a former wound. The county never furnished a better soldier to any cause. His uniform is in the Smithsonian Institute at Washington, D. C.

John A. Barrow married Mary Smith. Issue: Albert and Mabel.

Pete Tom Barrow moved to Danville, Va., and mar. Dora Guerrant. Issue Ben, Nannie, Tom, George, John, and Elva.

Ben F. (Nib) Barrow was born Dec. 1, 1847, married Judith, the daughter of Col. William Sheffield, on Dec. 20, 1871. He was a large man weighing nearly 250 pounds, smoothe featured, had a ruddy complexion, and possessed a jolly disposition that spread sunshine everywhere he passed. The county never had a better citizen. He died June 11, 1914. The children of this union were: William who died upon reaching maturity, Ben. F., Katie, Susan, and Pete.

Mary Barrow married Dr. Jesse H. Turner. They reared their family at the old Barrow homestead at Barrow's Mill. Issue: Walter, Lelia, Edd, Ella, Orrin, Lottie, Jesse, Watt, and Irvin.

Nannie married Capt. Willie F. H. Lee of Franklin county. Issue: Dr. Charles Lee, of W. Va., Benjamin, Dr. Robert R. Lee of Martinsville, Lula Watkins, Annie Page, Willie L., and Nannie Sue.

Cassandra Barrow married Clack Stone. He was a self educated and self made man in every respect who was a success in life and accomplished much in everything he undertook, but was stricken down early in life by disease and died, leaving his widow with the following children: Dr. Alvah Stone of Roanoke, Va., Orrin, Nannie, Edd, Dr. Harry Stone of Roanoke, Va., Mamie, and Page.

BAILEY FAMILY

The English Baileys were descended from a general of William of Normandy, France. This general was intrusted with the great treasures of the king. The office of stewardship was often called bailey instead of steward,

HISTORY OF HENRY COUNTY, VIRGINIA 127

hence the name,"Bailey." Quite a number of them were crusaders who achieved a large number of escutcheons, as many as eleven being recorded in Burke's General Armory. One claimed by this Bailey shows the strong Norman preference for parts of the human body, or of the brute creation, while the Anglo-Saxon leaned to Cabalistic designs.

The tradition back of the crest is that this general successfully defended a tower filled with women and children. On the coat decoration is found a representation of an animal skin, ermine, and bars, which, in any number means protection, taken in 35 as they are here, they mean a pilgrimage to the Holy Land.

The English Baileys intermarried with the royal family of Ireland, lineal descendants of the kings of Leinster (MacMurrough), Ireland, and lived near Dublin.

Samuel Bailey, the son of Sarah Lewis, and a descendant of the English—Irish Baileys was a large, handsome man, and a true Virginia. He married Augusta Parks in 1744, and built a home in Albermarle county Virginia, which he called Hedgelands and where his children were born and raised. One, Sarah Judith, born in 1745, married I. Y. Hill. It was during the French and Indian Ware he earned the title of General Bailey. He was a patriot, every inch of him, for he spent his means, too, in the last named, as well as in the Revolutionary conflict. It is unfortunate that we have only a record of his being Quartermaster of the 11th Virgiia Regiment. He died in 1781.

John Bailey, the eldest son of Samuel, was born at Hedgelands in 1746. He was a member of the Albermarle Guards in the Revolution. He did not marry early, but was a great trader, traveling to Richmond, Norfolk, Savannah, and New York, on horseback to the boats. Other times he went on stage from state to state, but always accompanied by his body-servant, "Chester Wade", who was purchased from Wade Hampton, of S. C. He was an artist in his line as servant.

After he was wealthy and a bachelor, he married, on March 8th 1790, Mrs. Sarah Smith Allen, a widow with six children, but the latter were well provided for. She was the widow of William Allen, who reared 20 children. In time she became the great grandmother of "Private

John Allen" of Miss. Her father was Henry Smith, a lawyer, who left his former home in Prince George county to live near his daughter in Henry, but he soon died suddenly while conducting a case in court.

John B. built a large house where Dr. W. W. Morris's garden is located in the western part of Henry county. Here they resided for a number of years and one daughter, Tabitha, was born and reared. She married John C. Traylor, a Methodist preacher. A beautiful home, about one mile away, was given to her by her father along with an annuity in her name which kept her well provided for all her life.

He was always neat in personal appearance, keeping his hand-bag ever at hand packed with the requisites to keep that way. He was devoted to his wife and one day while talking to her about the characteristics of a true woman said, "A true woman is to be like you, dear".

His estate was a large one near Mt. Bethel church of which he was the chief backer. On one of his trips to Savannah, he heard it whispered that there were cases of Yellow fever in that city, and he left immediately on a boat to Washington, thence hurried home only to die of this fearful disease in 1817.

After his death, their large house was burned and Mrs. Bailey's daughter and husband did all in their power to induce her to live with them, but she refused and had a cottage built in front of the site of the burnt home, and here she lived with her grandaughter, Martha Hairston Allen, till the marriage of the latter to her cousin Dr. Allen. Then until her death, about ten years, she lived at the home of her daughter. They buried her beside her husband, near the old camp ground, and there they lie till the last trump shall call. A servant, a descendant of "Chester Wade, just before his death erected a fence around the ashes of John Bailey, the model husband, and father and his wife.

Parks Bailey, a brother of the above, was the youngest son of Samuel and Augusta Parks Bailey, and named for his grandfather, David Parks. He was born at Hedgelands Oct. 13th, 1763. He married May 5th, 1786 in Amelia county Virginia, Mary Cabiness, the daughter of Charles, Cabiness, the inventor of plug tobacco, who was both a planter and manufacturer. Parks Bailey was a soldier, took part in the battle of Yorktown, Va. This couple lived several years in his native county, then moved to Henry, but finally went to Pulaski, Giles county, Tenn., to a grant of land given for his services in the Revolutionary War. Here he built a commodious residence. A Virginian did the building and on one of the stone lintels, he carved the letters "P. B.: W. C. These letters were often jocularly rendered", Plenty of Bacon Well Cured. He was six feet two inches tall, and weighed over three hundred pounds. He was a kind and indulgent father and very fond of entertaining. He claimed to have attained his highest ambition which was to be a success in private life. He walked twice during the day of his death to his daughter's home, Mrs. Sarah Lewis Bailey Pullen, and without a day's illness, died while at evening prayers, Feb. 9th, 1833. His wife died June 1st, 1819.

Rev. Robert Parks Bailey, a son of Parks, and Mary Cabiness, lived with his parents after his marriage to Miss Green of S. C., till their death.

William Bailey, another son of Parks, and brother of the above, married Valerine Neven, of Lyons, France. She had a son William Adolphe, who was entered at Yale and graduated as valedictorian in 1842. The president, Wolsey, stated that the valedictory was the ablest since the days of John C. Calhoun.

William Adolphe Bailey after his graduation at Yale returned to New Orleans, studied law, and before this, was Supt. of Public Schools, and soon thereafter was appointed Judge of the 18th Judicial District. He was elected to Cangress but counted out by the Republicans in Reconstruction days. After this, he returned to Opelousas, La., and continued the practice of law the remainder of his life. His wife was Cecile Lastropes, and came from one of the most prominent and influential Creole families.

Charles Cabiness Bailey, son of Parks and Mary Cabiness, married Martha Hairston Rowland of Henry county Virginia. His daughter Mary was born in this county, but was taken to Ga. in infancy and finally married J. H. Traylor, the youngest son of Rev. J. C. Traylor, long of Henry Co. Va.

Patience Bailey, a descendant of Samuel and Augusta Parks Bailey married T. Patterson Traylor, and they had a son Albert Washington, who married a Miss Adams.

The last named reared a son Robert Lee Traylor, who had a daughter Anne, who married a Mr. Larus of Richmond, Va.

CALLAWAY FAMILY IN ENGLAND

Arms: Norman. Fesse between 3 daggers. The Shield is black. The Fesse, a band of Metal or color that crosses the Shield horizontally and is one of the nine honorable Ordinaries, Daggers or Conveys. The Daggers are gold.
Crest: Helmet.
Motto: St. Callay Ora pro me.

In working up the pedigree of the Callaway family, searchers date back to early 14th Century where Calwey was a Monk at Monticute Monastery, Somersetshire. He was of the Cluniac order of Monks confirmed by King Henry 1 and emigrated from Normandy to St. Neots, Cornwall, where other members of the family took interest for a century afterwards.

During 1500 John Callway placed a window in the church at St. Neots to his ancestor and his own family and canonized the Monk., hence "St. Callaway Ora pro me". This window is still existing, Jan. 1915. Wm. Callwaye, a brother of John Callway, mar. at St. Kew, 1577. In Patrynimica Britannica (Names of Britain) it is stated that Calway and Callaway are of one origin. In an "Historical Sketch of St. Neots" there is much information regarding the family at this period. In a list of books written by the Callaway family taken from the Library of the British Museum there is evidence of both education and literary attainments. One Henry Callaway, 11th child of a Somersetshire parent, was born Jan. 17, 1817, was a teacher, a chemist, M. D., D. D. and Bishop of Kaffraria. Died Mar. 26, 1890, buried, Ottery Church, Devenshire. The only living descendant of Ann Hathaway is Miss Marian Calaway, of Council School, Stratford-on-Avon. An entry at St. Kew, Cornwall gives three brothers: Daniel Calaway 1620, Richard Calaway 1621, William (Guliel) Callaway, 1624. To this Guliel Callaway the ancestry of the Callaways in America can trace clear and direct. It is believed they visited this country with Sir Walter Raleigh and his brother-in-law Sir Humphrey Gilbert. These three families were associated in Eng.

HISTORY OF HENRY COUNTY, VIRGINIA

CALLAWAY FAMILY IN VIRGINIA

The original ancester of the Callaways in Va. was Col. Wm. Callaway, of Bedford Co., Va. He mar. Elizabeth Tilly. They had five sons, b. in Va. Richard, James, Thomas, and others.

SECOND GENERATION

Richard Callaway b. 1719, mar. 1st., 1740. Patented lands in Brunswick and Lunenburg counties, Va., 1747-1754: sergeant, lieut. Major in French and Indian Wars, 1755-1763: trustee of the new town of New London, then in Bedford, now in Campbell county, 1761: patented lands in Bedford, 1762-1770; went several times to Ky.; moved to N. C. possibly between 1771-74; to locate, early in 1775; a member of the Transylvania Convention, held in Boonsboro, May 1775. His family reached Boonsboro Sept. 26, 1776. The first ferry (Boonsboro) was placed under his charge. He was killed by the Indians near Boonsboro, Mar. 8, 1780. Callaway Co. Ky. was named for him. His children: Sarah, Elizabeth, Frances, Flanders.

James Callaway, of Bedford Co., b. Dec. 21, 1736. mar. Elizabeth Early, who was a descendant of Jeremiah Early, emigrant from Ulster, Ireland, and settled in old Culpeper, now Madison Co., Va. The emigrant had ten sons and every one began his name with "J". One of these, Jubal, was the grandfather of Jubal Early, of the C. S. A.

Referring to Col. James Callaway of Bedford: (These committees first recommended by the convention of Aug. 1774, were soon chosen in each county. They met at varying dates, and their proceedings became of increasing importance. Col. Wm. Cabell was chairman of the Amherst Com. Thomas Jefferson of the Albermarle; Col. J. Cabell of Buckingham; Col. P. Carrington, of Charlotte, Col. Jas. Callaway of Bedford. Col Jas. Callaway served in French and Indian War; built first iron works above Lynchburg; also owned and operated lead mines from which were supplied the patriotic armies of the Rev., and was constantly employed in all that pertained to those important offices. In 1780, co-operating with other faithful citizens, he helped suppress a conspiracy against the Commonwealth. The conspirators (tories) were tried, Col. Charles Lynch acting as judge. This was the origin in our state of the term "Lynch Law". Col. James Callaway was the founder of New London, Campbell Co. Va., where he died Nov. 18, 1809. Issue: Geo., John and others.

Rev. Thomas Callaway was an Episcopal clergyman. He mar.—. Issue: John, Jacob, Isaac. They moved from Va. to Halifax Co., N. C.

THIRD GENERATION

John Callaway, son of Rev. Thomas Callaway mar. Bethany Arnold and was an officer in the Rev. army.

Jacob Callaway was the father of Joshua Callaway. Other descendants of these 3 brothers are now living in Ga., among whom are Judge Enoch Callaway, of Augusta Ga., Rev. Enoch Callaway, Brantly Callaway, and Fuller E. Callaway, of LaGrange, Ga. They first settled in Wilkes Co., on land granted them by the State of Ga., which land is still kept in the family.

Children of Richard Callaway: Sarah, Elizabeth, Frances, Flanders. Sarah Callaway mar. Sept., 1761, Gabriel Penn, of Amherst Co. Va., who was a first cousin of John Penn, the signer of Declaration of Independence. This Gabriel Penn was b. July 17, 1741, was a sergeant in 1st, Va. Regiment under Col. Wm. Byrd, 1764; member Rev. Convention, etc., and d. 1798.

Elizabeth and Frances Callaway, with Jemima Boone, were captured by the Indians July 14, 1776, and retaken by Boone the next day. The incident is made use of by James Fenimore Cooper in "The Last of the Mohicans". On Aug 7, 1776. Elizabeth Callaway mar. Samuel Henderson one of her rescuers, and their dau. Fanny Henderson was the first white child b. in Ky., to parents mar. in Kentucky.

Frances Callaway. (It is not certain that this is the same Frances who mar. James Steptoe, of Bedford Co., but rather likely it was).

Regarding Frances Callaway, grand daughter of Sir. Wm. Callaway. She mar. James Steptoe, of Federal Hill, Bedford Co. He was b. in Westmoreland Co., July 16, 1750; clerk of the court, 1772-1827; connected with the Washington, Lee, and Ayletty families. His grandfather was Sir Philip Steptoe, of Teddington Hall, Eng. His half aunt mar. Samuel Washington, brother of Geo. Another half aunt mar. Philip Ludwell Lee, ancestor of R. E. Lee. Frances Callaway Steptoe is the great-great grandmother of Lady Nancy Astor, M. P. as her dau. mar. Henry Langhorne. In this home have been entertained Andrew Jackson, Patrick Henry, and a boyhood friend, Thomas Jefferson. A granite stone which marks the grave of his son bears the inscription: "James Callaway Steptoe, b. Dec. 10, 1781, d. Oct. 24, 1827, etc." It is said that Sir Wm. Callaway was the father of 22 children. (This can not be the Col. Wm. Callaway there is an article which reads: who mar. Elizabeth Tilly unless he was mar. twice, which is possible).

Flanders Callaway mar. Jemima Boone, dau. of Daniel Boone, the Ky. Pioneer.

Children of Col. James Callaway and Elizabeth Early: Geo. and John.

Dr. Geo. Callaway, of Bedford Co., mar. Mary Elizabeth Cabell Apr. 11, 1811, at Union Hall. They lived first at Lynchburg, on estate inherited from his father (since belonging to the Langhornes, but now to the corporation of the city of Lynchburg). About 1818 they moved to Nelson Co., Va., leaving no living descendant.

John or Jack Callaway, b. Aug. 1 1721, came to Rocky Hill Henry Co., from Horse Shoe Farm on Yadkin River, N. C.

In a miniature picture of John Callaway, painted in London, there is enclosed a stamp resembling a king's seal. The design contains the crowned head and name of Geo. III and inscription in Latin: "Shame on him who evil thinks"; also, "God and My Right". The former is the same adopted by the old English order, "The Knights of The Garter".

Hairston, b. Feb. 25, 1793, Mar. Dec. 14, 1809. Issue: Samuel Hariston Callaway, September 9, 1810. Elizabeth Mary Callaway, Jan. 26, 1812, James Callaway, Jan. 18, 1814.

Polly Hairston Callaway d. July 10, 1816.

SECOND GENERATION

To America Hairston, dau. of Bethenia Letcher and Col. Geo. Hairston. The 1st. dau. after many sons. She was b. Feb. 21, 1801, and mar. Jan. 14, 1821. Issue: Geo. Hairston Callaway, may 23, 1822 and Bethenia Ruth Callaway, b. March 1, 1826. Both she and Bethenia

Letcher Hairston are buried at "Beaver Creek, Henry Co. In the hands of a descendant of America H. Callaway

"LA FAYETTE BALL"

"The pleasure of Mrs. Callaway's company is solicited at a Ball to be held in the Long Room of the Court House, on Wednesday evening, the 23d inst. in compliment to Col. Thos. Polk's Volunteer troop of Cavalry, now on their march to meet the nations' guest, Gen. La Fayette."
Salisbury, N. C., Feb. 21, 1825.

Geo. Locke
D. F. Caldwell
James Huie.
    Managers."

John Giles
R. H. Alexander
Junius Snead
John Beard Jr.
Charles Fisher

FOURTH GENERATION

Children of John Callaway.—Samuel H. Callaway, d. Aug. 9th, 1846, on his farm in Yancy Co., N. C. James Callaway, d. Dec. 17, 1829, after an illness of only 37 hrs. Geo. H. Callaway's mind became disordered 1832, resulting from a blow on the head by a baseball bat at school. He d. Nov. 3, 1894. No Issue from these three.

Elizabeth M. Callaway mar. Evan Davis, of N. C. Issue: Elizabeth, Katherine, John Henry Davis, Bethenia Ruth Callaway, at the age of 15, mar. Geo. Pannill of Pittsylvania. Issue; (See Pannill Family in this volume).

FIFTH GENERATION

Children of Elizabeth Callaway and Evan A. Davis: Elizabeth, or Betty Davis, mar. Mr. Eaton, her teacher in a boarding school in N. C. Issue: Callaway Eaton. (2) Baker, Katherine, or Kate Davis, mar. 1st., McCorkle; 2d, McLaury. Issue; May McCorkle and John McLaury. May lives in Salisbury N. C. and New York City.

John Henry Davis mar. his half-first cousin, Mary Pannill, dau. of Bethenia Ruth Callaway and Geo. Pannill. Issue, five children also recorded elsewhere in this work.

CAHILL FAMILY

John Cahill, the progenitor of the Henry county family, came from Ireland, born about 1760, married Dianah Garner born Oct. 10, 1769, and who was the wealthiest lady in the northern part of the county. This marriage was in 1789. He died April 1, 1817. The children of this union were as follows: Nancy, Peregrine, Thomas, John, Susannah, Mary, Nathaniel, Dianah, Maria, and Sallie, who died an infant.

FIRST GENERATION

John Cahill, Jr., was born Feb. 15, 1797, married, and reared the following children: Thomas, Peregrine, and Jack.

Susannah Cahill was born June 21, 1799, married Geo. K. DeShazo in 1822, and died Dec. 8, 1862. (See DeShazo family).

Mary Cahill was born Nov. 9, 1804, married James Price of Franklin Co. Issue: 5 children, among them William, of Roanoke, who reared a large family, and Thomas P. Price, of Natural Bridge.

Nancy Cahill married David Philpott. Issue: Columbus. She was born about 1800, and lived on Smith river, in Philpott settlement.

Nathaniel Cahill was born in 1807, and died in 1826.

Mariah Cahill was born Nov. 25, 1811, married Columbus King, Dec. 13, 1829. She died June 28, 1833, and left one son, John W. King.

Peregrine Cahill was born Sept. 19. 1792, married Ann Purdle. Issue: Mary, Sallie, Lucinda, Dianah, Mariah, Thomas, Perry, John Car, who was killed in the Civil War, Jesse, and Obediah.

Thomas Cahill was born Oct. 20, 1794, married Clementine Turner, who was born in 1803, and died in 1892. Issue: Nancy, Eliza, neither married, Jane, who married Ashworth Dove Sr., Thomas who married Ann Eliza Draper, Marshall, John W. and Taylor Z.

SECOND GENERATION

Of the children of Perry Cahill we note as follows: Mary J. Cahill married Capt. Thomas G. King in 1830. Children of this union were: Susan Ann, John Lewis, Thomas Jesse, Mary Jane, Anna, George Perry, Sallie Lou.

Sallie Cahill married James Turner; Lucinda married Joseph Thomasson; Dianah, and Maria never married; Thomas Cahill married Margaret Thomasson; and the others, not married.

Zachary Taylor Cahill, who was born May 26, 1847, married first Sallie Akers, (No issue) 2nd, Harriett Bousman, had the following children: Bessie W., John Taylor, Lorenza Dow, William Price, and Gustavus B.

Of John William Cahill, who was born about 1830, married Betsy Ann Finney, we note children as follows: Victoria Cahill, married John Burgess; Lenora and Thomas not married; Jennie Lily Cahill, married Thomas Jesse King; Zachariah Cahill, married Florence Williams; Benjamin Marshall Cahill, another son of Thomas Cahill, Sir. was born about 1832, married Tamesia Young. He was in the 10th, Va. Cavalry during the Civil War. He lived in the southern part of Henry county, on Smith river most of his life, as a progressive farmer, and reared the following children: B. M. Cahill, Jr., married Kate Lewis, and moved to Winston, N. C.; Loula Cahill, married Joe. L. Trogdon, of North Carolina; Dora Cahill married Hugh Binford, a merchant of Madison, N. C.; Lelia Cahill married A. B. Poindexter of this county; Tarmesia Cahill married Walter Dunn; Dr. James Semple Cahill, a dentist, married Marie Chappell, and located at Richmond, Va.; Dr. William Cahill, dentist, married Ann Richardson, and located at South Hill, Va. Beatrice Cahill married Jesse Richardson of Leaksville, N. C. A. Holt Cahill married Lettie Carter, of Stoneville, N. C. Edgar Cahill married Fannie Flynn, of North Carolina.

CLARK

Gideon Clark married Cassandra Stultz, dau. of Thomas J. Stultz. Issue: Tom, Lettitia, Sarah, Nathaniel, William, Patty, Joe, and Carnetta.

William Clark married Miss Wyatt. Issue: Ernest E., b. Nov. 7, 1872; Marion E., b. May 20, 1876, d. Feb. 1914. Cassandra C., b. Oct. 19, 1878. Ruby, b. Jan. 29, 1881. Charles S., b. Aug. 17, 1883. Joseph E., b. Sept. 7, 1886. Annie, b. Oct. 14, 1889 (Now Mrs. T. S. Moore). John D., b. May 10, 1892; Nina G., b. Feb. 3. 1895 (Now Mrs. J. W. Lovell).

C. S. Clark, son of Wm. and Miss Wyatt, md. Miss Trout, and is a faithful servant of the people of Martinsville, in the capacity of mail-carrier.

CRAGHEAD FAMILY

John Craghead was of English descent. He was born in 1804, in Franklin county, where he spent his entire life. He married Sarah Powel when she was quite young. He died in 1859, but his widow lived to be 102 years old. They had a large family of children as follows: Thomas Lodowick, John, who died while a child, Robert, Charles, Townley, Alexander, Virginia, Catherine, and Lily.

SECOND GENERATION

Virginia Craghead married a Mattocks; Emily Craghead married John Morgan; Catherine married Dr. Spencer James. Issue Dr. John James, of Pittsylvania county.

Thomas Lodowick Craghead was born in 1819. He married Lucinda Baker, grandaughter of Henry Koger and Mary King, and their children were: Sallie, Angeline, Pocahontas, and Loula. He lived on the Staunton river in Franklin county, where he dispensed old Virginia hospitality. He had a large farm and nearly a hundred negroes. He was a great hunter, and enjoyed chasing foxes and other game so plentiful in those days. He joined the Confederate Army, and was a good soldier, but was captured and taken a prisoner to Point Lookout, Md., where he died in 1864.

THIRD GENERATION

Sallie Craghead married John H. Matthews, in 1867. (See Matthews family).

Loula Craghead married Sam Hill, and their children were: Sam, Robt., William, Lucy, Loula, Thomas Lodowick, and Catherine, Overton.

Pocahontas Craghead married John Coleman. Issue: James, All, Harrison, Loula, and Ethel.

Ruth Angeline Craghead married in 1870, Morgan A. Coleman, of Henry county, where they lived all their happy days. He reared a large family by the splendid help of his wife, and had a good time through life. He was fond of sport very energetic, and known as a real hustler and a splendid trader. The children of this union were as follows: George, Robert, Thomas C., Bruce, Morton, Sallie, Ida, and Alice.

FOURTH GENERATION

George Coleman married and died while young, and left the following children: Burwell, Clyde, Ruby, and Alvis;

Thomas C. Coleman married Azzie Davis, of Bassett, in 1912, and lived at Ridgeway.

Sallie Coleman married Joseph Bassett of Charlotte, N. C.; Ida Coleman married Thomas Calvin Mathews, of Martinsville; Bruce Coleman married Essie Hodnett, of Reidsville, N. C., Morton Coleman married Lottie Hundley, of Pittsylvania county; Alice Coleman married G. C. Pratt, a merchant of Martinsville, Va.

CLANTON FAMILY

The Henry branch of this family came from Brunswick, and is of English descent. Wm. Clanton was born in that county, about 1799, and came to this county when a young man, and accumulated about 3,000 acres of land. He married Polly Thornton, of Cascade: Issue; George Washington, Jesse, Eliza, Bessy, and Dolly.

SECOND GENERATION

Geo. W. Clanton, b. Mar., 25, 1818, married Mary Ann, daughter of Jeremiah Hylton. Mr. Clanton was a planter in the western part of the Co., and owned a large boundary of land, and many slaves. He was one of the county magistrates prior to the civil war, and died May 5, 1907. Issue: Mary E., Nancy Hylton, Geo. William, and Hylton Claude.

Jesse Clanton married 1st., Kinnie, dau, of Camillus King, 2d., Columbia, dau. of Columbus King. Issue by 1st. marriage, Willie C., by 2d., Mary, Lillie, Nannie, Bessie, Geo., Robert, and Jesse.

Eliza Clanton married John Salmons, and died in 192— after passing the century mark. Issue: Edmund, Geo., Jesse, Lou ,Dolly.

Dolly Clanton married Franklin Griggs. Issue: Greenbury, Robert, Samuel, Edmond, Mary, Sallie, Julia, Adelaide, (See Griggs family).

Mary Clanton married John Graveley, Betsy married Garret Philpott.

THIRD GENERATION

The children of Geo. W. Clanton are as follows: Nancy Clanton, married Will Rangeley (See Rangeley family). Mary E. and Geo. Wm. died unmarried. Hylton Claude, owner of the old homestead, married Mary Bennie Jones. (See Jones Family). Issue: Claudia, Lucille, William, and Geo.

Mr. Clanton is one of Henry's substantial conservative gentlemen, and the compiler is proud to own him as one of her "Boys".

*DAVIS FAMILY

The forefathers of Charles Davis came from England, and settled in Charles County, Md. Chas. Davis md. Sarah Moreland in Trinity Parish, May 11, 1762, in Charles County, Md. Issue: Moses, Rachel, Lydia, and Joshua.

Charles Davis md. (2d) Anne, Dent in 1775, Issue: Benjamin Thomas Blackburn, Eleanor, Anne, and Peter. They came to Va. prior to 1785, and settled at Reed Creek, Henry County.

Peter Davis, son of Charles md. Mary, dau. of Wm. Heard, Dec. 6, 1807. Issue: Joathan, who married three times; 1st, Nancy Turner, 2d, Elizabeth Turner, 3d, Nettiee Smith. Nancy Dent md. Capt. Tom Draper. Peter Perkins md. twice, 1st, Emily Wade, 2d. Mary Frances Holland. Thomas Blackburn md. Martha Coleman, Wm. Heard md. Bettie Napier, Laban J. md. Letitia Pedigo, David H. md. Nancy Mcghee, Margaret Carr md. Joseph Jones, Jane Hickey md. Jesse Lavinder, and Benjamin S. md. Anne Hunter.

Peter Perkins Davis md. Emily, dau. of John Wade, of Franklin County, 1850, and settled at Oak Level. He was a merchant, tobacconist and landowner. During the Civil War he was made Capt. of Detail, his duties being to look after deserters and supplies for the soldiers' wives and families. Issue: John Peter Davis, b. March 2, 1852.

John Peter Davis md. Mary Jane, dau. of John Mitchell and Elizabeth Napier Mitchell, Dec. 22, 1875. Issue: Emily Wade, John Mitchell, Mary Elizabeth, Sarah Jane, Charles Peter, Anne Ursula, and Robert Brown.

He was elected sheriff for three terms and died while serving his third term, Feb. 17, 1898, at the age of 45 yrs. It was said of him at his death "He died without an enemy".

Emily Wade md. Ernest Lynwood Kelly, Jan. 15, 1903. No issue. John Mitchell unmarried. Mary Elizabeth unmarried. Sarah Jane md. James Webb Kelly, June 10, 1907. Issue: Mary Davis Kelly, b. Oct. 28, 1911. Emily Ball Kelly b. Oct. 18, 1915.

Charles Peter Davis md. Kate Decottes, Aug. 28, 1916.

---

*On the authority of Thomas J. Draper, one of the oldest citizens of Henry County, a near relative of the Davis family, David Davis, the father of Charles, was a grandson of Lord Baltimore.

Issue: Charles Peter Davis, Jr., b. Feb. 13, 1918. Anne Ursula Davis unmarried. Robert Brown Davis d. March 13, 1918. Jane Davis Kelly d. Aug. 5, 1918.

Robt. E. Davis, half brother of John Peter was appointed to serve the unexpired term as sheriff, and was afterward elected to the office for one term.

John Mitchell, son of John Peter Davis, was elected to the same office at the age of 24 and served three terms, being the youngest sheriff at the time of election in the State of Va.

Peter Perkins was md. 2d. to Mary Frances, dau. of John and Sarah Holland, of Franklin Co. Aug. 24, 1864. Issue: Robert E., Sallie Elizabeth, Thomas Holland, Chas. W., Fletcher A., Robt. E. Davis md. Lillian Trent. No issue.

Sallie Elizabeth Davis md. Everette J. Davis. Issue: Frank Payne, Harry Holland, Maude Wall, Mary Sue, Walter E., and Jesse Guy. H

Thomas Holland Davis md. Lily Heard. Issue. Thomas Holland Jr., Robt. E., and Julian.

Chas. W. Davis md. Ida Townes. No issue. Chas. W. Davis md. 2d, Virginia Grantham.

Fletcher A. Davis md. Julia———.

Frank Payne Davis md. Ellye Walker, Oct. 9, 1910. Issue: Frank Payne Davis, Jr., and Sarah Elizabeth Davis.

Harry Holland Davis md. Lena Seward Feb. 7, 1917. Issue: Lewellyn Davis and Everette Holland Davis.

Maude Davis md. Sidney P. Childress. Issue: Mary Anne Childress, Sidney P. Childress, Jr., and Vincent Davis Childress.

Jesse Guy Davis not married. Mary Sue and Walter E. Davis d. in infancy.

Benjamin Davis, son of Charles and Anne his wife, was born Sept. 19, 1778. Benjamin and Peter sons of Chas, and Anne Davis married sisters, daughters of William Heard.

Benjamin Davis and Nancy Heard were married December 13, 1800. They lived about one mile north of Oak Level, on the road leading to Arnold Walker's mill. To this union was born the following children: Benjamin, William, Charles, Jesse, Mary, Peggy, Betsy Anne, and Winnie.

Benjamin married Eleanor Hicks, and moved to Rome

Ga. William married Lucy Craig, Charles never married, Peggy married a Mr. Minter. Mary, Betsy Anne, and Winnie married three brothers, Wootson, Tandy, and Thomas Ramsey, of Franklin County, and to these were born and reared large, prosperous, and influential families, now scattered to the four corners of the earth.

Benjamin Davis and his brothers were farmers by trade, and were prosperous and good livers. The Davis family was noted for its kind and generous disposition. Their homes were often the scenes of large gatherings of friends and relatives. They responded to the call of duty. Many of their sons fought bravely throughout the Civil War, and a great many gave their all to the Lost Cause.

Jesse Heard, youngest son of Benjamin and Nancy Davis, lived near the old homestead and married Susan Koger, daughter of John Koger, in 1848. To them were born seven sons and two daughters, namely: John Benjamin, Gillie Coleman, Pinkney Gilmore, Rufus Franklin, Everett Jesse, Lloyd Tilman, George Thomas, Doctor W., and Lula.

The following article taken from the Henry Bulletin in 1904, will represent the character of the man. "An Old and Respected Citizen Gone."

Jesse H. Davis, one of the oldest men of Henry County, died at his home near Oak Level on Saturday morning, March 26th 1904.

The deceased was born on March 12th 1820, making his stay on earth 84 years and 14 days. He was born near where he died, having lived his entire days in Henry County, and on an adjoining farm to his father's old home. He was brought up on the farm and spent his whole life in farming. He was married at the age of 28 to Susan Koger, daughter of the late John Koger of this County. His widow still survives him. He and his companion lived happily together fifty-six years. To them were born seven boys and two girls, of whom five boys still survive him: Pinkney G. Davis, of Reed Creek, E. J. and Geo. T. Davis, of Martinsville, Lloyd T., and D. W., of Oak Level, Mrs. Hailey W. Ramsey, of Ramsey, Va., and Mrs. N. S. Goode of Alumine, Va.

He was laid to rest in the family burying ground, near the old homestead, in the presence of a large concourse of relatives and friends. The funeral services were conducted by Rev. A. B. Philpott, of the Primitive

Baptist Church, of which the deceased had long been a member. He paid a glowing tribute to the memory of the man whom he had known all his life, and said that he did not know of another man like him. He said when he was a young man leading a wayward life he was often counseled and admonished by this good man, which wielded a great influence over his own life. One of his texts was, "Mark the perfect man, and behold the upright, for the end of that man is peace."

He joined Town Creek Baptist church at the April meeting 1877, was baptized by the late E. B. Turner in June of the same year, and chosen deacon of that church at the July meeting 1880, which office he filled until his death. He was devoted to his church, and whenever he was able to attend, always filled his place. While he was deeply and well grounded in the faith and doctrine of his church, yet he was charitable to all other denominations. To his family he was a kind affectionate father, to his wife a loving husband, to his neighbors he was generous and obliging, to his country a loyal citizen.

He never had a quarrel with any man, never warranted any man for debt, never had a law suit. His conversation was chaste never indulged in blackguard, in fact he would not repeat in a conversation profane language used by others.

He was successful in his business. His home was always open to his friends and to the traveling public. He never turned off any weary traveler, but took him in his home and gave to him of the best he had. He was a man possessed of good common sense. His counsel and advice were sought by many. His motto was: Rather suffer a wrong than to go to law with a neighbor. The Golden Rule was the tenor of his life. So lived the man, a friend and favorite of all who knew him. He said that he enjoyed life, his family and his friends, but that the future had no terror for him. In his old age he was bright and cheerful, and leaned heavily upon the arm of the Lord.

D. S. Davis, son of Benjamin S. Davis, has been elected to the office of Treasurer of Henry County for six successive terms, and is the present incumbent.

James P. Davis his brother, who moved to the state of Indiana, a good many years ago, is a prominent business man of Kokomo, and has represented his County both in the Legislature and Senate, and is now the nominee of the Democratic party for Congress in the 5th Congressional District of the state of Indiana.

Hon. B. A. Davis, son of David H. Davis, is a prominent attorney of Rocky Mt., Franklin County, has represented his County both in the legislature, and Senate. His sons are all prominent attorneys. His two brothers also reside in Rocky Mt., and are prominent business men and bankers. Chas. J. Davis is Cashier of Peoples National Bank, and Raymond Davis is Cashier of First National Bank.

E. L. Davis, son of Laban J. Davis is a prominent business man of Martinsville, Va., being a contractor and builder.

Everett J. Davis, son of Jesse. H. Davis, was married the second time to Minnie Heard Davis, daughter of Obediah and Eliza Heard, November 14, 1900. Born to this union is the following children: Evelyn, Elizabeth, Everett Jesse, Jr., and Ernestine.

He came to Martinsville in 1890 and engaged in the warehouse business as bookkeeper, afterwards engaged in the warehouse business for a number of years as manager and proprietor. In 1900 bought the Orinoco Warehouse (now the Banner) and is one of the most prominent tobacco warehousemen in the state of Virginia. He is a leader in all public, civic, and religious affairs.

THE DANDRIDGE FAMILY

ARMS: Azure, a lion's head erased or, between three mascles argent.
CREST: A lion's head erased charged with a mascle argent.
MOTTO: In Adversis Etiam Fide.

The ancestor of the Dandridge family of Henry Co., Va. was Col. William Dandridge, of the British Navy. He and his brother, Col. John Dandridge, the father of Martha Washington came to Va. about the same time and settled on opposite sides of the Pamunkey river. Col. John in New Kent Co., and Col. William in King William, near West Point, which was named for his wife's (Unity West) ancestors. They bore the Arms of the Dandridges of great Malvern, Worcestershire, the first of whom on record (see Foster's Alumni Oxonienses) was John Dandridge, (son of William Oxford) born 1679, who matriculated at New College, May 13, 1696, became M. A. 1702, and vicar of Weston Beggard, Co. Hereford, in 1705. In a deed of 1719 Wm. Dandridge is descended as "Late of Hampton, Now of King William, Gentlemen". In 1717 July 19, William Dandridge and Gov. Spottswood, sign a charter, party for a vessel belonging to Dandridge in which the latter engages to transport 20 men to South Carolina Colonial Va. State Papers, I., 176 lb. p. 190.

July 11, 1719, Wm. Dandridge and Thomas Wythe obtain grant of a water-front in Hampton Land Registry, Vol. X., page. 450.

In 1727 we find him a member of the Colonial Council, and one of the commissioners appointed with Col. Wm Byrd to settle the dividing line between Va. and North Carolina.

A few years later he entered upon a distinguished naval service. In 1737 it is stated in the Virginia Gazette that Wm. Dandridge, Esq., would be given command of one of his majesty's ships, and later there occurs mention of the presentation to him of a sword by the Duke of Montagu. In Feb., 1741 he commanded the Wolf, 12 guns, on the Va. station, and in Nov., 1741, he was transferred to the command of the South Sea, of 40 guns, and served in Oglethorpe's attack on St. Augustine, and Admiral Vernon's siege of Cartagena, he subsequently commanded the man-of-war, Ludlow Castle. Wm. Dandridge died in 1743 while on a visit to his Hanover estates. He married Unity West (2nd wife) great granddaughter of Gov. John West. They had two sons and two daughters.

Reference: "The Dandridges of Va."
by Wilson Miles Cary.
William and Mary College Quarterly-1896.

FIRST GENERATION

Descent: Nathaniel West Dandridge, Capt. in the British Navy, born in King and Queen Co., Va., 1729, died in Hanover Co., Jan. 10, 1786. He was Capt. of the Va. Association, May 28, 1756, Burgess of Hanover Co., 1758-1764 (Colonial Families of the U. S., Page 117). Nathaniel Dandridge was one of the "Knights of the Golden Horseshoe." He married Dorothea Spottswood born 1733, died Sept. 1773, daughter of Major General Alexander Spottswood, Gov. of Va., and Anne Butler (Brayne) Spottswood.

SECOND GENERATION

Descent: William Alexander Dandridge the eldest son of Nathaniel West Dandridge and Dorothea Spotts-

NANNIE ANDERSON DANDRIDGE
(Mrs. P. W. Dalton)

Daughter of Wm. and Mary Hamner Dandridge. Great, gt. gt. grand-daughter of Maj. General Alexander Spottswood, Gov. of Virginia.

HISTORY OF HENRY COUNTY, VIRGINIA 145

wood, was born April 6, 1750. He married Anne Bolling, born Feb. 5, 1752, daughter of Major John Bolling, M. H. B., J. P., and his wife Elizabeth Blair Bolling. Elizabeth Blair was the daughter of Dr. Archibald Blair, and a niece of the Commissary James Blair, D. D., founder of William & Mary College (see "Pocahontas and her Descendants", by Wyndham Robertson.) William Dandridge was Major of Militia in the Rev. war. (Historical Register of Officers of the Continental Army, 1775-1783). For other services see "Major Wm. Dandridge," Council Journals, beginning with 1776 thru the Rev. (Council Journals 1777-1778) "Major William Dandridge (York M) War23 (1773)" This is a collection of M. S. Volumes bearing on the Military Establishment during and after the Rev. Sargent Allen captured a Cremona Violin in the Redoubt at Yorktown and presented it to Wm. Dandridge, as he was a very fine "fiddler." His brother-in-law, Patrick Henry, and Thomas Jefferson were also good violinists, and they often joined him in playing for the stately minuet at "Elsing Green", his grandfather's home. (Wirt's life of Patrick Henry). The fine old violin is now in the possession of a great granddaughter of Wm. Dandridge.

THIRD GENERATION

Descent William Alexander ("Little Dover") Dandridge was born in Hanover Co., 1772, died 1842. He married Nancy Pulliam, born in Goochland Co., Va, 1782, died in Henry Co. Va.

FOURTH GENERATION

Descent:: William Alexander ("Little Dover") Dandridge, born in Hanover Va. 1812, died in Henry Co., Nov. 1865, was a planter and large slave owner. He was a great, great grandson of Alexander Spottswood, Gov., of Va., 1710-1723. Thru this family his ancestry has been traced back to Duncan, King of Scotland (who was waylaid and killed by Macbeth, but not in the manner as stated by Shakespeare) 1034. He was 17th in direct descent from Robert Bruce, king of Scotland; 7th in descent from Pocahontas; and 7th from Col. John West, Gov. of Va. in 1635. Thru the West family he was descended from Egbert, the first Saxon king of England, who reigned 827-823. He was also descended from

HISTORY OF HENRY COUNTY, VIRGINIA

"Alfred the Great," Henry Percy, the renowned "Hotspur" of history, Edward III, William the Conqueror, and three of the Plantaganet Kings Henry II, John and Henry III. After his marriage to Sarah Nicholds, sister of Greenberry Nicholds, William Dandridge settled in Henry Co., near Martinsville, Va. Five children were born to this union: Thomas West, Robert Bolling, Clay, John, and Sarah Virginia, who was only a few weeks old at the time of her mother's death in 1845. In 1847 he married his second wife, Mary Jane Hamner (daughter of Nancy House Hamner) born in Brunswick Co., Va., died in Tate Co., Miss. 1879. After his second marriage, Wm. Dandridge moved to his plantation, "Locust Grove" near Spencer, Va. He was preparing to build a commodious house for his large family but was prevented from carrying out his plans by the outbreak of the Civil war. The death of John, his youngest son, who died in service, and great financial losses left him so broken in spirit and health that he never recovered. He died in 1865, at the age of 53 yrs. William and Mary Dandridge had nine children: Nannie Anderson, Mary Pocahontas, Emma Louise, Martha Washington, and Bessie Lee; sons, James Spottswood, Samuel Hamner, George Gilmer, and Walter Alexander. After the death of her husband, Mary Dandridge and family moved to Tate Co., Miss, where she lived until the time of her death in April 1879.

FIFTH GENERATION
CHILDREN OF Wm. & SARAH NICHOLDS DANDRIDGE

Descent: Dr. Thomas West Dandridge, the oldest child, was born in Henry Co., about 1836, died in Madison N. C. about 1880. After graduating in medicine at the Virginia Medical College, Richmond Va. he attended lectures at the University, Charlottesville, Va. He was in Texas at the outbreak of the Civil war, so he entered service with the "Texas Rangers". The silver star with which he pinned his hat, is one of the heirlooms of his family. Later Dr. Dandridge was transferred to Salisbury N. C. He was one of the surgeons in charge of the Federal hospital there. After the war he located at Madison, N. C. He was a splendid physician; and soon built up a large practice. Dr. Dandridge was an unusually handsome, cultered man, and his death brought sorrow to hundreds of admirers and friends.

MARY POCAHONTAS DANDRIDGE
(Mrs. J. W. Wilborn)

FIFTH GENERATION

Descent: Dr. Robert Bolling Dandridge was born Aug. 6, 1838 in Henry Co., Va. He graduated in medicine at the Virginia Medical College, Richmond Va., March 8, 1860, after which he took a post graduate course at the University, Charlottesville, Va. Later he returned to his home "Locust Grove" Henry Co., Va. where he had an office and established a practice in the surrounding country. He enlisted for service in the civil war June 5, 1861 at Lynchburg. He entered as a private, Co. "H". 24th, Regiment, Va. Infantry, C. S. A. Nov. 24, 1861 he was promoted to Hospital Steward; discharged from service June 3, 1862. (see records War Dept.). Dec. 1866 Dr. Dandridge was married to Susan Rangeley, daughter of John Rangeley and Mary Webster, of Rangeley, Va. Susan Rangeley is of English descent on her father's side, he having come to this country when a young boy. On the maternal side she is a lineal descendant of John Endicott, Gov. of Mass. from 1644 to 1665. The children of this union were William R., John, Thomas, Harry C., Una, and Annie.

Descent: Clay Dandridge was born in Henry Co. about 1840. He married Mattie Dodd, daughter of Nathaniel and Maria Woodson Dodd of Rockingham Co., N. C. She lived only a year or two , dying when their only child, Nathaniel, was a few weeks old. In the Civil war Clay Dandridge served in the 42nd Va. Cavalry. After the death of his wife he moved to Missouri, where he married again. He died in 18—, survived by his widow and several children. His son "Nat" Dandridge married a Miss Watson, of South Carolina. They had one child, Nell Dandridge.

Descent: John (called "Dude"), was the youngest son of Wm. Dandridge and Sarah Nicholds. In the war between the states he was in the 42nd Va. Infantry. Being only about eighteen years of age, and of a frail constitution, he couldn't with-stand the hardships of the war, and he soon contracted typhoid fever; and after a short illness died at Corbin's Plantation, near Fredericksburg, Va.

Descent: Sarah Virginia, the youngest child and only daughter of Wm. and Sarah Nicholds Dandridge, was born in Henry Co., the 20th of August, 1845. She was educated at Powell's School for girls, an Episcopal school in Richmond, Va. She was in Pontotoc, Miss., at the outbreak of the war, but her brother Clay went for her, and they finally reached their home in Henry Co., after a dangerous and exciting trip across the country, in which the Federal lines were crossed several times. Later she spent a lot of time nursing the sick and wounded in Richmond. She taught school in her own state, also in N. C., for several years. In 1874 she was married to Samuel Wall, of Stokes, N. C. He was born June 28th, 1847, died Nov. 14, 1900. Their early married life was spent on a plantation adjoining his old home near Sandy Ridge, N. C. They moved to Winston, N. C., in 1883, where Samuel Wall engaged in the leaf tobacco business. Sarah Dandridge Wall was a member of the Christian Church. After the death of her husband she moved to Darlington S. C., where she lived until the time of her death, Dec. 7, 1908. Five children were born to this union: Thomas, Elizabeth Roseboro, Samuel S., Nannie Spottswood, and Robert Edward. Sam S. Wall is the only surviving member of this family.

CHILDREN OF Wm. & MARY HAMNER DANDRIDGE

Descent: Nannie Anderson Dandridge was born at the Dandridge homestead in Henry Co. Va., April 15, 1848. When a little girl she went to school at "Penn's Store", boarding in the home of Dr. Staples. At the age of eleven years she was sent to eastern North Carolina. There in the home of her great uncle, Henry House and with his children, she had the advantage of a splendid governess for two years. On their return to Va. she prepared to enter Salem Academy, but the sudden death of her father changed her plans. She taught school in Rockingham, N. C. in 1868. On May 18, 1869, at her home "Locust Grove", she was married to Peter Washington Dalton, of Patrick, Co., Va. He was a son of James Hunter and Nancy Critz Dalton, a grandson of Col. Haman Critz, who was an officer in the Rev. (see Muster Roll of Col. Abram Penn's Regiment) war. He was a great grandson of Major James Hunter, of Guilford, County, N. C. James Hunter was in the "Battle of Alamance". By one historian he was called the "General" of the Regulators. A handsome monument on Guilford Battleground bears testimony to his presence there. He represented Guilford County in the Legislature from 1778-1782. For other services see: Colonial records of North Carolina. In the Civil war P. W. Dalton was 1st, Lieutenant in Co. "H" 42nd Va. Infantry. He volunteered in 1861, and was in service from then until he was discharged from duty in 1865. He was one of the Confederate officers, prisoners of war confined in the stockade on Morris Island, S. C., under fire of our own guns shelling that island. (see—"The Immortal Six Hundred" by J. Ogden Murry). Nannie Dandridge and husband, P. W. Dalton spent the first year of their married life in Atlanta Ga. Later they returned to Va. and spent several years in Henry and Patrick Counties, before going to Winston, N. C., to make their permanent home. Nannie Dandridge Dalton died in Winston-Salem, June 4, 1922. The children of this union were Edgar Elliot, Harry Lee, Chas., and Ada Dalton, Nannie Anderson, Hunter and Irene died in infancy.

Descent: Mary Pocahontas Dandridge was born in Henry Co., Va. July 24, 1849. Mary Pocahontas stayed in Va. some time after her mother and family left for Miss., joining them in 1873. On Dec. 23, 1873 she was married to James W. Wilborn, who was one of the most successful business men of Tate Co. They settled at Senatobia, Miss., making this their permanent home. Mary Wilborn died October 29, 1915. She was survived by her husband and four children, Willie, Durward, Marcus, and Bessie.

Descent: James Spottswood Dandridge was the eldest son of Wm. and Mary Hamner Dandridge. He was born in Henry Co. Jan. 27, 1851. When about twenty one yrs. of age he went to Tate, Co., Mississippi, to make his future home. On Jan. 4, 1881 he was married to Miss Mary Cathey. Of the six children born to this union only two, Cathey Spottswood, and Jimmie Ophelia, are now living. James Spottswood died 19—.

Descent: George Gilmer Dandridge, the second son, was born Jan. 29, 1853 at the Dandridge homestead, near Martinsville, Va. In Nov. 1872 he went to Thyatira, Miss., where he made his home for a good many years. Dec. 23, 1879 he was married to Miss Mattie Norfleet. After their marriage they went to Paris, Arkansas to live. Having always taken an active part in the affairs of town and state, he has held several offices of trust-having recently been postmaster. The children of this union are Merle, Jessie, Beatrice, Edward, George Gilmer, Samuel Clark, Mattie, Pattie Washington, Zelia Lightfoot, and James Spottswood.

Descent: Samuel Hamner Dandridge was born in Henry Co., Va. Jan. 1st, 1855. When about 17 years of age he went to Tate Co. Miss., to live. For the last 34 years he has been in the mercantile business at Thyatira, Mississippi. Dec. 4, 1890 he was married to Miss Nannie Cathey. They had five children: Mildred Hamner, William Cathey, Lightie Louise, George Samuel, and James Spottswood, who died in 1903.

Descent: Emma Louise, the third daughter, and Walter Alexander, the youngest son of Wm. and Mary Hamner Dandridge were both born at the Dandridge homestead in Henry Co., near Martinsville, Va. With their mother they went to Tate Co., Miss., in 1872. Sometime after the death of their mother they moved to Pontotoc, Miss. Where they are still living. Neither of them have married.

Descent: Martha Washington Dandridge was born in Henry Co., Va., but was reared in Mississippi, her mother having moved there when she was a little girl. August 1st, 1888 she was married to J. W. Thornton, of Littleton, N. C. They had three children, Dandridge, Margaret, and Mary, who died in infancy. Martha ("Pattie) Dandridge Thornton died Jan. 31, 1918.

Descent: Bessie Lee the youngest child of Wm. and Mary Hamner Dandridge was born in Henry Co. Va., Sept. 1865. She was reared and educated in Mississippi. On May 26, 1881 Bessie Lee was married to Walter G. Cumpton, of Paris, Arkansas. Walter Cumpton was born May 15, 1865. They had four children: Dandridge, Mary, Anna Lou, and Walter George who died 1906.

DESCENT OF Wm. ALEXANDER DANDRIDGE FROM POCAHONTAS

Pocahontas, the Indian Princess, daughter of the mighty Indian Chief, Powhatan, was born about 1595, was married to John Rolfe, gentleman, 1614, died and was buried in Gravesend, England 1617. She was called "The Nonpareil of Virginia," by the English. History does not offer, or has fiction ever depicted, a lovelier character. John Rolfe is now mainly remembered as the husband of Pocahontas, but he was undoubtedly one of the capital figures of the great epoch; the first permanent English

MRS. J. W. THORNTON
Nee Martha Washington Dandridge

settlement in North America. The place of "Secretary and Recorder-General of Virginia," was first instituted for, and filled by him. At a later period he was a member of the Governor's Council. When in London we find Pocahontas provided for as the guest of the Va. Company, the honored recipient of the marked notice of the Queen and ladies of the Court, and entertained with special and extraordinary "state, festival, and pomp", by the Lord Bishop of London (as described by Purchas, who was present); closing entirely her finer and beautiful life at Gravensend when about to embark for Virginia, in a vessel of the Virginia Company, specially provided for her accommodation. In one of the Registers at Gravensend, England is still found this brief record: "1616-March 21, Rebecca Wrolfe, wyffe of Thomas Wrolfe, gent. A Virginia lady borne, was buried in the chauncel".

FIRST GENERATION

Descent: Thomas Rolfe born 1615, reared by his uncle, Henry Rolfe, of London, married Jane Poythress. They left one child.

SECOND GENERATION

Descent: Jane Rolfe born—,died 1676; married 1675, Col. Robert Bolling, born 1646. He was the son of John and Mary Bolling, of "All Hallow's, Barkin Parish, Tower Street, London. They left one child only.

THIRD GENERATION

Descent: Col. John Bolling, born 1676, died 1729, member of the House of Burgesses, married Mary Kennon, daughter of Dr. Kennon, of Conjuror's Neck (Member of the House of Burgesses). They left one son and five daughters.

FOURTH GENERATION

Descent: Major John Bolling, M. H. B., J. P., born 1700; died Sept. 6, 1757; married Aug. 1, 1728, Elizabeth, daughter of Dr. Archibald, Blair, and niece of the Commissary James Blair, D. D., founder of William and Mary College.

FIFTH GENERATION

Descent: Anne Bolling, born Feb. 7, 1752; married Major William Dandridge, born 1750.

SIXTH GENERATION

Descent: William Alexander Dandridge, born 1772, died 1842; married Nancy Pulliam in Goochland Co. Va. 1782, died—.

SEVENTH GENERATION

Descent: William Alexander Dandridge of Henry Co. Va. married first Sarah Nicholds, secondly Mary Jane Hamner of Brunswick, Co., Va.

Reference: "Pocahontas and Her Descendants", by Wyndham Robertson.

DILLARD FAMILY

The Dillards trace their family back to 1660, in the enrollment for the militia at Jamestown, Va., when George Dillard, 26 years of age, from Wiltshire, England, first appears. He was given 250 acres of land for military services against the Indians, and this was added to, till in his will he gave 389 acres to his son, James Stephen, of James City county, and two girls.

James Stephen Dillard was born in Wiltshire, Engalnd, in 1658, and married a Govan, or Page, records indistinct, and settled in James City. He with the Carys, Wises, and Pages, were granted 25,000 acres located in a body and known in history as "The Williamsburg Plantations."

James Dillard, the son of James Stephen, was born in 1698, and married Lucy Wise in 1724. Issue: Thomas, Nicholas, James, who was born in 1727, Stephen, John, William Terry, who was born in 1742, and two girls, Mary and Sally, date of birth not given.

James Dillard, Jr., settled in Amherst county, this State, and there he and his wife spent their days and were buried.

Of the children of James Dillard (1727-1794) and his wife, 1734-1748), of Essex county, Virginia, soon after their removal to Amherst county, was born a son, Capt. John Dillard. In succeeding years he came to Henry county during the Revolutionary period, and bought a large boundary of land on Horsepasture creek.

Captain John Dillard (See Biography Chap.) was born in 1751, married Sarah, the daughter of George Stovall, of Pittsylvania county. Their children were as follows: James, George, Ruth, Pattie, Jane Athey, Elizabeth, Mary Ann, Peter Hairston and John.

HISTORY OF HENRY COUNTY, VIRGINIA

James Dillard the eldest son of the above, was born in 1779, married Lucy Moorman in 1809, and died in 1859. He was the father of Judge John Henry Dillard of the Supreme Court of North Carolina, who was born in '19, and married Ann Isabelle, the daughter of Gen. Joseph Martin.

George Dillard married, Elizabeth, the daughter of William Hill, and settled in Mo., where he has numerous descendants.

Ruth Dillard, the eldest daughter, married John, the son of Moses Spencer, who was a soldier in the Revolution.

Pattie Dillard married Captain Peter Shelton, a distinguished soldier of the War of 1812.

Jane Athey Dillard married a Mays.

Elizabeth Dillard married a Hairston; and (2nd,) Capt. John Dillard.

Mary Ann Dillard never married.

Peter Hairston Dillard married Elizabeth, the daughter of Maj. John Redd. She was born in 1792, died in 1837. Her husband died 30 years later. Issue of this union were: John Redd, Overton Redd, Martha Ann, Sarah, Mary, Lucy, George Penn.

John Dillard (see Biog. Chap. Len Dillard) was born, 1783, married Matilda Hughes, daughter of Col. Archelans Hughes and Mary Dalton, of Patrick County. Issue: Peter Francisco, John Lea, James Madison, and Geo. Penn.

Archilous Rughes Dillard was born in 1817, married Martha Ann Dillard, who was born in 1822, married in 1840. He moved from this to Franklin county prior to the Civil War, and was defeated as a Secessionist by Jubal A. Early for the Convention of 1861. About ten years later, he moved again, to Chatham a popular lawyer there, till he retired from legal practice. He was educated at the University of Virginia. He was Democratic Presidential elector in 1854, and represented this county in the legislature in 1855-56. He died in 1901. The children of this union born in this county, were: John Lea, Elizabeth Redd and Matilda Hughes.

SECOND GENERATION

Of the children of Peter Hairston Dillard, we note as follows:

Dr. John Redd Dillard was born about 1830, married Margaret Brown, and after her death married Adele Lee, a cousin of Gen. Robt. E. Lee. He was a graduate of the Jefferson Medical College of Philadelphia, and practiced at Spencer, Virginia, all his life, and was one of the most popular physicians in the county. His children by his first marriage were; Elizabeth, Lucy Martha Hughes. By his second wife there were: George, Peter, John, Carrie, Annie, William, Robert J., Chas. H., Adele, and Helen.

Overton Redd Dillard married Sallie Martin; Martha Ann married Col. Hughes Dillard; Sarah Dillard married William P. Watt; Mary Dillard married Harrison Spencer (see Spencer family); Lucy Dillard married Lewis Williams of Charlotte, N. C.; George Penn Dillard married Fancy Penn.

Of the children of Gen. John Dillard we record these: Dr. Peter Francisco Dillard married Elizabeth Hairston. Issue: Dr. Peter Francisco Dillard, Jr., who went to Miss. soon after the Civil war. John Dillard who moved to W. Va.; Lula who died unmarried at maturity. Dr. P. F. Sr., died in the forties, and his widow married John Reamey, and there were many children. John Lea Dillard, the second son of Gen. John, married Isabella Jones of Eastern Va. There was no issue. He was a gallant Confederate soldier and was promoted to Lieut. Colonel.

James Madison Dillard, the 3rd son, died unmarried; Dr. George Penn Dillard married Maranda Brooks. Their children were (9) as follows: George, Matilda, Miranda, Wilthem, Sarah, who married Nicholas Hairston; Matilda Hughes Dillard, married Shelton Penn; Mary Dalton Dillard never married; Jenny Dillard married William Watkins; Ann Dillard married Dr. Richard Watkins.

Of the children of Archelaus Hughes Dillard we record the following:

John Lea Dillard was born in 1847, married Lucy Spencer, of this county, and there was an only son, Harry Dillard who died of small pox in early manhood.

He was in the corps of Virginia Military Institute in the memorable battle of New Market, and continued in the Confederate Army till the War was over. He studied law at the University of Virginia, was admitted to the bar, and was the first Judge of Henry County Court. He died at the age of 27, in 1875.

HISTORY OF HENRY COUNTY, VIRGINIA

Elizabeth Redd Dillard married Col. Daniel Arrington, of Franklin county, gallant soldier for the Southern Cause.

Matilda Hughes Dillard married Capt. William Chamberlain of Norfolk. Issue: Mary married Ferguson Reed of Norfolk; William married Miss Frank. William attended West Point, and was Brig. Gen. in the World War. Ann married Maj. Gen. Coe of U. S. Army; Martha Ann married Capt. Wm. J. Penn, of Botetourt county, Va.; Mary died in infancy.

Judge Hughes Dillard was born in 185—, married Mattie Wilson, of Chatham, Va. He was Commonwealth Attorney of Pittsylvania county for many years and at the time of his death in 19— had been Circuit Judge of Henry county for several years. Their children were: Ann Garland, Elizabeth Redd, and John Wilson.

Judge Peter Hairston Dillard was born in Martinsville in 1849, married Lydia Adela Nash, daughter of Thomas Nash and Lydia Adela Herbert, of Norfolk, Va., in 1872. He was admitted to the bar and practiced in Henry and Franklin counties principally, has lived at Rocky Mount for many years, and is Judge of the Franklin and Bedford Circuit courts. His wife died Jan. 19, 1924.

THIRD GENERATION

Of the children of Judge Hairston Dillard we record the following:

Herbert Nash Dillard married Mary C. Greer; H. Dalton Dillard married Ethel C. Hale; Percy Dillard married, like the two named, a lawyer; Carter L. Dillard died unmarried; John Lea Dillard married Mary Taylor of Winston-Salem. He was in the railroad construction business; Adela Nash Dillard married Kent Shepherd, of Winston-Salem, N. C.; Louie Frances Dillard married Harig Dangerfield, of Philadelphia, Pa.

We note the following of Dr. John R. Dillards family:

Bettie Brown Dillard married, 1st, Tyler Hairston, 2nd, Chas. Angle, 3rd, Lum. Ayers; Martha Hughes Dillard married Robert Jordan of Charlotte, 2nd, P. P. Watson; Lucy Ashton Dillard married Thomas S. Brown of Wytheville, Va. The Second wife's children: Judge George Lee Dillard married Florence Echols, of Bluefield, W. Va.; Caroline Dillard married Charles Wilmut, of Texas. 2nd Walter H. Penn. Annie Dillard Married

J. Murry Hooker Member of Congress, U. S.; William Dillard married Nellie; John R. Dillard married Nell Prince, of Bluefield, W. Va.; Robert Jordan Dillard never married; Charles Harden Dillard, unmarried; Adelle Dillard married William L. Pannill, of Reidsville, N. C.; Helen Dillard married Thomas Morris.

DESHAZO FAMILY

John de Shazeau and his wife came from France in the great tide of 1700 to 1720 of Huguenots that were driven by the religious persecution from that country. They landed at Yorktown, and settled in King and Queen county upon the York river. Here he reared his family, and died about the beginning of the Revolution. Issue: William, John, Robin, Clem, Edmund, and another, who remained in their native county.

Robin de Shazo settled in Person county, N. C., accumulated wealth, but died without issue. He gave his land and 20 slaves to his nephew Geo. K. DeShazo and his children, of this county.

John de Shazo was a noted horse-racer, and migrated to Miss. Clem, his brother, also went to the West to an unknown location.

Edmund and the others of this family remained in King and Queen county.

William de Shazo was born in 1759, married Jane, (Gincy). King of Leatherwood, daughter of George King, at Roxbury, N. C., Nov. 5, 1794. She belonged to the family of Kings that came with the first settlers to Virginia; and she lived to be nearly 90 years old, her death occurring in 1864.

He came to Leatherwood when a young man and accumulated about 600 acres of land, lying on the north side of the Patrick Henry estate. On this he spent three score years and reared his family. The records at Washington, D. C. (War Dep.) show that he joined the Second Virginia Infantry in the spring of 1777, served with Lafayette, under Washington, during his northern campaign, was in many battles, the most noted Monmouth, and with Gen. Wayne at Stony Point when it was captured. He was honerably discharged in 1780. He died April 24, 1839, and left the following children: George King, Tabitha Jane, Sallie, Fannie, and Richard.

SECOND GENERATION

Tabitha Jane DeShazo married a Conway, next a Degrafenried, then a Nance, and the last marriage was to an Albritton. The only child was a son, Robert Albritton, a distinguished tobacconist of Bowlingreen, Ky. Sallie DeShazo married a Pace. No issue. Fannie DeShazo married Coleman Allen, a cousin of Private John Allen of Miss. She died in Mo. and her daughter returned to this county, and married Obediah Minter in 1851. Her sons, Lef and O. Coleman, were the remainder of this line in the county.

Richard DeShazo was born in 1804, married Elizabeth Conway, moved to Mo., settled in St. Clair county, reared II children, and died in 1854. He was a Baptist minister. Issue: Martha, Wm. A., Virginia A., G. K., Nancy M., Chas I., Ben L., John W., Mary E, and Elizabeth E.

George King DeShazo was born in this county in 1796, married Susanna, the daughter of John Cahill, and Diana Garner, who was born in 1769, the wealthiest lady in the northern part of the county.

He was a large man, a 200 pounder, delighted in sports, the ring "Fights" at Henry Court House being his favorite. He did a general transfer business from Lynchburg, the only way freight was moved in those days. He attended the religious Associations and engaged in too much diversion to accumulate much property. His farm contained 330 acres on Reed creek, where he reared his family; viz, John, Sallie, William T., Larkin, Nathaniel C., George, Richard T., and Mary.

THIRD GENERATION

Mary DeShazo, the youngest daughter, married Ben. Jones (See Jones Fam.). Richard Tazwell DeShazo was born in 1843, married Mary Napier. He was a Magistrate, and a Prince at his home on Mayo river where he died in 1881. His children were: Laurie, W. T., G. B., and Mary Reid.

George DeShazo was born in 1839, and never married. He was a brave Confederate soldier, wounded at the battle of Gaines Mill, and died.

Nathaniel C. DeShazo was born Nov. 29, 1837, married Virginia, the daughter of Walker Smith, Rockingham, Sheriff, in 1865. He was in the 42nd, Virginia Regiment, fought in many battles; however, escaped capture at the last, Five Forks. He was a most hospitable and public spirited citizen, and never shirked a public duty. His estate was in this and Rockingham county, N. C. He died in 1922. His children were: Prof. Geo. W., C. N., J. F., J. W., P. L., G. B., W. T., and H. F. The girls were: Sallie who married Harvey Glen and died in 1924, Mary who married Frank Flynn, and Rosa who married Sam Taylor. He died in 1922, leaving a daughter, Irene. Bebe and J. F. both died after reaching maturity.

Larkin DeShazo was born in 1831, married Susan Dalton, and died Oct. 20, 1906. He was well educated, a splendid conversationalist, and owned a large farm on Horsepasture creek where he reared a large family. He was First Lieut. in May's Company, in the 45th, Virginia Regiment, and saw much hard service in the Civil War. Issue: Rufus, who died when grown, R. A., Job., J. S., W. D., C. E. and T. D. (twins). The daughters were Mary Virginia, who married Judge Geo. P. Pell, of the Corporation Commission of North Carolina, Raliegh, Annie D., who married W. P. McMichael, who died leaving her with seven boys; Minnie, who married Sam Watkins, who died leaving one child, Geo. Hairston Watkins, and two unmarried, Dora and Mattie. The young, brilliant brother, W. Dalton DeShazo, graduated in medicine at Richmond, Va., practiced at Stokesdale, N. C. one month, and died of typhoid fever in 1905, age 24.

William Thomas DeShazo was born Dec. 13, 1829, married Sallie Finney, and died July 18, 1910. He had but three months at school. He took charge of his father's farm at 12 years of age and conducted it successfully for 12 years. With the slave labor of the family to which was added in 1850 twenty given by their Uncle Robin DeShazo, he soon took from the soil enough values to purchase nearly a thousand acres in the Anglin farm on Mayo river where his father died. The slaves numbered over a 100 at the surrender.

He served in the 10th Virginia Cavalry under Gen. Wm. Henry Lee, taking part in the campaigns till captured at Five Forks in April 1865, and imprisoned at Point Lookout, Md. till summer time. When liberated, he returned to his little farm on Reed Creek, his earthly possessions less than $500. He commenced raising tobacco again, and in 1875 had accumulated enough to purchase Red Plains, a thousand acre farm formerly belonging to Tyler Hairston, lying on Marrowbone creek. He and his son, H. A. manufactured tobacco several years, at Red Plains. Here he lived subsequently, reared and educated his four boys, the fifth one, Robert Noble, being killed accidentally when in boyhood. These were: Homer A., William T., J. Beverly, and Dameron F. William T. DeShazo, the second son, died when 42 with pneumonia. There was never a better hearted man. He left an infant daughter, Hilda.

Sallie Finney, the wife of William T. DeShazo, Sr., was endowed with a strong mind and a most wonderful memory, and retained her faculties till she died on Jan. 4, 1922, age nearly 87. She was the daughter of John Finney and Frances King, of Franklin. The Finneys have been in Virginia since the first settlers landed on the Eastern Shore. (See Finney fam.).

REV. JOHN E. DeSHAZO

From Edmund, or a brother, remaining in King and Queen county, of the sons of John, the progenitor of the Virginia family, descended a son, Larkin DeShazo, of that county, and his son Charles Henry became the father of Rev. J. E. DeShazo, who was born there Aug. 23, 1850, and married S. Lou Zentmeyer of Patrick county, in 1879. It was while a Methodist minister in that county, his children were born; Viz, Edwin Penn, John E., M. Florence, Peter H., and Mary Hunter. After his services in this and Patrick county as a circuit rider he was transferred. Several years after, he was made by the bishop the presiding elder of the Danville district.

His first wife died and he married a second time, Lucy Bishop. He returned as local minister for the Henry circuit and lived at Ridgeway. A few years later he was retired from the active work and built a home at Gloucester Pt., in sight of the Monument at Yorktown, where he is spending his declining years.

He is a devout man, that preaches and practices godliness, and is a power in the pulpit. He is industrious, wholesouled, and wholehearted in everything he undertakes, and numbers his friends by the thousands throughout the State.

DYER FAMILY

The Dyer family is of English-Scotch origin, and came to this country in the 17th, century. The progenitor of the family in this country was James Dyer, who was born in 1720, his son George was born in Prince George county Md., in 1753, and died in Henry county, Va. in 1827. He was a Lieut. in the Revolutionary War, going from Maryland June 15, 1773, in Capt. Chas. Williamson's Company. After settling in the county, he married Rachel Dalton, and their children were: James, Benjamin, Frances, Phoebe, Joel, David Dalton, Elizabeth H., Louisa B., Rachel M., and David P.

SECOND GENERATION

James Dyer married Sarah Reynolds. Issue: Coleman, Joseph, Fountain, James, Benjamin, Hugh, Elizabeth, Ann, Mary, Grief, and George.

Benjamin Dyer was born in 1778, and in 1801 married Mary Gravely. Issue: George, Eleanor, Joseph, Rachael, James, Jabez, Sacville, Benjamin. He was in the War of 1812, and represented this county in the legislature of Virginia in 1822. He died in 1823.

Frances Dyer married Edward DeLazier; Phoebe Dyer married Arnold Thomasson; Joel Dyer married Mary Salmons. Issue: Nancy, Mary, Sallie Martha, Susan, Joseph, George, Benjamin, Fanny, and Rachael.

David Dalton Dyer (See Biography Chapter) was born in 1791, married in 1810 Nancy Reynolds Salmons. Their children were as follows: George W., Joseph F., Martha C., John S., Sarah A., Janes C., Nancy J., Elizabeth H., Mary B., Louisa B., Rachael M., and David P.

Martha Dyer married in 1822, Lewis Gravely. She died in 1876. (See Gravely family).

Joab Dyer was born in 1801, and married Mary Salmons in 1824. Issue: Margaret, Ann, Rebecca, Rachael. By his second wife, Nancy Harvey, two, George V., and Elizabeth C. He died in 1875.

Jefferson Dyer was born in 1803, married Margaret Salmons, who had an only child, Mary. By his second marriage to Elizabeth C. Custer in 1829, there were 7 children, George L., Malinda, Minnie, David L., Zanie, Virginia, and Missouri.

HISTORY OF HENRY COUNTY, VIRGINIA 161

THIRD GENERATION

Of David Dalton's descendants we note as follows:
George W. Dyer was born in 1811, married in 1833, Mary Philpott. Issue: Martha, Nancy, David, Sinai, Mary, Virginia, Fredonia, Trusten, and Minnie.

Joseph F. Dyer was born in 1813, married in '33, Elizabeth Dyer. Their children were: Mary, Sarah, Martha, Joseph, Harriet, Nancy, and James.

Mary B. Dyer was born 1814, married in 1833, Bailey Martin; Martha C. Dyer born in 1817, married 1835, Nathaniel Spencer.

John S. Dyer was born in 1819, married Martha Bassett in 1839. Issue were: Mary, Nancy, David A., James, George, Cherokee, Choctaw, Pocahontas, Luella, Cora, Ida, and Eloise. He died in 1880.

Sarah Dyer was born in 1822, married in 1841, Albert Mason.

James C. Dyer was born in 1824, married in 1849, Martha Camp. Children were: David A., George C., Joseph W., John H., Leonidas C., Mary, Nancy, Anne, Virginia, and Emma.

Nancy J. Dyer was born in 1827, married in 1845, to Douglas Wyatt; Elizabeth Dyer was born in 1829, married in 1850, John E. Ball; Louisa B. Dyer was born in 1833, married in 1854, W. L, Carter, and 2nd, in 1882, J. E. Carstarphen; Rachael M. Dyer was born in 1834, married in 1853, Dr. J. M. Foreman.

David P. Dyer was born in 1838, married in 1860, Lizzie C. Hunt. Issue: Ezra, Emma Grace, Lizzie Logan, David P., Horace Levi, and Maria Louise.

Of the children of Benjamin Dyer, and Mary Gravely, we note as follows:

Benjamin Franklin Dyer was born in 1821, married Martha Walker in 1849. Issue: Mary, Sallie, Fannie, George, Alice, Henry Gustavus, David, Lulu. By his second wife there was one, Kate. He was a gallant soldier in the Civil War, promoted to Captain. He also represented the county in the legislature in 1875-76. He died in Mar. 1914.

Jabez Dyer was born about 1823, married Martha Eliza Ivie. Issue: Willis Dyer married Harriet, Jack Jones' daughter; Mary, and George never married;

Ben married Agnes Strong, of Rockingham county, N. C.; Susan married a Taylor; Eliza married Doctor Franklin King.

James Dyer, the son of Hugh and grandson of Geo. Dyer, married Lucy Jane Holt, their children were Sallie, Ella, Ballard, Hugh, John, Holt, and Tom.

Sallie married Hughes Oakley; Hugh Dyer married Kate Garrett; John Dyer married Julia Williamson; Ella Dyer married Ben Hundley, and he died leaving two daughters; viz, Mamie, and Mattie who married Irvin Groves. Holt Dyer married Annie Bone; Ballard married Diana Movae; Tom married———.

DAVID DALTON DYER

The smoke of battle and strife of the Revolutionary War had just passed into history when David Dalton Dyer was born in 1791. His father George Dyer was a lieutenant in that war. When 19 years of age he married Nancy Reynolds Salmon, also of Henry county. He had hardly begun his home life whe he answered the call to arms, leaving his young wife and one child to shift as they could, and fought through the War of 1812. When peace was declared he returned to his farm and built up his family and splendid home where he accumulated wealth and became one of the most influential citizens of his county.

For twelve consecutive years, he was a representative either in the House or Senate from Henry county, and made an official record of which his descendants will always be proud. He was a true friend without any taint of deceit, and in honor of one of his warm friends in the Senate of Va., named Patterson, he named a son. He died in 1844.

Mrs. David Dyer was of Irish descent, and was a woman of strong mind and wonderful constitution. On the trip to Mo. she traveled over a thousand miles in a four-horse wagon. She was the mother of twelve children. She lived under every presidential administration from Washington to Benjamin Harrison. She had in all living and dead 277 descendants before her death.

DUPUY FAMILY

Bartholomew Dupuy, the immediate progenitor of the Virginia family entered the army under Louis IV. of

HISTORY OF HENRY COUNTY, VIRGINIA

France at the early age of 18, and after 14 years' service, married Susanne Lavillon and retired to his country seat.

The revocation of the Edict of Nates made it imperative for him to flee with his wife to Germany where he spent two years before migrating to America. They came in a company of 170 other Huguenots on board the good ship "Peter and Anthony", of London, reached Jamestown Sept. 20th, 1700, and finally settled in King William Parish above Richmond on James River, his home subsequently.

SECOND GENERATION

John Bartholomew Dupuy, the second son, married a Miss La Garronde, and they had three children, viz: John, Peter, and Magdalene.

THIRD GENERATION

John Dupuy married Mary Watkins, and reared only one daughter, Susane. He was a noted soldier of the Revolutionary war, and attained the rank of Captain.

Peter Dupuy married Margarett Martin, Nov. 13th, 1789, and settled in Powhatan county. Issue: Anthony Martin, Sarah Holman, and Harriett Amasia. Magdalene Dupuy married Thomas Watkins of Pittsylvania county. Issue: John, and Benjamin.

FOURTH GENERATION

Susanna Dupuy married Benjamin Watkins. No children.

Anthony Martin Dupuy was born Dec. 21st, 1791 and died Dec. 19th, 1869. He was a citizen of Martinsville, Va., for some time, and died at the site of the H. C. Lester home on Church street.

Sarah Holman Dupuy was born Jan. 6th, 1800, and married Stephen Dupuy Watkins. She died without issue, July 13th, 1862.

Harriett Amasia Dupuy was born June 8th, 1807, married April. 21st, 1825, to Ptolemy Lefebre Watkins, and died near Cascade, Va., April the 9th, 1872.

FIFTH GENERATION

The male line became extinct in the last generation, and the Dupuy blood descended from Magdalene Dupuy through John Watkins and his wife, a Miss Wilson, to her grand-children, as follows:

Sallie Watkins married a Plummer; Betsy married a Southall; Peter W. Watkins married a daughter of "Rusty" Hairston, and died at "Shawnee" farm on Marrowbone creek.

Magdalene Watkins married Peter Shelton March 21st, 1832, and lived in Henry county near Spencer, and reared a large family, 12 children.

Thomas Watkins md. Letitia Hairston, daughter of Samuel Hairston.

Susan Watkins md. Benjamin Barrow; Nancy md Nat. Mullins.

DREWRY FAMILY

John de Drewry first came to England with William the Conqueror and fought in the battle of Hastings. His name appears in the Roll of Battle Abbey, prepared by the order of King William himself to perpetuate the valor of all who distinguished themselves on that occasion.

He rewarded his officers by large grants of land; consequently we find the descendants of John de Drewry settled at Thurston, in Suffolk county. His family held this domain for 600 years.

Sir Drewry was a member of Queen Elizabeth's cabinet, and one of her councilors. He was appointed by her to the Court of Mary Queen of Scots. He was appointed Governor of Fotheringay Castle, and he with two others were the Committee who had charge of the details of her execution.

The first Drewry, who came to America was John Drewry, about 1650, and received grants of land in York and Nansemond counties. Samuel, James, and William were among his descendants.

William moved to N. C., where his son John was born. The latter returned to Virginia, and married Sallie Slaughter, and became the progenitor of the Drewry family in King William county.

Henry T. Drewry owned land that once belonged to Col. William Byrd, and "Westover" is now owned by the heirs of the late Maj. A. H. Drewry, son of Capt. Martin Drewry, of the King William family.

Henry T. and Martin Drewry, were brothers and soldiers in war of 1812, with England.

Major A. H. Drewry married Mary Harrison, a lineal descendant of Col. Wm. Byrd. He gained his title by distinguished services in the war between the States.

Dr. Henry Martin Drewry, of Martinsville, Henry Co. was a cousin of Major A. H. Drewry. He was born in 183— in Chesterfield and was the progenitor of the family in Henry county. On his mother's side he was fourth in lineal descent from Rev. Samuel Davies, the President of Princeton College in 1759. This eloquent ancestor was called from Delaware to the Presbyterian church in Hanover in 1748. He gained pre-eminence in an argument "On the Rights of Protestant Dissenters from the Established Church in Virginia". He rebuked the King himself on one occasion in his church for speaking too loud. He was for 11 years the pastor of Patrick Henry when the latter was attaining manhood.

Dr. Henry Martin Drewry married Flora, the granddaughter of Maj. John Redd, one of the first settlers of Henry Co., Nov. 10, 1859.

He graduated from Princeton College in 1855, and then studied at the University of Virginia one year; afterward graduated, in 1858, at Jefferson Medical College and located at Martinsville, immediately thereafter, where he practiced till he was retired by the infirmities of old age. He also had extensive real estate holdings and profited by them. He died and was buried at Martinsville.

Flora Redd, wife of Dr. Henry M. Drewry, was born Feb. 14, 1832 at Stuart. She was the daughter of James Madison Redd and his wife Ruth Staples. She was educated at Dr. Dame's private school in Danville, and that of Madame Le Fevre in Richmond.

She was the first member of the Episcopal Church to be confirmed in Henry County, and was a prominent member all her life. She was large hearted, hospitable, cheerful, and of brilliant intellect ready with rare powers of conversation, and a social charm which won the love and esteem of those who knew her.

She died in 1915 and was buried in Oakwood Cemetery at Martinsville. The Drewry issue was as follows:

Ruth, who married Judge Stafford G. Whittle; Flora who married John A Wright; Keziah, who married John W. Carter, Atty-at-law; Milly, who married James P. Lewis; Plummer who married Miss Freda Williams; Dr. Madison R. Drewry of Cascade, Va., who married Miss Starling.

DILLON—CAMPBELL—HODGES

Dr. Dillon married Miss Witt, and lived near Preston. He was a large landholder and lived to a good old age. Was an invalid for years before his death. His children were Patsy, who married Starling Wells, Betsy who married Geo. Baker, and Polly, who married David Campbell, Nancy who died unmarried, and Tommy, a son, who never married. Patsy, Betsy and Polly lived to be from 75 to 93 years of age. Nancy and Tommy died much younger.

Mrs. Wells raised a large family. Mrs. Baker had an only child, a daughter Martha, who married Henry Jarrett. David Campbell came from Scotland in his boyhood. They settled in Leaksville, N. C. One day they bought some beef that happened to be unwholesome from some cause. The entire family were severely stricken, and the young man David was the only one that lived. He was sick for a long time, but finally recovered. He married Polly Dillon and settled in Henry County. His children were William A., who married America Pannill, James P., who married Kate Mitchell. Robert, the youngest son, died very early, unmarried. Mary T., the only daughter, married Hiram K. Hodges, of Franklin County, Va. When quite a young man he came to Henry County, and was considered one of the foremost farmers of his day. He served through the Civil War and never received a wound. He died Nov. 15, 1915, age 79. His children were Pattie, J. D., William, Walter, Alice, and Ida. All married and have families.

The compiler recollects from her earliest days that there has never been a time when there was not a young family taking care of an old, infirm person in that home. Mrs. Campbell took care of her father many years. She in turn was taken care of by her daughter Mary, and now Mary is being cared for by her son William. However, these old people all had means of their own but lived beyond their days of activity. Mr. Campbell was considered a very fine tailor. He was one of the "Sons of Temperance" reclaimed by this order organized near Mt. Bethel. The old hall is still standing but looks forlorn and dilapidated.

EGGLETON FAMILY

The Eggletons are of English descent. Mike Eggleton was brought to America by his grandparents when he was a small boy. He married a Miss Robertson, and had two children Jane Abigail, who married Silas Minter, son of the Baptist minister of that name, Polly married E. B. Draper, and had 4 children Mike, Keziah, (Mrs. Prunty), Lucy Frances (Mrs. R. F. Mcmillion), Eliza Susan (Mrs. Pete Prillaman). Mrs. McMillion has three sons, James, Joe, Mike, Mrs. Prillaman has ten children, Theodora, Nick, Lafe, Jim, Hassie, Vance, Geo., Mary, Ruth, Robert.

Mike Draper's children are as follows: Truman, Leslie, Mary, Everett, Vaughn, Hass.

William Draper, father of E. B. Draper, married Lucy Meredith. She baked cakes, and he sold them here in town. The compiler can testify that they were good cakes. Mrs. McMillion has in her possession an old trunk more than a hundred yrs. old that was brought from England. She also has an old Bible which her ancestor learned to read in. Mrs. Marshall Hairston once wrote Mrs. Eggleton a letter in figures which she read, and sent word back that she would do the work as requested. She could not read with letters, but she could with figures.

ESTES FAMILIES

Estes is de Este in French. The family descended from the French nobility, and like hundreds of others, came to America in the tide of Huguenots in 1700 to 1720.

There are two families to note, so distantly related, if at all that no record has been discovered.

BENJAMIN ESTES FAMILY

Benjamin Estes, the progenitor of the family in this county, was born about 1740, married during the Revolutionary War period Selah Thorpe, and settled in Bedford county, Va. Their issue: Triplet, Nancy (Mrs. Fears), Elizabeth (Hughes), Lucy (Morton), Joel, Benjamin, Thomas, William, Elisha, Edmund, Thorpe, Selah (Cowherd), Martha (Nance), Sarah (Mrs. Noel), and John who died young.

He was, according to the family tradition, a soldier in

the Revolution with his son-in-law, Jesse Fears who married his daughter Lucy, in 1792. He lived to a good old age and died in 1816.

SECOND GENERATION

Benjamin Estes, the son of the above, was born toward the close of the eighteenth century, married Peggy Neal, who died without issue. He next married Eliza M., the daughter of Thomas Dix and Lucy Miller of Henry county. Mrs. Estes's sister Martha married Mr. Winston, a grandson of Patrick Henry, and another sister, Nancy married Dr. Houston, a cousin of Gov. Sam Houston of Texas. The family settled in 1816 in Halifax county (now Pittsylvania), where he died in 1868, and Mrs. Estes ten years later. Their children were: Joseph; Thomas who died young; Edward; Elisha who never married; Benjamin; James Dabney; Lucy, and Emma.

THIRD GENERATION

Joseph Estes was born in 1838. He never marrried but was a gallant soldier in the War Between the States, and rose to the rank of Lieutenant.

Edward Estes was born in 1840, and when about 25 married Unie Fontaine, a great grand daughter of Patrick Henry, and settled in Henry county, his wife's home all her life, and reared his family. He too was a fearless soldier, rising from the ranks to lieutenant. Issue of this union: Edward Harrison, James Dabney who married Bettie Price Starling, and William Dix who married Marion Holden, rearing two children, Dixie, and Marion.

Benjamin Estes Jr., was born in 1848, married Bell Rodery who had before married a Collier. Issue: Lucy who married Harry B. Grimsley of Greensboro, N. C., and Emma. He died in Miss. in 1907, his wife six years before. These daughters were reared by their uncle, Dr. Estes, of Cascade, Va.

Dr. James Dabney Estes was born Jan. 31, 1836, no issue to his marriage, to Nannie Leake, of Rockingham, N. C. He studied medicine at the University of Virginia, and began practice in 1856, at Cascade, Va., near the Henry county line, continuing it for sixty years. He was a surgeon in the civil War under Gen. R. E. Lee for four years, and never was wounded.

DR. G. W. G. ESTES

He was a fine physician, good business man, and accumulated property. He retained all his faculties, till around 90 years his hearing was not good, but in the evening of life enjoyed the company of his nephew and his nieces he had reared, and all of whom were untiring in his service.

JESSE ESTES FAMILY

Jesse Estes, the progenitor of this Henry county family, married Betsy, the sister of Champion Napier, who married Gov. Martin's daughter, of N. C. His second wife was Mariah, the daughter of John Fortune, of Montgomery county, Va., who died at the age of 75 in Martinsville. Issue of this union: George W., Girard, Francis, and William Alexander.

George Washington Girard Estes was born in 1830, and died in 1882. He was a graduate of Medicine but preferred teaching, and was a distinguished educator in Henry county many years (See High Schools of Henry County).

William Alexander Estes was born in 1834, married Sarah Louise Davis, of Stokes, N. C. in 1855, but his wife died, and he again married Sadie Martin of Winston, N. C. He was a prominent citizen of his county, and was elected Sheriff of Stokes county, where he died. Issue of first union: John Francis, Lilla Elizabeth who married Jesse H. Prather, James W. G. issue of the last: Charles Watt, Jesse Edward, and Annie Lelia.

I. W. FRYE FAMILY

I. W. Frye came to Henry Co. Va. from N. C. His 1st, wife was Miss Preston. Issue: William, Allen, Isom, Jesse, Lusinia.

Second wife was Elizabeth Patterson. Issue: David M., Peter W., John C., I. J., Annie L., Henry A., Rufus P., Franklin I.

GRAVELY FAMILY

Joseph Gravely, the ancestor of the Henry county family, was born in England in 1744. He and his two brothers came to America when quite young. He settled in the county prior to the Revolutionary War, and here he lived till his death at the ripe old age of one hundred years. He belonged to the "Landed Gentry" in early life, and continued a farmer after coming to this county. He left quite a large estate. On this he had built the first brick chimney in this section, and it attracted visitors for miles around. He was a noted patriot that gave both of his time and means to help establish American Independence. In the list of Henry county soldiers, his name appears in that gallant body of men from this section of the State assisting Gen. Greene at Guilford Court House. His descendants have inherited the qualities of the soldier, and have proven worthy of bearing his name in every conflict to the present time.

He married Eleanor, the daughter of Capt. Francis Cox, Sept. 1, 1775. Of this marriage there were: Jabez, Frank, Joseph, Jefferson, Eleanor, George, Edmund, Polly, Lewis, Peyton, and Willis.

SECOND GENERATION

Jabez Gravely married Judith Wells. Issue: John W., who married Frances Marshall; Joseph married Eliza Dickerson; Judith married Ephraim Riddle; Eleanor married William Moore; Jabez Leftwich married Miss Hankins; Francis Cox married Sallie A. Holman; Benjamin Franklin married Julia C. Thomas.

Frank Gravely, the second son, was a soldier in the War of 1812, and died near Norfolk.

Joseph Jefferson Gravely married a Miss King. No issue.

Eleanor Gravely married Maj. Arnold Walker. Issue: Logan, the father of Maj. J. A. Walker, and Betsy who married a Philpott, the father of Ben.

George Gravely was born in 1788, married Mary Hughes. Issue: Letitia, born in 1826, and married George D. Gravely; Mary, who married Dr. Henry D. Peters, of Leatherwood. Issue: Judge George D. Peters of Franklin Co., Robert, Mrs. Alice P. Lavinder, and Hon. H. G. Peters, of Bristol, Va., formerly representative from Henry county; Nancy who married William Dickerson in 1847; Eleanor never married; Lilian, and May Bud, children by second wife, Elizabeth Jones, died unmarried.

Edmund Gravely, the twin brother of George, was born in 1788, and married Susan Robinson who was

HISTORY OF HENRY COUNTY, VIRGINIA   171

born in 1800. Issue: Mary Jane who married Elijah Richardson; Joe Morton never married; Eliza married Joseph Richardson; George, and William, neither married; Jabe married Anna Towler; Susan married John Belcher; Judith Elizabeth Gravely, the youngest child of Edmund, was born in 1844, married Capt. John Cox, of the Virginia militia, and only one child, Joanna, was the issue. The latter married Gustave A. Giles, died, and left the following issue:

Emma who married Henry Clay Eanes; Harry who married Fairy Law; Susan married Dr. F. Paul Turner, a dentist of Martinsville, Va; Elizabeth married William J. Childress; Richard married Woody Ramsey; Ruth married Alcin Fisher, of Montana; George, and Edmund, unmarried.

Polly Gravely, another daughter of Joseph Sr., married Ben Dyer. For issue see Dyer family.

Lewis Gravely was born about 1795, and in 1822, or 3, married Martha Dyer. Their children were: Spottswood, who married Alice Williams; Joseph Jackson Gravely, born about 1832, married Martha Marshall, a daughter of Dennis Marshall. He was elected to the legislature of Virginia over Geo. Rusty Hairston, later moved to Mo. before the Civil War, being a captain in the Union Army, elected member of Congress from that State, and also Lieutenant-Governor. His children were: Benjamin, died in infancy, Nannie, Jackson, Joseph W., Pattie, Ella, Minnie and Lutie.

Lewis Gravely Jr., was born about 1830, moved to Mo. before the Civil War, married Sarah Sherrill. Issue: Eugenie Gravely, of Oklahoma; Eleanor married Mr. Donegan; Rachael married a Cheatham, he died, and she next married J. F. Pedigo. Issue: Edd Pedigo. Martha was the first wife of J. F. Pedigo. Issue: Dr. Lewis G. Pedigo a distinguished physician of Roanoke, Va.;Emma Pedigo, who married C. B. Gravely; Mary married Patrick Martin; Frank married Sallie Hughes Dillard; Thomas married Georgia Stultz; George D. married his cousin, Letitia Gravely.

The father of this family was a distinguished citizen in his day, and with his brother Frank, took part in the War of 1812.

Peyton Gravely was married about 1830 to Matilda

Thomas, a sister of C. Y. Thomas. He was a member of the Virginia legislature when the Ordinance of Secession was passed. He was a great tobacco manufacturer. He and his brother Willis made famous the Gravely plug tobacco which they produced at their Leatherwood factory.

Willis Gravely, the youngest son of Joseph Sr., married a second time, Anne Nancy Marshall Barrow, daughter of William Barrow and Susan Marshall, who was a grandaughter of Col. Thomas Marshall of historic fame. Issue: Susan Ellen married Abner McCabe; Peyton B. married Mary Walters; William Armistead married Sarah Morrison, Julia Cassandra died in infancy, infant boy died young and Francis Marshall, never married; Joseph Henry married Francis McCabe, and next Eliza Griggs, and last married Miss Henick; Mary Elizabeth married Dr. William Allen Holman; Chester Bullard married Emma Eugenia Pedigo; Willis Lewis married 1st, Berta Treadway, 2nd, Mrs. Mattie Smith Ivy; Martha Annie married Royall Washington Morrison; Edward Bonner, and sister Matilda Jane, never married.

THIRD GENERATION

Of Willis Gravely's children we record as follows:

Capt. Peyton B. Gravely enlisted in the Confederate Army in the Danville Artillery April 9, 1861, and later became Capt. of Company F., 42 Regiment, and served through the War.

Joseph H. H. Gravely enlisted in the same regiment a month later than his brother, became orderly sergeant, and was a good soldier, in many battles.

Marshall Francis Gravely was a member of the Danville Grays, entered the army in 1862, and was in the first battle of Manassas. He died in the service.

William Armistead Gravely entered the Southern Army in 1862 from Henry county, was in the 24th, Regiment of volunteers, and died in the cause.

Chester Bullard Gravely was in the 10th, Virginia Cavalry, went in before he was of legal age, and served till the Surrender.

Admiral Silas Wright Terry, the well known Navy fighter, was a great-grandson of Joseph Gravely.

Of the descendants of Lewis Gravely we note as follows:

HISTORY OF HENRY COUNTY, VIRGINIA

George D. Gravely, the oldest, was born in 1823, married Letitia Gravely in 1853, and their children reaching maturity were: Mary Hughes, George L., William H., and Albert S. He was a lawyer of wonderful natural capacity, and noted for his candor and fine judgment. He did not favor Secession, but was loyal to his state, and hoped always that the Union might be preserved. He was one of the real builders of Martinsville and lived to see it one of the most substantial Southside towns in the State. He was clerk of the Court of Henry county for two terms, and filled other positions of honor and trust. The county has produced a more brilliant type, but never a more substantial citizen, on whom every one depended knowing that they would never be deceived. He died in 1904. Of his children were reared: Mary Hughes Gravely is unmarried; George L. Gravely, a lawyer, married Minnie Walker Gregory; Hon. William H. Gravely married Caroline F. Ansen; Albert S. Gravely, editor of the Henry Bulletin, married Alice Kennon Williams, the daughter of H. S. Williams and Susan Withers who was a daughter of United States Senator, R. E. Withers, of Virginia.

The Gravely Coat of Arms is found in the British Museum, and in the possession of the Virginia Gravelys which is:

AM · Sable. A Cross pointed argent, In the dexter Chief point a mullet of the last, meaning a black shield with a silver cross and a silver spur.

MOTTO: "Mihi Solicitudo Futuri."

FORD FAMILY

In reviewing old Virginia families, we come upon the first Ford in Charlotte county, Samuel Calvin Ford, who married a Miss Pentecost. There was one child only, Hezekiah.

Hezekiah Ford was born between 1815 and 1820. He married Sarah Armistead, a sister of Mrs. Robt. Anderson, of Campbell county Virginia, and came to Henry about 1870. He was not physically strong and was much handicapped in the agricultural enterprises he attempted. However, he taught school and trained many of the county's young of those days of the first free schools. Every one of his pupils remembers him as a kind hearted good teacher, and an elegant Virginia gentleman. Of this union there were: Samuel Calvin, James, Joseph, Henry, Lena, William, John, and Sallie.

SECOND GENERATION

Samuel Calvin Ford was born about 1843, married Jane, the daughter of Overton Dillard and Sarah the daughter of Col. Joseph Martin. Issue: Obe Dillard, who married Miss Cecil Witten; H. A., who married Miss Patricia Packard; Tom who married Dorothy English; and Pete, married Blanche Walker.

James Ford md. Lizzie Dillard, and moved to Fla. and reared a large family, among them Geo., Mattie, Lucy, and Hezekiah.

Joseph Ford md. Margaret Alzira Lavinder and died young. Issue: Annie, Joseph who md. Anna Allen, Nov. 25, 1908; Jesse died 1921; Jane Hickey died Nov. 27 1917; and Mary Sherman who md. Arthur B. Gathright June 30, 1908.

John Ford d. unmarried. He was a lawyer, partner of his brother Judge Ford.

Lena md. Sydney Hamlett, and settled in Charlotte Co., Va. Issue: Sarah, Joe and Ellie. She d. 1920. Prior to her marriage she manifested much interest in art.

Willie Ford was a farmer and Mail carrier at Axton. He md. the widow of Tom Dillard. Issue: Sarah, Annie, John, Lewis, and Lena. He d., and his widow is living at Axton.

Henry Ford taught school at Ironside and read law at the same time. He was County Judge of Henry for some time. He married and settled in Lynchburg, where he died at an early age. His grandmother came from one of the best families in the State and he appeared to inherit many of her good qualities.

FONTAINE FAMILY

The Fontaine family in Virginia descended from the Rev. De la Fontaine, one of the Huguenot families from France, who came in 1716, and became Rector of King William and Westover Parishes. He had a son, Rev. Peter Fontaine, a minister and, also, county Lieutenant of Halifax when that county extended to the mountains. He married Elizabeth Winston and of their six children John was the eldest.

HISTORY OF HENRY COUNTY, VIRGINIA

John Fontaine married Martha, the daughter of Patrick Henry, the great orator, and their children were: Patrick Henry, Charles, Martha, William Winston, and Rev. John I. Fontaine.

John Fontaine was a soldier in the Revolutionary War, and was promoted to the rank of Captain. He died not long after this, and his widow was given the Leatherwood home by her father, where he formerly lived. Patrick Henry Fontaine, the eldest son, married Nancy Dabney Miller, and their oldest child who became the Rev. Edward Fontaine, was born on Leatherwood, in Henry county, Aug. 5, 1800.

William Winston Fontaine, another grandson of the Orator, married Martha Dandridge, and their children were as follows: William Spotswood, Patrick Henry, and Anne.

Martha Dandridge was a descendant of Gov. Spottswood also of Col. Gov. John West, whose administration was in 1635. She was a first cousin of Mrs. George Washington. Her husband died and she married a second time, a Perkins, and lived by the Presbyterian church site in Martinsville. In fact, most of her life was spent in that place.

SECOND GENERATION

Patrick Henry Fontaine, son of William Winston and Martha Dandridge, married Sarah Miller Cole about 1830, and their children were: Samuel Cole, Watson Hale, and Nathaniel Cole.

Samuel Cole Fountain was born in 183—, married Mary Morton, the daughter of Rev. Robert C. Anderson. Issue: Robert, Willie, Samuel C., Justina and Henry.

Sam Fontaine, as he was called, was a gallant Confederate soldier, distinguished for his bravery, and was promoted to Lieutenant for merit. He was captured and imprisoned in Cincinnati. After the war was over he was liberated and walked from there to his home at Fontaine on Smith river, a flag stop on the N. & W. Railroad, named in his honor.

Watson Hale Fontaine was a brother, and one of the truest sons who fought for the South from this county, and died in line of service.

Nat Fontaine, the youngest, like his brother, never

married, but distinguished himself on the field of battle for the Confederacy. He was brave and quick witted and captured a whole squad of Union soldiers single-handed without getting a wound. He died a few years ago.

THIRD GENERATION

Robtert Fontaine married Genevieve Kearfott; William Fontaine married Gretchen Welty; Samuel C. Fontaine never married. He was accidentally killed by an electric current when nearing maturity in 1912; Justina Fontaine married Arthur B. Richardson; Patrick Henry Fontaine was killed accidentally while hunting.

FINNEY FAMILY

The first on record of this English family was Richard Finney, who came to Accomac county in 1639, and there you find his descendants like those elsewhere in the State distinguished by their blue eyes, fair skin, fine hair, and it often scarce, and withal good natured, and genuinely hospitable. The old records show three spellings of last syllable, "ney" "ny," and "nie".

One of the earliest Episcopal preachers, the Rev. William Leigh, married into this family. In 1719, we come upon Rev. William Finney who was an important member of the Episcopal Convention of that year. One year later he became rector of the church at Dover, in Goochland county, where during his four years' stay, Thomas Mann Randolph built a new church which cost 54, 990 pounds of tobacco.

Twenty-five years brings us to the Revolutionary period with John, James, William, and Ruben Finney listed as soldiers. This William Finney spelled his name "nie" style, and registered from Amelia county, and was on Gen. George Washington's staff. He was the Col. Finney Patrick Henry sent special messages by to the Commander-in-Chief.

From Amelia county came the first Finneys to this and Franklin county about 1750, and of this family we note specially three brothers and a sister; viz, John, Zack, Peter, and Nancy.

FIRST GENERATION

John Finney was born Sept. 17, 1774, married Elizabeth Prunty (Born Aug. 24, 1809, died Mar. 24, 1850), lived and reared his family in this county and died June 18, 1844, and was buried near Mt. Bethel church at the family cemetery. Children of this union were: John, Thomas, Franklin, Robert, Joshua, William, Nancy, Betsy, and Polly. He married a second time, Susan Mitchell. Issue: Marshall, and Jane.

Zack Finney was born in 1776, married Sallie Brown. He lived in Franklin county. Issue: Jackson Finney, who married a Miss Muse and represented Pittsylvania in the legislature of Va.; Sanford married Miss Swanson; Zack Jr. never married; George married Miss Frith; Betsy Ann married John Finney, a cousin; Dolly married John Smith; Jane married John Ward; and Caroline married Bolin Brown.

Peter Finney was born in 1778, married Ann Walker about 1818. Issue: Wesley L. who married his cousin, Martha Finney; Louisa, married Charles Lee, and reared a son, Capt. W. H. F. Lee; and Ann married Robert Prunty.

Nancy Finney was born in 1780, married Jesse Prunty, Sr., of Franklin county, Clerk of the Court, and issued his own license. Issue: Thomas, Robert, Jane who married Frederick R. Brown and became the mother of Hon. John R. Brown of Martinsville; Betsy married a Wingfield and had two daughters, Ann Wingfield and Jane Wingfield. She next married her cousin Amos Finney. There were two more, Susan Finney who married Col. William A. Brown of Franklin county, and Elizabeth, called Betsy, who married a Bowman, and spent her last days in Lexington, Ky.

SECOND GENERATION

Of the children of John Finney Sr. we note as follows:

John Finney was born in 1803, married Frances, the daughter of John King and Mary Love, lived on Snow Creek in Franklin county where he manufactured tobacco for many years, and died in 1883. Issue: Mary who married Frank Fralin; Sallie Ann married William T. DeShazo (See DeShazo Family); James L. married Susan Napier; John killed at the battle of Seven Pines; Jacob; and Babe.

Joshua Finney was born June 15, 1812, married Caroline Staples, and lived in the western part of Henry county where he died April, 20, 1856. Their children were: Mollie who died at maturity, and George, a business man of Danville for years, who died in Fla. about 1880.

Franklin Finney was born 1806, and settled in Ky.; Robert Finney was born about 1908, married Mary Morris and went to Ky.; William Finney was born 1832, married Ruth, the daughter of Jacob Clark, the wealthiest man in Patrick county. He settled near Ridgeway but moved to Martinsville where he died in 1890. Issue: Mollie and Annie, both died unmarried, and Carrie L., who married Charles J. Angle, and located in Greensboro, N. C.

Polly Finney was born about 1838, married Geo. Napier. (See Napier fam.).

Jane Finney, the only girl of the last union, born about 1826, married a Thomas, and lived near Mt Bethel most of her days.

Marshall Finney, a half brother to the boys, was born Jan. 5, 1824, married Mary East and reared three children. He died, and was buried at the Finney cemetery in the western part of the county, April 17, 1864. The children were: Annie Finney married William D. Hill; Callie Finney married Polk Mills; John J. Finney married Mattie Philpott, built a fine settlement on Smith River west of Martinsville, and reared a large family.

GRIGGS FAMILY

The Griggs family of Virginia is of English origin intermingled with a strain of Scotch-Irish blood.

"The will of Michael Griggs, county Lancaster, colony of Virgina, "Gentleman," was proved in London Sept. 10, 1688, and a few years later, the will of Robert Griggs, of Gloucester county, left a "Thousand pounds of tobacco to the poore".

Among the earliest emigrants to this country were four Griggs brothers; one came to Boston Mass., and one to New York, and later to New Jersey, and there formed the nucleus of the large Griggs family of that section. The other two, Michael and Robert, came to Virginia and settled in Lancaster county.

The Virginia branch, as well as the northern, was well represented in the Revolutionary war. From Virginia appeared the names of, George, Peter, Philip, William, Lewis, and Lee Griggs.

The Henry county branch of the family descended from Michael Griggs. Three brothers, Jeremiah Michael, Peter, and John, came from the eastern counties of the State to Henry county just after the Revolutionary period. Peter Griggs never married. John Griggs married Phoebe Ackelas and was the progenitor of Peter Griggs, owner of the celebrated "Snow Bird" mill, of Henry county. Here he spent his days as a bachelor, practically a recluse, and died in 1921.

Jeremiah Michael Griggs first married a Miss Minter, from which union there were two children, Jeremiah, and a sister, Mariah, who married a Pace and died in young womanhood. His second wife was a Miss Stultz and she bore him five children; viz, Wesley, Peter Franklin, George, Ira, and Susan. His last marriage was to Miss Pedigo, and from this union there were three children Brice, Lewis, and John.

SECOND GENERATION

Jeremiah Griggs, son of Jeremiah Michael, and his first wife was one of the county's leading citizens. (See Biograph. Chap.).

As in the Revolutionary, so in the Civil war, the family of Griggs did not fail to answer the call of their country to arms. Jere W. Griggs served faithfully, and was at the battle of Gettysburg. So was another son of George Griggs, William, in the thickest of that great battle and scores of others during the four years of service, losing a leg at the famous charge at the latter field of carnage.

George King Griggs, son of Wesley Griggs, and Susan, his wife, the daughter of William King, enlisted in June 1861 and participated in nearly all of the battles fought by the army of northern Virginia. He was several times wounded, severely at Gettysburg. He rose rapidly from captain to Colonel of the 38th, Regiment of Infantry, and surrendered at Appromattox in charge of the Brigade.

Greenbury Thornton Griggs, son of Franklin Griggs, only 16 years old when war was declared, served as Captain of Company H. 47th, Va. Regiment in Kemper's Brigade, Longstreet's Corps. He was captured before Appomattox and held a prisoner on Johnson's Island, from which place he was paroled.

In civil life, the Griggs family have responded to every call of their country for uplift or advancement, not only commercially, but also in an educational or political field. Samuel J. Griggs, son of Franklin Griggs, was elected to the legislature from Henry county for the years 1881-82.

Col. George King Griggs, war record above noted, late of Pittsylvania county, was distinctly a man of great executive force and rare judgment. He was for several years connected with the Danville and Western railroad, gradually being promoted till he became General Superintendent and Treasurer. Besides his distinguished career for the public Col. Griggs was a member of the Baptist church and active in church work. He was a Mason, being a Past High Priest of Euclid Chapter, and Past Eminent Commander of Dove Commandery, Knights Templars. He left two sons, Archie, and George.

Perhaps no greater service was ever done the county than that of Greenbury Thornton Griggs in his untiring and persistent efforts in behalf of public school education. In collaboration with Dr. Ruffner, when the system was adopted in 1871, he canvassed the state. Soon thereafter he was appointed the first school superintendent of Henry. As the result of his efforts Martinsville had one of the first High Schools in the State. It was named in honor of Dr. Ruffner, and called "Ruffner Institute" until 1904, when it was changed to the Martinsville High School.

Every son of Michael Griggs lived and died in Henry county. They all married and reared large families except Brice, who went to Texas. All were farmers and bore by inheritance and by deed in truth the title of gentleman. Every one lived up to the motto inscribed on the family Coat of Arms: Gules-3 ostrich feathers argent. Crest-A sword in pale enfiled with a leopard's face, all ppr. (See old pen-ink copy in possession of Miss Lila Griggs now in Roanoke).

George Griggs, brother of Jeremiah, and a son of Jeremiah, Sr's 2nd, wife, settled near Ridgeway. He was born in 1816, and married Francis Wills. He died Dec. 23rd, 1882, and his wife in 1854. Issue: William, Jerry W., Frances, Susan, and Geo. Ira.

HAMILTON HOTEL
Martinsville, Va.

THIRD GENERATION

William Griggs, a cripple for life from the loss of leg at Gettysburg, reared a large family as follows, Tom, William, Kate, Ida, and Sam.

Jerry W. Griggs was born in 1844, married Emeline King. Issue: George K., and an adopted daughter, Lina. He was a successful farmer and a good citizen. He died in 1920.

Frances Griggs married Judge Moir. No issue.

Susan Griggs was born in 1842, married Sol Franklin, of Irisburg, who died young, leaving her with the following children; viz, Joe, Sol, George, Ben, John, Clay, Rosa and Kate. The climate being destructive to the children after Rosa, Kate, and Clay died, Mrs. Franklin moved to New Mexico where they had good health except Ben, who died soon, and the greatest of the world's blessings, good health and great wealth, at last came to nearly every one of the name.

George I. Griggs was born in 1846. He married Susan Churchill Nov. 10, 1878, and conducted a general merchandise business at Ridgeway for a long period of years. The firm of Jones and Griggs was the oldest business house in the county when he died on Jan. 11, 1912.

His children were as follows: Katy, Susie, Margie who died in early childhood, May Bud, and George named for her father, George Ira.

HAMILTON FAMILY

Wm. Hamilton, the father of the Hamiltons of Henry Co., Va., was born in Bath Co., Va. 1811, mar. May 14, 1834, Medora Sabina Beard Price,* who was of Scotch descent. Issue: Virginia Agnes, Sue Margaret, Alice M., Martha Sophia, John, Wm., Ellen Frances, Rose L., Eugenia, Charles Atley, and Paul Price.

After some years near Mountain Cove, this family moved to Blanco, Texas, 1855 and the father was made Sheriff of that county. The Comanche Indians went on the war path during his term of office, and he had many narrow escapes. His wife died Nov. 1882, and he followed her 1894.

Paul Price Hamilton, the youngest, enlisted in U. S. Army 1865, and served in Montana against the Nez Perces Indians. He developed heart disease, was honorably discharged, and died 1892.

Charles Altley Hamilton was born in Virginia May 15, 1851. He mar. Mary I. Henderson of La., lost her, and came to Henry Co. in 1876. Married Mrs. M. W. Lavinder 1879.* He became a tent evangelist in 1911. Their children were as follows:

William Wirt Hamilton, b. in Martinsville, Va., June 25, 1882, mar. Jessie Turner, of Henry Co. Jan. 21, 1905. She died in Lynchburg, Va., Feb. 4, 1920. His 2d. wife was Oneta Augusta Templeton, of Lynchburg, Va. They were married Sept. 14, 1921.

Charles Atley Hamilton Jr. b. in Martinsville, Va., May 2, 1884, md. Anne E. Retzack, of Oshkosh, Wis., Dec. 17, 1902. She was born Jan. 17, 1884.

Medora Hamilton b. Oct. 4, 1880, md. Charles Eugene Crist Aug. 25, 1905. He was born in Va. Aug. 1, 1880. Issue: Medora Woodsen Crist, b. Mar. 14, 1923.

Virginia Ray, born July 18, 1919, of good parentage, was adopted at the age of six hours by Mr. and Mrs. Charles E. Crist.

John Waddey Hamilton, b. in Martinsville, Va. Dec. 21, 1885, md. Nora Southall Weisiger, of Richmond Va., June 16, 1915. She was born March 1, 1885, and is a descendant of Major Anderson De Witt, of Rev. Fame. Issue: John Waddy Hamilton, Jr., b. at Jefferson Hospt., Roanoke, Va., Sept. 23, 1916.

Southall Weisiger Hamilton, b. at the Memorial Hospt., Richmond, Va., Jan 24, 1919.

*Rev. C. A. Hamilton's 3d wife was Mrs. Elizabeth Jackson, of Atlanta, Ga.

* The Beards were Scotch. The name Price is a blending of two Welsh words "ap" and "Reese". "Ap" means "son", and reese means "a strong man". Apreese would mean "The son of a strong man. Price is a short way of saying "Apreese".

Thomas A. Price md. a Beard, and from this marriage descended the Hamiltons.

HILL FAMILY

The Hill family is of English descent. The founder of the family in Va. was I. Y. Hill, of Amherst Co., who md. Sarah Judith Bailey, dau. of Sam Bailey and his wife Augusta Parks Bailey.

Among their children were two sons, Samuel C. and William, both of whom were in the troops sent to the relief of Gen. Greene at Guilford Court House, and who afterwards settled in Henry.

Samuel C. married Lucy Mitchell. Issue: Catherine Ann, Judith Parks, Matilda Winston, John Parks, and Sallie.

In 1801 he sold out his Amherst property and came by wagon train to Henry Co., attended by outriders to drive the cattle and serve as protection to the wagon train.

Arriving at his destination, near where Snow Bird Mill now stands, he built a house hastily of logs right in the woods, but near water. He died before he could make a better home. He was devoted to his motherless children, his wife having died before he left Amherst. But he taught them to be good housekeepers, and they took pride in being fine needlewomen. Judith often boasted of having received five dollars for making the neatest darn in her Father's silk stockings. None of the children married until after Mr. Hill's death, which took place April 11, 1815. Rev. J. C. Traylor preached his funeral Oct. 8, 1815, from a text in last Chapter of Revelations, 14th, verse.

William Hill, the brother of Samuel C, came to Henry somewhere about 1793. He had married Elizabeth Saunders, and settled on Horsepasture Creek. He built the house long occupied by Dr. J. R. Dillard. Issue: Thomas, JohnWaddy, David, Sallie Parks, and Elizabeth Saunders.

SECOND GENERATION—S. C. HILL'S LINE

Catherine Ann Hill, b. Dec. 26, 1786, md. W. A. Taylor 1817. Mr. Taylor was a farmer, but a shining light in the Methodist Church and a blessing in the community.

Judith Parks Hill b. March 20, 1789, md. her cousin, John Waddy Hill, and lived at Horsepasture for years till her husband's health gave out, when she moved to the home left her by her father. Issue: Samuel Robt., Wm. Wirt, John Waddy Jr., David Parks, Hester Ann, Elizabeth Saunders, and Catherine Matilda.

Matilda Winston Hill, b. July 24, 1791, md. Henry G. Mullins, and settled near her father's old residence.

John Parks Hill, b. July 11, 1793. md. Eliza Morris, no issue. He was a soldier in war of 1812.

Sallie Hill, b. April 7, 1796, d. May 27, 1796, and the mother Lucy Mitchell Hill, d. Oct. 2, 1799.

David Hill died unmarried. (Son of Wm. Hill, the pioneer).

THIRD GENERATION

Wm. Wirt Hill, b. March 8, 1822, md. Mary Catherine Bassett, 1840. Issue: Judith Parks America, Mary Catherine, Martha Woodson, Elizabeth Saunders, Lucy Matilda, John Waddy (3), Eliza James, Sarah Alexander, Samuel Robt., Frances Ruth, Wm. Wirt (2).

Elizabeth Hill (3), b. 1824, md. 1854, James Harden Carter, b. 1826, and d. 1901. She joined the church in early life at a Methodist camp meeting near Meadow Church. For years she was the only member of the church in her family. She lived a consistent Christian life, and died firm in the Faith. She was the mother of 3 children, Judith Parks, who md. Edward Henry Booker. Issue: Walter Shields, Byrd, Harold, Lowry, Harden Chapman, James Carter, Lena Alma, and Edward Henry.

Sallie Ann Carter, 2d, dau. of Elizabeth 3d, md. Wm. A. Latimer. Issue: Bessie May, Cora Alyce, Louisa Hamilton, James Carter.

John Waddy Carter b. Nov. 16, 1858, studied law, and was successful at the bar. He held many prominent positions in life, and was held in high esteem by his countymen. At the time of his death he was considered the best lawyer of Martinsville. He md. 1st, Mary Lavinia Smead, dau. of an officer of the U. S. Navy. Mrs. Carter d. leaving two sons, J. W. Carter Jr., a lawyer, and Louis Gordon, a business man. By his 2d marriage to Kizzie Drewry, there are two daughters, Keziah Drewry, and Ruth Redd, Catherine Matilda Hill md. W. A. Sheffield. Issue: Judith Parks md. B. F. Barrow (see Barrow family). Lucy Wootton d. in infancy, Elizabeth md. Starling Thomas, Leonard md. Bettie Coan, John W, md. Lucy Withers.

Hester Ann, Samuel Robt., (1) John Waddy Hill (2), and David Parks, d. unmarried.

FOURTH GENERATION

Judith, b. Feb. 20, 1842, unmarried.
Mary Catherin b. Nov. 24, 1843, md. M. M. Koger (see Koger family).
Martha Woodson, b. July 14, 1845, md. 1st, S. H. Lavinder (see Lavinder family.) 2nd. C. A. Hamilton (see Hamilton family).
Elizabeth, b. Oct. 21, 1847 d. March 10, 1910, unmarried; Lucy Matilda, b. May 4, 1850, died 1885; John Waddy b. May 12, 1853, d. 1857.
Eliza James, b. June 14, 1855, md. O. R. Gregory Aug. 11, 1878; Rev. J. W. Crider officating. No issue.
Sara hAlexander b. Feb. 20, 1857, unmarried.
Samuel Robt. b. Dec. 18, 1859, md. 1st, Loulie Craghead July 15th, 1885, Rev. J. L. Pribble officiating. Issu: Samuel Robt., (3) Wm. Wirt, (3) Lucy M., (2) Loulie C., Thomas L., Mary C., Ruth Angeline, Overton Gregory; 2nd wife, Sallie Bryant. Issue: Joseph Wilson, Edith Parks, and Francis.
Wm. Wirt (2), b. April 21, 1866, md. Grace Fish. Issue: Wm. Nathan.
Frances Ruth, b. Sept. 25, 1861, md. T. A. F. Mitchell. Issue: Wirt who md. Miss McClintoc, issue, two sons.

FIFTH GENERATION

Samuel Robt. (3), b. June 26, 1886 md. Sadie Bryant, Oct. 26, 1915
W. W. Hill (3), b. Aug. 14, 1888, md. Loula Price, Dec. 22, 1915. Issue: W. W. (4).
L. M. Hill (2), b. Feb. 9, 1890, unmarried (Trained Nurse).
Loulie C. Hill, b. Feb. 22, 1892, md. Will Asbury, no issue.
Thomas L. Hill, b. Feb. 28, 1894, md. Stella Brandt, July 6, 1914. Issue: Judith Parks, Catherin Bassett, Nancy Langhorne, and Samuel Robert, (4).
Mary C. Hill (Kitty), b. Sept. 5, 1895, md. J. Moorman Shepherd March 10, 1923.
Ruth Angeline, b. April 18, 1897, died in infancy.
Overton Gregory Hill b. July 25, 1899.

DEATHS

Loulie T. Hill d. Sept. 3, 1899; Rev. W. W. Hill d. July 22, 1891; Mary C. Hill d. July 9, 1922; S. R. Hill (2) d. May 1, 1921.

SECOND GENERATION (WILLIAM HILL'S LINE)

Thomas S. Hill md. Lucinda Payne. Issue: Mary, Lucinda, Thomas, William David, Martha, and others.

John Waddy Hill md. his cousin Judith Parks Hill. Issue: enumerated above.

Sallie Parks md. Billy Spencer. Issue: America, Sallie Ann, and Harrison.

Elizabeth Saunders md. Geo. Dillard, their oldest dau. md Daniel Stone, and when Mr. Dillard died Mrs. Dillard and her entire family moved west.

David Hill d. unmarried.

THIRD GENERATION

William David, son of Thomas Saunders Hill and his wife Lucinda Payne, md. Catherine Donovant. Issue: T. J. b. Sept. 8, 1850, Lucy J., b. June, 1853. W. D., (Burke) b. Sept. 19, 1854, G. W., b. Oct. 18, 1856. M. M., b. Oct. 19, 1858, S. S., b. March 19, 1860. E. W., b. July 1862, J. P., b. June 23, 1865. Katherine, b. March 7, 1867.

Mr. Hill was a tall man, so he was nick-named "Long Bill Hill". As were most young men of his day he was extremely fond of fox-hunting and kept a pack of hounds: careless in dress but industrious and energetic, provided well for his family, though rather careless with his money, evinced by his losing $500 out of his pocket on one occasion. As a boy he had a great distaste for school, and once hid in a tree all day till time to go home.

Another time his mother wanted him to wait on the table. He was so obstreperous that she locked him up in the corn-crib till after supper, when she found that he had beaten to death, with ears of corn, an old rooster put up there to keep from fighting. However he made a kind hearted man, never refusing a helping hand when called upon.

FOURTH GENERATION

W. D. (called Burke), md .Annie Marshall Finney Nov. 18, 1880. Issue: Mollie Finney, d. unmarried Nov. 7, 1904; Peter Marshall died, unmarried, Oct. 7, 1904; John P., b. July 10, 1836; Harry M., b. Jan. 14, 1889; D. W., b. Nov. 16, 1891; Ethel Maud, b. May 30, 1894;

Ruby Lee, b. Feb. 5, 1896; Ernest, b. Aug. 12, 1901; Russell, b. Dec. 13, 1905.

G. W. Hill b. Oct. 19, 1856, md. Ambrosia Marshall Dec. 10, 1882. She was b. May 8, 1856, d. April 10 or 16, 1904. Issue: Ida. b., May 7, 1884, d. Jan. 11, 1904; T. J., b. June 29, 1886 md. Annie Dunbar, Dec. 11, 1912; Mary M., b. Feb. 8, 1888, md. Royer Poteat, Dec. 3, 1911; Kittie, b. Feb. 7, 1892, md. Thomas Wells, Dec. 18 1912. Ambrosia Hill, b. March 29, 1893; Mabel C., b. Feb. 6, 1895; Helen Hill b. March 22, 1904, d. July 3, 1904; on Nov. 6, 1906, G. W. Hill md. his 2d. wife, Mrs. Matilda Moore.

T. Jefferson Hill, b. Nov. 20, 1851, md. March 22, 1870, Susan Jarrett, dau. of Henry Jarrett and his wife Martha Baker. He died April 14, 1890, and left one child, Willie, b. July 10, 1880.

Katherine Hill, youngest child of W. D. Hill, Sr., b. March 7, 1867, md. B. D. Moore, who was b. May 1, 1862, and died Feb. 12, 1903. Issue: Four children. The oldset girl b. Dec. 11, 1892, died Oct. 17, 1903. Hilda D. Moore b. July 17, 1894; Mary E. Moore, b. April 13, 1896; Berry Scott Moore, b. Oct. 18, 1902.

John Payne Hill, son of W. D. Hill, Sr., md. Fannie Marshall.

HAIRSTON

There was a Peter Hairston who came from Ireland to Penn.—somewhere about 1715—There is a town in Penn. named for Donegal, Ireland—but Henry Co. Hairstons came later to Norfolk, Va.

HAIRSTON

Virginia was settled by families from the Old World. Family names are so much alike that it is difficult to distinguish one from the other. George, Peter, Sam and Robert are old Hairston names. In Pennsylvania 1742 there was a Peter Hairston from Donegal, Ireland. Many thought that his descendents finally came to this county, but there was another Peter that came here after the battle of Culloden. He came to Norfolk. All are descended from Robert Hairston a friend and kinsman of Robert Bruce, king of Scotland. The Hairston coat of arms is 3 Keys. The story goes that Bruce wanted his heart buried in Jerusalem but owing to deaths and disappointments this heart was finally burned and the ashes enclosed in a casket and placed in Melrose Abbey and was locked with 3 keys, one kept by Robert Hairston, another by the son of the good Douglas and I do not know who the other Knight was.

The Hairstons were originally Scotch. Nearly three centuries after the first we know of them, they were staunch Royalists as well as adherents to the Stuart dynasty. When this was overthrown by William, Prince of Orange (1688), being men of prominence, they were subjects for the displeasure of the House of Hanover and had to flee to Wales. When James II, called the Pretender, invaded Scotland to seize again the throne of his ancestors, the Hairstons crossed into Ireland, joined the Irish Army, and came again to Scotland. After sharing the horrors of the fatal field of Culloden, the Hairstons came to America about 1746.

The first whose name we have on Va. records, was Peter, whose wife was spoken of as an "Irish Lady of Rank They had two daughters. One died at sea, the other married a Shelby, of Ky. He finally settled in Bedford Co., with his four sons, Robt., Peter, Andrew, and Samuel.

SECOND GENERATION

Samuel, son of Peter, was Lieut. in the Militia, also represented Bedford Co., in House of Burgesses, 1769, and while his will was probated in Bedford in April, 1782, he is recorded as first Presiding Justice of Campbell Co., Feb. 7, 1782. He was never married (See Bedford Co. records).

Peter, son of Peter and brother of Samuel, died unmarried. He is said to have accumulated considerable wealth. His will was probated in Bedford Co. March 27, 1780.

Andrew, son of Peter, and brother of Samuel and Peter (2) died June, 1782, leaving large estates, and in his will mentions his wife, Elizabeth, and daughters, Priscilla, Margaret, and Susannah. He moved to Ga.

Robt. (son of Peter) first settled in what is now Campbell Co., which Co. he represented in House of Burgesses. (See Acts of Assembly) and was an officer in Colonial Army, 1758. (Henning's Statutes, Vol. 7, page 204). In Va. Historical Magazine Vol. 9, Robt. Hairston was "Commissioner of Peace) and on page 145 is spoken of as "Justice in 1778; and on page 417, Gov. Thomas Nelson appointed him the first High Sheriff of Henry Co. He married Ruth, dau. of Capt. Geo. Stovall, of Amherst Co., Va., and had three sons, Geo., Sam, and Peter; and six daughters. Martha married Alexander Hunter, Sarah mar. Baldwin Rowland, Elizabeth mar. Michael Rowland, Agnes mar. John Woods, Ruth mar. Peter Wilson, Rebt. Hairston died 1783, and is buried in Franklin Co.

THIRD GENERATION

Geo. Hairston, 1st, son of Robert and Ruth Stovall Hairston, was born in Bedford Co., Va., in 1750, and came to Henry about 20 years later, bought the Beaver Creek home with 20,000 acres of land, fifty acres of which he donated, 1790, to Henry Co. Va., as a site for the Court House and "Public Halls" (see Va., Magazine of History and Biography, Vol. 10 P. 329). This purchase laid the foundation of the great wealth he accumulated. A large quanity of this property is still in the possession of his descendants.

He was brave, patriotic, and farsighted. When the Revolutionary war raged we find his name enrolled in the list that went to death or glory. His deeds are a part of the history of this great struggle and will not be repeated here. He was Capt. of a company in Col. Abraham Penn's regiment, marched from Beaver Creek in March, 1781, and hurried to Gen'l Greene's assistance.

During that month these soldiers covered themselves with glory at the battles of Guilford Court House, and Eutaw Springs, and others.

When the war was over, he returned to his plantation, and by careful attention gathered great wealth rapidly from his vast estate. However, he responded to his country's call once more. In the war of 1812 he was acting Brigadier Gen'l in command of the 3d, 4th, 5th, and 64th Virginia and 38th, N. C. regiments with the rank of Colonel. He saw much service and was in the engagement that repulsed Gen'l Ross who burned Washington and who was killed at Bladenburg.

For the second time he left the field of battle after peace was declared and resumed the quiet life of a planter. But soon the public called him again, and he served his county as High Sheriff and later still, he was elected a member of the legislature from his county. This closed his long public career; and from this period he dwelt in peace by his own fireside. Col. Hairston was married Jan. 1781 during the war of Independence and soon after the tragedy was enacted that changed his career in life. In August, 1780, Capt. Letcher, a friend in the army, came home on a furlough, and had hardly put up his gun on the rack when he was shot through the window (his wife, with a little girl three years old was an eye-witness) by a band of tories lying in wait. Geo. Hairston gathered his band of men, caught the tories, convicted them before a drumhead court martial and hanged every one of them. This spot in Patrick county is still called "Drumhead".

This baby, in the course of time, became the grandmother of Gen. J. E. B. Stuart, the great Confederate leader. The widow Letcher, in the following Jan. became the wife of the avenger of her husband's death and presided over the great hospitable home on Beaver Creek with true Virginia grace. She came of distinguished families herself, for she was a Perkins, a dau. of Nicholas Perkins, the pioneer, and her grandmother was a Harden, of the House of Buccleugh.

Col. Geo. Hairston died at this home where he lived for over half a century, 5th of March, 1827, and not many years later his good wife followed him.

THIRD GENERATION

Samuel Hairston (2) son of Robt. and brother of

HISTORY OF HENRY COUNTY, VIRGINIA 191

Geo. Sr., mar. Judith Saunders. He attained the rank of Col. in war 1812. Issue: Robt., Peter, Geo., Sam., Ruth, Mary, Ann, Letitia.

Peter Hairston, 3d son of Robt. and Ruth Stovall Hairston, married Alice Perkins, and settled Upper Saura Town in N. C. Issue: one dau. Ruth Stovall.

Sarah, dau. of Robt. and Ruth Stoval Hairston, mar. Baldwin Rowland.

Elizabeth mar. Michael Rowland; Martha mar. Alexander Hunter; Ruth mar. Peter Wilson; Agnes mar. John Woods.

The children of Geo. Hairston Sr. will be considered as follows: Robt., the oldest son, was in command of a company in war of 1812 in Scott's army at the battle of Lundy's Lane. After this he married Ruth Stovall Wilson and settled at Berry Hill. He was elected to the Va. Legislature before moving to Miss. where he died 1852. No issue.

Geo. Hairston, Jr., "Old Rusty", graduated from Princeton 1805, mar. 1811 Louisa Hardeman, a ward and relative of President John Tyler, and settled 1st., at Marrowbone, a thousand acre estate in the Marrowbone valley. Years afterwards he moved to Hordsville, another farm up Smith's River. He was a member of the Legislature from this county longer than any one before or since his day. He originated the Smith River Navigation Company and the Union Iron Works. He gave to the Methodist, Presbyterian, and Episcopal churches, the land upon which the churches in Martinsville were built; and also gave the land on which Odd Fellows Hall was built. His wife was the first Episcopalian confirmed in the "Old Episcopal Church", in Henry Co. He also gave Rev. Robt. Anderson 138 acres of land upon which to build his home. Issue: John Tyler, Geo., Nicholas, Robt., Samuel, Elizabeth, Susan, Louisa.

Samuel mar. Agnes J. P. Wilson, settled at Oak Hill, had 2,000 slaves, great landed estate, and died 1875, and left 7 children, viz., Peter W., Geo., Robt., Samuel, Henry, Ruth Stovall and Alcy.

Henry Hairston mar. Mary Ewell a relative of the great Gen'l of Confederate fame, moved to Miss., and died without issue.

Nicholas, Constantine and Peter all died young.

John Adams mar, Malinda Corn, lived in Patrick.

Moved to Miss. and died 1836. Issue: Geo., Marshall, Elizabeth, Ruth A. and Susan A.

Marshall, the tenth son, b. 1802, mar. Ann Marshall Hairston and lived all his life at his father's old home, Beaver Creek. Issue: John A., Elizabeth Perkins., Ann Marshall, and Ruth Stovall.

Ruth Stovall mar. Peter Hairston of Franklin county. Issue: Samuel, Geo., Peter, and Elizabeth Perkins.

America Hairston mar. John Calloway. Issue: Geo. and Ruth.

The children of Samuel Hairston and Judith Saunders as follows: Robt. mar. Elizabeth Woods. He was a soldier in the war of 1812.

Peter Hairston mar. Ruth Stovall Hairston of Henry Co. Geo., another brother died without issue.

Samuel mar. Elizabeth P. Hairston, dau. of Harden Hairston of Miss. He was appointed Col. of Militia. He was a large planter and reared 12 children, nine of them reaching maturity.

Ruth Stovall Hairston mar. Joab Early. Issue: Jubal Early, afterward the great Lieut. Gen'l of the Confederate army.

Mary mar. John Calloway; Ann mar. Marshall Hairston as above stated; Letitia mar. Thomas Watkins.

The children of Harden Hairston and Sarah Staples were as follows: Geo. was an A. M. of Chapel Hill, N. C., a class mate of Thomas Ashe. He died in Miss., unmarried; John H. b. 1812, was killed by lightning.

Samuel Harden, 4th, son, b. in Patrick Co., 1822, graduated at William & Mary, studied law, nominated County Judge and served with the rank of Major on the staff of J. E. B. Stuart in the Confederate army. He was attending the Legislature and was killed at the Capitol disaster. He early mar. Alcey Hairston dau. of Samuel of Oak Hill. He left three children, Harden, Ruth, and Sallie.

Peter C. Hairston b. in Patrick Co. 1823, was highly educated. He studied medicine and graduated at Medical College of New York. He mar. Miss Moseley of Miss. and reared six children to be grown.

Nicholas mar. Keziah Staples, sister of Judge Waller Staples. They had only one child, Bettie Waller.

Robt. A. Hairston b. 1838, graduated at Chapel Hill and mar. Mary Hays, of Ala. Issue: Percy and Ada.

J. W. T. Hairston b. 1835, mar. Elizabeth Perkins dau. of Marshall Hairston of Beaver Creek. He was on Gen'l J. E. B. Stuart's staff as Major, and saw much service in the Civil War. He left one child, Watt Harden Hairston, who died unmarried.

The children of Peter Hairston of Franklin County were as follows: Samuel b. 1829, issue only by his 1st. wife, Henrietta Jones, viz. Wm., Geo., Peter, Marshall, Robt., and Caroline. His 2nd wife was Lucy Estes.

Geo. mar. Pattie Smith, dau. of James M. Smith, Sr. No issue. Elizabeth Perkins Hairston's children by her 1st. husband: Peter Dillard, son of Gen. Dillard, were Dr. Peter Dillard and his brother John, a farmer. Her 2d husband was John Reamey, brother of Dr. Peter Reamey.

Geo. Hairston's children ("Old Rusty") were: John Tyler of Red Plains on Marrowbone creek md. Pocahontas Cabell. Issue: Mrs. James S. Redd, Mrs Libb Clayborn, Mrs. Virginia Williams, Hardyman, Tyler, Powahatan, and Cabell. Dr. Geo. Hairston was an eminent physician, and lived at Marrowbone farm, his father's old home. He mar. Matilda Martin. Issue: Geo., who died at Hordesville leaving, 3 children Rusty, Peter and Mattie.

Judge N. H. Hairston, of Roanoke, Va.; Mrs. C. H. Ingles; Mrs. Flem Saunders, Mrs. John Draper, of Draper's Valley; Mrs. R. C. Tate, of Wythe Co. Two died very young.

Robert Hairston, of Roundabout farm, near Martinsville mar. Elizabeth Saunders of Franklin. Their two daughters were: Lizzie and Louisa, Lizzie mar. W. S. Gravely. Louisa mar. H. M. Darnall, of Roanoke.

Samuel Hairston mar. Miss Eliza Penn, of Patrick Co. Issue: Mrs. E. P. Zentmeyer, of Patrick, Mrs. Judge Hairston, of Roanoke, Geo. died young; John Tyler died after marrying Miss Watkins, leaving two daus. and a son; Lydia, Nannie, and Watt who mar. Lelia Price. He left 4 children.

Elizabeth Hairston, the 1st. dau., mar. a lawyer, John Seawell, of Gloucester county. Issue: Louisa, Hairston, and Mollie, a noted writer.

Susan mar. Col. Wm. Martin (See Martin Family). Louisa mar. Peter W. Watkins, of Shawnee farm (see Watkins Family).

Marshall Hairston's dau., Ruth Stovall, left a dau. Ann Marshall who mar. Rorer James. Elizabeth P. md. J. W. T. Hairston. Ann never married.

John A. was a lieutenant in Civil War, and was killed at the battle of Williamsburg.

JONES FAMILIES

Three Jones families are considered in this chapter, Benjamin Jones, Charles Jones, and Ambrose Jefferson Jones. The two last mentioned are related.

In 1679, David Jones, from Wales, entered land where the City of Baltimore now stands, and gave name to the stream that runs through the City. His grandson Joshua Jones lived in Culpepper County, Virginia, and married in 1751, Isabel Norman. Their children were Benjamin, John, James, and Thomas.

John Jones reared two sons, John and Martin, and a daughter, Sally, who married a Houston, from which union General Sam Houston was descended.

James Jones went to Tennessee. Thomas Jones located in Georgia.

Benjamin Jones, (See Biography Chapter), was born in 1752, married Elizabeth de Remi, in 1776, and settled on Jones Creek near Martinsville in this County, rearing the following children: Thomas, Sanford, Gabriel Remi, Bartlett, George Washington, Pamela, Benjamin Churchill, and Elizabeth.

FIRST GENERATION

Thomas Jones married Elizabeth Lyell, of Pittsylvania County, where he afterwards resided and reared the following children: Benjamin, Bartlett, Mary Decatur, Elizabeth, and Martha.

Sanford Jones married a Miss Hodges, and reared a family in Pittsylvania County.

Gabriel Remi Jones married in 1809, Mary Bryant, and there were two children, Jane Elizabeth, who married Moses Carper, Clerk of Franklin County Court, and a son Beverly.

Dr. Bartlett Jones married Eliza Dunlap, and settled in Lancaster, South Carolina. Issue. Benjamin Rush, Constantine, Mary Theresa, and Virginia.

George Washington Jones married Salina Dunlap,

of South Carolina, located at Leaksville, North Carolina, where he practised many years, and reared two sons Erasmus Dowen and Adolphus Dorsett. Descendants of the first mentioned live in Little Rock, Arkansas. A. D. Jones has descendants in Rockingham, County, N. C. A daughter, Mrs. Nora Winston, lives at Stoneville, North Carolina.

Pamela Jones married John Menzies, and settled in Tennessee. Issue: Mary and son Remi.

Dr. Benjamin Churchill Jones located in Lancaster, S. C., married a daughter of General Davis, United States Minister to the Court of France.

Elizabeth Jones married James Kyle, and settled in Georgia. Her son Col Robert Kyle became a wealty car builder and foundry proprieter of Gadsden, Ala., and died in 1922, when 94 years of age.

SECOND GENERATION

Children of Thomas Jones: Benjamin Jones had a daughter Nannie who married John Anthony of Axton, Virginia; Decatur Jones married Harriet Kean, and lived at Bachelor's Hall, Pittsylvania County and reared the following children: Araminta Jones, married John H. Holcomb, Danville, Va.; Maria Louisa Jones married H. B. Haase; William Henry Jones married Elizabeth Kean; Bettie A. Jones married M. C. Cunningham, of Greensboro, N. C.; Nannie Witcher Jones married Victor McAdoo first, second married R. R. King; Emmie Jones not married; John Kean Jones married Mary Flain Wilkinson of Md.; Thomas D. Jones married Mattie Southgate, Durham, N. C.; Kate Jones married Joseph Morehead, Greensboro, N. C.; Charles Jones never married; Dorsey Jones married Mary Glenn, Halifax, Virginia.

Bartlett Jones of Pittsylvania married Miss Keen, lived in that County and reared the following children: Witcher Jones, of California; Keen Jones of Pittsylvania County; Elisha Jones, of Danville, who married Annie Robinson; Annie M. Jones married Dr. John James, Danville, the parents of Lt. Jules James, U. S. Navy.

Elizabeth Jones married Capt. George Gravely, of this County. (See Gravely family.)

Mary Jones married James O. Martin, Pittsylvania

County; Martha Jones, never married was a typical aristocrat of the old South. She died 1910.

Children of Dr. Bartlett Jones: Benjamin Rush Jones, practiced medicine in Montgomery, Ala.; Mary Jones married Judge James Witherspoon, of South Carolina; Theresa married Dr. J. Marion Simms, famous New York surgeon and physician to Empress Eugenia, of Paris; Virginia married Mr. Wm. Hooper, son of Gen. Wm. Hooper; her daughter Theresa, married Governor Joseph Johnson, of Alabama.

Children of Gabriel Remie Jones: Jane Elizabeth, md. Moses Carper. Issue: Robert Beverley went west at close of Civil War; James Jones md. Mary Wilson; Moses J. md. Lily Turnbull. These four are deceased. Mary J. Wilson and Emma are the living children of James Carper.

Dr. Beverly Jones, son of Gabriel Remi Jones, was born Aug. 18, 1811, read medicine with his Uncle, Dr. Jones, Leaksville, N. C., graduated at the Jefferson Medical College, Philadelphia, 1838. He began practise of medicine, Germanton, N. C., and in 1843 married Julia Conrad, a great granddaughter of Jacob Lash (Loesch), one of twelve founders of the Moravian Colony of Wachovia, 1753, and long connected with its governmnet. Dr. Jones and wife moved from Bethania to Oak Grove, 1848, where he practised medicine fifty years over a wide territory. He was a man of sound common sense, rare judgment, and robust constitution, a close observer of nature as well as of men, and an untiring student of his profession. These characteristics combined to make him a successful physician and surgeon. He died November, 1902, and is buried at Oak Grove. The children of this union were: Abram Gabriel, James Benjamin, Alexander Conrad, Robert Henry, Erastus Beverly, Ella Mary, Virginia E., Julia P., Kate E., and Lucien G.

THIRD GENERATION

Dr. Abram G. Jones was born 1845, married Nannie Dalton, saw service in the Civil War. He is practising medicine at Walnut-Cove, North Carolina.

James B. Jones, also in Civil War, was for years a minister of the Christian church, married Mary Frances Rogers first, and second Carrie Anderson. He died in 1911, and had been president of William Woods College,

DR. BEVERLY JONES

Fulton, Missouri, fifteen years. Two daughters survive him, Eleanor Conrad and Frances Adair.

Alexander C. Jones, Military Cadet Horner Institute, died 1865.

Robert H. Jones married Sallie Wayt, practised dentistry in Martinsville, Va., a number of years. In 1890 moved to Winston-Salem, N. C., continuing his professional work. His second marriage was to Amelia Holland.

Erasttus Beverly Jones married Ida Matheson; his second wife was Sue Barbour. He was a prominent lawyer as well as politician, was elected to the House and Senate of North Carolina, several times For seven years he was Judge of the Superior Court taking rank with the eminent jurists of his State. He died August, 1922, leaving a daughter, Hervey Louise.

Virginia E. Jones married H. L. Sullivan, died 1893, leaving one son Beverly N. Sullivan.

Ella, Julia, Kate and Lucien Jones live at the old home, Oak Grove.

Descendants of Dr. Benjamin Jones living in Henry County: James O. Martin, Jr., a great grandson of the founder of this family was born 1851, and came back to this County when a small boy. In 1874 he married Ella Turner, and they reared the following children: Lucy Martin married Dr. Fagg, Axton; Mary Martin married Ainslee J. Lester, Martinsville; Susie Martin married J. P. McCabe, D. D. Martinsville; Rorer James Martin married Margaret Slawron.

CHARLES JONES FAMILY

The family is of Welsh descent, but by marriage claims lineage direct from Lord Bacon of England. This family can be traced to the first settlers in Eastern Virginia.

Charles Jones, the progenitor of this family in the county, was born in Grayson county, in 1768, and came to Henry after the Revolutionary War, settling finally just south of Ridgeway. He acquired a large boundary of land and, married about 1790, Polly, the sister of George King who married Gen. Joseph Martin's daughter Susan, and daughter of Rev. John King who came from Brunswick county to Leatherwood. Their children were: Betsy, Polly, Jane, Nancy, another daughter who married an Allen and went to Mo., and George King.

FIRST GENERATION

George King Jones was born Nov. 11, 1803, married Ann, the daughter of Hon. John King, of Henry county, in 1827, and settled just on the border of Ridgeway, where he reared his family, and died in 1881. He was a large farmer and for a long time magistrate, and was generally known as Esquire Jones. His official acts were generally legal, and popular in his district. Nancy Jones married Robert Anderson. Issue: King, Charles, Seward, Betsy Ann. Jane Jones married John Ziggler. Issue: Charles, Eliza, and Mary. Betsy Jones married Sill Webb, no issue.

Polly Jones married William Dalton, of Rockingham, N. C., and their children were as follows: William; Robert who died early in life; John who died in the Confederate Army; Rufus who was killed in the same conflict; Lou who married Robt. P. Price; Susan married Larkin DeShazo: Jane married Sheriff Walker Smith; Mary married Valentine Hylton; Sarah married Edd Foster; Puss married Francis Stone; Elizabeth married Edward Matthews; Charlotte married Dave Matthews; and Walter.

SECOND GENERATION

Of the children of Charles, and Polly Jones his wife, we record as follows: Benjamin Seward Jones was born Oct. 8, 1828, married first Mary DeShazo, daughter of Geo. K. DeShazo, and lived the life of a very successful farmer near Ridgeway, where he reared a large family by the aid of his second wife, Nannie Price, who was a model step-mother. Their children, of the first union, were as follows: Sallie, Ann, George King, Nathaniel L., William B., Lelia, Mary Bennie, Henrietta, and Robert L. He died in 1917.

John C. Jones was born Dec. 6., 1830, married Ann Coan of South Carolina, and settled in Ridgeway where he was a farmer, and Supervisor for a long term of years. He was the first postmaster of Ridgeway when it was established in 1850, and after that he was in the mercantile business with Smith, and Hairston in the Brick Store this firm built. He died in 1919. Their children were: Anna, Mollie, John William, Estelle, and Charlie Coan.

Mary Ann Jones was born June 6, 1837, married

John O. Coan of South Carolina who did a mercantile business at Ridgeway besides that of a farmer. He was a popular teacher, but later in life was several times elected Mayor of Ridgeway, in fact, was the first one when the town was incorporated. He died in 1909. The children of this union were: Bettie, Loula, George William, Posey, Bird, and John O., Jr.

George Osborne Jones was born May 27, 1846. (See Biog. Chapter.) He married Mary Churchill, and died in 1922. Their children were: Annie S., George Byron, John Brengle, Thomas King, James Benjamin, Mary Churchill, Daisy, Gertrude, and Paul who died in infancy.

THIRD GENERATION

Of the children of Benj. S. Jones we record the following: Sallie Jones married William H. Norman; Ann Jones married Robert Hall of Reidsville, N. C.; George King Jones never married. He was a fine business man traveling in Georgia in the interest of Geo. O. Jones, Tobacco Factory products, and made these brands popular and very renumerative. He accumulated a large estate, and developed typhoid fever and died in 1889.

Nathaniel Jones married Anna Perry, daughter of M. F. Perry, of N. C.; Lelia Garrett married Thos. J. Garrett of Rockingham county, N. C.; Mary Bennie Jones married Hylton C. Clanton of Spencer, Va.; William B. Jones married Bettie Rachael Garrett. He was a popular merchant at Ridgeway for years where he died in 1899. Issue of this union were: Dr. W. Clyde Jones of Salem, Va.; Mayor Ben S. Jones, of Leaksville, N. C.; Thomas G. Jones, Do.; Mrs. T. D. DeShazo; Mrs. Jesse Hall, of Mebane, N. C.; Mrs. Alphis Jones, of the Valley of Virginia.

Henrietta Jones married George W. DeShazo, of Rockingham county, N. C.; Robert L. Jones married Bettie Meadows.

Of the children of John C. Jones we note as follows: Anna Jones married William D. Mitchell of Franklin county; Mollie Jones married Dr. Dorsey B. Downey of Frederick Md. He was a popular physician at Norfolk, where he died, in 1920, leaving two children, Elizabeth, and Mary Dorsey.

John William Jones married Loula Grogan, of Rockingham county, N. C.; Estelle Jones never married;

Charlie Coan Jones married Bessie Strother, of Culpeper county, Va. He was a good business man at Ridgeway where he spent his life. He was accidentally killed by a car while on the way to the cemetery in the funeral procession with the remains of his brother-in-law, Dr. Downey. His only child was an infant, John C. Jones.

Of the children of Mary Ann Jones and Capt. John O. Coan we record: Bettie Coan married Leonard Sheffield; Loula Coan married Mayor A. H. Bousman of Ridgeway; George William Coan married Loula Brown, of Franklin county, Va.; Posey D. Coan, married J. J. Coxe, of Tenn.; Bird Coan, not married; John O. Coan Jr. married Mary Montague, of Winston-Salem, N. C.

The children of George O. Jones and Mary Churchill are: Annie S. Jones married Dr. J. B. DeShazo; George Byron Jones, a cashier of the Bank of Ridgeway, never married; Thomas King Jones, merchant of Ridgeway, married Ethel Grogan, of N. C.; James Benjamin Jones married Lina Griggs; Mary Churchill Jones married William J. Mitchell, a merchant of Ridgeway; Daisy King Jones married Dr. Andrew F. Tuttle, of Spray, N. C.; Gertrude Jones married C. S. Oakley.

KOGER FAMILY

From 1725 to 1775 there came to Pennsylvania alone from Germany 30,000 to find new homes. Four brothers came and founded the Koger family in America. Jacob came by way of Philadelphia in 1728; Nicholas came later and reached the same city in 1732; Joseph came by way of Charleston S. C., in 1734; Peter came into Philadelphia, in 1738; and a younger brother came when a child, with Jacob, but unfortunately lost its life by climbing a pear-tree. A dead limb caught its clothing in such a way as to suspend it till life was extinct.

The brothers first tarried in Pennsylvania after taking the oath all immigrants took: "We subscribers, natives and late inhabitants of the Palatinate upon the Rhine and places adjacent, having transported ourselves and families into this province of Pennsylvania, a colony subject of Great Britain, in hopes and expectation of finding a retreat and peaceable settlement, to which therein do solemnly promise to his Majesty, King George the Second and his successors, kings of Great Britain, and, will be faithful to the proprietor of this province and that we will demean ourselves peaceably to all his Majesty's subjects and strictly observe and conform to the laws of England and this Province to the utmost of our power and best understanding."

Jacob Koger married Lucinda Crumb about 1737, and their children were as follows: Michael, Henry who was born in 1742, Peter, Nicholas, Joseph, and Mary. The latter married Dr. Stone and is lost to history.

He soon moved from Pennsylvania, but was prosecuted in that State for driving hogs on the Sabbath, according to the family tradition. Next he is located in Augusta county Virginia, accumulating property, or else he could not have given his son Michael 455 acres in that county on the Shenandoah river.

By 1762 he was 20 miles west of Martinsville on his new home ground. This land was hilly and especially adapted to tobacco. He built his house over a spring so as to get water without being exposed to the Indians. One of his children while just a baby, was drowned in this spring.

He dreamed one night three times in succession that the Indians came and killed his children, so he got his family up and took them to a neighboring hill and spent the remainder of the night. Next morning he found his house had been plundered and a fine horse gone. He paid a thousand acres of land for this animal. Fortunately it escaped from the Indians in Floyd, and was returned.

A fort was built three miles below his home and here his family took refuge during savage raids. Wild animals were plentiful in these pioneer days. He often killed 4,000 pounds of bear meat and with other small game supplied his family with meat, as it was impossible to raise hogs on account of depredations of the wild beasts of the forests.

He was too old to be in the Revolutionary army, but his son Jacob was. He had been constable and here are some of the returns he made: "Not executed on account of an axe, Williams vs. Bulger, John Lewis D. S."

"May 1753, Williams vs. Bulger, not excuted by reason of a gun, J. Lewis D. S."

"Nov. 1756, not executed by reason of the defendant outrode me so I could not catch him, Sampson Mathews, D. S."

"Feb. 1763, Reed vs. Clendenning not executed by reason of the heathen Indians ranging so I could not get there, William Brewer, D. S."

It should be recorded that he worked for a very strong man, who paid his way to this country. He could lift 5 bushels of wheat at once. On one occasion a man living entirely out of Harnom's vicinity, took offence at something and came to fight it out with him, and in Koger's presence Harnom's took the enraged man up with one hand and threw him over the garden fence.

One of his contracts shows the relative price of corn and currency in Virginia at this period in the Revolutionary times of 1779; "Know all men by these presents, That I, Susannah Reynolds, of the county of Henry, am held and firmly bound to Jacob Koger of the county aforesaid, in the just and full sum of one thousand pounds Virginia Currency. I bind myself, my heirs, executors, and administrators jointly and severally by these presents, sealed with my seal and dated this date Anne Domini 1779.

The consideration of the above obligation is such that if the above bound Susannah Reynolds does well and truly pays or causes to be paid unto the above named Jacob Koger, his heirs or assigns, thirty barrels of good merchantable corn delivered at the said Koger's dwelling house on or before the 25th, of December next ensuing the date hereof then the above obligation is void. Otherwise to remain in full force and power. Signed sealed and delivered in presence of _____Seal."

In 1782, fifty-four years after coming to this country, he gave his son Henry the tract of land where he lived, being a certain parcel of land lying on both sides of Stone creek. It was here as a farmer, mechanic and machinist, he had spent so many years of a very active and useful life. He died the following June the 13th, 1783.

SECOND GENERATION

Henry Koger was born in 1742, and married twice, but no issue by the first wife. His second wife was Mary King, sister of John King, a Revolutionary soldier, and this marriage must have occured about 1780 or 90, if she and her brother were about the same age. Issue: John, Catherine, Betsy, Polly, Sallie, Joseph, Henry, Abraham, Jacob, and Billy.

Jacob Koger married a Philpott; Billy married an Anglin; Abraham married a Luttrell; Betsy married a Slaughter; Sallie married a Philpott; and all the above went West

Henry Koger was a builder among the wilds of the forest, and to rid the woods of bears he burned the woods every spring. He was energetic and thrifty and accumulated every kind of property. He owned a grist mill, a powder mill, a cotton gin, and a distillery. He also kept a tavern every Patrick Court, carrying everything needed for the term from home. His wife was a great help-mate and milked 8 cows made cheese and had much milk and butter to sell above home needs. By their joint efforts they accumulated much land and gave each boy a home and each girl the equivalent in negroes and money. His wife survived him and had a plenty for her days and the property left her increased very much in value. He died in 18—.

THIRD GENERATION

John Koger, the son of Henry and Mary King, his wife, was born about 179— and married Gillie C. Napier, daughter of Tarleton Napier, about 1819. Issue: Susan, Woodson, Bettie, Moses Marion, John Jr., Kittie, Emily, Gillie, Lute, Hill, Victoria, and George.

Joseph Koger, brother of the above, married in 182— a Miss Slaughter. Issue: John S., called "John Bucket", who had triplets, two living, William who married an Ingram; Mary who married an Ingram; Joe Henry born in 1834 married Mary Turner; Daniel King, and James both killed in Civil War; Kittie born in 1845 married James Via and died in 1919

Henry Koger Jr., was born 1793, and married Lucinda Thomas, and died in 1868. Issue: Thomas who married a Webb; Middleton married Margarett Mills, served in Civil war, died 1912; Mary born in 1824 married William Corn; Perry married Emily Burgess; Lucinda was born 1832; Lee, and Edd were both killed in the Civil War; Susan md. a Shelton; Caroline b. 1836, d. unmarried; Emily, b. 1840, md. John Ziegler; Pink md. in 1868, Emma Ford.

Mary Koger dau. of Henry Koger and his wife Mary King Koger md. A. H. Bassett. Issue: Martha A., Woodson, John Harden, Eliza, and Mary C.

Katie Koger md. James Baker. Issue: Ruth md. J. P. H. Taylor, Lucinda md. Lodowick Craghead: Polly md. Mr. Via; John md. in Ga.; James md. twice, 1st, Miss Ingram, no issue; 2d wife, Fannie Kelley, issue one dau., Minnie.

Leftrage Baker had a son William by his 1st, marrige, 2d wife, Dolly Burgess. Issue: Lucy, Henry Clay, Daniel Webster.

FOURTH GENERATION

Moses Marion Koger, son of John and Gillie Koger, b. March 9, 1832, and md. Mary Catherine, dau. of W. W. Hill, b. Nov. 24, 1843. This marriage was in 1861. Issue: Kora Koma, b. March 4, 1862; Minor Botts, b. Jan. 17, 1865; Mary C. Koger, b. Dec. 17, 1866; Marion (called Carson), b. Feb. 27. 1867; Gillie N., b. April, 1871; Judith Koger, b. Nov. 15, 1875; Emma M., b. Jan. 21, 1878; Woodson Hill, b. Jan. 24, 1882.

Emma married John Lewis, of Ohio. Issue: Hilda. Woodson md. and has one son, Maurice Hodges. Minor Botts md. Virginia Morris. Issue: Geo. A, b. May 17, 1888; Wm. M. b. Oct. 24, 1890; Mary Annie b. Aug. 15, 1893; John M. Koger, b. May 28, 1895. Served thru World War and was in the Occupation forces left in Germany for a time; Kit Carson b. July 15, 1898; Kate O., b. Nov. 24, 1900; Bennie, b. May 7, 1903; Bland S., b. Aug. 21, 1905; Martha V., b. Oct. 8, 1909; Minor Botts, Jr., b. April 10, 1913. Mary C. Koger dau. of Moses Marion, md. James W. Matthews. Issue: Mary L., b. Dec. 7, 1888; Sadie E., b. Sept. 24, 1890; Robt. M.; Warren; Botts; Celia; Catherine.

Special record should be made of the following children of John Koger and Gillie Napier: Kittie Koger, b. 1838; Emly, b. 1840 Gillie C., b. 1842; Lute H., b. 1844; and Victoria, b. 1845, never married, but took care of their parents in their old age, and inherited their property. They are thrifty, of unquestionable integrity, and noted for their kindness to their neighbors and relatives not so fortunate as themselves. Gillie and Victoria attended the St. Louis Exposition to represent old-time industries as a part of the great show.

GEORGE KING FAMILY

George King, the pioneer, a first cousin of Rev. John King, was born in Brunswick county Virginia in 1730, married Mary Niblet and settled on Leatherwood creek, where he reared his family. He was a soldier in the Revolutionary War, and there is an old land grant on parchment made to him by an early Virginia governor still in the possession of his descendants of the fourth generation, Misses Terry of Nance Mountain.

His children were: Thomas, George W., Columbus, John, Jane born in 1775, Fannie, Thenie, Mary, Susan, Tabb, Mrs. Benj. Marshall, Mrs. Peyton Nance, Mrs. Jones, Mrs. Howchin, and Sallie who never married. He died in 1837 in Henry county Mo.

FIRST GENERATION

George W. King, the eldest son, was born in 1768 or 69, married Susan, the daughter of Gen. Joseph Martin, and saw much service under his father-in-law fighting Indians. He died on one of these expeditions out West. For this service the goverment was due him a bounty of land but he nor his children ever got a title to it. He accumulated much property and reared a large family. He died in 1838. Issue: Susan C., Lewis Graves, Elizabeth, Thomas H., Sallie, William E., and George W. Jr.

Thomas the next son, married Charity Stockton. He was a prominent farmer and delighted in hunting fox. In 1826 he was killed by his friend and neighbor Jack Hairston, over a frivolous affair. His faithful dog guarded his remains for two days before returning home, and led relatives to a large thornbush where the body had been secreted. Issue: Camillus, Columbus, Cephas, Martha, and Elizabeth.

John King, the youngest son, was born around 1774, Married Mary Love, of Pittsylvania county, settled on Leatherwood and reared a large family and accumulated much property. Issue: Thomas, George, William, John, Frances, Columbus, Jane or "Gincy", Sallie, and Jacob Love who was born in 1800.

Columbus King and his wife Susan's history are lost. He died in 1838.

Jane or "Gincy", King was born in 1775, married William DeShazo, the progenitor of the family in this county (See DeShazo Family), and died in 1864.

Fannie married James McCullock; Thenie and Susan married a Wills; Mary, "Polly" married Charles Jones

(See Charles Jones Family.); Tabby married John DeGraffenreid, no issue, and while a widow was killed by a negro for her money.

SECOND GENERATION

Of George W. King and Susan Martin's children we note: Susan King married Wesley Griggs. (See Griggs Family). Lewis Graves King, the eldest, son was born in 1819, married Eliabeth King born in 1825, and lived on Leatherwood. He was a Confederate soldier, being in the 42nd Va. Regiment, was wounded and died from the same at Ft. Monroe, Va. Issue: George W., Emeline, John M., who died early, and Lewis Graves Jr.

Neither Elizabeth, William, Nancy, or George King Married. Sallie King married Ira Griggs (See Griggs Family.) Thomas H. King was born in 1830, married Mary Jane Cahill in 1855. He was a prominent farmer, public spirited, and served the county as Sheriff. Children were: Susan Ann married Wingfield Byrd; John Lewis never married; Thomas Jesse King married Lily Cahill; Mary Jane married William Hundley; Anna married Thomas Stultz; Sallie Lou married G. H. Thomasson; and George Perry married Eliza Dove.

Thomas King's children were as follows:

Camillus King was born Nov. 24, 1811, married Sallie J. Hylton Sept. 17, 1838, and died __ov. 18, 1880. He was a successful farmer on his large estate on Horsepasture creek in this county where he reared the following children: Nannie H., Jeremiah C., and Thomas J.

Columbus King, the second son and nephew of Columbus Sr., was born April 5, 1805, married Maria Cahill who died June 28, 1832. Issue: a son, John. He married a second time, Sallie Stockton, Jan. 4, 1838. Issue: Susan E. who married George W. Hylton, and Sallie who married Jesse Clanton. He died in 1845, and his widow survived him many years.

Cephas King, the next son, settled in Henry county, Mo; Martha King was born about 1812, and married William Barrow (See Barrow Family.); Elizabeth King, the youngest married a Cabaniss.

We record the following of John King and Mary Love's children: Thomas King was born around 1790, married Mary Cahill who was born Nov. 9, 1804, and moved to Henry county, Mo., where he reared a family.

George King, married Mary Smith, a step daughter of Ballinger Wade, settled in Ky., and reared four children. A letter reported him in health there in 1842, in Christiana county.

William King, the third son, married a Stockton, and he, too, settled in Mo. He was a Baptist minister, visited this county in 1851, and died soon afterwards. He left issue.

John, (Jack) King married and reared a daughter, Helen, who married a Gravely. Issue: John King Gravely.

Columbus King was living at Marrowbone, Ky., in 1838 and had issue. Jacob King was born May 3, 1800, married Jane Thornton Dec. 16, 1824, and died in 1842. He was a prominent farmer, business man, and lived on Leatherwood. Of the issue; a daughter, Louisa, died at 17, Susan at 8, James R., Isaac and their mother died in a few days of each other of measles. Mary Elizabeth alone survived of the family.

Jane King married Daniel Pace (See Pace Family); Frances King married John Finney (See Finney Family); Sallie King married William Cooper of Franklin county. Issue: Starling, William, and George.

THIRD GENERATION

Lewis Graves King's children were as follows: George W. King was a Confederate soldier, born in 1845, and fell a victim to disease and died in middle life; John M. King his brother died in early manhood; Emaline King, the only daughter, married Jerre W. Griggs, and settled at Ridgeway where both died and were buried. Issue: George K.

Lewis Graves King, Jr., married Lucy K. Gibboney, of Wytheville, Va. Issue: Lucy Elizabeth, and Estelle G.

Of the children of Camillus King, we note as follows: Thomas J. King was born in 1839, married Alice Martin Dec. 7, 1876, and died Mar. 31, 1908. He was a prominent farmer on Horsepasture creek. He was public spirited, and elected several times Commissioner of the Revenue for Henry county. Their children were as follows: Thomas J. King of Roanoke, married Gertrude Shipman Clare; Minnie King married Horace A. Bass of Roanoke; Charles R. King married Mary Cromer; and Annie King married Samuel L. Byerly of N. C.

Nannie H. King, the only daughter, married Jesse R. Clanton in 1861. (See Clanton Fam.).

Jeremiah C. King, the second son, was born Sept. 25, 1845, married Eliza Rangely in 1870. He was a large and prosperous farmer on Horsepasture where he reared the following children: John C. King, M. D., of St. Albans Hospital, Radford, Va., married Fannie Price; Clare L. King of the First National Bank of Pearisburg, Va., married Katherine Oglesby; Nannie King married John W. Price, a merchant at Price, N. C.; T. B. King, Vice-President and Cashier of Marion National Bank, married Margarett Painter; Sallie R. King married J. D. Miller, a merchant of Newport News, and died in 1921; Mamie King married Charles H. Price, merchant of Leaksville, N. C.; Gertrude C. King married W. H. Wheelwright of the Federal Reserve Bank of Richmond, Va.; and Helen King married Dr. Harvey V. Price, a dentist of Martinsville, Va.

Columbus King's only heir by first wife, John C., will be recorded:

John C. King was born in 1831, married Abba Farmer of Mo. where he settled and reared the following issue: Columbus, Willie, Richard, Herbert, Theodore, Mollie, Mattie, Myrtle, Sallie and Pearl.

Of his, Columbus's, children by his second wife we record as follows: Susan E. King married George W. Hylton; Sallie King married Jesse Clanton (See Clanton Family).

Of Jacob King's issue, an only daughter, Mary E., survived. We note here: Mary Elizabeth King was born Aug. 3, 1828, married Maj. William Parker Terry, a great grandson of Sir William Parker, Admiral of the British Navy, died in 1869. Their children were: William, Benjamin, Lou, Jacob, Annie Scales, Mary, Edward Starling, James N., Corinne died from an accident when a child, and Thornton. The latter was born in 1865, a most distinguished youth, and a graduate of the Virginia Military Institute with special honors, but died in 1894.

WILLIAM KING FAMILY

William King was a brother of George King the pioneer, and lived in several places during his life but died in this county in 1798 as evidenced by the inventory of his estate in the Henry County Clerk's office. Issue two children John, and Mary.

FIRST GENERATION

John King was a soldier in the Revolutionary War, and gave the bounty given him by the Government to a nephew, but the latter never gained the title to the land.

Mary King, the only daughter, married Henry Koger and reared a family in the western part of the county (See Koger Family).

THE KING FAMILIES

From an Irish King who lost his throne before Surnames became general many centuries ago, the King family claim descent. This family is found at all times from the earliest Virginia settlements, and has spread over many states.

The Henry county families came through the Stafford and Prince William county progenitor, William King and his wife, Judith Peyton. Saunders King of Brunswick county is closer down the line of the families of this county that begin with two Kings, George, and Rev. John, who were cousins. The two branches will be considered separately.

REV. JOHN KING FAMILY

Rev. John King was born in 1758 and married Mary Seward, both of Brunswick county Virginia. He came to the county around 1780, settled, and preached at Leatherwood about 40 years, and died in 1821. He was known as the one-legged preacher, having lost one in early life.

Semple's History says of him, "Few men open their mouths in the pulpit to more purpose than Mr. King. His language is strong, his ideas clear, his countenance grave and solemn. Though modest and unassuming out of the pulpit, when he ascends the stand, he speaks as one having authority. The children of this union were: Benjamin S., John, and Joseph Seward.

FIRST GENERATION

Benjamin Seward King, the eldest son, was born about 1785. He was a member of the Legislature of Virginia, the House of Delegates, the session of 1817-18.

John, called "Jack', King was born Jan. 11, 1788, married Polly Wills Jan. 18, 1810. He settled near his parents on Leatherwood, accumulated property and reared a large family. He, like his brother, represented this county in the House of Delegates of Virginia in 1842-43, but was defeated in the following election by Elkanah Turner a Whig. He died Nov. 13, 1862, and his wife in 1874. Issue: Benjamin S., John O., Joe, Dolly, Ann, and Elizabeth.

Joseph Seward King, the other son of Rev. John, was born about 1794, settled on Leatherwood, married first, Sallie Clanton. Issue: Martha, Betsy, Susan, and John Seward. He married a second time, Mary Lester. Issue: Jesse, Benjamin S., William, Joseph Bouldin, John Tyler, and Doctor Franklin. It is worthy of special note that of these sons Jesse O., William, and Benjamin Seward, were killed in the Civil War in which the seven sons were distinguished in the line of unshirked duty.

He, too like his two brothers, represented Henry county in the House of Delegates of Virginia, and died while his last children were very small in 1853.

SECOND GENERATION

We note the following children of John, "Jack", King:

Ann King was born in 1810, married George King Jones (See Jones Family).

Dolly King was born in 1820, married James Trent. Issue: William, John Tyler, King. Benjamin, George W., Mary V., Marthy, and Roxy.

Eliabeth King was born in 1825, married Lewis Graves King in 1841, and they reared four children: George W., Emmerline E., John M., and Lewis Graves Jr.

Benjamin Seward King was born in this county in 1812, married Mary Jones, of the Ambrose Jefferson Jones family, and they reared the following children: George Shelton, William, John, Benjamin S. Jr., Ruth, Sallie, and Bettie.

John O. King was born in 1834, married Roxy Alexander, of Charlotte, N. C., issue: Joseph. He married a second time, Miss Booker, Joseph B. King was born in 1837, never married, but was a Confederate soldier in the 10th Virginia Cavalry, and died at the Soldiers Home in Richmond, Va.

Of the children of Joseph Seward King we record as follows: Martha King was born about 1820, married Daniel Taylor (See Taylor Family); Betsy King married Joseph Bason. No issue; Susan King married John Francis Gregory. (See Gregory Family.); John Seward King married Sallie Ivie. Issue three chilren; viz, Joseph W. King married Roxy Stultz; Elizabeth King married George Penny, of Ga.; and Mary Lodosky King married D. M. Moore.

William King, of the second wife's children, married Maggie Morris, of S. C., and reared a son, Herman. He was killed in the Civil War.

Captain Jesse O. King never married. He was one of the bravest of the brave soldiers in the Confederate Army, and died for his country.

Joseph Bouldin King was born in 1840, married Mary Henrietta Critz, and after spending many years in this county late in life moved with his family to Leaksville, N. C., where he died in 1922.

He was a member of the 10th Virginia Cavalry and was a gallant soldier of the South four years. After this career, he settled on Matrimony creek and became a prominent planter, miller, and influential citizen, noted for his quiet manners and sterling character.

The children of this union were: Nannie King Married A. H. Ould; Edward Burdett King; Jesse C. King (See Biog. Chap.); Berta King married Rufus P. Ray, a prominent merchant of Spray, N. C.; Frank King married Katie Milliner; Hattie died young. and William Brengle King married Elsie Smith, of Texas.

John Tyler King, a younger brother, married Eliza Whitlock. Issue: William King married Hattie Grogan; Frank King married Malissa Aaron; Herman King married Sallie Grogan; Robert L. King married Ida King; Mollie King married Willie Grogan; Mattie King Married Jack Stultz; and Joseph King married Alice Grogan.

Doctor Franklin King (See Biog. Chap.) was born in 1844, married Eliza Dyer and died in 1922. He was a Lieut. in the 42nd, Va. Regiment in the Confederate Army, and was a brave soldier, serving the whole period of strife. Afterwards was a highly successful business man at Leaksville, where he died distinguished for uprightness and Christian career.

Children of this union were: Irene King married Jesse Ben Taylor, a prominent business man of Leaksville. Issue: a daughter, Sunshine; Lottie King married Rev. S. J. Beeker. Issue: a daughter, Mabel; Daisie King married Hayes Barker, a capitalist of Leaksville; Myrtle King married J. Platt Turner, of Leaksville-Spray, N. C.; Mary Lily King married Lester A. Martin of N. C; Frank King married Anna Adelle Neal, of Reidsville, N. C.

THIRD GENERATION

The children of Benjamin King, Sr. will be noted:

William E. King was born in 1844, married Eliza Matthews in 1866, and died in 1876. He lived near Ridgeway and reared the following children: Edgar King married Lelia Seamore; Earnest King married Laura L. Robertson; and Annie Adelle King married first M. Thrasher, and the second marriage was to Jesse Carter, of Stoneville, N. C.

George Shelton King was born in 1846 married Eliza Jane (Mitt) Matthews. Issue: Bulah, Sarah E., Anna, James, George, Caleb, Charlie, and Frank. (See Matthews Family).

Benjamin King, Jr., was born in 1850, married Laura Smith in 1872. He lived in Patrick county most of his life, but died in Danville, Va., in 1918. Issue: Minnie King, of Danville; George King married Dorothey Bondurant, settled at South Boston; Mary Edna married W. B. Hundley, a merchant of Draper, N. C.; Caleb King of Pensacola Fla, manager for years for the Associated Press, married Harriett Bondurant; Annie Ruth King married F. I. Dovell of Virginia, later of Lake City South Carolina, where he practiced law.

The issue of Elizabeth King, who married her cousin Lewis Graves King, a son of George W. King, will be recorded next:

George W. and John M. died. Emaline King married Jere W. Griggs and they left one son, George K. Griggs; Lewis Graves King Jr. married Lucy K. Gibbony, of Wytheville, Va., and reared two daughters, Lucy E., and Estelle G.

LAVINDER FAMILY

After the revocation of the Edict of Nantes, which occurred in 1685, owing to persecution on account of religious views, great numbers came to America, some historians say 30,000. In 1700, five hundred came to Virginia at one time. They landed at Norfolk and Yorktown, therefore it is easily understood why a good colony was located at Manakan Town near Richmond.

They were industrious, clannish, honest and as a rule names show "de" in French means of the (royal) house. The change to beginning their names with a capital resulted after they learned English forms of writing family names.

They were idustrious, clannish, honest, and as a rule too liberal to amass great fortunes, distinguished for hospitality, and every one a model of politeness, and many brilliant in writing and oratory.

Philosophic students of history say that France has never recovered from the loss of the Hugenots, who took from that country the very best part of its citizenship. With such an inherited type in a virgin country, it is no wonder that to-day nearly every prominent old family in the State is connected in blood with some of the Hugenots.

Among these families we note:

The Lavinder Family.

de La Vinder in France in 1572.

Lavinder and Lavender in England and America today.

In Normandy a province of France, before and until the St. Batholomew massacre of Huguenots in Paris on the nights of 23 and 24 of Aug. 1572, lived a family of nobles who bore the name of de La Vinder, the male members of which were a father and four sons.

Owing to treacherous intrigue on the part of Catherine de Medicis (queen Regent), widow of King Henry II of France (wife of one king and mother of three), the nobles of the surrounding provinces who professed the Protestant faith, were invited (for the purpose of being massacred) to be present at the Royal feast in celebration of the marriage of Margaret de Valois to Henry of Navarre, later King Henry IV of France and Navarre. Margaret de Valois was the daugther of Catherine de Medicis and sister of Charles IX, then King of France under his mother's tutelage. Charles, at the instigation of his mother, actually took part in the massacre, hurling weapons from his window upon the unfortunate victims on the streets below.

Among the Protestant nobles enticed from home, this momentous day where the De La Vinders, who escaped, two brothers with their father to England, another to Belgium, while another emigrated with other Huguenots to America, one settling in South Carolina where the family still write their names with a capital "V" although they have long ago dropped the "de".

The two brothers in England, Richard and William, married and settled in the counties of Bedford and Hertford. Richard was the eldest and, of course, used the paternal Coat of Arms in France before 1572, and granted in England by William Delthick in 1580. The Coat was granted by Sir William Segar to Nathaniel Lavinder in 1628, likewise the crest which was a demi-horse rampant colored with a garland of the flower lavender. The Coat was "Per fesse Gules", and or a pole and three buckles of the second tongues pendant—Motto: Dieu defend le droit—"God defend the Right."

Richard Lavinder, of Felmersham in Bedford County, married Anne, daughter of Risley of Risley. Issue: Richard, of Bedford, John, of Stewsbury, Thomas, of London who married Margarett daughter of Ambrose Salisbury of Ravernston, Richard, Annie, who married Henry Jay.

The children of Thomas and wife Margarett were as follows: Thomas, born in 1630, Elizabeth, Margarett, Mary, Sarah, John, and Anne who married Samuel Ball, a relative of Geo. Washington's mother.

William, of Standon married Judith, the daughter of John Jenks, of London, and their children were as follows: Nathaniel who married Judith daughter of Thomas Tyler of London, Hester, who married Humphrey Browne, of London, and Sarah, who married Henry Westere of London.

The grandchildren of William, and Judith of Standon, and children of Nathaniel, above noted, were Nathaniel born in 1632, and Elias who married Ellen, daughter of Henry Bennett, of London.

The Lavinder family of Virginia are direct descendants of Richard and William, two of the Lavinders, brothers, who came to America after the close of the

Revolutionary war. They were wealthy and cultured and set about to ameliorate the then existing rural conditions.

Thomas, settled in Roanoke County and constructed the first iron works foundry, in that part of the State. The rest of his life was spent defending the interest of the people in warfare with the Indians, etc., and his descendants include many F. F. V's. The old site of his foundry is pointed out to strangers to this day.

John Lavinder settled in Franklin County and developed a large plantation. He spent much time uplifting the community, and was noted extensively for his kindness to his slaves. He built a chapel for them, and often preached to them. After the Gospel was spoken, each slave enjoyed the never-failing Sunday morning "dram of good old brandy served by Marse John's own hands".

Many of the family slaves clung to their "White Folks" all their lives. One who was a child at her master's death, still lives with the aged granddaughter of John, of England, Mrs. Margarett Alzira, Ford, of Martinsville, daughter of Jesse Lavinder.

John Lavinder of Franklin, married Mary Depity. Issue: Thornton, William, James, Joseph, Chilton, John, Mary, Frances, Nancy, Emily, and Jesse the youngest who survived the others.

Jesse md. Jane Hickey Davis, and died May 25, 1876, at the age of 85, after having lived with his wife 62 yrs. They lived happily together thru all these yrs., cherishing for each other a love that did not wane or grow cold, for even in their extreme old age they were just as attentive just as solicitous of the other's comfort and pleasure as most people are who are just beginning life together. Mrs. Lavinder lost all interest in life when he died and followed him in 6 weeks, dying July 5, 1876, at the age of 81.

They moved from Reed Creek to "Park Place" two miles south of Martinsville in 1874, where old Va. hospitality was never more truly meted out. Issue: Mary Letitia, John Peter, Sam Henry, Emma Jane, Margaret Alzira, and Jesse Ben.

Mary Letitia md. Mr. Hurd and moved to Mo.; Emma Jane md. Frank M. Wells March 14, 1867. Issue: Harry, who md. Cora Fleming; no issue; Jane Hickey md. Anthony Hundley and reared a large family.

Sam Henry Md. M. W. Hill (see sketch of M. W. Hamilton). Issue: two girls, Mary Catherine who died young, and Janie Hickey b. 1875, and now living.
Margaret Alzira b. Nov. 25, 1848, md. J. C. Ford, at Park Place, March 29, 1876 (See Ford Family).
Jesse Ben Lavinder b. Sept. 22, 1842, md. Alice Peters, dau. of Dr. Peters, a well known physician of the county, on Dec. 6, 1877, and reared 3 children as follows: Henry Geo., Mary Peters, and Alice Greyson.

Henry Geo. was educated at Randolph Macon and the University of Va. After graduating in law at the University he went into partnership with his uncle, the Hon. Herbert Peters, of Bristol. He md. M. Katherine Haynes, dau. of Judge Hal H. Haynes, of Bristol. Issue: Laura, Alice, and Katherine.

Mary Peters Lavinder md. Richard B. Semple; Greyson md. D. H. Pannill (See Pannill Family).

Jesse Ben Lavinder was a successful business man, distinguished for devotion to parents, family, and neighbors. He was the pioneer of modern Martinsville, and was made of the highest order of civilization. For his loving disposition, hundreds of children were named for him in the county (see Martinsville Methodist Church).

John Peter Lavinder md. 1st. Mary Louisa Jones, 2d., Miss Annie Fleming. No issue. He was owner of and builder of what is known as the Central Building, in Martinsville.

Joseph Hereford was Capt. of the Leatherwood Fencibles, and in his company were the bros., John Peter and Jesse Ben, who served through the war in the 42 Regiment. They were with Jackson at Chancellorsville. The reins of "Old Sorrel" were tossed to John Lavinder as Jackson was brought in mortally wounded. Only a few years before his death Mr. Lavinder paid a visit to the Old Soldiers' Home in Richmond, and there stood Old Sorrel, saddled and bridled just as he had last seen him when he turned him over to the stable boy at Chancellorsville. (See Martinsville Methodist Church).

MORRIS FAMILY

Samuel Coleman Morris was of Welch descent. After marrying a Miss Wade, he came from Goochland to Henry county about 1776. Issue: William, Ben, John, Joseph, Nancy, and Rebecca.

HISTORY OF HENRY COUNTY, VIRGINIA 217

SECOND GENERATION

William Morris married Tabitha Cheatham. Issue: William, Ben, Tabitha, Susan, Booker, Eliza, Patsy, and Eleanor.

Ben Morris married Nancy Haygood. Issue: William Wade, Gregory, Eliza, and Virginia.

John Morris, another brother, married Reamey Pharis. Issue: William, James Madison, John Wesley, Dandridge Wade, Logan.

Joseph Morris, the fourth son of the senior Morris, is unaccounted for; Nancy Morris, a sister of the above, married a Brewer; Rebecca Morris, the other sister, married a Bradley.

FIRST GENERATION

Of Cap. William and Tabitha's children: Ben Morris was a successful business man, of Alabama. He was a Colonel of the Confederacy, and prominent in the State of his adoption, and where he married.

William Morris, another brother, died in the Civil War unmarried; Tabitha Morris, married Andrew Jackson Smith. Issue James R. Smith, J. T. Smith, Susan who married Howard Owens, and Janette who married Shadrack Washburn; Susan and Eliza, two other sisters, never married.

Booker Morris married a Miss Finney. Patsy Morris married Daniel Price. Issue: two sons, Sam and Marion. Eleanor Morris, who married Joseph Cheatham. Number of children —. All moved to Miss.

Of Ben and Nancy Haygood's children we record the following: William Wade (See Biography Chapter) married M. E. Schoolfield. Issue: Ben married Lulu Hyatt and died without issue; William married; Addison married in Oklahoma, and has two children, Helen, and Jennie; Annie married a Smith. Issue: Emily, Martha, and Vincent Smith. By her second marriage to a Graham, no issue; Virginia married Minor Botts Koger.

Of the issue of John and Reamey Pharis Morris we note as follows: William F. Morris never married; James Wesley Morris married Elizabeth Mitchell. No issue; Dandridge Wade Morris married Ann Waller. No issue; James Madison Morris married Mary Hill, daughter of

Thomas S. Hill, the Rev. John C. Traylor officiated, Dec. 20, 1834. He was born 1811, and his wife in 1820. Issue: Ann Eliza, Mary A., John T., William W., Samuel A., James M., Robert S., David H., Sarah E., Walter C., and Virginia Dare.

FOURTH GENERATION

Ann Eliza Morris daughter of James Madison, married John Hill Matthews. No issue.

Richard Hairston Morris, was born Feb. 4, 1852, married Emma Lou Coleman 1874, died in 1912. Issue; Maggie, Ellen Morton, Emma Hairston, James Harrison, Dewy and Grace.

Virginia Dare Morris was born in 1861, daughter of James Madison, and Mary Hill Morris, married B. D. Grogan in 1878. Their childern were Lillian, William D., Mary L., Virginia B. Robt. P., Ollie B., Emmett M., Ernest V., Jennie L.

John T. Morris, a brother of the above, married a Miss Miles. Issue: Hairston, William, Thomas, and Edgar.

Robert Sanders Morris, another brother, married Mary Campbell Mason. Issue: Samuel Madison, Martha Louisa, Thomas Hill, Robert Ernest, Ann Eliza, Bessie Haymaker, and Henry Sanders.

Samueel Anderson Morris Md. N. E. Forbes. Issue: Melissa, Mary Emma, Georgie M., John Wm., Kellie Reed, Mattie, Rosa P. md. Sam Hill, Brooksie, Edgar.

FIFTH GENERATION

Samuel Madison Morris md. Miss Philpott. Issue: Martha Louisa, John Thomas Hill, Henry Sanders, and Bernard.

John Thomas Hill Morris, b. Feb. 14, 1874, md. Feb. 23, 1898, Annie Lou Vaughn, b. Feb. 17, 1880. Issue: Robt. Vaughn, Geo. Emerson, Mary Evelyn, Katherine Leak, and Thomas Hill.

Ann Eliza Morris, b. Dec. 6, 1878, md. James R. Wray; Robt. Ernest Morris, b. July 20, 1877, md. Dec. 25, 1902, Ruth Dillard Donevant, b. March 10, 1886.

Bessie Haymaker Morris, b. May 11, 1882 md. C. M. Stone, b. Oct. 15, 1877.

Henry Sanders Morris, b. Feb. 23, 1886, md. Nannie Elizabeth Craig, b. Aug. 23, 1882.

James Walter Morris, b. Aug. 17, 1879, md. Sallie Elizabeth Bouldin, Feb. 6, 1901. She was b. March 26 1882. Hairston Morris md. Daisy Reamey, and died early. He was a popular merchant in Martinsville till his health gave down. Thomas Morris md. 1st., Helen Dillard, 2d. Miss Smithson. William Morris married Virginia Wells, and raised a family of worthy girls and boys. Edgar died when a small boy.

Annie Elizabeth Morris md. Pinckney Cox. Pocahontas md. Elijah Richard Nelson, Mamie J. Morris md. Robt. B. Winn. Lucy Matt Morris md. Jesse Thomas Byrd. Ellen Morton Morris md. John Wm. Wingfield. Maggie Morris md. Watt Wade Smith. Grace Forest Morris md. Harry Dillard Smith. Emma Hairston Morris md. John Harrison Frye.

MITCHELL FAMILY.

Two families of Mitchells are recorded in Henry county, both beginning with the name of William.

William Mitchell, a cousin of the other of Henry, was born near the line between this and Franklin county, and married Mary Bondurant, of the latter county, and they peared the following family: Benjamin Franklin, Thomas Bondurant, William J., Eliza, Sarah, and Edwin who died young.

SECOND GENERATION

Thomas B. Mitchell was born in 1829, married Katherine Price, of Ridgeway, and died in 1916.

He was a member of the 10th. Virginia Cavalry, and fought through the War Between the States, surrendering near Appomattox, returned and resumed the life of a successful farmer, and reared the following children: William D., Anna, Belva, and Edwin. The latter died in early life.

Benjamin Franklin Mitchell, married Nannie Abingdon, and lived near Mt. Bethel church. Issue: Bettie and Virginia died in infancy; Annie md. a Cannaday; Ella md. Edward Craig; and Richard married a Miss Shumate.

William, called "Buck", Mitchell married Mary Price, daughter of Maj. John Price, of Ridgeway, Va., and reared the following children: William, Fletcher, Robert, Mollie (married a Hines), Laura, and Kettie.

Eliza Mitchell married James W. Trent, and moved to Strawberry Plains Tenn., and reared three children: William, Charlie, and Mollie.

Sarah Mitchell married, Robert Trent, a brother of the above, and settled with the latter in Tenn., and reared two daughters.

THIRD GENERATION

William D. Mitchell married Anna Jones, daughter of John C. Jones, of Ridgeway, where he finally settled and was in the mercantile business for many years. He married a second time, Mrs. Jennie McKiver. Issue by the first union as follows: William J., and Bessie.

Anna Mitchell, married James P. Garrett, of Ridgeway, Va., and there the following children were born: Alma, Kate, Paul, Annie May, Peter G., Rachael, William, and Ruth.

Belva Mitchell married Jeff Sparrow, of Martinsville, and died in young womanhood, leaving two daughters: Kathleen, and Rose. The former married Alex Mahood, Rose died with typhoid fever.

William Mitchell, of Mt. Bethel section of Henry county was born in the early twenties, married Lucy Trotter, and reared the following children: Joseph T., Edward R., and Elizabeth. He married a second time, Annie Haygood. Issue: Mary Frances, Sallie Ann, Wade, and George.

SECOND GENERATION

Joseph T. Mitchell married Frances Stovall and reared the following children: Willie and Jubal never married; Edd died in young manhood; Trotter died in infancy; Joseph married Mrs. Hurd, (Nee Loula Lester; Landis Married Mary Garrett, of N. C.; and Nannie married George D. Craig.

Edward R. Mitchell married Martha Schoolfield. No issue. He was a soldier in the War Between the States, took part in the Gettysburg battle, and spent some time in a Federal prison.

Elizabeth Mitchell married John W. Morris, and died without issue.

Of the second family, Mary Frances married Jack Dillon. Issue: Joe, married a Miss Blackwell and lives at the old home; Lizzie married Jesse Davis, no issue; and Annie died unmarried.

Sallie Ann Mitchell died unmarried; Wade died in the Civil War.

George Mitchell married Florence Stovall. Issue: Dora, Annie, and Elizabeth who mar. and settled in the South; Harry, the eldest married Maud Cahill; James married Brooksie Frye; Hughes married an Overton; and Wade married Miss Bouldin.

MATTHEWS FAMILY

Three brothers came from Wales, but Tandy Matthews was the only one that stopped near. He settled in North Carolina, near Germanton, born 1773, married Betsy Hill, and they reared the following children: Robert, William, James, Tandy, Caleb, Eliza, Patsy, and Calvin. He married a second time, Pink Coffer, and there was only one child; Marcella. He was the owner of 2,000 acres of land and 150 slaves. He died in 1855.

FIRST GENERATION

Robert Matthews the eldest of the family was born about 1797, married Mary Critz, and reared one child only; William. He also gave a home while his grandson John Hill Matthews, was finishing his education, to the latter, at Germanton, N. C., where they had a good High School.

William Matthews married Mary Staples, a sister of Col. Geo. Staples, of Spencer.

James Matthews was born in 1799, married Eliza Allen, daughter of Robert Alllen, and bought the old Allen home place near Ridgeway, "Lewiston", when the Allens moved to Mississippi in the thirties, nearly a century ago, and here he reared his family. (Dr. Brengle Place). Issue: Robert, Edward, Mary, William, Celia, David, Caleb, and Eliza Jane. Two died in infancy, and James when seven years of age fell from a rail fence and died instantly.

Tandy Matthews, Jr., and Eliza, never married.

Patsy married Col. Bitting, of North Carolina.

Caleb Matthews was a lawyer, and located at Germanton, N. C.

Calvin Matthews married Lucy Mullins, daughter of Henry Mullins of Henry county, and reared two children, John Hill, and Thomas Calvin. The latter died in early life, unmarried.

SECOND GENERATION

Of the children of James Matthews, and Eliza Allen we note as follows: Robert Matthews married Sarah Abingdon. Issue: James married Mollie Koger, Bettie and John neither married, Celia married William Marshall, William never married, and George md. Miss Purdy

Edward Matthews married Elizabeth Dalton. Their children were: Eliza who first married William King, 2nd, Hannibal Simpson; Mary married Thomas Seamore, of Virginia; Ginnie married a Heggie; Thomas married Sallie Adams, and was killed in the Civil War; William married Sallie Stuart; and Mary married a Dalton no issue.

William Matthews married Mrs. Antoinette Conrad. Issue: Sallie, and Frank. The latter never married.

David Matthews married Charlotte Dalton, of Stoneville N. C. Their chilren were: Robert who died; Caleb married Sarah Elizabeth (Trottie) King; Leonard Matthews married Elizabeth Price; John never married; Walter married Nannie Davenport.

Celia Matthews married Zachary Wall. Issue; James, Walter, Mollie, Nannie, Charlie, Granville, John, Hunter, Muncey and Cartrina.

Eliza Jane Matthews (Mitt) married George Shelton King of Patrick, county, in 1868. Their children were: Beulah married John Smith; Sarah Elizabeth married Caleb Matthews; Anna married Mat Holland; James King married Mattie Holland; George married Mamie Pulliam, of Kings, N. C.; Caleb married Fannie Hunter, of Kernersville, N. C.; Charles married Lily Pratt; Frank married Minnie Taylor, of Stoneville.

THIRD GENERATION

Sallie Matthews, the only daughter of William Matthews, and Mrs. Antoinette Conrad, married William Glenn, nephew of Gov. Glenn of N. C.

John Hill Matthews, son of Calvin Matthews and Lucy Mullins, was born on Meadow creek in Henry county, Dec. 7, 1837 (See Biography Chapter). He married, Annie, the daughter of James M. Morris; 2nd, Sallie Craghead, the daughter of Thomas and Lucinda Craghead, of Franklin; 3rd, Loula Shelton, daughter of Peter Shelton, of this county. Children of second union only were: Lucy Matthews married T. P. Parish of Smithfield, Va; Minnie Matthews married George Akers Brown, (See Brown Family); Annie Matthews married Dr. Rob. R. Lee, of Martinsville; Thomas Calvin Matthews, married Ida Coleman. He has been Circuit Court Clerk of Henry county many years.

MARTIN FAMILY

Wm. Martin, of Bristol, Eng. was a wealthy merchant, and sent his son Joseph on a trading expedition to America in the 18th Century. While here he met and married Susanna Childs, a dau. of a wealthy planter, and settled in Albemarle county. In 1760 he died and left a good estate to five sons and six daughters.

Two of his sons settled in Henry county. Brice purchased the farm on the south side of Smith's River, and Joseph, later General, purchased the north side, "Scuffle Hill". He moved to his plantation from Orange Co., 1773, where he had previously md. Sarah Lucas, who died in 1782, leaving him seven children; Viz: Susannah, b. 1763, md. Jacob Burrus, Mar. 13, 1781. He d. Oct. 1832. She d. at her brother William's, in Tenn., June 16, 1844.

William Martin, b. in Orange Co., Va., Nov. 26, 1765, d. in Tenn. Nov. 4, 1846. He went on expedition against the Indians with some of Wm. Campbell's men 1781, was in Powell's Valley 1785, and remained 2 years. He did much to aid the country in his day. He came back to Henry Co., md. Franky Farris, dau. of Jacob Farris, in 1791, went to S. C. He was a Jefferson elector 1804 and a Madison elector 1808, and was the Whig vice-presidet in convention 1844. He was in war 1812. He served against the Creeks and took command when Col. Pillow was wounded.

Elizabeth Martin, b. Oct. 13, 1768 d. on Leatherwood, Henry Co., Va., June 11, 1805; md. Carr Waller, son of Thos. Waller and Sarah Dabney, of Spottsylvania Co.

Brice Martin, Jr. b. 1770, d. Dec. 10, 1855, md. Matilda Perkins, of Tenn., 1811. He was promoted major at battle of New Orleans, and was in Creek war.

Polly Martin md. Daniel Hammock. He d. 1820. She was living 1840.

Martha Martin md. Wm. Cleveland, son of Ben Cleveland one of the heroes of King's Mountain.

Nancy Martin md. Archelaus Hughes, d. 1835.

Gen. Martin md. Susannah Graves, Feb. 24, 1784. She gave him 11 children as follows: Joseph Martin, known as Col. Joseph Martin, b. Sept. 23, 1785, md. April 30, 1810, Sally Hughes, b. April 27, 1810. He was a member of Va. legislature 1809, and of the Constitutional Convention, 1820-1830; a farmer by profession and d. at Leatherwood, Henry Co., Va., Nov. 3, 1850. He had 8 daughters and 4 sons.

Jesse Martin was in war of 1812, was a farmer, md. 1st, Annie Armistead, and had one son; 2d, Cecelia Read. Our townsman, Dr. J. M. Shackelford, is a great grandson of Jesse Martin, and is named for him.

Thomas W. Martin went to Tenn. and md. Miss Carr.

Lewis Martin went to Tenn., saw military service, d. in Lincoln Co., Mo., about 1850; md. Miss Rucker.

Alexander Martin d. in Mo. about 1850; md Miss Carr. 13th, child md. Miss Rucker,

Geo. Martin, better known as Major Geo. Martin, md. 1st., Miss Starling, 2d., Miss Watkins moved to N. C., d. about 1860. Sally Martin md. Rev. Samuel Armistead Feb. 7, 1807, d. 1813.

Susannah Martin (Gen. Martin adopted the Puritan custom of giving the same name to more than one child) md. Geo. King, She survived her husband, and left among her children, Capt. Thomas King, of Reed Creek.

Polly Martin md. Reuben Hughes, d. 1830.

Patrick Henry Martin, was taken to Tenn. by his half brother Brice, Jr., and educated by Wm. and Brice. He studied law and went to the bar at beginning of war 1812. Joined Jackson's army, d. unmarried, after returning from New Orleans, 1814.

SECOND GENERATION

Joseph Martin's children were: Sallie md. Obe Dillard; Matilda md. Dr. Geo. Hairston, of Marrowbone; Susan md. Cook; Ella md. Robertson; Ann md. John H. Dillard; Eliza md. Samuel Williams, of Wytheville, Va.; Jane md. McCabe; Col. Wm. md. Susan Hairston, dau. of "Old Rusty"; Archie and Sam never married; Tom md. Thenia Pannill, and was killed at Malvern Hill, 1862; Joseph md. Susan Pannill.

The father of this large family was a farmer and lived on his plantation in great luxury. His home (Greenwood) was the scene of many brillian social affairs for which Leatherwood in those days was celebrated. He died 1859.

THIRD GENERATION

Col. William Martin, of "Magna Vista", on Marrowbone creek, was one of Virginia's most gifted orators and but for a habit of his would in all probability have been Governor of the state. He was elected a member of the Legislature of Va., before he was 21. Some member of that body objected to his being seated on account of his youth, but his reply, an oration unlooked for, overwhelmed the opposition, and he became as a result, famous. He was later elected several times Commonwealth's Attorney for Henry County. He married Susan Hairston, and their issue was: Joseph and Samuel, who both died without issue; and Loula, who late in life married Sam. G. Sheffield; and Bettie Martin who married Dr. W. D. Brengle of Ridgeway. The latter are survived by two daughters, Maizie, and Bettie Martin.

Four generations of Joseph Martins were buried at "Belle Monte" on Leatherwood creek during the last century, and the male members in the county have about become extinct. However, the sons of Eliza inherited talent, and Judge Martin Williams was several times elected to the legislature from Giles county, and his brother Samuel Williams was elected Attorney General of the State.

MARSHALL FAMILY

The first of this family to settle in America was Thomas Marshall, whose will is on record in Westmoreland county, and dated May 21st 1704. His son William married Elizabeth Markham, and their son Thomas was a soldier in the Revolutionary war attaining the rank of Colonel and was the father of Chief Justice John, and another son, Sam.

Sam Marshall m. Cassandra Alfriend and moved from Mecklenburg county and settled in this county on the head waters of Leatherwood creek. Their Issue: Dennis, Lewis, John, Ben, Susan, Sally, and Nancy.

They spent the remainder of their lives at their home in Henry educating and establishing their children in life, and were buried nearby on the Wesley Griggs place west of Dyer's store.

SECOND GENERATION

Dennis Marshall was born in 1768 and died in 1843. He married Frances Harper, and to them were born ten children; viz, Sam, Benjamin, Alfriend, Lewis, Dennis, Polly, Sally, Frances, Cassandra, Nancy, and Patsy.

Lewis Marshall moved to Ky.

John Marshall never married. He had a store and a tobacco factory at Shady Grove in Franklin. He had as his partner his brother Ben.

Ben Marshall married Sallie Dugger, and their only child died.

Susan Marshall married William Barrow, (See Barrow Family).

Sallie married Elisha Arnold, and their children were: Sam, John, James, Elisha, Franklin, Nancy, Cynthia, and Lucy.

THIRD GENERATION

Sam Marshall the oldest son of Dennis Sr., never married. He worked tobacco on the north side of Nance mountain. He died of cholera in Baltimore, the year of 1834 or 5.

Lewis Marshall, the youngest son of Dennis Sr., married Mary Ann Nance, a half niece of his brother Ben's wife, moved to Mo., and their children were Hugh, Sam, Nancy, Giles, and Ben. He lived last near Hannibal.

Dennis Marshall, another son, died in infancy.

Benjamin Alfriend Marshall was born Nov. 13th, 1800, and educated by his father Dennis Sr., and married Nancy Nance, a daughter of Ruben Nance from whom Nance Mountain took its name. The latter married twice, and was the father of 22 children, two died in infancy. All were born between 1765 and 1809. Does he not deserve this landmark for a monument?

To Benjamin and Nancy, 5 sons and 11 daughters were born; viz, Mary B., born '22, Reuben D., '23, Nancy M. '25, Frances M. who married a Stultz and preserved these records, was born Oct. 22nd, 1827, Peyton S., Sarah L., Benj. A., Martha J., Susan B., Edmond S., Julia E., Abigail M., Cassandra A., Melissa L., William H., Eliza L., April 17th, 1846.

They moved from the county with all their family except two, Martha, and Frances. The latter married

HISTORY OF HENRY COUNTY, VIRGINIA   227

William David Stultz See Stultz Family). He died at Bear Creek, Cedar Co., Mo., Oct. 31st, 1833, his wife Mar. 31, 1865, at their far western home where they were both buried.

Polly Marshall married Dubartis Dempsey, and their children were: Sam, Marshall, Fletcher, William, Rufus, Mary, Hamala, and Ann Eliza.

Sallie Marshall married Charles M. Wingfield. Issue: Francis, Mary, Ann, Jane, Julia, Sally, Louisa, Walter, and William.

Frances Marshall married John Gravely in lower part of Henry, near Mt. Vernon church. He was a very successful business man. Their children were: Judy, Marshall, Jabe, Harriet, Sally, and John W.

Elizabeth Cassandra Marshall married William Clark in 1826, after his death, went to Texas. Their children were: Ann, Cassandra, Nat, Howell, Mary, and John.

Patsy Marshall married Ben Connoway, and they moved afterwards to Mo. Their children were: Dennis, Francis, Sally, and Martha.

Nancy Marshall, the last of the family died in infancy.

MULLINS FAMILY

The Mullins family trace their fathers to Ireland from the Duke of Connaught. One of the branches of the family is found in New England, and the other in Virginia. David Mullins who was born in 1760, was the first of the family in this State.

He married Susanna Herndon, and settled in this county. Their issue were: Celia, John, and Henry Green. He married a second time, and two were left of this union, Burwell and Nathaniel. He was a soldier in the Revolutionary War, and was with General Greene in hhis many campaigns. He named one of his sons in his honor.

SECOND GENERATION

Celia Mullins married Robert Allen, son of William Allen and Sarah Smith, and of their children, David Allen married Sallie Spencer and went to Miss.; Henry Allen died during the Civil War; and Eliza Allen married James Matthews.

John Mullins married in Fayette county, N. C., and became wealthy.

HISTORY OF HENRY COUNTY, VIRGINIA

Henry Green Mullins married Matilda Winston Hill, daughter of Samuel C. Hill of Henry. There were several children.

Burwell Mullins moved to Indiana.

Nathaniel Mullins married Nancy Watkins daughter of John Watkins.

Of the 8 children of Henry Green Mullins we note as follows:

Lucy Catherine Mullins was born in 1818, married in 1837 to Calvin Mathews, and he died leaving two children, John Hill, and Calvin. She married a second time, to Robert Walker, who died in 1857, leaving Susan Matilda, Alice who married a Dean, and another daughter who married a Nelson.

David Hill Mullins married Virginia Wood, of Troup county, Ga. He died in 1880, leaving 5 children, Anna, Henry Hill, Willie, Winston, and Jack.

Susan Mullins married Tandy Mathews, and after he died, she married Pink Hays who died in 1850.

Patrick Henry Mullins married Mary Wood, of Ga., and had two daughters, and a son who was a good business man and public spirited citizen.

Celia Mullins married Robert B. Traylor. Issue: Jno. H., and Matilda Traylor. Who married Mr. Wright. Another son was Hill Mullins Traylor who was killed at battle of Chancellorsville.

Samuel Jesse Mullins was born Nov. 22, 1831, and married Sarah Hay Athey, and their children were: Henry, Peter, and Sallie. After she died, he married Minnie Martin. Issue: Jesse, Alice, Hatttie, and James, besides other children who died in early life. He died in 1889.

"Con" Mullins, as he was known, was public spirited and patriotic. He was one of the first to organize a company and join the confederate army, but after some service with his company, as captain, he resigned to accept a seat in the legislature of Virginia. After the war was over, he became county Judge of Henry and held this office for years.

Elizabeth Matilda Mullins married John A. Hardie, of Halifax. Issue: Dr. Henry Hardie, and two daughters, Ella and Susan.

America Augusta Mullins was born in 1841, and married James Penn in 1860. Issue: Matilda who married

Mr. Chaney, and James who married Lilly Kirby; and of this union Hunter Penn became Clerk of Rockingham Co., N. C., Courts. The sister Gussie did not marry early.

FOURTH GENERATION

The children of Samuel Jesse Mullins are recorded in this order:

Henry Green Mullins the oldest, studied law, married Annie Whitten McCabe and located in Martinsville. Here he built up a good practice, and accumulated a snug fortune. For a long time he was president of peoples National Bank and looked after the financial affairs of this institution. He became Judge of the County Court of Henry and held this office for years. Children of this couple were: Sadie who married Richard Gravely; Nellie who married Dodson, an army officer; Marion, Henry, and Peter.

Dr. Peter Mullins graduated at the Medical College of Virginia, married, a daughter of Dr. Stiggleman of Floyd, Va., and was a successful practitioner of medicine at the several places he practiced. He died in 1923 leaving two children, Con, and Ellen.

Alice Mullins married Wm. Edwards. No issue. He died young.

Hattie Mullins married John Gravely. They lost their only child, Virginia.

James married ———. Issue: Preston Martin, and James Rosa.

NANCE FAMILY

(Reuben and Descendants)

The following list and data is copied from the Bible, which bears the notation in the front pages:

"This Bible is the property of Reuben Nance." Marriages.

Reuben Nance was married to his wife Nancy (Brown) this 3d day of February, 1786". (Reuben Nance was first married to Amy Williamson, whose death is not recorded in the Bible).

"Births":

Sally Nance was born 14th day of July, 1767; William Nance b. 24th day of Dec., 1768: Mary Nance b. May 30, 1770, Bud Nance b. July 24, 1772; Issac Nance b. Febuary 13, 1774; Allen Nance born January 18, 1776;

Joham Nance born November 18, 1777; John Nance b. May 24, 1779; Suhanna Nance b. Aug. 10, 1781; Tabitha Nance b. April 21, 1783; Reuben Nance b. July 8, 1785; Clement Nance b. Sept. 20, 1787; Joseph Nance b. Feb. 1790; Nancy Nance b. May 19, 1767 (wife) ; Sally Nance b. Nov. 2 1791; Stephen Nance b. June 11, 1793; Payton Nance b. Feb. 18, 1795; Edmund Nance b. Aug. 20, June 8, 1797; Sofronby Nance b. Aug. 20, 1801; Nancy Nance b. March 22, 1804; Ruben Nance b. May 28, 1808.

Deaths:

Reuben Nance d. Jan. 13, 1812; Nancy Nance d. Dec. 26, 1825.

Reuben Nance was b. evidently in what is now the section of Va., comprising Henry County in part in the year 1745.

Joseph Nance, b. Feb. 5, 1790, wife Polly Philpott, b. Sept. 17, 1788, md. Oct. 25, 1810. A son Barton Garrett Nance, b. Nov. 27, 1822, md. Lovicy S. Harrison (b. Feb. 4, 1820) Feb. 18, 1847. William E. (son of Barton G. Nance, b. Oct. 22, 1849) was the father of the contributor of this data—Emmett Warren Nance, of Peoria, Ill. the last named being the great-great grandson of Reuben Nance, the first known ancestral head of the Nance family in America.

NAPIER FAMILY

The Napier family were formerly Irish, but came from England to America. The first we note is Champion who was born about 1750 and lived in North Carolina and married the daughter of Gov. Martin of that state. He had several brothers and sisters; viz, John, James, Boothe, Tarleton, and Valentine. The latter never married, and was a soldier in the War of 1812. After that, he taught school in the county for a long period. He died during the Civil War.

Of the sisters there were: Nannie who died in 1863; Betsy married Jesse Estes, no issue; two Pollys, and Frances.

SECOND GENERATION

Robert Napier, a distinguished lawyer and son of Champion, was Superior Court Judge of Rockingham county, N. C.; Betsy Napier, a sister never married; another sister married a Wall; John died insane.

Tarleton Napier, a brother of Champion, married Susan Smith, of Franklin county, Virginia. They lived near Mt. Bethel church in Henry county. Issue: Gillie C. Napier married John Koger, son of Henry Koger and Mary King (See Koger Family for issue); Ruth Napier married George Terry; Betsy married John Mitchell; Frances, Ann, and Polly never married; Tom married Sinai Philpott; Moses md. a miss Poindexter; George Napier son of Tarleton, was born in 1810, and married Polly Finney, daughter of John Finney Sr., of Franklin county. He lived on Reed creek. Issue: Moses who died in Mo.; Betty Napier married William Davis and went to Indiana and died; Susan Napier married James Finney, a cousin, of Franklin county Va.; Mary Napier married R. T. DeShazo, (See DeShazos),2nd, J. C. King; George Napier, Jr., went South in 1875 and was lost to history.

Of the children of all the Napiers, Champion, son of Tom, is the last one of the name in the county. He married Mrs. Prilliman. No issue.

PENDLETON FAMILY

The Pendleton family descended from Henry Pendleton, of Norwich England, where two sons were born, Nathaniel and Philip. The former was a minister, and died without issue. Philip emigrated to New Kent, now Caroline county, Va., in 1674. He visited England in 1682, a second time, and married Isabella Hunt. He died in 1721. Issue: Elizabeth Rachel, Henry, Isobelle, John, Philip, and Edmund.

SECOND GENERATION

Elizabeth married Samuel Clayton, of Caroline. Issue: Philip.

Rachael married John Vass, and Caroline married John Taylor: No issue from either union.

Henry Pendleton married Mary Taylor, in 1711, and they were the parents of Edmund Pendleton, the Revolutionary patriot and eminent jurist.

Isabella Pendleton married Richard Thomas from these descended Gov. James Barbour, and Judge Philip P. Barbour, of Orange county, Va.

John Pendleton was born in 1691, married Miss Tinsley of Madison Co., and died in 1775. Issue: Benjamin, Isaac, and John who went to Ky.; Edmund unmarried;

Richard married his first cousin; Reuben married Ann Garland, of Amherst Co.; James married a Rucker; William not married; Polly married a Witten; Sarah married a Mahone; Frances married a Candem; Betty married a Baldock, and Margaret married a Miles.

THIRD GENERATION

Of the children of Richard Pendleton and Mary: Glen Alexander, we note:

Alexander Garland Pendleton married Selina Christiana Dickson. He was Prof. of Mathematics, Naval Officer, and connected with U. S. National Observatory.

Douglas pendleton was an engineer in the United States Navy.

Mary Pendleton married a Hightower. No issue.

Frances Pendleton married Dr. Robert A. Read of Spencer, Va.

FOURTH GENERATION

John Read, son of Dr. Read, Married Josie Withers, daughter of U. S. Senator R. E. Withers; Charlotte Read married Rev. R. A. Haymore; Mary married Mr. Austin; Francis married a Morefield; Janet Read married Read Taylor. Issue Jesse Read Taylor, Virginia Dare Read md. a Thurman; Louise unmarried; Taylor Pendleton married Lizzie Boyd; 2nd Lizzie Royal.

Charlotte Pendleton never married; Taylor Pendleton, a noted teacher of Richmond, Va.

Manson, the oldest son of Dr. R. A. Read, and his wife Francis Pendleton moved to Missouri and became a famous physician.

PENN FAMILY

The Penns are English, and trace their family back to one of the early settlers of this State, when Moses Penn married Katherine Taylor and located in Caroline county. Their children were: Frances, George, Philip, Gabriel, Abram, William, and Moses.

Frances Penn married a Rucker, and died in Patrick county. No issue.

Philip Penn had several daughters who married into the Lee, Pendleton, and Cabell families.

Gabriel Penn was a soldier in the Revolutionary War,

and was promoted to Colonel of Amherst militia, and served with same to the surrender at Yorktown.

Col. Abram Penn married Ruth Stovall, a daughter of James Stovall and Mollie Cooper. His sword is in the possession of his descendants (See Biography Chapter). His children were: George, Lucinda, Gabriel, Horatio, Polly, Greenville, Thomas, Abram Jr., James, Luvenia, Edmund, and Phillip.

SECOND GENERATION

This large family was reared three miles north of Martinsville and will be recorded as follows:

George Penn was born in 1770, married a Miss Gordon of Manchester, this State,, and moved to New Orleans. A son of his went to Congress from that district.

Lucinda Penn married Samuel Staples, Clerk of the Patrick Court for years, and died in that county.

Gabriel Penn was born in 1773, and married Jinsy Clark of Patrick county, where they both spent their lives.

Horatio Penn born in 1775, married Nancy Parr, and reared a family. He moved to Mississippi where he died.

Polly Penn married Charles Foster, reared a family, and died in Patrick county.

Greenville Penn was born in 1779, married Anna Leath, of Manchester. Issue: Gabriel. He married 2nd, Martha Read of Bedford. He had several children. Two sons went to Edgefield, S. C.

Thomas Penn was born June 15, 1781, married Frances Leath, of Manchester, Va; 2nd, married Christine Kennerly, of Amherst Co. During the War of 1812, he was promoted to captain of minute men, but peace was made before he saw any service

Abram Penn, Jr., born 1783, married Sallie Critz. They had several children, but the family moved to Tenn., where he died.

James Penn, born in 1785, married Miss Leath, of Manchester. His second wife was Polly Shelton of Henry county. He had several children. He died in Patrick county.

Luvenia Penn died when a small child.

Edmund Penn married Polly Ferris, of Patrick county and raised a large family. He moved to Ky., and died there in 1841.

Philip Penn was born in 1792, and married Louise Briscoe, of Bedford county, and is lost to history.

THIRD GENERATION

Gabriel Penn, the fourth child of Greenville Penn, was born in 1814, married in 1833, Susan L. Frants, and died in 1844. Issue: William Leath, and Col. John Edmund.

Joseph G. Penn was born in 1831, married Ruth Shelton in 1867, and died in 1906. Issue: John T., Magdalene, Annie, Edwin G, and Sallie L.

He was a soldier in the civil war and a good fighter. He was captured in 1865, and taken to Point Lookout, Md. His experience here, like thousands of others, was indescribably terrible. After this he returned home and manufactured tobacco for years at Martinsville where he died.

FOURTH GENERATION

John T. Penn, the oldest child of Joseph G. Penn, married Anna Bowe, of Richmond, and settled in Martinsville. Where he has been interested in the tobacco business for years. He has the original muster roll of Col. Abram Penn, dated March 11th., 1781.

Magdalene Penn, Married White Blair, and moved to Texas.

Annie Penn married Mr. Blair, and died without issue.

Edwin G. Penn married Laura Hughes Hairston, in Martinsville.

William Leath Penn, the son of Gabriel Penn, was born in 1834, and married Priscilla Jane Tatum, a great grandaughter of Gen. Joseph Martin, Oct. 4, 1863, and died in 1910, in Roanoke, where he moved to from Henry county in 1898. Fortune smiled on them thereafter. Their children were as follows: William F. Penn; Robert Leath Penn married Mag Moore, of N. C.; Hattie M. Penn married P. L. Zentmeyer; Hugh C. Penn married Jennie Carson; Earnest G. Penn married Annie Penn; John Harrison Penn; Mary Tatum, and Susie Letitia Penn.

PRICE FAMILY

Among the early settlers just over in North Carolina, south of Henry, was Reece Price, on Matrimony creek. He was born about 1750, and died in 1824. His home was near the church of the same name. He married twice. By his first wife, there was only one son Drury. By his second there was only one with children, Tom; the other, not married. Tom Price's children were: Pleas, Whit, and Frank who never married. Drury Price was born in 1785, and died in 1856. He lived near his father's home on Little Matrimony, where he reared the following children: Duke, John, Allen and Reece. There were three girls; Nancy, Sallie, and Polly.

SECOND GENERATION

Nancy married a Joyce, Sally and Polly moved further down in North Carolina.

Reece Price was born in 1829, married Cindy Moore, and died at Stoneville, with his daughter, Mrs. Jim Moore, age 91.

Esquire Allen Price was born about 1812, and married Biddy Moore. Issue: Joe Henry, Drury, James, and John Allen.

Major John Price was born about 1808, and married Matilda Eliza Hampton, of North Carolina. He bought a large farm on the Madison road, in Henry county, in the 40s from the Hairstons, built his residence soon thereafter, and here he reared a large family, and died in 1881. He was a noted citizen in his adopted county, fond of military, and was promoted to major of the Virginia militia. Children were as follows: John H., Nannie who married Buck Mitchell, Mary who married Woodson Bassett, (See Bassett Family). James M. Price who married a Fields, Robt. P., and Sallie who married Barzellai Smith.

Esquire Duke Price was born Jan. 1, 1804. He married Rachel Trent, Issue: William, Mary Ann Eliza, Preston, Katherine, Dolly, Allen G., and Hanna Price, the only child by his second wife, Harriet Shackelford. He reared this large family on Matrimony creek, in Henry county, and was a noted magistrate and patriotic citizen. He died in 1891.

THIRD GENERATION

Of the children of Esquire Duke Price we note as follows: William Price married Rebecca Kane, of Stoke, and resided two miles south of Ridgeway, near his father's home.

Preston Price married Mary Smith. He was a soldier in the civil war serving in the North Carloiina regiments.

Katherine Price married Thomas Mitchell, of Franklin county. Issue: William, Lula, Anna, and Belva.

Dolly Price married Madison Evans. Issue: Georgia, Daniel, Alice who married Jeff Roberts, Polly, Yancey, and Duke.

Allen G. Price married Minerva Roberts. Issue: Steve, Loulie, Samuel, and Anna who married Dr. Luther W. Kallam, a dentist.

Hanna Price, the only half sister, married Milliner Baughn. No issue.

Mary Ann Eliza Price was born in 1829, and married William A. Garrett, who lived near the State line in N. C. Their children were as follows:

James P. Garret Married Anna Mitchell; W. A. Garrett married, first Susan Trent, next Emma Garrett, no issue from either marriage; Alice Garrett married Frank Joyce; Thomas J. Garrett married Lelia Jones; Bettie Rachael Garrett married Willie Ben Jones, next Homer A. DeShazo; Loula never married; and Susie married Robert Loftis, a minister.

Robert P. Price, the son of Maj. John Price of Henry county, was born in 1847. He married Loula Dalton, the daughter of William Dalton, Sr., of North Carolina. He saw service in the civil war in the 16 year old company going as far as Salisbury, N. C., before the surrender. He was a fine business man and practically founded Price on the Va-N. C. line. He was a successful merchant, and accumulated much property, besides rearing a large family, many of them living in Virginia. He was a great Methodist, and lived his religion in his daily walk in life. He was the real founder of the Church at Price, and nurtured it generously all his life. He was distinguished for his earnestness, honesty, and sobriety, and the world is better off for his having lived in it. He died in 1913, and his ashes lie in the family cemetery in this county in sight of the place where he was born. Their children were as follows:

Robert Price who married Alice Tatum; John W. Price who married Nannie King (See King family); Annie Price who married Robert Grogan; Preston Price unmarried; Loulie Price unmarried; Charlie Price who married Mamie King; Ada Price not married; Elizabeth Price who married Len Matthews; Dora who married Ira Humphreys, a lawyer of Reidsville; Dr. Harvey V. Price, dentist of Martinsville, married Helen King; Lelia Price who married Watt Hariston, now deceased; Bert Allen unmarried.

John H. Price, the eldest son of Maj. John Price, married a Miss Dalton, and settled in Rockingham county, N. C., and was known as "Beaver Island John," and lived a successful life of a planter, and reared the following children: Anna Lee, Hattie who married a Tech, and Robert who married—.

PANNILL FAMILY

Two Pannill brothers fought around the person of Charles I, and when he was defeated at Naseby, they fled to America.

One settled in Maryland, where some of his descendants may be found to-day. The other, Thomas, settled in Va. on the Rappahannock. In his will, which is on record in Richmond, Va., he mentions a son, Wm. (1) who, when he became of age, sold his property and moved to Richmond Co. Va. and mar. Frances Mills, dau. of Col. Mills. His son Wm. (2) mar. Sarah Bailey, of Urbanna, Middlesex Co., Va.

Wm. (3), Son of Wm. (2) and Sarah Bailey, mar. Ann Morton. Issue: Morton, David, Samuel.

Samuel died unmarried. Morton Mar. Mary Johns, of Lynchburg, Va. Issue: Geo., Joseph, Wm., Ann, and Morton.

David mar. *Bethenia Letcher dau. of Col. Wm. Letcher and Elizabeth Perkins. The latter was a relative of "Bigbee" Perkins, of Tenn. who captured Aaron Burr on the Perkins plantation, and carried him to Washington, D. C., in an open gig. Issue: Wm. and Elizabeth.

Geo., son of Morton and Mary Johns mar. Bethenia Ruth Callaway, dau. of John Callaway and America

---

*The name Bethenia came through the Perkinses, handed down as a family name from the House of Buccleugh, of Scotland, who were dukes, or lords.

†Miss Milly Rodgers was the housekeeper at Claremont, whom all the family remember and love for her true service and constant devotion. She too sleeps in that quiet spot, and on her tomb are the words: "The faithful are sure of their reward."

Hairston. Their home was at "Claremont", Henry Co.,
Va. Issue: George, Jack, America Hairston, William
Hairston, Mary, Betheniah Ruth, Loulie, Hardin, Edmond
Johns and Sarah Ann Catherine.
Joseph mar. Sarah Shelton dau. of Peter Shelton and
his wife Magdalene. Issue: Magdalene and Peter Shelton.
Magdalene was burned to death when a young girl.
Peter S. died of typhoid, was buried in Hollywood, Richmond, Va., by the masons.
Ann died unmarried.
Morton mar. ——. No issue.
Wm. mar. Mildred Purcell, of Bedford Co. Issue:
8 daughters Elizabeth, Alice, Lutie, Katherine, and
others.
Elizabeth, eldest dau. of Wm. Pannill and Mildred
Purcell mar., Wright, and lived in Bedford Co. Va. Issue:
Della, Vera, and brothers. Her children are living in
Mexico where they have amassed quite a fortune. Alice
died in Sheltering Arms Hospt., Richmond, where she
was in training for a nurse. Lutie mar. ——. Issue:
2 daughters. Katherine mar. Richard Smith, of Norfolk,
Virginia.
Children of Geo. Pannill and Ruth Callaway. Geo.
Jack, Willie, Hardin and Loula died unmarried. Willie
belonged to Capt. Graham's Company K., 10th, Va.
Cavalry, and was killed near Reams' Station, Aug. 25,
1864.
America Hairston Pannill mar. Wm. Campbell. Issue:
Bethenia, Wm. Pannill, and Ruth Janet.
Mary Pannill mar. John Henry Davis, a half first
cousin, and lived at "Rocky Hill", the ancestral home of
the Callaways of Henry Co. Issue: Geo. Evans, John
Henry Jr. Elizabeth Ruth, Edmond Pannill, and Ernest.
Bethenia Ruth Pannill mar. Martin Penn. Issue: Geo.
Jackson, and Robert Edmond. Sara Ann Catherine Pannill (Kate), mar. Dr. Wm. T. Woodley, of Charlotte, N.
C. No issue.
Edmond Johns Pannill mar. Eliza Reamey, dau. of
Dr. Peter Randolph Reamey and Sallie Waller, Jan. 28,
1885. Issue: Sallie Reamey, Ruth Callaway, Bethenia
Letcher, Mariah Waller, Katherine Langhorne, Geo. Edmond, Jeb. Stuart, Mary Elizabeth, and America Hairston.
Children of America H. Pannill and Wm. Campbell

are: Bethenia mar. Charlie J. Stanley. Issue: Royal and Gertrude. They live in Roanoke, Va.

Wm. Pannill Campbell mar. Erie Brodie, of Franklin. Issue: Edwin Ruthven, Wm. Arthur, Frances Pannill, Raymond, Norman, Evelyn, James, Ruth. They live in Richmond.

Ruth Janet Campbell mar. Norman Taliafeno Shumate, of Henry Co., Va. Issue: Joseph, Ruth, Louise, Betty,and others. They live in Charlottesville, Va. where he is president of Farmers & Merchants Bank, of which he is founder, or rather was an organizer.

Of the children of Bethenia Ruth Pannill and Martin Penn. Robt. was killed by a train at the age of 21. Geo. Jackson mar. Susie Lee, dau. of Capt. W. H. F. Lee and Susan Barrow, of Henry Co. They live in Roanoke. Children of Edmond Johns Pannill and Eliza Reamey: Sallie Reamey mar. John Redd Smith, an attorney of Martinsville, Va. Issue: Patsy Pannill Smith.

Ruth Callaway Pannill is a registered nurse, trained in Johnston & Willis Hospt. Richmond. Bethenia Letcher Pannill, teacher in W. Va., educated at Randolph Macon Inst., Danville, Va.

Mariah Waller Pannill mar. Wm. Brumfield Read, son of Taylor Pendleton Read and his wife Lizzie Royal. No issue. Katherine Langhorne Pannill, teacher in Winston-Salem, N. C., graduate of State Normal, Farmville, Va. Courses at Art School in Chicago and Columbia University, New York City. Mary Eliabeth Pannill, sixth dau., lives in Martinsville, educated at Martinsville High School, and Chatham Episcopal Inst. America Hairston Pannill (Amy), youngest of these nine, teaches in Boydton, Mecklenburg Co. Grad. State Normal at Farmville, Va. Geo. Edmond Pannill and Jeb Stuart, respectively, enlisted in 2d Div., Co. K. 9th, Infantry, A. E. F. Geo. was killed in action July 18. 1918, in Chateau-Thierry drive near a small town Vierzy, at 9 A. M.. Jeb Stuart Pannill was wounded about that same time, and died in a Hospt. near Paris. August 4, 1918. Geo. b .Mar. 2, 1896. Stuart b. Aug. 1897.

The children of Mary Pannill and John Henry Davis we note: Geo. Evans mar. Miss Galloway of Philadelphia, dau. of Dr. Galloway. They live in Bristol, Va., where he is engaged in lumber business. Issue: Mae Galloway, Edith and Geo. Evans, Jr.

John H. Davis, Jr., mar. Hilda Forsberg, dau. of Col. August Forsberg, one of the old families of Lynchburg. Issue: Jack and August.

Elizabeth Ruth Davis mar. John Spotttswood Taylor, son of Dr. W. F. B. Taylor and Fanny Bishop. He was County Clerk for many years in Patrick. Issue: Frances Pannill, John Davis, Wm. Clayborne, Katherine Langhorne, and James Spottswood.

Edmond Davis mar. Emily Rangeley, of Henry Co. No issue. Earnest never married.

Returning to Wm. Pannill and Elizabeth, children of David P. and Bethenia Letcher: Elizabeth Pannill mar. Alexander Stuart, brother of Archibald Stuart who was father of Henry Carter Stuart Ex-Gov. of Va. Issue: Columbia and James Edward Banks Stuart. The latter became the famous cavalry leader in C. S. A. Wm. Pannill, brother of the foregoing Elizabeth, mar. Maria Bruce Banks, dau. of Wm. Bruce Banks, whose mother was Frances Bruce, and was descended through James Bruce, the immigrant, from Sir John Bruce, the uncle of Robert Bruce. History states that Robt. Bruce had no son and only one dau. There is in the possession of Miss Lucy Duke Ballard, of Chatham, Va., the silver cream pitcher belonging to the silver service that James Bruce, the immigrant, brought over in 1680. The first wife of Thomas Nelson Page was also a descendant of this line.

Children of Wm. Pannill and Maria Bruce Banks: David, John, Bethenia, and others.

Bethenia Pannill Mar. Martin. Another dau. mar. a Ballard. Issue: Lucy Duke. John mar. Dillard, and lived in Reidsville, N. C. Issue: Wm., Gordon, Cora, Anne, etc. David Pannill mar. Augusta Roberts. of Eastern Va. Issue: Maria, David Harry, Augustus Hunter, Wm. Banks, and Samuel Roberts. Wm. Pannill, son of John Pannill and Dillard, mar. Adele Dillard dau. Dr. J. R. Dillard, of Henry County. They have several children.

Gordon Pannill mar. ———; Cora Pannill mar. Nissen, Winston-Salem, N. C. Annie Pannill unmarried.

Children of David Pannill and Augusta Roberts: Maria mar. Dr. Jones, Chatham, Va. Issue: Mary, Stuart. Geo.; Marion mar. Lucy Charles Jones, of Chatham and is now living in Martinsville, Va.

David Harry Pannill mar. Greyson Lavinder, and lives in Martinsville. Issue: Alice Christina, Wm. Banks, and Mary Lavinder. Wm. Banks Pannill mar., and lived in N. C. till his death. Issue: several children. Samuel Banks Pannill mar. Bessie Hudspeth. They also live in Martinsville. Issue: Robt. and Lucy Moir. Augustus Hunter Pannill lives in Toronto, Canada, and is unmarried. He enlisted in the World War as Lieut. with the Canadian troops, was wounded at Vimy Ridge. For bravery there, was made Capt. Later joined the aviation corps, and once fell with his plane, fracturing both hips. While in Hospt. received the "Croix de Guerre" for extraordinary bravery under fire.

The Pannills are as a rule modest and reserved people. Few only have been in politics, though it is on record that Lieut. Thomas Pannill was a member of House of Burgesses 1758-61. In 1850 there was a Pannill in State Legislature. He mar. Miss Lottie Lee, of Richmond, and lived at corner Grace and Fifth Sts.

I. Article from William & Mary Quarterly—Published 1898—by David H. Pannill, Volume now in New York City Library—Comes under head of J. E. B. Stuart ancestry:

"On battle roll of Battle Abbey will be found the name of PAINELL and from him are supposed to be descended the Pannells of Ireland and England. Those of England were churchmen and Royalists, those of Ireland Roman Catholics.

"On the accession of Cromwell, the three English Pannells emigrated to America, one to Maryland, one to Norfolk, Va., the third to Rappahannock, Va. The orthography of the Rappahannock branch was changed from ELL to ILL. The other kept the ELL. General Stuart is descended from the Rappahannock branch."

II. William Pannill, 1735, married Sara Bagley, of Urbanna, in Middlesex County, Virginia. He settled in Orange County. There were six children: I. Sarah, 2. William, 3. John, 4. Joseph, 5. Frances, 6. David.

Joseph was a colonel in the Revolutionary war, serving under General Greene, of Carolina. His descedants now live in Louisiana.

Frances married —— Farrish, and removed to North Carolina. Gov. Holt of that state was one of her descendants. The first five children were mentioned in William's will, David was born later.

After William died, his widow married William Strother. From the record of Culpeper County, Feb. 20, 1752, a dower was assigned Mrs. Sarah Strother, who was widow of William Pannill; at the same time her husband, William Strother qualified as guardian of the six orphans. William Strother's widow died in 1774, and bequeathed all her property to Susanah, William Dabney, Frances Banks, and Sarah. William Dabney Strother was killed in the battle of Guilford Court House. His sister Sarah married Richard Taylor, and was the mother of Zachary Taylor.

III. William Pannill, second son of the first William, was born in Orange County, Virginia, October 30. 1738. In 1748 Culpeper County was cut off from Orange County, divided by the Rapidan River. William resided on the Orange side. He married Anne Morton, daughter of Jeremiah Morton, whose wife was Sarah Mallory. William was sheriff of Orange County, and as such made proclamation from the court house announcing the accession of George III to the English throne. He died after the Revolutionary war, his youngest child being born in 1790. His wife survived him and died in 1804. He had fourteen Children:

1. John, b. March 20, 1763, Halifax County, Va., married Miss Wimbish; had three daughters, one of whom married William Bruce Banks.

2. Elizabeth, b. Oct. 24, 1764.

3. Frances, died in infancy. There was another Frances.

4. William or the 3d William, b. Jan., 1768, settled in N. C.

5. Samuel, b. January, 1770, died 1861. He lived at "Green Hill", Campbell County, Va., and for many years was president of the Roanoke Nav. Co. One of his daughters married Robert Rives, of Albermarle County, brother of Hon. William C. Rives.

6. David, maternal grandfather of Gen. Stuart, b. 1772.

7. Sarah Bagley Morton Pannill, March 1774, married John E. Fitzpatrick.

8. Joseph, b. Jan. 26, 1776.

HISTORY OF HENRY COUNTY, VIRGINIA

9. Frances, b. March 1778, married Samuel Nowlin.
10. Morton Pannill, b. May 14, 1780, married Miss Mary Johns, of Lynchburg, Va.
11. Jeremiah, b. July 1783, married Miss Payne, of Campbell County. His descendants still live in Orange County.
12. George, b. July, 1784, married, 1806, Miss Blackwell. His sons, George, Dr. David, and Joseph; the two former represented Orange County several terms in the State legislature.
13. Anne, b. July, 1786, married —— Keartley.
14. Mary, b. January, 1790, married John Herndon.

IV. David, fourth son and sixth child of William 2nd, b. 1772. In early years, he and his brother Samuel, emigrated to Kentucky, their father having given them valuable Bluegrass region of that state. They were troubled with malaria, sold out in disgust, and returned to Virginia, and David married Bethenia Letcher. Bethenia was an old name in the Perkins family of England, from whom Mrs. Letcher descended. She was an only child of Col. Wm. Letcher, of the Revolutionary Army. In the spring of 1781, when she was an infant in the cradle, he returned to his home in what is now Patrick County, to see his family and collect recruits for General Greene's army, then encamped near Halifax (old), Virginia. A British loyalist, named Nichols, collecting beef cattle for Cornwallis' army encamped near the North Carolina border. Hearing of Col. Letcher's arrival and his object, he repaired to his house and shot him dead, in the presence of his wife and child. Nichols was pursued by friends, captured and hanged.

Colonel Letcher's wife was Elizabeth Perkins. Her family were from England and settled in Buckingham County, Virginia. Afterwards she married Major. Geo. Hairston of Henry County, Virginia, and from her descend those large antebellum slave holders, the Hairstons of Virginia, North Carolina, and Mississippi. Col. Letcher's parents were from Scotland, and settled in Petersburg, Virginia.

David died in Pittsylvania, Nov. 1803, aged 32, of typhoid. In his will, recorded in the clerk's office of

Pittsylvania County, he bequeathed his sword to his younger brother, George, with the injunction "that it should never be drawn in behalf of any rebellious or Jacobinical party". He left a widow and two small children. The children, Elizabeth (oldest), Letcher, and William Letcher. Elizabeth married Archibald Stuart.

ARMS: Panill Az—on a fesse between six martlets or—two martlets of the first. also Sir Walter Panell made a Knight of The Garter, 1348, and bore arms: Barry of six or an az. a bend or (another ceoat Az—a cross palonce or.)

WILLIAM I.

PRILLAMAN FAMILY

Two brothers, Daniel and George Prillaman, were the progenitors of this family in America. They came from Switzerland.

We have no record of George's descendants. Daniel settled on Smith river and lived to be 105 years old. His son George was the only issue.

SECOND GENERATION

George Prillaman was born 1790, married Miss Dicie Ross, a sister of Capt. Lee Ross who served through the Civil War and died 1875. Issue: Christopher, Lieut. in Civil War, died at White Sulphur Springs. F. M., Geo., Gabriel, Callie, Martha, Nannie, Lydia, Xeonia.

THIRD GENERATION

P. M. Prillaman born 1832, married Drusilla, daughter of Meshack Turner and Sallie A. Deshazo. The latter was a daughter of Geo. K. DeShazo (See Deshazo Family). He was a Sergt. in Co. B. 67th Reg. of Va. and was wounded at the battle of Gettysburg 1863. After the war he was elected Commissioner of Revenue for Franklin County 8 years. He lives on Reed Creek where he has spent his declining years well into the 90's. Issue: Jacob, Geo., Benjamin, Shields, Letcher, Cliff, Loula, Nannie, Sudie, and Hortense.

Geo. and Gabriel Lived in Franklin County, reared families and were successful farmers and good business men. Callie married John T. Cannady; Martha married Andrew Turner; Nannie married John W. Bowlin; Lydia married Bailey Cannady; Xenia married Geo. C. King (See King Family).

FOURTH GENERATION

Jacob Prillaman married Beulah Dillard; Geo. married Maggie Philpott; Loula married A. D. Yates; Nannie married Chas. S. Turner, a prominent business man of Axton; Sudie married A. V. Neblette; Hortense married N. J. Brown; John married Sallie Garrett; Benjamin married Ellen Ross; Shields married Nannie Coleman; Clifford married Bernice Prillaman. Letcher never married.

FIFTH GENERATION

The children of C. S. Turner and Nannie Prillaman, his wife, are Douglas, Morton, Vera, Mable, Conway, Howard, and Edwin.

There were two children by a former marriage Minnie C. and C. Roy Turner.

PACE FAMILY

John Pace married Polly Baker in 1815 and this is the earliest known of this family in Henry. Issue: James Baker, Green, and German. His will dated in the late twenties is all that is recorded of him.

SECOND GENERATION

James Baker Pace was born in 1820, married Caroline Hunter. Issue: Reed, Charles P., and William, By his second marriage to Lucy Taylor the children were: Samuel Green, Grief, Spottswood, Kitty Ann, Judith C., and Callie.

THIRD GENERATION

Reed Pace married and went West, and reared a family; Charles Pace died during the Civil War; William Pace was burned in the hotel fire in Richmond a few years ago. Of the second family of children: Samuel Green Pace was born in 1850, and married. He had a son who settled at Mt. Airy; Grief Pace died while young; Spottswood Pace married. He had three children, Kitty Ann, Corinne, and Judith, who located in Danville, Va. Kate Pace, Callie and Judith C. never md.

Pace married Dr. Reed Stovall. Issue: John, T. (Tony), and James who died young.

DANIEL PACE FAMILY

Daniel Pace, a nephew or cousin of John Pace, the founder of the other branch of the family, was born in 1797, married Jane King of Leatherwood, reared his family in this county, and died in 1880. Issue: Lafayette, Geo., Matilda, and Christine.

SECOND GENERATION

Matilda Pace married William Dillon; Christine Pace married William Pettit; And Lafayette Pace married Leatha Ann Stultz, daughter of Joseph Stultz of Leatherwood. Issue: Joseph, George, John T., Lucy, and Nannie.

THIRD GENERATION

George Pace married Martha Tolly Shumate, of Reed Creek. Issue: Raymond, Joseph, Nellie, Cassandra, and George.

John Pace, a brother to the above, married Nannie Eleanor Wyatt. Issue: Emma, Henry C., Allie, Lily, and John.

PURCELL

James O. Purcell came from England to America when a boy and md. Elizabeth Kent, of Pittsylvania Co., Va., Oct. 27, 1825. Issue: Mildred V., b. Jan. 26, 1827, d. young. Peter b. May 12, 1828, d. unmarried. Entered civil war in company of S. J. Mullins, wounded at Gettysburg, but returned home and lived a useful life. Elizabeth Ann, b. Aug. 11, 1830, d. young. Mary S,. b. Nov. 16, 1831 d. unmarried. James, b. May 28, 1835, lost sight of in Civil War.

Charles Rufus, b. May 9, 1837, d. in youth.

Martha F., b. Sept. 7, 1839, d. unmarried. Thomas Hill, b. Dec. 13, 1841. Geo. Dallas, the youngest child.

Thomas was in Civil War, served throughout the struggle, md. Miss Ferguson. Issue: One son and 3 daughters.

Nannie (Mrs. Henry Warren); Minnie, (Mrs. Archie Wells), Annie (Mrs. J. C. Minter), and Arthur.

Dallas was the only other member of the family that left heirs.

Mrs. Purcell d. May 16, 1857. Rufus followed in Dec. of same year. She, Rufus and Miss Ann are buried in the Hill Cemetery.

HISTORY OF HENRY COUNTY, VIRGINIA

REDD FAMILY

Major John Redd, the progenitor of the family in Henry county, was born in Albermarle, Oct. 25, 1755. He came to this county about the time of the Revolutionary War. (See Biography Chap.) He married Mary, the daughter of Col. Geo. Waller, of Henry county. Their children were as follows: Annie, James Madison, Elizabeth, Martha, Waller, Edmund Burwell, Polly C., Lucy Dabney, Dr. John Giles, Overton and Carr, killed in childhood by falling from a see-saw. He finally settled at Belleview, in the Marrowbone valley, and here he reared his family and died in 1850.

SECOND GENERATION

Annie Redd married Thomas Starling, and from this union we enumerate the Starlings, Thomases and Reameys' (See Reamey Family).

Col. James Madison Redd married Ruth Penn Staple. (See Drewry Family); Elizabeth Redd married Peter Dillard. (See Dillard Family); Martha Redd married a Clark, 2nd, JamesM. Smith. (See Smith Family); Waller Redd married Keziah Staples, one of whose children married a Preston. He was the second Clerk of Henry County Court soon after the Revolution. His father, Major Redd, bought the office from the former Clerk, John Cox, at the price of eight hundred pounds.

Polly C. Redd married Jack Fontaine and reared a family; Lucy Dabney Redd married John Taylor Wootten, 2nd, Wm. Bullard; Dr. John Giles Redd married Apphia Fauntleroy Carter; Overton Redd married Martha Fontaine.

Edmund Burwell Redd was born about 1795, and married Sarah Ann Fontaine. Their children were: Martha, Mary, Celestia, Polly, Ella, John, Wm. Spottswood, James S., and Edmund Madison.

THIRD GENERATION

Martha Redd married John Francis Wootten; Mary Redd married Dr. John Wayt; Celestia Redd married Samuel Caldwell; Nannie Redd married Patrick Fontaine; Ella Redd married John Wattlington; Dr. John Redd married Marion Fontaine; William Spottswood Redd married Mary Wootten; James S. Redd married Sallie

Hairston, daughter of Tyler Hairston, of Red Plains, on Marrowbone creek; Edmund Madison Redd married Annie Richardson.

Of this large family, James S., and W. Spottswood, were soldiers in the civil war, and both rose to the rank of captain.

FOURTH GENERATION

At the old home, Belleview, on Marrowbone creek, Capt. W. S. Redd reared his family and died in 1909, age 70. He was a great hunter, took much interest in public affairs, and was a public official for several years. He reared the following children:

Edmund B. Redd, a fine handsome young man, who fell a victim of fever. He was kind-hearted, sociable, a good mixer, and possessed a charming manner that attracted every one who came in contact with him; Lucy Redd never married; Pattie Redd married Overton Reamey, 2nd, J. B. Walker, and dispensed Virginia hospitality at Belleview for years; Ella Redd married R. Fischer and reared a large family as a widow, her husband dying quite early in middle life.

THE REAMEY FAMILY

The progenitor, of the Reamey family in the county, was Abram deRemi, French form, and his wife. They came on a ship bearing 169 emigrants, mostly Huguenot refugees who landed at Jamestown, Va., Sept. 20th, 1700.

Abram de Remi was a descendant of Count Raoul de Remi, of Piccardy France. He settled with other refugees at Manican Town, where there was quite a colony of French planters. This was not far from Richmond, and here he resided and reared one son. This was probably Pierre.

SECOND GENERATION

Like most of the new-comers, knowing only the French, the history of the first two generations is preserved by tradition, as they learned English slowly without schools, hence the knowledge of Piere de Remi is hazy. From him however, only one son is known, Daniel.

THIRD GENERATION

Daniel Remie, as the spelling was in the colonial militia of Augusta county, Va., was a Revolutionary sold-

HISTORY OF HENRY COUNTY, VIRGINIA

ier under Washington, at Valley Forge, and in subsequent campaigns (See Rec. War. Dept.). He was promoted to colonel as evidenced by his uniform; and besides he left his sword to his posterity.

Two sons and a daughter survived him; Viz, John, Daniel, and Elizabeth. The latter married Benjamin Jones and they lived and died in Henry county. Their ashes finally found a resting place in the cemetery at Martinsville.

FOURTH GENERATION

John Reamey, as spelt, married a Pace, and lived to a good old age and died near Irisburg. No issue.

Daniel Reamey Jr., was born —— in Henry county, and married Susan Starling, —— 18——. His wife was a grandaughter of Maj. John Redd, and with her sunny disposition assisted him in educational work. As teachers, they filled a great want in the county educational field prior to the free-school system era.

A record of their labors can never be complete, for the good they did lives on and on, and will never be forgotten by their pupils and their descendants. Their children were as follows: Peter, Mary Ann, John Starling, Kate, Overton Redd, Henry Clay, Daniel Webster, and Lucy. All the children were born between 1825 and 1845.

FIFTH GENERATION

Peter R. Reamey, 1929-1891, married Sallie Waller, and their children were: Starling, Jack, and George deceased, Florence, Henry, Eliza, and Sallie. Of his issue by his second wife, Bettie Kesee, there are Walter, and one sister dead, Mattie, also Jasper.

Mary Ann Ramey married Christopher Thomas and their children were: L. Starling, John. Jane and Lucie, deceased. and Hope. Faith. Kate. and Frank.

Kate Reamey married Dr. James Semple of Irisburg, Va. Issue: Reamey, Baylor. Lucy. Muscoe, George, and Kate, all dead; andJames, Susie. and Richard B. Kate left a daughter, Kathleen Eggleston.

Overton Redd Reamey married a Smith. Issue: a daugther, Alice; Henry Clay Reamey died in civil war unamrried; Lucy Reamey married James Smith, of Ohio, and their children are John, dead, Lucy Bell, Lyne Starling, James, and Edith; John Reamey married Elizabeth Hairston. Issue: Overton, dead, Sam. Sue Starling, and Pattie Ruth.

Daniel Webster Reamey was born Aug. 18th, 1838, and married Bettie Redd Dillard in 1870. Their children are as follows: Overton D., Daisy Martin, Annie, Lucy, S., James W., Lyne Starling, and Frank G.

He was a true son of the county and every inch a patriot. He was a member of the Tenth Virginia Cavalry under Gen. Wm. Henry Lee, and fought with great gallantry for the Confederacy. He died June 2nd, 1908.

Of this generation of Reameys, two, Peter and Mary Ann, Mrs. Thomas, developed quite a literary talent. Dr. Reamey will be noted in the chapter of noted men of the county in this volume.

Mrs. Mary Ann Reamey Thomas was a pupil of Dr. C. F. Deems, completing her studies at Greensboro Female College, N. C., and was a talented conversationalist and distinguished writer for many publications. She left many warm friends in her home town and community when she passed away in April 1910.

Mrs. Thomas was for 31 yrs. the teacher of the infant class in Sunday School, and the president of the Woman's Foreign Missionary Society from its organization. Her associates, when recently determining a name for a Bible woman in Soochow China, who is supported by the Martinsville Society, unanimusly agreed upon that of Mary Anne Thomas. Mrs. Thomas was Pre-emiently the preacher's friend. Her last visit before her fall, was to the parsonage to inquire how the pastor's family, during his absence, was getting on.

RANGELEY FAMILY

This family traces back to James Rangeley, a wealthy Englishman of Leeds.

He reared a son (James the 2n) who crossed the Atlantic nine times, looking after the large landed estates, of his fater, in America.

This James (2) married Mary Newbold, dau. of William Newbold, of Sheffield, England.

Both families were of aristocratic blood, and belonged to the "Smart Set" that attended the Court of St. James. Some of the American descendants have the plumes worn on the horses heads of their coach-and-six at the last function they attended at Court.

Mr. Rangeley brought his family to America about 1820, and remained in New York City for a number of years. In 1825 he bought large landed estates in Maine, and moved there. This section is now known as the "Rangeley Region." His little settlement was named Rangeley in his honor; so were the Rangeley Lakes.

Mr. Rangeley was of a restless disposition, and after living at Rangeley a few years, he moved to Portland, where Wm. Newbold had given his sister (Mrs. Rangeley) a beautiful home. But the climate was too severe, and so he left Portland and bought land in Henry Co., Va., where he settled in 1841, and died and was buried here.

Two of Mr. Rangeley's sons John and James came south before the family did. They bought a home together near Stuart and accumulated much property. They conducted a tannery, saw-mill, and store, successfully.

The children of James (2) and his wife Mary Newbold, were Henry, James, John, Hannah, Mary and Sarah.

Henry was adopted by his uncle William Newbold, and remained in England, only paying one visit to America. He reared a son William, who left 2 daughters.

Hannah married Reid Ayres, no issue; Mary Rangeley married Dr. Noel, no issue; *John Rangeley md. Miss Webster, a lineal descendant of Daniel Webster of Ipswich, Mass. Issue: John, Susan Webster, Eliza Caroline, and Wm. H. Rangeley.

James Rangeley (3) married Miss Were of Bangor, Maine. Issue: James, Joseph, William, Sarah, and Emma who died.

SECOND GENERATION

James Rangeley (4) married Alice Via. Issue: Dr. Walter, Fred, John, Frank, Clarence, Hattie, Maggie, Lily, Annie, and Carrie. Joseph md. Miss Connor. Issue: Samuel, Eliza, Willie, Nellie, Ida, and Ada.

William married in Texas and raised a large family. Sarah md. Murray Turner. Issue: Lillie, Noel, Harry, Nellie, and Edward.

John, the oldest child of John Rangeley and his wife

Miss Webster, died in Civil War. Susan Webster Rangeley md. Lr. Robt. B. Dandridge. Issue: William, John, Una, Annie, Thomas, and Harry.

Eliza Caroline Rangeley md. J. C. King. Issue: John, Clarence, Nancy, Sallie, Mamie, Thomas, Gertrude, and Helen.

W. H. Rangeley, b. Nov. 2, 1850, died 1913. He married Nannie Clanton. Issue: Raynie, John, Annie, George, Alice, Emily, Eliza, William and Nancy.

*John Rngeley, son of James (2), married 2d, Miss Annette Stone, of England. No issue.

ROWLAND FAMILY

The name Rowland is of Norman origin and was brought to England in the train of William the Conqueror. From England branches of the family spread to Wales and Scotland and is identified with the literature of Europe.

Thomas Rowland, of Baconstrope, England, had a son, John Rowland, who married Scolis Pemberton, and their son John, Jr., emigrated to America in 1635, on the ship Dorset, John Flower, Master, and settled in Virginia.

Andrew Rowland was a descendant of John Rowland, Jr., who was a native of Egham, England. His children were, John, Michael, and Baldwin.

Michael Rowland married Elizabeth Hairston. He was a soldier in the Revolutionary War and marched with the Henry county troops that went to Gen. Green's assistance at Guilford Court House in time for that battle. He had a son named Creed T.

Creed T. Rowland married Matilda Brewer, and they lived in their native county of Henry till 1840, when they moved to Aberdeen, Miss., and on his plantation near that city he finally settled and died in 1866. He had a son, William Brewer.

Dr. William Brewer Rowland married Mary Bryan, who was a direct descendant of Charles Moorman, of Louisa county, Va., who emancipated his slaves in 1778. They had a son named Dunbar.

Dunbar Rowland, Director of the Department of Archives and History of Miss., was born August 25, 1864, at Oakland, Miss. He studied at the Memphis private

DUNBAR ROWLAND, LL. D.

MRS. DUNBAR ROWLAND
(Eron O. Rowland)

HISTORY OF HENRY COUNTY, VIRGINIA 253

schools, and prepared for college at Oakland Academy. In 1882, he entered the Freshman class of the Miss. A. and M. College and was graduated in 1886, with the degree of B. S. He was the first anniversarian of the Philadelphia Society the year before graduation, and delivered the second alumni oration in 1888.
In 1886 he entered the Law department of the University of Miss., and two years later was given the degree of L. L. B., being the senior debater at the Commencement June, 1888. The same year in Nov. he located in Memphis, Tenn., where he remained four years, and attracted many friends by his culture and scholarly attainments, but in 1893, he returned to Miss., and opened a law office in Coffeeville. In 1902 when the Department of Archives and History was created he was elected Director, and re-elected in 1907. He has written and edited a number of historical Volumes. In recognition of his services to the State, the University of Miss. conferred upon him the degree of L. L. D. in 1906. That summer he went to Europe to investigate the official archives of England, France, and Spain which relate to the provincial history of his State.

Dr. Rowland is a member of the Episcopal church, of the Sons of the Revolution, of the The Delta Epsilon Fraternity, and of a number of historical societies in the United States. On Dec. 20, 1906, he married Eron Pha Gregory, daughter of Benjamin Moore and wife Ruth Rowland Moore. Maj. Benjamin Moore was a son of Lemuel Moore and wife Eron Byrd Moore, his mother descended from the Byrd family of Westover; he was a soldier of both the Mexican and the Civil War, and at one time associate editor of the Wetumpka Argus, with William L. Yancey, of Alabama.

John Rowland, a brother of Michael, and Baldwin, married Elizabeth Hampton in 1728. Their children were Benjamin, born in 1720, Andrew, born in 1731, and John, who was born in 1730. He was a prominent citizen, and when Henry county was created, the legislature required the courts of the county to be held at his house till a court house could be built.

Baldwin Rowland, another brother of the above, married Sarah Hairston, daughter of Robert and Ruth Stovall Hairston. She died leaving him two girls, Elizabeth Hampton, and Martha Hairston, the latter an infant. Their Grandparents kept them till the death of the grandfather, Robert, after which grandmother Ruth took them to her son, Samuel and his wife, Judith Saunders, till they were grown. Martha H. Married C. C. Bailey, son of Parks Bailey and Mary Cabiness, and their daughter Mary Bailey was born in Henry county, but was soon taken to Georgia. She became the wife of John H. Traylor, son of Rev. J. C. Traylor, formerly of Henry for years, a prominent minister.

Baldwin, was a bright and handsome man, and a very fine penman. He was in great demand for this accomplishment at schools and public functions. He did the first work as clerk of the court of Henry county at the home of his uncle, John Rowland, where the first Henry court was held. He went west not long after his wife died and is afterwards lost to history.

Kate Mason Rowland, was the first woman in Virginia to be honored with the degree of L. L. D. She was a noted writer. She died in Richmond, Va., age 78.

Tradition relates that the Rowlands were the first to manufacture woolen goods on the Virginia Coast.

SALMONS FAMILY

John Salmons, the progenitor of the Salmons family in Henry Co., was of Irish descent and served in the Revolutionary War. He was one of the men of Henry Co. when it was cut off from Pittsylvania, and was its first sheriff.

At that time the best men in the county were made justices and the oldest of these was appointed sheriff. At one time Mr. Salmons was a man of wealth, but lost much of his land and property.

Among his children were Capt. John Salmons, Jr., Thaddeus, Hezekiah, Betsy Holt and others.

Capt. John. Jr., married Polly Davis, of Stokes Co., N. C. He was born Sept. 25, 1772. His wife Polly Davis Salmons was born Feb. 12, 1779, and died Oct. 17, 1857. Issue: Margaret, b. Oct. 24, 1799, md. July 31, 1823, d. Oct. 17, 1824 leaving an infant daughter (Mary Dyer); James, b. Oct. 21, 1801, md. Dec., 1825; Thaddeus, b. Feb. 24, 1803; Polly, b. Aug. 5, 1805; Elizabeth, b. Sept.

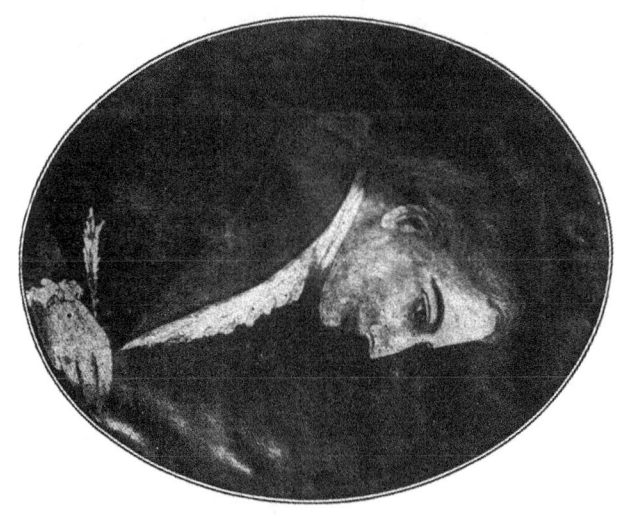

BALDWIN ROWLAND
From a painting made about 1777

MRS. BALDWIN ROWLAND
(Nee Sarah Hairston)
From a painting made about 1783

29, 1805; Bethenia, b. July 12, 1811; Rebecca Ann, b. Aug. 25, 1813; Wm. J. Salmons, b. August 14, 1816, Virginia Salmons b. 1819. Margaret Dyer, b. March 2, 1826, Ann Dyer, b. April 7, 1828; Rebecca Dyer, b. April 27, 1830; Rachel Elizabeth, b. Oct. 8, 1832. Caught on fire when very young and burned to death before aid could reach her. These Dyers were grandchildren of John Salmons, Jr., and his wife Polly Davis.

Hezekiah Salmons married a Miss Philpott, and had several children.

Thaddeus also married, and had sons and daughters, among them was John (3) called "Pea Ridge John" to distinguish him from the other Johns. He married Miss Eliza Clanton, dau. of William Clanton. She had sons and daughters, and lived to be 102 years old. She left children, grandchildren, and great grandchildren behind, all worthy citizens. Her husband preceded her many years.

Children of Pea Ridge John Salmons were: Elizabeth; Eliza; Martha md. Mat WingUfield; Susan md. John Salmons, a cousin; Dollie md. Geo. Jamerson; Lou md. Tom Jamerson; Issue: Sam, Geo. W., Jesse, Thomas, and Harry. Henry Clay d. young. Will Salmons, Edd Salmons. Geo. md. Bettie Robertson. Issue: J. W., Fannie, Geo. C. Annie, Kemper. Special notice should be made of the second son of Lou Salmons; viz, Gen. Gerge H. Jammerson, b. in this county 1868, attended school at Martinsville till old enough to teach a free school a year. He was appointed to the U. S. Military Academy and graduated in 1893.

He was appointed Lieut., and ordered to many of the Islands and States of the United States, being gradually promoted. During the World War he was commissioned a Brigadier General and was noted for the careful consideration he had for his men. He made a brilliant campaign and was cited for bravery and given the Distinguished Service Medal for meritorious conduct very recently.

SCHOOLFIELD FAMILY

Three Skulfeels' as spelt then, came to America with Lord Baltimore. They were Catholics, but some of their descendants became Quakers and others Methodists. The latter finally located around Lynchburg, Va., and from there migrated to this county.

David and Rachel, his wife, were the first known in this section. Their children were as follows: Samuel, John, Enoch, Benjamin, Sidney, Jane, Aaron and David.

FIRST GENERATION

John Schoolfield, the second son of the above, was born Feb. 1, 1765, married Sarah Thurman, Sept. 5, 1799. Issue: Henry Asmond, James Lorenzo, Emaline Anne who left no heirs Martha, and William Miranda.

SECOND GENERATION

Martha Schoolfield married George W. Humphries, and left one son, John Humphries.

William Miranda Schoolfield married Sarah Ann Harrell, of Bertie Co., N. C., on Dec. 11, 1834. The latter was the daughter of Josiah and Rachel Harrell. The former died in Henry county June 12, 1855, 31 years before his widow.

He was a Methodist minister and after joining the conence, was sent to Henry circuit as its pastor, soon after his marriage. His services over, he settled permanently in the western part of the county near Mt. Bethel where he preached once a month the remainder of his life. The children of this union were: Martha Ann, John Harrell, Mary Emeline, Sarah Elizabeth, Laura Virginia, William Henry, James Edward, and Robert Addison.

THIRD GENERATION

John Harrell Schoolfield was born Feb. 18, 1838, married Susan France, Mary Emeline Schoolfield married Dr. W. W. Morris. (See Morris Family). Martha Ann b. in Bertie Co., N. C., Oct. 1, 1835, md. E. R. Mitchell. No issue.

Sarah Elizabeth md. 1st, James France, 2d, James Carter. Issue by 1st, husband: Gordon and Henry France.

Laura Virginia d. unmarried. Wm. Henry md. ——.

---

*Dr. Joseph Schoolfield was the first surgeon of the U. S. Navy commissioned by the government between 1797 and 1800. This information obtained from the first U. S. official register of the U. S. N., published in 1800, or 1801.

Issue several. James Edward md. Lucy France. Was first a successful business man, but joined the ministry, and became a noted evangelist. Robert Addison, the youngest md. Annie France, 2d. Miss Vass, 3d. a sister of his 2d wife, Mrs. Van Wagener.

SHEFFIELD FAMILY
(By Susan Sheffield)

Behind this family lies a long line of ancestry dating back to Duke John Sheffield, of Buckinghamshire, England, whose statue stands in Westminster Abbey.

The exact date on which the three brothers came over from Sheffield, Eng., has been lost. However, one of them settled in New York, one in Virginia, and the other in Georgia.

Jesse Sheffield, the founder of the family in Henry county, came from Nottoway county, where he was born in 1746. He married Susan Cheatham, nine years his junior. Issue: Leonard, Susan, Joseph, Nancy, Nicholas, and John.

FIRST GENERATION

Leonard Sheffield, the eldest, was born in 1779, married Lucy Wootten born in 1795, and distinguished himself in the war of 1812. Issue: Jesse, Martha Ann, Col. William, Henry, Thomas, James M., John A., Frances Jane America W., Lucy O., and Susan C. (twins), Samuel G., and Leonard born in 1836. He reared this large family in Henry county, and several of them achieved distinction in the civil War. He died in 1837.

SECOND GENERATION

Jesse Sheffield was born in 1810, was a good soldier for the South; James M. Sheffield was engaged in the historic battle between the Merimac and Monitor, was wounded severely and never fully recovered; Thomas Sheffield settled in Oklahoma and achieved great wealth; Samuel G. Sheffield was born in 1836, married Loula Martin, daughter of Col. William Martin, of Magna Vista. No issue. He was Lieut. in the Civil War, and later engaged in the mercantile business at Ridgeway. In the early eighties he moved his business to Martinsville. He was a fine financier and prominent merchant until his death about ten years later.

Leonard Sheffield, the youngest of the family, reared a son Leonard, who married Mary McFadden, of S. C. The latter died leaving a son, Leonard, born in 1871, the popular postmaster of Spray, N. C., and deputy sheriff of Rockingham county. He married a second time, Mandy Edmund. Issue: William E., John T., James R. and Edward C.

William A. Sheffield was born in 1814, married Catherine Hill,, daughter of John Waddy Hill, and Judith Parks, who was born in 1827. Issue: Judith, Elizabeth, Leonard, John W., and Lucy Wootten who died in infancy.

He was a devoted son, husband, father, and neighbor, and a man of intellectual ability and foresight. During the Civil War while others were satisfied with paper currency, he turned it into gold and when the War was over, bought vast boundaries of land, making him at that time the largest land owner in his community. This land increased in value with time, and when he died he left his children provided with good farms. He was a Col. of the 64th, Reg., 12th Brigade 1st, Division of Va. Riflemen in the Confederacy. Althought he was advanced in years, he gave freely of his means for his country's cause. He lived at the Sycamore on Marrowbone creek, and was distinguished for his princely entertaining; truly old Virginia hospitality, which is known all over the world as unequaled in its charming purity. He died in 1897, and on a high hill above his old home on the National Highway by the side of his devoted wife, he lies sleeping.

THIRD GENERATION

Judith Parks Sheffield married Benj. F. Barrow, in 1874, and reared a family. (See Barrow Family.)

Elizabeth Sheffield married Lyne Starling Thomas in 1881 (See Thomas Family.)

Leonard Sheffield married Bettie Coan. He had a frail constitution wholly unfitted to battle with agricultural enterprises, and died at the time he should have been in the very prime of life. Issue: Mamie who died in young womanhood. Kate, and Annie Coan.

John Waddy Sheffield was born in 1863. He developed into a man of great courage, sterling character and integrity. At the age of 33 he married his beautiful and talented cousin, Lucy Withers. The old Colonial home of his parents fell to him, together with many broad and fertile acres of land. He was a scientific farmer, and met with much success. He was one of the most influential, political and educational leaders of the county, and did much to promote the welfare of the county along these lines. In his early manhood, he was a correspondent for a Richmond paper; and was noted for his elegant English, polished manners, and loyalty and devotion to his family and friends.

He died before reaching the meridian of life. A year later his beloved wife followed him. Their children were: William A., John W., Susan E., and Lucy Wootten. William A. Sheffield, the eldest of these is a World War veteran and fought in the battle of the Meuse Argonne and others, with the same bravery which marked his heroic forefathers.

SHELTON FAMILY

William Shelton and his brother Nathan came to Henry from Goochland prior to the Revolution. Nathan did not tarry, but William married Peonia Critz and settled, and thus became the founder of the Henry County Shelton family. He raised 3 sons: James, Nathan (2), and William (2).

SECOND GENERATION

James was born 1750. He married Fannie Allen, youngest dau. of Wm. Allen, the founder of the Allen family in Henry Co., 4 children were born to this couple: Pines Henderson, Nancy, Polly and James. Mr. Shelton had the distinction of fighting in both the Revolutionary War and that of 1812. He rose to the rank of Capt. In the latter, but died and was buried in Norfolk. His widow married Wm. Abingdon, and in 1830 the entire family moved to Missouri.

William Shelton (2) married Pattie Dillard, dau. of Col. John Dillard, the pioneer of the Dillard family in Henry Co. Issue: Peter, John, Geo., Ruth, Polly, and Susan. Nathan Shelton (2) married Mary Hatcher, and raised 4 children: Alfred, Joseph, Judith, and James.

THIRD GENERATION

Peter Shelton b. in Henry Co. Nov. 12, 1798, not far from Spencer. He married, on March 21, 1832, Magdalene Dupuy Watkins, dau. of John Watkins and Miss Wilson. Twelve children were given to Mr. Shelton: Wm. Henderson who married Nancy Jane Hylton; Sarah Martin md. Joseph Pannill; John Watkins md. Rhoda E. Howard; Annie Wilson md. James S. Martin; Virginia Magdalene md. Dr. R. R. Robertson, Peter Fowler md. Laura Howard Mary Elizabeth unmarried; Ruth Stovall md. Joseph G. Penn; Susan Louisa md. John Hill Matthews; Thomas Meade md. Fanne Clopton; Geo. Hunt died unmarried; James Buchanan md. Miss Price.

Pines Henderson Shelton md. Rebecca Carter, a descendant of Robert Carter (King Carter). Rebecca died and left 2 children, George James, and Rebecca. Mr. Shelton md. 2d., Mary Wyatt. Issue: James Lamertine, and Fredonia. The latter md. Pabner Greenwade. Losing his 2d wife, P. H. Shelton md. 3d, Mary O. Scales. Issue: Wm. A. Shelton of Windsor, Mo., and Thomas Marvin. The latter died leaving a dau. who md. Harper Stephens, of Temple, Texas.

George James Shelton, a brother of Pines, md. Ann Bailey Allen, of Wirtzville, Mo. April 26, 1889. Issue: Mrs. Norman Campbell, Colorado Springs, Col.; Alcie Bobinreith, Kansas City, Mo.; Miss Byrd Shelton, Kansas City, Mo.; Mrs. J. W. Dawson, Eldorado Springs, Mo.; Mrs. W. C. Lamping, Denver, Col.; Mrs. Todd M. Pettigrew, Bronxville, N. Y.; James Lamar Shelton, Kansas City, Mo. The father of this large family served in the Confederate army 4 years. He enlisted at Waco, Texas. He was a prominent citizen in his time, and left a record his posterity will ever be proud of. He died June 2, 1913, and was buried in Windsor, Mo.

James Lamertine Shelton, a half brother of the above, Md. Janie Pomeroy. They left 3 daughters, of Windsor, Mo: Lula Shelton, Mrs. Alvin Winsureid, and Mrs. John Harris.

Of Nathan Shelton's children we record as follows: Alfred md. Susan Shelton, sister of Peter Shelton. Joseph

HISTORY OF HENRY COUNTY, VIRGINIA

Shelton md. Narcissus Astrop. Judith md. John Pinckney Scales, father of Miss Sue Scales, of Sandy Ridge, N. C.

James Shelton md. Adeline Taylor. Issue: Wm. Nathan, Geo., Lucy, Martha, Fanny, Chester, Ben and Joe.

FOURTH GENERATION

Wm. Nathan Shelton md. Martha Wells dau. of John and Matilda Wells, granddaughter of Baker Wells. Issue: Addie md. Fred Doyle, son of Sam and Maggie Bouldin Doyle; Mollie md. T. J. Glenn; Dean md. Geo. L. Price; Annie md. Thos. M. Fair; Maggie md. W. A. Stanford; Daisy md. Joe Scales, son of John Pinckney Scales and his wife Judith; James Taylor Shelton md. Sallie Loving; William P. md. Beulah Basham.

SMITH FAMILY

The family is English and has been represented in every epoch, both in war and peace, from the colonization of the State till the present time. The progenitor of the family in this county was James Moss Smith who was born in Halifax county Feb. 8, 1798, married Mrs. Martha Redd Clark, a daughter of Maj. John Redd, in 1828, and spent three score years in Martinsville before giving up his earthly burden.

He was a farmer, merchant, and good business man. On his large estate he was different from other men in not letting his slaves call him master.

He was opposed to secession, but followed his State. His home during the Civil War was the hospital of Gen. John M. Palmer (Palmer Buckner Gold Ticket fame, 1896) when the Federals were stationed in Martinsville, then a very small village.

He was Commissioner in Chancery for years. He settled up more large estates in the county than any before or after him. Administrators were not always over honest. His settlement of the Maj. John Redd estate was so far, square, and eminently satisfactory, he was given a loving-cup by the legatees. This souvenir will be held in the family, a precious memento of his sterling honesty, generation after generation.

He was an official of the Methodist church, and so have his descendants been, their combined services being over a hundred years in one organization. He died on Dec. 17, 1883. The children of this union were as follows: John Redd, James Moss, and Pattie.

SECOND GENERATION

John Redd Smith was educated as a lawyer, was admitted to the Henry bar, and married Letitia Claiborne, but fate decreed that both should die young, and without issue.

Dr. James Moss Smith was born in Martinsville, in 1830, married Corinna Smith, of Petersburg, Va., and lived in this county all his life. He was elected Mayor, of Martinsville, and was one of its most efficient and popular officers. He practiced medicine continually after his graduation at Jefferson Collegee of Philadelphia, in 1854. He was a surgeon in Stonewall Jackson's Army, and participated in his wonderful evolutions in the valley of Virginia.

It was while Supervisor from the Martinsville district that he did his greatest public service for the county. He was the father of improved roads. He secured the State convicts by whose aid he finally succeeded in getting the people won over to his policy, and thus began the county era of better roads that continues to this day. He died May 19, 1919. The issue of this union were as follows: Charles Purnell, James Moss, Jr., Pattie Hairston, Electra, Will, John Redd, and Elizabeth.

Pattie Smith, the only daughter of James M. Smith, Sr., married George Isham Hairston who went into the mercantile business at Ridgeway with John C. Jones, and Dr. John Smith. The lands of the three cornered at a point, and on this their "Brick Store", now standing, was built.

He owned much land on the east of the road to Martinsville where he did extensive farming. He was apparently destined for a highly successful career, but was stricken by disease when young, and died and his popular wife followed him, and both were buried across the Marrowbone valley at Belleview, the home of Major Redd in the days of slavery.

THIRD GENERATION

Of the children of Dr. J. M. Smith we record as follows: Dr. Charles Purnell Smith married Nannie Jane

Brown; James Moss Smith married Mattie Gravely; Pattie Hairston Smith married John Andrew Brown, (See Brown Family); Electra Smith married Hon. Herbert G. Peters, a lawyer of Bristol; W. C. Smith, twin to the latter, died in early manhood; Attorney John Redd Smith married Sallie R. Pannill, a grandaughter of Dr. Peter R. Reamey; Elizabeth Smith married Thomas N. Barbour.

SPENCER FAMILY

The Spencers are of English descent. The first of the line recorded in Henry county was William Spencer. He married Sallie Parks, the daughter of William Hill and Elizabeth Saunders. Of this union there were three children; America, Sally Ann, and David Harrison.

SECOND GENERATION

America Spencer married Greenbury Nichols, a son of Thomas Nichols and Sarah Lane, daughter of Dutton Lane a Maryland family. Greenbury was born in 1808. This marriage was about 1830. Issue: Bettie who married Henry Clay Wootten; Sallie married John Fontaine Nichols and went to Mo.; William Nichols never married.

David Harrison Spencer married about 1834, Mary Waller, the daughter of Col. Peter Dillard and Elizabeth Redd, the latter the second daughter of Maj. John Redd, of Belleview, on Marrowbone. Issue: William David, Peter, John, Robert Lee James Harrison, George Overton, Lizzie, Annie, Lucy, Mary, Mattie, and Maggie.

Sallie Ann married David Allen. (See Allen Family).

THIRD GENERATION

William David Spencer never married but was the chief factor in the firm with his father, D. H. Spencer & Sons, tobacco manufacturers at Spencer, this county for about forty years. Bill Spencer as he was usually called was a young soldier, in the 16-year old company that went as far as Danville before the surrender, and after this short career, returned to the old home where he built up a great paying tobacco business. He added greatly to the family fortune, was one of the county's most popular business men. He died in 1912.

Peter Spencer was never married. He was associated in the manufacture of tobacco with his brothers at Martinsville. He was loyal to his friends.

John D. Spencer was one of the most handsome men the county produced, was a very popular business man, and a member of the firm of Spencer Bros., tobacco manufacturers. He married Annie Clark and moved to Danville, where they reared the following children: Wm. Clark, Margaret Allen who md. Lieut. John Hazzard Carson, Mary Waller, unmarried, Ann Dillard who md. Lee Overman Gregory.

Robert Lee Spencer was possessed of a lovely disposition that endeared him to every one that came in daily contact with him. He died young.

James Harrison Spencer was born March 8, 1858, married Blanche Williamson, daughter of Col. James N. Williamson of Durham, N. C. April 18, 1894. Issue: Margaret who married Dr. John A. Shackelford; Mary Holt married Kennon Whittle, a lawyer of Martinsville; James; and Blanche. "Hass" Spencer, as he was usually called was one of the county's fine moral men, possessed of splendid business capacity, public spirited, and an example as a father, friend and neighbor, loved by a large circle of people throughout this section of the State who grieved at his death in middle life.

Gerge Overton (Tobe) Spencer lives unmarried at Spencer attending to business as well as his farming interest, and serving his friends.

Lizzie Spencer married Rufus Penn, and he died leaving their children as follows: Birdie who married a Pendleton, 2nd, was married to Richard W. Lindsey; Arthur; Hardy; and others besides Walter Penn, of Martinsville, who married Carrie Dillard.

Annie Spencer married Frank, the son of Jefferson Penn. They spent their lives in Reidsville N. C. At their death, their tobacco manufacturing business had expanded till it became a part of the American Tobacco Co. Their children Jefferson and Charles lived in New York and accumulated great wealth. Both are noted for their devotion to their kin.

Lucy Spencer married Judge John Dillard. He died leaving one son, Harry Dillard who fell a victim to smallpox. She married again Mr. Bill and died leaving two children, David S. and Lucy, who married Lawrence Holt and died without issue. David Bill married Catherine Wilson and went West.

Mattie Spencer married John Lee. He died leaving her with two children. The son, Robert, died early, leaving the sister, Mary Anderson.

Maggie Spencer married Hails Janney and reared a large family.

Mary Spencer married Henry C. Buchanan. He died early. She is the owner of the old Homestead at Spencer and looks after business successfully and enjoys dispensing old Virginia hospitality with rare grace and elegance.

STANLEY FAMILY

The Stanleyi are English in descent. The oldest member of this family to live in this county was Samuel Stanley from Franklin county. He was born about 1800, married Martha Lovell who was born in 1822, and spent his declining years in Henry county, where he died. Their children were: Crockett, William Green, Cynthy Ann, Abigail and Jane. The two last named died in infancy.

FIRST GENERATION

Crockett Stanley was born in this county Jan. 8, 1838, married Susan Matilda Walker, daughter of Lucy Catherine Mullins, Matthews and Robert Walker, on Feb. 8, 1872. Issue: Robt. Hillie, Lucy Matt, Jessie Roberta, John Walker, Samuel William, Berta Anna, and Thomas Bahnson.

He was a member of Co. H. 24th, Va. Regiment, and served through the war. A review of his services would but tell the doings on the field of battle of one of the greatest body of men in the War between the States. He was always interested in public affairs, and was Commissioner of the Revenue on the north Side of the county for several years, and filled every public duty carefully and conscientiously. He died in 1915.

William Green Stanley married Nannie Philpott and moved to Giles Co.

Cynthy Ann Stanley married James Thomas.

SECOND GENERATION

Robert Hillie, Berta Ann, and Lucy Matt, died before maturity; Samuel William Stanley died in 1906 with typhoid fever; Jessie Roberta Stanley married John Reid

Aaron; John Walker Stanley married Addie Vaughan. She died in 1924; Thomas Bahnson Stanley married Ann Pocahontas Bassett. Swin David Stanley, Nephew of Crockett Stanley, md. Kellie Reed Morris, dau. of Anderson Morris and his wife N. A. Forbes. Issue: Callie Matt, Berta Annie, James Jefferson, Nellie Bee, and Helen Booth Stanley (dead).

STARLING FAMILY

The Starlings are of English descent. They begin their family history with Sir William Starling, who was Lord Mayor of London in 1670. He had a son, William, the father of Roderick Starling. The latter married Miss Hubbard and reared a son, William, who was the first of this family to come to America. He settled in King William county, this State, in 1740, and married Jane Gordon. They both died in a few years, and left three children; Viz, William, Roderick, and Sally.

FIRST GENERATION

William Starling was born Sept. 1756, married Susanna Lyne in 1774, and died in 1826. Without parents, he had as guardian Col William Lyne, a prominent neighbor, and his marriage to the Colonel's sister meeting with the latter's displeasure, he left the county, and settled near Boydton, in Mecklenburg county, Va. He filled the office of Sheriff of that county before moving to Ky. in 1794. He was made Colonel of the troops collected to attack Arnold in his raid in Virginia, but saw no active service. After his location in Kentucky, he represented Mercer county in the legislature, and in 1806, was appointed assistant Judge for that district. He was six feet three inches in height, graceful in figure, grave, learned, noted for his natural politeness and generous hospitality. Of the eleven children of this union we note one, Thomas.

SECOND GENERATION

Thomas Starling, the third of the family, was born in Mecklenburg county Sept. 3. 1779. When his father Col. Starling went to Ky., his uncle Henry Lyne adopted him and brought him to Henry county when 16 years of age. His education in school was over, but he was a great reader of books and became a dictionary of history according to family tradition.

He married, Annie, the daughter of Maj. John Redd, in 1903, and lived for years a life of ease, happiness, and hospitality in the finest and most refined part of this county. He was imposed upon by friends, and the notes he endorsed for them swept his fortune away. To add to this all his family died in rapid succession, but one daughter, Mrs. Reamey who cared for him in his declining years. His brother restored his finances to all the comforts, but his reverses wrecked his health and spirits, and he died in 1852. Issue: Susanna, William, Overton, John R., Elizabeth, Jane G., Lyne, and Edmund Thomas.

THIRD GENERATION

Edmund Thomas Starling was born in Henry county in 1818, married Mary Anderson from Prince William county, a sister of Rev. Robert Anderson, and settled in the southern part of the county on Smith's river.

He was a model citizen and known far and wide for his kindness to his slaves. He was quiet in manners, sterling in character, and a Methodist in religion, exemplifying in his daily walk in life a Christian spirit in deed and in truth. He reared his children with the help of his good wife to live and walk in the ways of their parents. They were: Leonard, Annie R., Thomas, and Ballard.

FOURTH GENERATION

Leonard Anderson Starling was born in 1846, and married Maria Ralls. There was only one child, Leonard Anderson who married Floria Anderson.

Annie Redd Starling was born in 1848, married Rexy B. Cabiness. Issue: Jack, Roy, Isabel, Annie Redd, Elizabeth, Starling who married Corrie Fitts, and Mary who married a Clay.

Thomas Starling was born April 17, 1850, married Permelia Daniel. Issue: Robert Anderson married Josie Lee Lightsey; Sallie Miller not married; Bettie Price married James Dabny Estes, a nephew and adopted son of Dr. J. D. Estes; Annie Maria, and Thomas, unmarried; Mary Anderson married Dr. Madison Redd Drewry (See Drewry Family); Alvis Daniel married Mary Withers; Jervin Daniel never married; and Edmund Thomas married Virginia Robey.

Ballard Preston Starling was born in 1860, married Agnes Deslin. Issue: Edmund, Annie Preston, Hallie Brown, and Pattie who married Snow Smith.

STOVALL FAMILIES

The Stovalls trace their ancestors back to England, and there are two distinct branches to be considered, and while both came from Goochland county to Henry they can not be connected as one family; so we first note the Bartholomew Stovall Family.

In the Henrico county records we find that Bartholomew Stovall married Ann Burton in 1693. They had a son, George Stovall, who we learn from Henning's Statutes, was granted permission to "run a ferry across the river". This was in 1752.

George Stovall married Polly Cooper, a descendant of Sir. Ashley Cooper, the first Earl of Shaftsbury, etc. He was clerk of the House of Burgesses of Virginia as late as 1688. Their daughter, Ruth, Married Robert Hairston, a member of the Henry county family in 1749.

James Stovall, the eldest son of George, married Mollie Cooper, a relative of his mother. Their daughter, Ruth, married Col. Abram Penn, of Revolutionary fame, who settled on Beaver creek in 1768. We record the other children as follows: 2, Joseph Stovall never married; 3, Brett Stovall married Nancy Hughes, and her descendants lived in Patrick County; 4, James Stovall married and settled in Georgia; 5, Thomas Stovall married Elizabeth Cooper and in time became the ancestor of Hon. Pleasant A. Stovall, Minister to Switzerland; 6, Sallie Stovall married George Dillard and had a large progeny; 7, Mary Stovall married a Farris and went to Tenn.; 8, Elizabeth Stovall married a France and moved to Tenn.; 9, Martha Stovall married John Staples, and had a distinguished progeny, Samuel, and John Staples, and many others, who adorned the legal profession and did honor to their family and State.

Dr. Stovall came from Goochland county with his wife, Mary Isabel, about the end of the 18th century and settled at Hordsville in this county. Issue: Joseph, Albert, Dr. Read, George, and Dr. Quince.

FIRST GENERATION

Dr. Quince Stovall was born about 1820, and married Mary Watson, of Danville. Issue: Annie who married a Garland; Bonnie, Jack. Dr. Stovall practiced in the Northern part of the county many years.

Dr. Read Stovall was born 1823, practiced medicine on Smith's river in Ridgeway district. Issue: James and (Tony), Alexander, 2nd marriage to Miss Wingfield. Issue: Sallie mar. Dick Jamerson; 2nd mar. was to Wm. Lawrence; Bettie mar. John Davis, 2nd, mar. was to John Edd Philpott; John, and Christopher, never married; Jennie Stovall married Frank Wells; Josepsh Stovall, the eldest son of Landis, married Nancy Grayer Mitchell, and lived all his life in Henry. His children were as follows: Landis, Tom, William, Francis, Mary, Sallie, Florence, Quince, and James Read.

Second Generation.

Landis Stovall married Virginia Watson of Danville. Issue: Callie died in infancy; and Melvina married Frederick william Townes of Danville.

Frances married Joseph Mitchell. Issue: William, Joseph S., Jubal Early, Landis P., Nannie Mitchell Craig, Eddie, and Trotter.

Sallie Stovall married John Jarrett. Issue: Mary who married a Wilkinson, Nannie married a Benton, Rosaline, Robert, and Charlie.

Florence married George Mitchell. Issue: Dora married a Redfern, Harry, Wade, Hughes, James, Annie married a Simpson; and Elizabeth married a Galleager; Quince Stovall married Willie Thomas. No issue.

James Read Stovall was born about 1865, married John Manassa Holt, the daughter of Mary Ann Powers, and John W. Holt, in 1886. He died in 1901. Their children were: Mary Green, Lucy Friend, and William Morris.

STULTZ FAMILY

The Stultz family originated in Germany, but migrated to Pennsylvania and thence to Virginia. The founder of the family in the county was Adam Stultz who was born about 1750, and settled on Leatherwood creek before the Revolutionary war. He married Mary

Gravely, an aunt of Peyton Gravely, the founder of a celebrated brand of tobacco. Their children were: Abner, Joe, Katy, and Polly.

SECOND GENERATION

Abner Stultz was born Sept. 7, 1770. He married Nancy Eggleton. To them were born: Thomas J., Adam, Joe, Synthy, Patsy, Nancy, Nellie, and Betsy. He was an exhorter in the Primitive Baptist church.

Joe Stultz was born Nov. 12, 1773, and while wagoning in Tenn. met and soon married Amy Withers. Their issue: Anderson, Zephania, Brice, Amelia, Thenia, Lucinda, and Sarina.

Katy Stultz married Michael Griggs of Henry county. Issue: Wesley, Peter Franklin, Irie, Geo., Joe, and Mariah.

Polly Stultz married Tom Haley. Issue: Jeff, Jim, John, Polly, and Leanna.

THIRD GENERATION

The 8 children of Abner will be considered as follows: Thomas J. Stultz was born Nov. 11, 1798, and married Susan, the daughter of Othniel Minter, a Baptist preacher. He moved from his old home on Leatherwood to the Ruben Nance place about 1840, where he died in 1842. Issue: Cassandra, Nancy, William Davis born April 26th, 1822, Delilah, Orthniel M., 1826, Joe. A., Martha Ann, Johnson W., Geo. H., Achilles M., and Thomas Leftwich, Oct. 1st, 1840.

Adam Stultz married Betsy Taylor. Issue: Martha Jane, Peyton W., and Sally. He lived on the head-waters of Leatherwood creek.

Joe Stultz married Lucy Eggleton. Issue: Ben, Saunders, Tyler, Lethy, Clarissa, Julia, Judy, and Louisa.

Cynthy Stultz married Anderson Purdy. Issue: Jim, Gen. Geo., Chester, and several girls not recorded.

Nancy Stultz married Silas Minter, a Primitive Baptist preacher. It is related of him that he preached so long to a Baltimore audience that they began to leave; whereupon he said: "I perceive you all can't stand strong doctrine". Their children were: Richard, Joe, Jim. William, Silas, John, Betty, Cynthia, Nancy, Martha, and Susan.

Nelly Stultz married Tom Hicks, the mason who built the Marshall brick chimneys in 1813. Their issue: William, Tom, John, Nancy, Betsy, Lucy, Nelly, and Melindy.

Betsy Stultz married John Richardson. Issue: Abner, Geo., Nelly, Nancy, Lucinda, Frank, John, Eliza, and Joe.

The 7 children of Joe Stultz will be noted as follows: Anderson Stultz was born March 16th, 1809, and settled near Dyer's Store. He married Polly Lester who was the mother of Geo., Brice, Malinda, Francis, Eliza, and died. He next married Jane Wingfield. Issue: Edd, John, Ben, Calvin, Joe, Amy, and Sally.

Zephaniah Stultz was born Apl. 2nd, 1815. He was commissioned a Capt. of State Militia. He was a successful tobacco manufacturer, and built the first brick factory in the county, 1860, near Dyer's Store. He married Sarah Virginia Stockton, a descendant of Sam Marshall. Issue: Georgia, Alice, Millard Filmore, Rufus Janifer, Jubal Early, and a daughter named Zeph.

Brice Stultz was a great factor in establishing the reputation of the brands of tobacco manufactured by his brother, as well as those of Geo. O. Jones of Ridgeway in later years. He resided at the latter place for a generation. Here he spent his last yeras, and is buried by his wife, Tamsy Wells, in the Ridgeway Cemetery. No man had a better heart, or had as few enemies. Their children are as follows: Zeph, Brice, and Henry, living, and Frank, John W., Daniel, and Ben, dead; and two girls, Alice and Anna.

Parmelia Stultz married Joe K. Gravely. Issue: Peyton, Frank, John W., Joe, Goggin, Jabe, and Eleanor.

Thena Stultz married Jeff Lyle. Issue: Joe Henry, Bartlett, and Ruth Anna.

Lucinda Stultz married John Atkins. Issue: Wm. Stultz, John Francis, Lucinda, and Lizzie.

Sarina Stultz married Daniel Pace. Issue: William, Sally, Ann, Henry, Mary Tabitha, Julia, Jimmie, Ballard P., and Pace.

FOURTH GENERATION

Of the 11 children of Thomas J. Stultz we will record the following:

Cassandra Stultz married Gideon Clark. Issue: Tom, Letitia, Sarah, Nathaniel, William, Patty, Joe, and Cernetta.

Nancy Stultz married John Beal. Issue: Eliza, Tom, and Julia.

William Davis Stultz married Frances Harper Marshall, and is noted further in chapter on biography of noted men of the county. Issue: Ruben Nance, Sam Johnson, Susan Frances, Abner Dennis, William Marshall, Thomas Benjamin, Nancy Missouri, Jesse Davis, Sallie Melissa, James Achilles, and Peter Hairston.

Delilah Stultz married Nat Eggleton. Issue: Wm. S., Peyton W., John H., Eliza, and Nathaniel.

Orthniel Stultz married Sally Griggs, the daughter of Franklin Griggs. He was a partner in the tobacco business with his brother Davis for some years. He was a big hearted man and was imposed upon by his friends and lost money by endorsing for them. Their children were Ida, Henry, Frank, Tom, Will, Anna, Bob, Jack, Lula, Betty, Janie, Mattie, Katie, Jim, and Julia.

Joe Abner Stultz was born in 1828, and married Mary Wingfield, a grandaughter of Dennis Marshall. Issue: Virginia, Achilles, Joe King, Mary Lou, and Nancy.

Johnson W. Stultz was born in 1832, and married Mary, the daughter of Girard Burch. Issue: Isabella, Girard, Nellie, Mary, Johnson, Davis, Lou, Shields, Walter, and Geo. H.

Achilles and Thomas were Civil war veterans and never married.

Geo. H. Stultz married Polly the daughter of Armisted Glass. Issue: Achilles, Eliza Ann, Beechy, Emma, and Betty.

TURNER FAMILY

Isaiah Turner the first member of this family of whom we have any record, was born near Irisburg in 1812 and died 1892. He married Elizabeth Gilly and to this union were born one son Geo. W. Turner, who was born 1837, married Sarah Greene in 1852. Issue: Spottswood J. married Sis Bullington; N. P. married Ninon Turner, Nannie Prillaman (See Prillaman family). Bettie married Geo. L. Mitchell; Anna Laura Md. S. T. Robertson; Chas. S. md. Nannie Prillaman.

TAYLOR FAMILY

The Taylor family came from Wales. The progenitor of the family in this county was George Taylor, who married Elizabeth Anyon before leaving his native land. He stopped a while in Lunenburg county, Virginia, but in 1774 obtained a grant of land on North Mayo river in the south-western part of the county. He later added to this during the time of Gov. Thomas Jefferson's administration of Virginia. He was a good citizen, and a great Bible student. Although his eyes failed him so he could not read print, he enjoyed quoting verses, and often chapters, of the Sacred Word. He spent his days at his new home, and died in 1823. He left the following children: James, Blagrove, George, John, Josiah, William A., and Reuben.

SECOND GENERATION

James, Blagrove, and George Taylor Jr. were in the War of 1812. The first two never returned. George came back but soon went to Tenn.

John Taylor settled in Kentucky; Josiah Taylor located in Stokes county, N. C., where he lived till he reached his ninety-seventh year; William A., "Uncle Billy", Taylor was born May 20, 1788, married Kittie Ann Hill Nov. 16, 1817. He died in 1854. He was a prominent citizen and settled at Traylorsville, Henry county. He was a prominent member of the Methodist Episcopal church, and exerted a great influence in county affairs, both general, and religious, holding the love and esteem of his fellow men till the final call.

The children of this happy pair were as follows: Spotswood, Samuel, "Jack", William F. B., Kittie Ann Hill never married, Judith Ann died in infancy, and Lucy Elizabeth married James Baker Pace. She died in 1900 leaving two sons and three daughters. Sam Green, the oldest son died in Mt. Airy N. C. His widow and his only son still reside there. Mrs. Pace, like her father, was a consistent member of the Methodist Church, and did what she could to further its interests. Her second son, Spottswood, and the 3 daughters, continue in the home in Danville, Va., where she left them. The girls never married. The son married, and has an interesting family.

Reuben Taylor, the youngest son of George Sr., was born in 1815, and married Nancy Gray, daughter of William Gray of Patrick. He retained the lands given him by his father and by the help of his industrious wife added to this until he was able to provide homes for his five sons; viz, Daniel G., George W., James I., Josiah F., and Samuel C. He did not attach sufficient importance to educating his children at first, but later as his family came on, he consented for a school-house to be erected on his land. He was a man of clean lips and generous heart. His son in after years wrote that he never heard him swear, or use an improper word in his life.

Through the influence of John Watkins of his neighborhood, in 1844, he donated a site for the Mayo Baptist Church, and he and his son did most of the building. Here Elder John S. Lee, a Missionary of the Baptists, and Elder John Robertson, of Leaksville, N. C., conducted a meeting, and Nov. 11, 1844 the church was organized and he and his son Daniel became members. His daughters were, Mary, Lucy, Adeline, Sarah, and Nancy.

THIRD GENERATION

We note the following in reference to the sons of William A. Taylor: Spottswood Taylor was a noted hotel man of Danbury, N. C.

Samuel Taylor went to Mt. Airy and served Surry county as Sheriff for several years satisfactorily.

"Jack" Taylor remained on his ancestral home a model citizen. He married Ruth P. Baker, daughter of James Baker and his wife Catherine Koger and left 3 children; J. W. B., John L., and Kittie Ann. J. W. B. married Ann Forbes who has passed away. He has been a prominent farmer and worthy citizen, doing much good among the sick and distressed. Two children remain to him, Kate, and Botts the latter married Lucy Wells, and has an interesting family. John L. has married twice, has one daughter, and is now and has been for some time treasurer of Danville. He is much loved and respected by Henry county people.

William F. B. Taylor, the youngest son, graduated in medicine, married Fannie, the daughter of Dr. Joseph Bishop, and located at Elamsville and represented Patrick county in the Virginia legislature. His son John S. Taylor married Ruth Davis and served in the legislature from the same county, and afterwards was elected clerk of the court of Patrick.

In reference to the careers of Reuben Taylor's sons we record: His sons, John L., Geo. W., Josiah F., Samuel C., besides his son-in-law, J. F. Lancaster, also a minister, served in the confederate army.

Daniel Gray Taylor was exempt from the Army, but filled a great want in his community. Besides preaching every Sunday but two, throughout the Civil War, he did every kind of labor with his hands to supply the needs of his community. He tanned leather and made harness, made wagons, coffins, and all kinds of household necessities, besides performing the usual duties of a minister of the Gospel, like visiting the sick, burying the dead, etc., he practically served the whole community. The service rendered in these sundry ways was incalculable.

Samuel C. Taylor was the youngest of the eleven children. He married first, Sallie Atkins, but she died within a year, After the war, he married again, Lucy Shelton, and reared a large family as follows: Joe, Tom, Sam, Lily, Nannie, Henry, Mollie, Jesse, Maggie, Ella, and Lucy.

He was a public spirited citizen served as magistrate, church trustee, sunday school superintendent, and exerted great influence in his section. He died in 1922.

FOURTH GENERATION

We note the children of Daniel Taylor and Martha King as follows:

Rev. John L. Taylor was a noted local minister for two generations, and also served his community as magistrate for 20 years. He died in 1924.

R. Reid Taylor while preaching in Roanoke county, died in 1887.

Sam Frank Taylor, D. D., was for ten years President of Stephens College, then moved to Mo.

J. Judson Taylor, D. D, L. L. D., was President of

Georgetown College Ky., then changed to several cities preaching. He wrote much, and his latest work was, "The God of War".

Dr. Tom. G. Taylor, and J. B. Taylor are successful business men of Leaksville, N. C.

It is worthy of note that seven of the grandsons of Reuben Taylor, including W. C. Taylor, D. D., the son of Jos. I. Taylor of West Virginia, were Ministers of the Gospel. A brother-in-law, J. F. Lancaster, too, was a local preacher, who spent most of his valuable life on Horsepasture creek in this county.

TOWNES FAMILY

The Townes family is English and traces its history back to 1700.

The father of the family in this county was Edward Townes who came from Pittsylvania county. His father, Stephen Coleman Townes, was born in 1797, and married Catherine Williams, of that county. He lived near Kentuck, and died at an advanced age. Their children were: James, William, George, Nathaniel, Robert, Edward, Stephen Halcot, Daniel Coleman, Wilmoth, Martha, Sarah, and Rebecca.

FIRST GENERATION

James Townes went to Tenn., married and left a large family:

Four of the boys, William, George, Nathaniel, and Robert went south—the latter two to Texas.

Stephen Halcot lived and died near his old home. He left a large family in that county.

Daniel Coleman Townes married and left a daughter who married Thomas W. Lanier.

Edward Townes was born Jan. 1, 1820, and spent most of his life in this county. In 1848 he married Harriet Gravely. Issue: George, Jabe, John Stephens, Daniel Marshall, J. Edward, Thomas J., Mary, Frances, Kate, Sallie, and Nettie Willie.

He was for years the manager for Marshall Hairston, and was known for his tact in dealing with men and for his fine judgment in financial affairs. He had thousands of friends who mourned when he died in 1886.

THE HOME OF REV. JOHN COUSINS TRAYLOR
1815-1841

SECOND GENERATION

George J. Townes was born in 1851 and married Martha Jane Davis. Issue: Florence Ann, Ben Marshall, George Edward, Ida May, James, Stobie, Lucy Ellen, John Willie, Charlie Davis. He died in 1901.

Florence Ann Townes married first John O. King, Jr. Issue: Willie Townes, and Gracie May, later adopted by her second husband, Michael Richard Hennessey, and bore his name. By her second marriage one child, George Thomas, was born. She married a third time to William J. Beard. No issue.

Ben Marshall Townes was born in 1875, and married Zela Davis, in 1901. They had three children to live; Viz Elizabeth, Benjamin Hairston, and Zela. He like his grandfather was a good business man, also, managed for the Marshall Hairston estate, and was so satisfactory to them, he was given a beautiful boundary of land above his salary.

George Edward Townes was born in 1879, and married Pattie Hundley. Issue: Frank Davis, Edwin, Ruth, and Harvey.

Frank Davis Townes married Helen Deitrick. No issue.

Ida May Townes married Charlie W. Davis. No issue. She was known for her kindness to others, whom she enjoyed serving.

James Stobie Townes went to Maryland, and married Mary Warren, of Baltimore. No issue.

Lucy Ellen Townes was born Feb. 22, 1886, and married Charles M. Hart in 1904. Issue: Charles M. and George Richard.

John William Townes was born in 1888, and married Elmer Holland.

Charlie Davis Townes was born in 1889. He married Mary Chamberlain, of Waverly, Virginia. They have one child. He left home when young and soon graduated in dentistry at the Medical College of Virginia.

TRAYLOR FAMILY

This line is Anglo-Saxon in name and escutcheon. The London Register does not record the name in the divisions for either peasant or middle class, but only among Court Circles. The escutcheon records three Crusaders.

Edward Traylor, of Hampton Parish, England, came to Virginia in 1663. He, with his wife Martha Randolph, and three children, were living in Henrico county when he died, in 1677. His widow married Porter, about 1780, and was again a widow as her will showed when probated at Henrico Courthouse in 1682. This document left her estate to her daughter, Mrs. William Hankins, and her two sons, Edward, and William.

William Traylor married Dec. 5, 1695, to Judith, the daughter of George and Elizabeth Harris Archer, son of George Archer, who was born in 1650, and lived on his land grant on Tunstall creek, in Henrico county. His grandson-in-law, William Traylor, lived on a grant of improved lands on Mooning creek in the same county. The first of this family was Gabriel Archer, whose name is the only one accompanying that of Capt. John Smith on a monument at the head of the oldest residential street in Richmond, Va. It is in a small park on the James river, and commemorates their landing in 1607. The name Archer is Norman-English and claims descent from Baron Archer, whose name is found in Battle Abbey on the Battle of Hastings.

The children of William and Judith Archer Traylor were Joseph, John, and Humphrey. The latter inherited his estate by will probated in 1753.

Humphrey Traylor married in 1736, and lived all his life on his estate in Henrico county, where he died in 1790. His children were as follows: George, Humphrey, Marjory, and Frederick. They inherited the estate by order of court, April 1791.

Humphrey Traylor, Jr. married in 1770, Sarah the daughter of John Cousins, son of Charles and Marjory Cousins, who came to Virginia from Lancasterhire, England, where they owned valuable lands. Their children were as follows: James who married a Sutherlin; Elizabeth who married a McDonald; Frances who married George Pegram; Martha who married Joseph Davis; Robert, not married; James who married a Cardwell, a

REV. JOHN COUSINS TRAYLOR
From a drawing made about 1840

first cousin of John Randolph, of Roanoke; Joel; Lucy; and John Cousins. This large family lived at Oakhurst, in Dinwiddie county, Virginia, near Petersburg. This city is built on a corner of the 17th century Traylor grant. At the beginning of the present century, the Traylors of Richmond still owned a part of the original estate.

John Cousins Traylor was born in 1788, and received his share of his father's estate by will, dated Sept. 13, 1802, probated October proximo. The will continues, giving to the 14 year old John, "a tract of land in the county of Chesterfield, left by the said John Cousins, which was to be sold and the money therefrom to be put at interest, for the benefit of said John Cousins Traylor".

Seven years later, a resident of Richmond then, he became acquainted with, and joined the Methodists. For two years he was a divinity student of the Virginia Conference.

In 1813, he was sent to Henry county as a circuit rider. Two years later found him married in this county. He was ordered by Bishop Asbury to locate and work for three things, to build a primary school house as a feeder to Patrick Henry Academy, to build a church, and a school for higher education, and a College for Methodists, in the western part of Virginia.

By 1841, all three commissions had been successfully accomplished, ably assisted by his life partner, Tabitha Bailey Traylor, who was born in Henry county 1791, married in 1815, and died in 1881. Their children were: John Humphrey, Sarah, Susan and Robert.

SECOND GENERATION

John Humphrey Traylor was born in 1824, and reared in the western part of the county where he spent the first seventeen years of his life. In 1841 he moved to Georgia where he was distinguished as a state senator, etc. He had previously married Mary Elizabeth Bailey. Issue: John C., Robert, George, Thomas Humphrey, Jerry, Martha, and Elizabeth.

THIRD GENERATION

John C. Traylor married a Miss Williams. There was one child, Mrs. J. C. Orr, Birmingham, Ala.

George Traylor married Mary Camper. Issue: Mrs.

R. J. Thiesen, Mrs. C. T. Dunham, Atlanta, Ga., Mrs. Allen Putnam, Brooklyn, N. Y., and Frances, a student at Mary Baldwin, Staunton, Va.

Jere Traylor married Martha Houston. Issue: Martha, a student of Randolph Macon, Va.

Martha Traylor married Thomas H. Northen. Issue: Capt. George Traylor Northen, signal corps, France, law student at Christ College Cambridge, England; realty, Atlanta, Ga.

Ruth Northern, honor graduate of Peabody Art School, School, Secretery of the South Atlanitc Musical Association, and National Arts Movement Committee.

Thomas Humphrey Traylor and sister, Elizabeth Rowland Traylor, are not married.

Geo. T. Northen b. in Atlanta, Ga., 1892, is the grandson of J. H. Traylor, born, reared, and educated in Henry Co., Va. He is also the great grandson of Rev. J. C. Traylor, long a Methodist minister in Henry Co.

Mr. Northen is a graduate of University of Ga., A. B. 1912; also a graduate of Atlanta Law School, L. L. B. degree, 1914.

Matriculate of Law Dept., Chicago University, and Cambridge University, Eng. He is a member of the Phi Delta Theta fraternity.

Mr. Northen served thirteen (13) months as Cap. in Signal Corps advance section A. E. F. in France during World War, and is now at the head of a real estate and loan company in Atlanta, Ga.

TURNER

Wm. and Green Turner were left orphans. Green md. a Davis, and moved to Indiana. Wm. was raised by Ben Davis. He md. Nannie Lee Draper, and died, 1910, leaving ten children, 8 of whom are living.

Lou Ella md. Robert Draper. Issue: Two boys, Wm. and Fletcher. Willie Lee Turner now living in Waynesboro, Va. Ben md. Emma Cobbler. Thomas Ira md. Celestia Winston, E. Homer md. Annie May Shumate. Mary md. Richard Yarber. Robert E., and Mallie Simmons, unmarried.

WALLER FAMILY

The Waller family has been in the State for three centuries. The first one of record was Dr. John Waller,

CAPT. GEORGE TRAYLOR NORTHEN

HISTORY OF HENRY COUNTY, VIRGINIA 281

who was born in 1617, and married Mary Key, and there came of this union nine children. Of these Col. John Waller, who married Dorothy King, and his second son, William Waller, the progenitor of most of the Henry county branch of the family, were the most prominent historically.

William Waller was born Sept. 24, 1671, and he had a son named George, who had a son named George Jr. George Waller Jr., came from Spottsylvania county to this county near 1750, and married Ann Winston Carr, who was born in 1733. Issue: John, Mary, Elizabeth Annie, George, and Edmund who was born in 1777. (See Biography Chap. of Col. Waller.)

Col. John Waller was born Feb. 23, 1653, married Dorothy King who was born in 1675. Issue: Mary, Edmund born in 1702, Thomas, John, William, and Benjamin born in 1716.

Edmund Waller, born 1702, son of Col. John, and Dorothy, married Mary Pendleton nee Curtis. Issue: John, Mary, William Edmund, Benjamin, Leonard, James Mourning, Dorothy Jemina.

William Edmund Waller, son of Mary P. and Edmund Waller, married Mildred Smith. Issue: Mary, Nancy, Stephen, Edmund, George, Richard and William.

SECOND GENERATION

George Waller, the son of Wm. Edmund, and Mildred Smith, was born in Henry county about 1773, and married Polly Staples, a daughter of John Staples, of this county. He accumulated much property and many slaves, and lived near Preston all his life. He was a surveyor and a good business man. He inherited from his father a half interest in a 1000 acre tract of land on Clinch river Tenn. After his death, his widow moved to Miss., where their descendants are to be found. Their children were: John who marrid a Miss Walters of Pittsylvania; Geoge Waller married Laura Fountain; Sallie Waller married Elam Williams; Mary died unmarried on a visit to the county in 1848.

William Waller, another son of William Edmund and Mildred Smith, was born in this county about 1775. He was highly educated and taught school. He married Mary Barksdale daughter of John Barksdale, of Revolutionary fame, who lived at the river ford of the name near Edgewood. He moved to his Clinch valley home given by his father. His descendants number in the hundreds in that part of Tenn., and all are good substantial citizens.

FIRST GENERATION, COLLATERAL BRANCH

John Waller, son of Col. Geo., and Ann W., was born in Spottsylvania county Oct. 12, 1765, married Polly Cooper, Nov. 30, 1790, and died, March 7 1842, near Horsepasture, Va., his old home.

His wife was born Aug. 5, 1772, the daughter of Maj. Thomas Cooper of this county who before this had been a member of the House of Burgesses, was Capt. of Militia during the Revolution, and, along with the distinguished John Marr, of Henry county, was a member of the Virginia Convention of 1788, which adopted the Federal Constitution.

Mr. Waller was a justice for many years. He was a very large man physically, as his measurement at the vest was seventy-two inches. His home abounded with good cheer, much company and rare old Virginia hospitality. Their children were: Penelope, Sarah, Thomas, Mary, Margaret, William D., Patsy, Judith, George, Nancy, Elizabeth, Edmund, John, James Anthony, and Winston.

SECOND GENERATION

George Waller, son of John and Polly Cooper, was born Sept. 2, 1782, married Eliza Finley Waller, a cousin, who was born Apl. 10, 1808.

Issue of this union: Maria, Sallie, Mary Eliza, John Stephens, George E., Samuel G., Judith A. M., William D., Albert R., Lewis S., the latter born Sept. 15, 1852.

Elizabeth Waller, a sister of George, was born in 1786, and married Jacob McCraw of this county, who was a brother of Wm. McCraw, a wagon-master of Gen. Greene's Continental Army, and settled with her husband in Surry county, N. C., then largely inhabited by Tories. Being loyal to American Independence and being a soldier of the Revolutionary army, he had many personal conflicts with narrow escapes from the numerous bands of tories, some he helped to hang.

His wife was possessed, too, of that unconquerable spirit for the liberty of her country. On one occasion when alone with her infant only nine days old, she was visited by one of these bands of marauders, and tumbled out on the floor, and her personal effects being appropriated by the thieves to their use, she exclaimed to them: "Thank God all my kinfolks are clear-blooded and none of them tories".

Edmund Waller, a prominent Henry son, another brother of the two latter, was born in 1777, and married at Kingston, Tenn., Maria Duncan, who was born in 1787. He was a gallant soldier of the War of 1812, being a member of Col. Edward Johnson,s Regiment, and took part in all the important engagements of that command about Norfolk. He lived only a few years after his war career, at his home, Waller's Ford, and here he died on Nov. 1817. Their children were: Eliza Finley, who married George Waller; Ann Winston Waller who married Dandridge W. Morris; Narcissus Jane who never married; Malinda Waller who married Burwell Bassett.

THIRD GENERATION

George E. Waller, a son of Geo. and Eliza F. Waller, was born Oct. 17th, 1838, and married Sarah Louise Putzel, Sept. 10, 1868. He was a graduate of the Medical College of Virginia, and practiced his profession all his life at Martinsville, where he died Feb. 2, 1915.

He was Hospital Steward in the 24th, Virginia Infantry, and was in the main identified with Pickett's and Longstreet's divisions in all their wonderful careers in the Confederate cause, till the disbanding at Farmville, Apl. 8, 1865. His services were on the battlefield and once a ball in the Fredericksburg battle, passed through the hair of his head, and a cannon ball passed between his legs wounding a surgeon behind him.

He filled other prominent positions besides being a practitioner of medicine, and health officer. He was elected councilman, magistrate, and mayor of his town, and in every position he measured up to the highest standard of the Virginian of the old sochol.

Mrs. Sarah Putzell, the wife of Dr. Waller was born in 1846, in Orange county N. C., but soon came to Martinsville, where she lived the remainder of her life. During Stoneman's raid through the county, she appealed to the officers of the Federal army and protected her invalid mother by her captivating manners, and in return for this kindness gave the officers breakfast. She was a charter member of the Mildred Lee Chapter of the United Daughters of the Confederacy, and with only 7 members undertook the building of the monument to the Confederate dead now standing in the Public Square at Martinsville. Thirty years after Stoneman's raid, the only Confederate killed on Jones' creek in the skirmish there was moved to the Oakwood Cemetery from the Episcopal Church yard. Mrs. Waller remembered this unmarked grave, and it was on account of this transfer the Mildred Lee Chapter came into being.

The children of Dr. and Mrs. Waller are as follows: William Lewis, Samuel Sigmund, Mary McCauley, Jean, and George.

FRANK WELLS

Frank Wells came to Henry County from Dinwiddie. He married Sarah Smith: his children were, William, Daniel, Robert, Frank, Tommy, Nancy, Susan, Eliza, William, and Daniel were both killed in Civil War. Robert married Miss Stockton. Frank married 1st., Emma Lavinder, 2nd Miss Stovall. Tamsy married Brice Stultz. She has two daughters living at Fieldale, and both doing well.

Nancy also married a Stultz. Susan married 1st., James Gregory who died in Civil War, 2d. Rowland Bryant. Issue of 2nd marrage: Wm. F., who married in Texas, and left two sons, Francis and Stafford; Rowland who married Miss Dillon, and lives at Pocahontas, no issue; Norvell who lives at Newport News, and has one daughter, Margaret, and Sallie who married S. R. Hill and has 3 children Joseph, Edith, and Francis.

Eliza Wells married Mr. Bowles, and has a grand daughter doing efficient work in the Post Office: Issue of 1st. marriage of Susan Wells, & James Gregory; Overton R. who married E. J. Hill; J. R. Gregory, who married Josie Rierson; Tom Gregory who married Minnie Walker; Joseph Gregory who md. Mary Norman.

STARLING WELLS

Starling Wells married Patsy Dillon, daughter of Wm. Dillon who lived near Preston, Va. The home of Mr. Wells was very near Mt. Bethel Church. Issue: Matilda, Mary, Caroline, Ann, Burwell, Geo., Robert, David. Matilda md. John Wells, son of Baker Wells; Mary married Thomas Wells; Caroline married Adolphus Weaver; Ann md. Obediah Bouldin; Burwell md., 1st., Mrs. Ben Morris, 2nd. Miss Franklin; Geo. Md. Miss Mitchell; Robert md. Miss Turner; and David md. Miss Turner.

Matilda's oldest daughter married William Shelton (See Shelton family). To Mrs. Mary Wells were given Martha, Mary Jane, Caroline, Lou, Starling, and Robert. Martha married Wesley Shumate and left a number of children, some of them in business in Martinsville; Mary Jane; married W. C. Shumate; one of Martinsville's business men. They have two children; Russell who is an important business man in town, and a daughter. Caroline who maried Robert Forbes and moved away. Lou married Mr. Eanes and lives at Fieldale; Robert unmarried. Starling married Fannie Campbell, dau. of James Campbell.

Robert Wells, son of Starling, Sr., married Letitia Turner. Issue: Callie, Victoria, Virginia, William, and John. Wm. married and is living in S. C.; John md. Miss Lavinder, and died leaving one dau.; Virginia married W. T. Willis. She has 3 children, Ebba, Robert, and Tom. Her boys are brick-masons, and Ebba lives near her mother, and the grandchildren are a great comfort.

Victoria married Geo. Willis. Some of her large family have passed over the line. Luther, her oldest son stands high with the business men among whom he works.

Callie md. 1st., Jack Cahill. Her oldest dau. md. Harry Mitchell, and has 2 daughters, Dora, and Mildred. Callie's 2nd. husband was Jack Oakley. No issue.

David Wells, son of Starling, Sr., md. Susan Turner, and raised 3 sons and one dau. Tom, the oldest, is a carpenter. David is a merchant, and Taylor lives in Washington, D. C.

Virginia, the only dau., md. William Morris, son of John Morris.

JOHN D. THOMASSON.

John D. Thomasson was b. in Henry Co. Va., 12, 1812. During his growing up his surroundings were primitive. His father died when the boy was quite young. On one occasion his widowed mother needing some one to drive her 4-horse team to Lynchburg with her crop of tobacco, put this 6 yr. old boy on the saddle mule. The neighbors who promised to watch over him and sell the tobacco, placed him in the middle so as to protect him front and rear, and when reaching bad places unhitched their mules and pulled him out. So he could say in after years that he drove a 4-horse wagon to market when he was only 6 years of age. He remained on the farm in Va. till he was 18 and finally settled in Indiana, where he made quite a name, and prospered. He filled many important positions, and was always faithful.

He married Jane Robertson, who made him a good wife. They had one dau., Maggie, b. Sept. 5, 1840, d. Feb. 28, 1864.

WOODS FAMILY.

Robt. Woods, b. 1720, d. 1811, was Capt. in Revolution in Henry County, Va. 1st High Sheriff of Franklin county. He md. Elizabeth Middleton.

Elizabeth Woods md. Francis Hill, of Henry Co. Josiah Woods md. Sarrah Cotton Hill; Jno. Woods b. 1760, d. 1800, md. 1st. Lucy Hawkins, no issue; 2d. Agnes Ann Hairston, dau. of Robt. Hairston and his wife Ruth Stovall. Issue: Elizabeth Hairston Woods who md. Robert Hairston, son of Samuel and grandson of Robert.

Rev. Charles Carroll Woods, the only surviving member of the family of Samuel Woods and Cicely Patterson, is now Jan. 1923., living at LaGrange, Ga. His wife, Annie Miller Nichols, is a dau. of John Fontaine Nichols, of Henry Co., Va.

The Nichols family descend from John Nichols, of Pittsylvania and Henry counties, who d. 1806, in Henry County.

WOOTTON FAMILY

The Woottons are from Kent, England.

The earliest recorded member of the family is Robert Wootton who married Annie, daughter and co-heir of

Henry Belknap. They had two sons, Sir Edward Knight; and Nicholas, Doctor of Laws. The latter was a great diplomat employed at the Courts of France and Spain. Sir Edward was equal in official honors, and had a son, Thomas Wootton, who succeeded his father in his vast estate, and also became Sheriff of Kent.

For forty years during Queen Elizabeth's reign Thomas Wootton, (born in 1521, died in 1587), was regularly included in the various commissions for the county.

From this period to the settlement at Jamestown, members of each generation held the highest positions of trust and honor.

The records of Richard Wootton, who was granted a tract of land in 1643, as kept by his family in Virginia, Carolina and Georgia, show they were among the first settlers. Thomas, of Georgia, was a surveyor and patented large boundaries of land. Records at the Capitol prove he was a Lieut. in the Revolutionary War, and was given a tract for that service.

The third generation in Virginia records Thomas Wootton in the Jamestown expedition; and William Wootton, at a much later period, as Lieut., in Sept. 1781, from Prince Edawrd county, Va., in the Revolutionary records.

The seventh generation of the family begins the real history of the Henry county branch. William Wootton was born in 1740, married Lucy Owens in 1763, and died in 1809. They lived in Prince Edward county, and reared the following family: Miles, Jesse, Samuel, William Taylor, Kesiah, Jeremiah, Martha, Lucy, Elizabeth, Nancy, Polly.

FIRST GENERATION IN HENRY
(Eighth of the Family)

Miles Wootton died young; Samuel born in 1770 married Tabitha Walton; William Taylor never married; Kesiah married Boler DeJarnette; Jeremiah married Simeon Walton; Martha born in 1764, married Henry Ligon; Lucy married William Carter; Elizabeth married Nathaniel Fowlkes; Nancy married G. Hamlet; Polly married Bass Fowlkes, and Jesse.

HISTORY OF HENRY COUNTY, VIRGINIA

Jesse Wootton was born in 1774, married Jane Jeffress, and died in 1810. Their children were as follows: Mary Grief, Lucy Owen, John Taylor, Jane, Samuel Grief, Martha Coleman, Jesse, and William.

SECOND GENERATION

Mary Grief married Bedford Hamlet in 1807; Lucy Owen Wootton married Leonard Sheffield, (See Sheffiield Family); John Taylor Wootton married, and his first wife died leaving, John Francis a son. He married 2nd, Lucy, the daughter of Maj. Redd. Issue: Henry Clay who married Bettie Nicholds, Overton, (Tobe) who married Kate Fontaine, and Taylor who married Spottswood Redd.

William Wootton married Kittie Trent. She died leaving two sons, John (Jack), and William, both cared for and educated by their uncle Jesse Wootton who never married. William entered the practice of medicine.

Col. Jesse Wootton was born in 1777 and spent his life in Henry county. He was a great success as a business man, purchased Patrick Henry's Leatherwood place and owned other valuable real estate. He gained his title in the War of 1812. He was Sheriff of the county and was a prominent and influential citizen for many years. At one time he was the proprietor of the Natural Bridge property, Leonard Sheffield being in charge of the resort for him. He died in 1810.

Martha Coleman, Wootton, a sister, married Dr. Thomas H. Averett. Issue: Martha Coleman, J. T., Edmond, and Lloyd Averett.

FIFTH GENERATION

John (Jack) Wootton was a distinguished lawyer at the Henry bar who swayed juries as none, before or after him could, had a bright future, but was disappointed in his affections, took to drink, and died in early life.

TRENT CONNECTION

Z Dr. John B. Trent, whose daughter, Kittie, William Wootton married, came from Amherst and settled at Horsepasture store in this county, and married Pattie Mitchell, a sister of Mrs. Lucy Hill, Mrs. George Staples, and Mrs. Saunders. A brother of Mrs. Wootton, Van R.

Trent, married a second time, Martha Cole, and reared three children; Mattie S., Virginia, and Kittie Wootton who married Samuel Shelton. Issue: Martha K., and Vann R.

WRAY FAMILY

The Wray family is descended from a long line of English and Irish baronets and knights (See Burke's Extinct and Dormant Baronetcies).

The American branch descended from Sir Christopher VII, and is among the early settlers of Va.

Adam Wray settled in Franklin Co. Va. during or soon after the Revolutionary War. He had a large family. His son, James Iredell came from Franklin to Henry Co. in early life, and located about 4 miles west from Martinsville, Va. He married Miss Virginia Salmons, granddaughter of the pioneer, John Salmons. Issue: Malinda, William, Pinkney C., Peter R., Molly, and Rebecca. Mrs. Virginia Wray died at about the age of 46, but her husband James Iredell lived to be 90 years old, and died June, 1904.

SECOND GENERATION

Malinda married Drury Bocock and died young, leaving one son, James Bocock. William Wray died young, unmarried. P. C. Wray married Cassandra Ward Davenport, Jan. 1873. Issue: Mary now Mrs. J. W. Dillon, a widow residing in Norfolk; James R. married E. A. Morris, now living near Martinsville; Martha, now Mrs. S. S. F. Harmon, of Tazewell Co., Va.; Jno. L. of Chattanooga, Tenn.; Wm. S., Northfork, W. Va.; P. C., Norfolk, Va.; Ernest Hunter at present pastor of the Richmond Ave. Christian Church Buffalo, N. Y.; Frank M., practicing law at Berryville, Va. He graduated at Randolph Macon College, Ashland, Va., and also at the University of Va. He served as Capt. of a machine gun Co. in 3d Division in World War. He went through into Germany with the Occupation force, and was military Major of Mayence, Germany during the occupation.

Irma Virginia, the youngest, now resides with her parents at the homestead. This homestead is probably one of the oldest places in Va. The original house was built by a Mr. Holt, and later acquired by W. J. Salmons The brother of Mrs. J. I. Wray and from him it descended to P. C. Wray.

Molly Wray married Tyler Franklin, and left a number of children, all worthy citizens. Rebecca the youngest daughter, unmarried.

P. R. Wray married Pocahontas Bassett, who died leaving 3 sons and 4 daughters: Everett Bassett, of Glen White, W. Va. now Mrs. W. G. Shackelford, Lynchburg, Va.; William, of Norton, Va.; Julia, Mrs. Ascough, a widow, at home with her father; Pocahontas, unmarried, at home with her father; Nellie, Mrs. Thompson, Charleston W. Va.

WRAY COAT OF ARMS.

Az. on a chief or. 3 martlets gu. Red Hand of Ulster on Center of Ulster on Center of each Shield.

*Children of Mollie Wray and Tyler Franklin are: Virginia, Lily, Mary, Laura, Geo., Dick, and Lewis.

Appendix

APPENDIX

ABSTRACTS OF HENRY COUNTY LEGISLATIVE PETITIONS

Made from the original documents in the Archives of the Virginia State Library By Marshall Wingfield for Miss Judith P. A. Hill's History of Henry County, Virginia.

PETITION

To the Honorable Speaker and Gentlemen of the United States in Congress assembled:

The petition of sundry of the inhabitants of Henry and Patrick counties humbly showeth that they find themselves oppressed by an act past last Assembly imposing nine cents a gallon on all spirits distilled, which discourages that branch of business and the consequence is that we must be deprived of one of the blessings God and nature have given us because we have not the money to pay the excise.

The policy of all good government is to enact such laws as to keep the balance of trade in their favor. Our system of policy would be to tax importing and exporting equal to any nation we are in commerce with and encourage our own manufacturing if not by premiums let them at least be free from tax.

One dollar laid out in our own manufacturing is not missed by the community so much as that laid out in foreign manufacturing, for the consumers pay all, but policy wants it where her money centers, if it centers with us we are enriched if not we are impoverished. We therefore pray that this law may be repealed and your petitioners in duty bound shall ever pray.

Joseph Anthony, Alexander Hunter, Jos. Martin, Markham Lovell, Jacob Ferriss, Geo. Waller Jr., Richard Stockston, Thomas Groves, Jesse Oscant, Joe Philpott, Charles Philpott, F. Garrett, Richard Adams, Wm. Collins Rea, Luke Adams, James Elkins, John Minter, James Whittritt, Thomas Jamison, John Norton, Abraham Payne, Joel Pace, Wm. Pace, Edward Daniel, John Cox, Tho. East, Reuben Nance, Edmon Toombs, Martin Bunch,

Tho. Gooch, John Lanier, John Philips, Thomas Cooper, Robert Watson, John East, Berry Moore, Benjamin McInney, Thomas Adams Jr., Thomas Leak, Robt. Anderson, Jesse Witt, Wm. Rea, John Mills, Hamon Critz, John McGee, Wm. Adams, Elisha Adams, Isaac Adams, Peter France, Daniel France, John France, John Randel, Geo. Pennilen, Robt. Quillen, Jacob Adams, Peter Adams, Wm. Adams, Hezekiah Shelton, James Shelton, Peter Shelton, Woody Burge, David Burge, Wm. Fortune, Peter Roman, Robt. Roman, John Roman, Munford Smith, Wm. Scott, John Jones, Isham Wells, Wm. Carter, Wm. Mitchell, Daniel Carlton, John Jarrett Jacob Lawson, David Lawson, Ben Rea, Edward Tatum, Nathaniel Smith, Joseph Pratt, Charles Ferriss, Joshua Ferriss, John Dillard, Mike Rowland, Wm. Shelton, Erasmer Alley, Wm. Reynolds, Joseph Carr, John Alexander, Major Runnells, John Salmons, Bartlett Reynolds, James Spencer, Henry Koger.

ABSTRACTS OF HENRY COUNTY LEGISLATIVE PETITIONS

Made by Rev. Marshall Wingfield, from the original documents in the Archives of the State Library of Virginia, at Richmond, for Miss J. P. A. Hill's History of Henry County Virginia.

No. 321. May 24, 1779. This petition prays for a division of Henry county, "By running a line from the head of Shooting Creek to the head of Turkey Cock Creek, thence to intersect the dividing line between Henry and Pittsylvania, thence along that dividing line to the mouth of Black Water River, which part of Henry will contain about 300. Further, your petitioners pray that, that part of Bedford which lieth on the Staunton River may be cut off and added to them, which proposal your petitioners are informed is much desired by those inhabitants of Bedford who reside on the south side of the Staunton ———". This petition bears nearly 500 signatures, many of them being names of families still represented in the county.

No. 330. May 28, 1779. A remonstrance against the division of Henry county, and praying that "Edm'd Winston, Paul Carrington, John Wilson and Benjamin Lankford, esqr's., Gentlemen having no connections, no property or concerns in this county, may be called upon to be examined concerning the premises." This petition is signed by Will Tunstall John Salmon, E. Lyne, Mordecai Hord, Henry Lyne, Wm. Gardner and Waters Dunn, and seemed to have more weight with the General Assembly than the petition of 500 names. On the back of this Petition the Clerk of the House wrote the word, "Reasonable."

No. 408. Nov. 2, 1779. Petition for division of the county with nearly 300 signatures.

No. 509. June 3, 1780. Walton King Coles represents that before the outbreak of the Revolutionary War his reputed father, Walter King of Great Britain, had assured him that he should be handsomely provided for out of the said King's, Virginia estate. That the said King's Virginia estate was confiscated by the State thus robbing him of what would have fallen to him. Prays House of Delegates to restore to him that which his reputed father's benevolence intended for him. Also sets forth his service as a soldier in the American army in the War of the Revolution.

No. 574. Nov. 23, 1780. Elizabeth Crowley represents that her husband was appointed a spy in the Expedition under General Lewis in 1774 against the Indians, and was killed. She was allotted ten pounds in consequence thereof, but prays such additional allowance as maybe adjudged reasonable.

No. 574-A. Nov. 23, 1780. Petition of James Armstrong represents that he lost a fine horse when he went out "on an expedition against the Tories," and prays compensation.

No. 778. June 8, 1782. Petition for the formation of a new county from Henry, and setting forth that the new county would contain 1200 tithables. App. 300 signatures.

No. 779. June 8, 1782. A petition remonstrating against a division of Henry County. Approximately 300 signatures.

No. 780. June 8, 1782. Petition prays that "the hollow which lies on the waters of the Yadkin may be added to Montgomery county." 39 signatures.

No. 850. Nov. 23, 1782. Petition for the division of Henry county, according to the lines of a remarkable pen-drawn map attached to the petition. 285 signatures.

No. 851. Nov. 23, 1782. Remonstrance against a division of Henry county. App. 260 signatures.

No. 901. June 4, 1783. Remonstrance against division of county. App. 135 signatures.

No. 939-A. Nov. 4, 1783. Petition for a division of the county. Over 1000 signatures.

No. 1123. June 12, 1784. William Ryan represents that. "In making his collection as Sheriff of Henry county he received two tobacco notes issued by the Inspection of Tobacco at Rock Ridge, which tobacco was burnt in the said Inspection." Prays relief.

No. 1268. Dec. 4, 1784. Petition for division of the county. 280 Signatures.

No. 1290. Oct. 27, 1785. A remarkable plot of the county. No petition is found with this drawing. Probably belongs with the following (No. 1291).

No. 1291. Oct. 27, 1785. Petition for the division of the county. This petition is on a sheet of paper nearly ten feet long and contains about 1500 signatures.

No. 1292. Oct. 27, 1785. Petition for taking that part of Bedford on the south side of Staunton river and a part of Henry on the North side of the river to form a distinct and separate county. 264 signatures. This territory became Franklin county.

No. 1293. Oct. 27, 1785. Advertisements of men who were employed by Richard Mitchell to go to South Carolina in search of horses which had been stolen from him.

No. 1551. Nov. 8, 1786. Petition sets forth that at the last session of the Assembly an Act was passed dividing Henry and Bedford counties, and forming Franklin from the territory, which division left the Henry Court House so near the north side of the county as to make it inconvenient for the majority of the citizens to attend. Prays for the establishment of the Court House at a more central point. 42 signatures.

No. 2056-A. Oct. 26, 1789. Petition against the division of the county. 300 signatures.

No. 2154. Nov. 14, 1789. Petition against division of the county. 525 signatures.

No. 2263. Oct 23, 1790. Praying that the county of Henry may be divided into two distinct counties, "beginning on the dividing line between Henry and

Franklin, one mile above where the dividing line crosses Town Creek, thence a parallel line with the Pittsylvania line." That part of the county east of the parallel line to retain the name of Henry. 705 signatures.

No. 2264. Oct. 23, 1790. A petition remonstrating against a division of Henry county setting forth that part of the public buildings have just been completed and that part are still unfinished, and that the tax is already too heavy to be borne by all the people, without a division. 528 signatures.

No. 2522. Oct. 28, 1791. Daniel Carlin represents that he was ordered by Col. William Tunstall, county lieutenant of Henry county, to march against the British in North Carolina; that he marched and served until March 10, 1788. Prays compensation. ---

No. 2592. Nov. 8, 1791. Petition recites that at last session of the Assembly the County of Henry was divided to the great satisfaction of the petitioners, and prays that the present session may pass an Act for establishing a town on forty acres adjacent to the Henry county Court House. 27 signatures.

No. 2625-A. Nov. 12, 1791. Citizens of Henry and Patrick join in praying that the line between these counties be run in the following manner: "Beginning one mile above Town Creek on the dividing line between Henry and Franklin counties, thence a direct course to the North Carolina line at the lower crossing Crooked Creek, a branch of Mayo River ____"—Signatures of James Armstrong and Jos. Martin.

No. 3201. Nov. 15, 1794. George Hairston prays remission of damages in sum of 150 pounds assessed against him for not turning in revenue tax within the time specified by law.

No. 3202. Nov. 15, 1794. Petition for the repeal of "an Act for the more effectual collecting of certain arrears of taxes and duties." App. 50 signatures.

No. 3253. Nov. 22, 1794. "The petition of the freeholders and others, the inhabitants of the county of Henry humbly sheweth that there is no Seminary of Classical learning in either of the adjacent counties or at any convenient distance; that the town of Martinsville is tolerably central to the counties of Patrick, Franklin, Pittsylvania and Henry in the State of Virginia, and that of Rockingham of No. Carolina. We therefore pray that the Academy which is now erected at Martinsville may have the sanction of your honourable House and that such men be appointed trustees as the Gentlemen Delegates from the counties of Henry, Patrick and Franklin may nominate." Signed by John Dillard, Robert Sharp, Jacob Lindsay, Joshua Dillingham, John Clemens, James Meredith, Jesse Atkisson, Ballenger Wade, Hezekiah Salmon, Joseph Morris, Burwell Bassett, Nathaniel Bassett, Richard Wade, Stephen Atkisson, Jesse Atkisson, Jr., Thos. Dickenson, Jonadab Wade, Wm. Shelton, George Hairston, John Ellis, John Staples, Benj. Jones, William Jones, Haynes Morgan, Jr., Wm. Paul, William Roberts, Fleming Saunders, N. W. Williams, Hugh Innis, Jr., John Stokes, Jr., J. D. Linsday, Lewis Bitting, Robert Cox, Wm. F. Mills and others.,

No. 3632. Nov. 23, 1796.* Petition for the holding of the District Court alternately at Franklin and Pittsylvania Court Houses. Nearly 200 signatures.

No. 3678. Dec. 7, 1797. Blizzard Magruder prays for an extension of the time allowed for the survey of lands and return of plats to Land Office. Names of John Salmon, Geo. Waller, John Cox, Henry Lyne, Sm'l Jennings, Wm. French, John Parr, Jr., Henry Smith, Nath'l Smith, Wm. Smith, John Smith, John Dillard, Wm. Hays, John Hays, Edw. Tatum, John Henly, Eliphaz Shelton, Gab Penn, George Clark, Samuel Staples, B. Stovall and others appear on this petition.

No. 3962. Dec. 24, 1798. William Wirt in behalf of his wife, Mildred, and the other children and devisees of Geo. Gilmer, dec'd, prays that the Assembly release the rights of escheat, so that lands of the said Gilmer may be shared by his devisees according to his will.

No. 4137. Dec. 19, 1799. Petition for an Act extending the navigation of the Smith's River by subscription. 24 signatures.

No. 5013 Dec. 9, 1806. A sheaf of petitions relative to the petition of Mrs. Polly Stone for a divorce from her husband, Jeremiah Stone. Several of these petitions represent that Jeremiah Stone is a worthy man and that there is no occasion for the granting of a divorce, while others declare him to be "the most abandoned wretch we ever knew." Nearly 200 signatures favor the petition of Mrs. Stone and about 75 names on petition opposing her plea for divorce.

No. 5035. Dec. 12, 1806. Citizens of Henry pray for an Act providing for the election, support etc. of a political convention. 78 signatures.

No. 5128. Dec. 11, 1807. Citizens of Henry and Patrick counties shew inconvenience experienced from lack of roads to communicate with the main roads, and pray that the County Courts of the said counties may be vested with the power to direct the width of any road thereafter established etc. 19 signatures.

No. 5352. Dec. 6, 1809. Petition of William Draper praying for right to bring from North Carolina a man slave belonging to him, and who belonged to him prior to the passage of the law against the moving of slaves into other states. About 50 signatures in addition to that of the petitioner.

No. 5395. Dec. 8, 1809. Elizabeth Rice Stacy petitions for a divorce from John Stacy on the grounds of brutal treatment. Petition is accompanied by a number of affidavits, among them being those of Zona Custer, Peter Garland, Robert Payne, George Taylor, Rachael Taylor, and also a petition in behalf of the said Elizabeth Rice Stacy signed by fifteen leading citizens.

No. 5396. Dec. 8, 1809. A remonstrance against the "Extraordinary innovations in our long established customs relative to the recommendation of sheriffs," and a prayer that the Assembly will "Hereafter regulate the principles upon which the recommendations of sheriffs shall be made in such manner" that the justices of the peace may receive in return for their long and inadequately compensated services "the emoluments which flow from his sheriffalty." 21 signatures.

No. 5466. Dec. 14, 1809. Petition of John Crunk for authority to bring his slaves from North Carolina into Virginia.

No. 5525. Dec. 21, 1809. Petition of John A. Verdel for authority to bring back into Virginia one of his slaves whom he had hired to a North Carolinian before the passage of the law against the removal of slaves from one state to another.

No. 6120. Dec. 14, 1812. Petition of James Patterson for authority to bring into Henry county those slaves of which his father living in South Carolina died seized and possessed. Petition accompanied by certificate signed by 14 men.

No. 6397. Nov. 15, 1814. Petition for the holding of the Quarterly Courts on the second Monday in March, June, August and November of each year, so as not to conflict with the sessions of the Superior Court of the said county. Signed by ten attorneys.

No. 6772. Nov. 20, 1816. Benjamin Jones prays for authority to keep a slave girl brought to Henry county from South Carolina by his married son, and for whom he gave his son a boy and a woman slave.

No. 8350. Dec. 8, 1825. Memorial praying right to ascertain the sense of the people as to whether there should be held a Convention for the purpose of revising or amending the Constitution of Virginia. 59 signatures.

No. 8727. Dec. 16, 1826. Petition of James Johnston an old Revolutionary soldier praying for a pension. Accompanied by the affidavits of Edward Eanes, George Hannah, and Dr. John Robertson.

No. 9165. Dec. 10, 1828. Petition of William Deshazo praying the Legislature to make some provision for paying him the value of One hundred acres of land which was promised him by the State for services rendered during the Revolutionary War.

No. 9587. Dec. 14, 1830. Petition of William Potter and wife, and of John Dillard, praying the liberation of a slave confined in the jail of Henry county, or else that some legal steps be taken at once to secure the services or the value of said slave to petitioners.

No. 10247. Jan. 16, 1833. Citizens of Henry, Patrick and Pittsylvania counties praying an amendment to the Act incorporating "The Danville and Evensham Turnpike Company." 48 signatures.

No. 10371. Dec. 6, 1833. Petition of citizens of Henry and other counties praying a repeal of the Act increasing tolls on the Manchester Turnpike. App. 300 signatures.

No. 10485. Dec. 30, 1833. The petition of citizens of Henry and other counties praying for an Act incorporating a company to improve the navigation of Smith's River. App. 125. signatures.

No. 10999. Dec. 14, 1835. James Johnston again shows his service as a Revolutionary soldier and prays for a pension.

No. 12324. Jan. 24, 1839. A petition of Daniel Stone and others asking for the construction of a railroad from some point on the Roanoke to the Tennessee line on State account. 32 signatures.

No. 14442. Jan. 28, 1845.* Petition for an extension of the jurisdiction of a single magistrate to all sums of fifty dollars and under. 39 signatures.

No. 14736. Jan. 3, 1846. Petition for the better organization and discipline of the militia and the revival of battalion musters. 3 signatures.

No. 15191. Dec. 23. 1846. Petition for the establishment of an election precinct at the house of Elkanah B. Turner. 60 signatures.

No. 15230. Dec. 31, 1846. Petition of voters of Henry praying that the Free School Law passed at the last session of Assembly be repealed so far as Henry county is concerned and the old system restored. 352 signatures.

No. 15231. Dec. 31, 1846. Petition for the repeal of the Free School Law. App. 300 signatures.

No. 15423. Jan. 25, 1847. Remonstrance of President and Board of School Commissioners against the law establishing district schools in Henry county.

No. 15541. Feb. 13, 1847. Petition for the construction of a rail road from Richmond to the town of Danville. 31 signatures.

No. 15666. Dec. 9, 1847. Petition for an amendment to the laws relative to licenses for retailing ardent spirits. Signed by Anthony M. Dupuy.

No. 15738. Dec. 23, 1847. Memorial of the Henry County Bar praying for a change in time of holding Superior Court in Franklin county. Signed by George Gravely, J. Griggs, C. Y. Thomas, John T. Hooker, Anthony M. Dupuy, John O. Redd, W. J. Hamlett, and two others whose signatures are illegible.

No. 16003. Feb. 3, 1848. Petition for incorporation of a joint stock company to improve navigation of Smith's River. 118 signatures.

No. 16051. Feb. 11, 1848. Preamble to Resolutions of the Henry Division, No. 15, of the Sons of Temperance. Signed by G. Pannill, J. H. Minor, and John Larmand.

No. 16315. Dec. 20, 1848. Petition of Lucy W. Norman from her husband James B. Norman.

No. 17119. Feb. 12, 1850. Petition of George Hairston, Pleasant Wilmontt, Josiah T. Mitchell, James M. Smith, John R. Fontaine, E. T. Starling, Hughes Dillard, H. C. Redd, W. J. Salmon, and J. G. Redd for a modification of the school law.

No. 17863. Jan. 22, 1852. Petition for the removal of election precinct from the house of William Pulliam to a more suitable place. 112 signatures, that of William Pulliam himself heading the list.

No. 18151. March 5, 1852. Petition for an election precinct at Ridgeway. 102 signatures.

No. 18252. April 5, 1852. Petition of James Smith, Hill M. Redd, George Hairston, P. R. Reamey and John King asking for a change in the school laws.

No. 18266. April 8, 1852. Petition of Anthony M. Dupuy, Jas. M. Smith, Sigmund Putzel, Jno. R. Fontaine, C. Y. Thomas, L. W. Redd, J. Griggs, Drury C. Dillard, W. F. Clark, Anderson Wade, and Hughes Dillard for the establishment of a savings bank at Martinsville.

No. 18730. Jan. 2, 1854. Memorial of citizens of Henry, Franklin and other counties for the incorporation of a company for the construction of a rail road from Lynchburg to a point on the Virginia-North Carolina line. 96 signatures.

No. 18950. Jan. 27, 1854. Petition of citizens for the establishment of a branch of the Bank of Virginia, the Farmers Bank, or the Exchange Bank, in the town of Martinsville. 23 signatures.

No. 19445. Dec. 17, 1857. Petition of the Bar and citizens of Henry county praying that the judges of Virginia may be required to hold the courts of their respective jurisdictions alternately. 65 signatures.

HISTORY OF HENRY COUNTY, VIRGINIA

INDEX TO ENROLLED BILLS, PERTAINING TO HENRY COUNTY, IN THE GENERAL ASSEMBLY OF VIRGINIA FROM 1776 TO 1910.

	VOLUME	PAGE
Forming from Pittsylvania	1776	27
For altering Court days of	1778	27
For dissolving vestries of	1782	10
Forming Franklin county from	1785	77
Changing place of holding court	1786	20
Changing court days of	1786	53
Changing time for holding court in	1788	17
For supplying loss of entry books and notes of surveyor	1789	30
Forming Patrick county from	1790	7
Adding part of Henry to Patrick	1791	7
For relief of owners of entries	1792	28
Amending Act relative to entries in	1793	25
Changing court days of	1809-10	115
Changing time for holding courts of	1814-15	92
Authorizing separate election in	1830-31	7
Authorizing separate election in	1830-31	60
Authorizing separate election in	1835-36	64
Authorizing separate election in	1846-47	6
Concerning free school system in	1848-49	10
Annexing part of Patrick to Henry	1857-58	60
Authorizing sale of district school house in	1863	188
Providing for sales of district free school house	1848-49	66
Authorizing subscriptions to incorporated companies by	1869-70	804
Repealing Act which declared Smith's River lawful fence	1872-73	18
For protection of fish in Smith's River in Henry	1872-73	150
Declaring Smith's River a lawful fence in Henry	1872-73	202
Amending Act declaring Smith's River lawful fence	1874-75	496
For furnishing convicts to work on railroad in	1877-78	208
Authorizing tax levy to pay subs. to Danville-New River Ry.	1879	54
Preventing obstructions to passage of fish in Smith River	1879-80	207
Amending Act declaring Smith's River lawful fence in	1883-84	455
For protection of game in	1885-86	278
Authorizing expenditure of school funds for buildings	1887	156
For protection of game in	1887-88	114
For working roads of	1897-98	1401
For protection of partridges in	1897-98	1750
For relief of sureties of Treasurer of	1899-00	1943
Legalizing subscription of $50,000 to stock of Mt. Rogers and Easter Railroad Company	1901-02	565
To permit the netting of partridges in	1902-03-04	1623

CITIZENS OF HENRY COUNTY WHO TOOK THE OATH OF ALLEGIANCE

The General Assembly of Virginia, when The United States was in its infancy, passed an Act to oblige all free male inhabitants of the State above sixteen years of age to give assurance of allegiance to the same. The following is a list of those who took the oath from the original record among the files in the Clerk's Office. At the time some were away fighting Indians, others hunting, and there were a few who refused to take the oath.

William Allen
John Abingdon
Henry Arnold
Bowles Abingdon
Jacob Adams
James Acton
Samuel Allen
Micajah Allen
Abraham Adams
Wm. Adams
John Alexander
Philip Augreen
Mark Adkins
Armsitead Anderson
Wm. Bohannan
Jno. Alexander, Sr.
Wm. Alexander
James Anthony
Joel Adkinson
Thomas Ashley
James Anderson
Joseph Anthony
Wm. Alexander
Daniel Allen
Francis Armstrong
David Atkins
Benry Baughn
John Briscoe
Christopher Boling
Joseph Boling
Christopher Boling, Jr.
Archibald Boling
James Blevens, Jr.
Aristophus Baughn
Reuben Baughn
Adam Cantwell
Samuel Byrd
Joseph Baker
Joseph Bradberry
Charles Burnes, Sr.
John Bolin

Martin Burch
David Burch
Wm. Blevens, Jr.
Willoughby Blevens
John Blevens
Dillon Blevens
Micajah Bool
Andrew Burns
Samuel Burnes
Truman Brisco
Charles Byrne, Sr.
Wm. Burnes
Thomas Bailey
Chandler Bailey
John Bailey
Carr Bailey
Wm. Bailey
Wm. Bohannan
Churchill Blakey
Michael Beel
Andrew Beel
David Barton
John Bryant
Charles Bonner
James Bolton
Augustine Brown
Peter Blanchett
Henry Bradberry
John Barker
Joel Barker
Charles Barker
Michael Barker
Joseph Blair
John Barksdale
Henry Barksdale
Thomas Bolton
Robt. Bolton, Sr.
James Bolton
Nathaniel Barnett
Jarvis Burdet
Wm. Breden

Charles Barnard
John Burks
Wm. Burks
John Brock
Aquila Baker
Edmund Baker
Josiah Bryan
Rowland Birks
Peter Bays
Sherwood Brock
John Curselly
Richard Copeland
Joseph Cooper
John Cooper
Thomas Cooper
Robert Cave
John Crouch
John Crouch, Jr.
Bailey Carter
Toliver Cox
John Cox
Cowler John
Thomas Collier
Wm. Collier
Charles Collier
Jesse Collier
Joseph Chandler
Jesse Chandler
Robert Chandler
Alexander Cavin
John Cantwell
Elijah Chism
John Chism
Geo. Carter
Josiah Carter
Joseph Cloud, Sr.
Joseph Cloud, Jr.
John Cunningham
John Corbitt
Adam Cantwell
James Charles
Thomas Callan
Joseph Cook
Ben Cook, Jr.
W. Choice
Tully Choice, Sr.
Tully Choice, Jr.
James Cooly
Adner Cockerhan
Wm. Chambers
Daniel Casey
Andrew Clark
John Koger

Nicholas Koger
John Campbell
Savarus Cotton
John Cotton
Thomas Cober
Enoch Conley
Raynes Carter
David Chadwell
Thomas Dooling
Thomas Dotty
Henry Dunlap
Waters Dunn, Jr.
Richard Francher
John Dobbs
Geo. Daniel
Gatewood Dunn
Richard Dunn
Jacob Dillinger
Wm. Dalton
John Davis
Solomon Davis
Wm. Greer
Joel Estes
James Estes
Alstrop Estes
Francis Gilley
Joseph Epperson
Charles Gates
Robt. Grimmit
John Grimmit
David Gibson
James Goddard
Richard Holt
Elisha Ivie
Jonathan Ison
Wm. Ison
Ambrose Jones
John Jamerson
Robt. C. Jones
Thomas Jamerson
Thomas Jones
Wm. Jamerson
Geo. Jones
David Clarkson
Wm. Davison
Wm. Finch
Henry Dillon
Benjamin Dillon
John Dillon
Carter Dillon
Thompson Dickson
Charles Dodson
John Doughten

John Duncan
Henry Diller
John Daniel, Sr.
John Fling
Wm. Denson
James Dicks
James Denson
Waters Dunn
John Farrell
Abraham Franklin
Thomas Garner
John Dillingham
John Good
Joseph Goodman
Samuel Gray
John Daniel, Jr.
Michael Dunn
Nathaniel Elkins
Wm. Elkins
Joseph Davis
Elisha Estes
Wm. Estes
Wm. Graves
Wm. Graves, Sr.
Wm. Estes
Andrew Gough
Howel Evoy
James Gates
Wm. Gates
Isham Hall
John Henderson
John Hall
Sam Hall, Sr.
John Ison
John Gussett
Wm. Graves, Sr.
David Graves
Wm. Graves
John Garrett
Belesworth Grafty
James Green
Wm. Green
Henry Harris
Thomas Hall
Peter Craghead
Samuel Canterbury
James Cooley
Thomas Finch
Mark Foster
Charles Foster
Bartlett Foley
Luke Foley
Geo. Foldy

John Fleming
Wm. Farris
Wm. Ferguson
James Frenor
Thomas Flowers
Samuel Fore
John Farrell
Moses Dotty
Moses Dillingham
James Duncan
John Duncan
John Gowing
Moses Dickerson
David Gowing
John Gowing
Edjecomb Guilliams
James Elkins
Aquila Greer
James Estes
Wm. Graves
Wm. Estes
Thomas Gough
Bottom Estes
Samuel Gates
Wm. East
Thomas Harbour
John Hickey
John Isham
James Ison
Clark Ison
Isaac Hill
Uriah Hardman
Adojah Harber
Ben. Hubbard
Lanceford Hall
Elisha Harbour
Wm. Hollinsworth
Peter Hudson
John Hall
Wm. Robt. Hinton
Jamey James
John Jones
Joseph Jones
Wm. Jones
Marry Heard Hall
Nimrod Hanbrick
John Hall
Thomas Henry
Thomas Hancock
Wm. Hay
John Hardman
Wm. Hardman
David Harber

Joseph Hammond
Joseph King
David Kirby
Elisha Keen
Samuel Hutt
Peter Hairston
Joseph Hunt
Moses Harris
John Holden
David Kirby
James King
Henry Haynes
Wm. Hutchinson
Paul Hutchinson
Elections Hardin
Lewis Hale
Nathaniel King
John Land
Thomas McKeen
John Luray
Joel Lyon
Samuel Loggins
Walter Marks
Wm. Lawson
James Lyon
Edmund Lyne
Henry Law
Jeffrey Murrell
James Meredith, Sr.
James Meredith
John Minter
Rodsham Moore
Alexander Lyle
Eli Landford
David Lawson
John Lawson
John Medlock, Sr.
Ambrose Mullins
Wm. Login
Wm. Mullins
John Long
Wm. Lake
Alex. Jarvis
Nathan Hall
Robt. Harris
Randolph Hall
Eusebius Hubbard
Lanceford Hall
Wm. Hodges, Jr.
Jesse Hurd
Ambrose Holt
Geo. Haynes
Wm. Haynes

Josiah Hodges
Jesse Hall
Peter Harris
Abner Harbour
James Hinton
David Hinton
Jesse Kirby
Richard Kirby
James Kinney
Benj. Kinney, Sr.
Jonathan Hanby
Samuel Hairston
Henry Haynes, Sr.
Wm. Harrell
Thomas Holt
John Handy
Joel Harbour
Daniel Howell
Barnabas Kelly
Geo. Lessieur
John Noe, Sr.
Lucas Luraya
Wm. Mavity
John Menifee
Wm. Menifee
John Neaville
John McQueery
Thomas Morrison
Wm. McAlexander
Samuel Meredith
Bristol Matthews
Geo. Phillip, Sr.
Abraham Parsley
John Philpott
John Payne
John Parr, Sr.
Wm. Meredith
Garrett Moore
Bradley Meredith
John Mullins
Ben. Potter
Richard Packwood
Michael Plaster
Thomas Mosley
Stephen Mays
Wm. Heard
Thomas Hollinsworth
Thomas Hamilton
Philip Hutchinson
John Heard
Hezekiah Jordan
John Litten Jones
James Johnson

John Jonakin
John Jenkins
Lewis Jenkins
John Jones, Jr.
John Jones, Sr.
Wm. Johnson
Robert Jones
Samuel Hinton
Augustine Hunnicutt
Robert Hairston
Francis Holt
Thomas Henderson
Mordecai Hord
Archelaus Hughes
Charles Hibberts
Charles Hardman
Joseph Hammond
Joseph Kirby
John Kindrick
Barnabas Kendrick
Thomas Kendrick
Benj. Kimsey, Sr.
John Kendrick, Jr.
James Newman
Brice Martin
John Lynd
Thomas Nunn
Joseph Nunn
Samuel Noe
Dennis O'Bryan
James Oakley
Ben. Oakley
Thomas Parsley
John Parsley
Nathaniel Law
Wm. Longs
John Livingston
Thomas Land
John Pelfrey
James Prunty
Thomas Prunty
Robert Powell
Richard Perison
Wm. Lawson
James Poteet
John Pace
Robert Pussy
Moses Parsell
Geo. Lawson
John Lane
Wm. Law
Thomas Madclaf
Daniel Prilliman

Samuel Packwood
Robert Perryman
Humphrey Posey
David Perwit, Jr.
Thomas Potter
Elijah Perwitt
David Perwitt
John Perwit
Archibald Prator
Jonathan Prator
Wm. Price
Daniel Newman
Francis Quarles
Richard Shores
Rowland Salmon
John Stokes
Randall Smith
John Smith
James Sams
Samuel Selmour
Zachariah Smith
John Simmons
Wm. Shrophire
Augustine Thomas
Wm. Thorp
Nathaniel Tate
Christian Rotz
Wm. Turner
Michael Rowland
Gideon Rucker
Charles Thomas
Wm. Tinch
Richard Ratcliff
John Ratcliff
Silas Ratcliff
John Rea
John Robinson, Sr.
Andrew Ray
James Ray
John Rennoe
Owen Roubies
Wm. Rentfro
Thomas Roberst
John Rentfro
Philip Ryan
David Rogers
Geo. Rogers
Peter Rickman
Jacob Read
Wm. Smith, Sr.
John Medlock, Jr.
Wm. McCoy
John Perryman

Richard Pursell
Jacob McCraw
Wm. McCraw
David Matlock
Patrick McBride
James Matlock
Hugh McKeen
Abraham Mays
David Mays
Henry Mays
Sherod Mays
Joshua Mayberry
Hance McKeen
John Noe, Jr.
Daniel Reamey
Daniel Ramsey
John Ramsey
Zachariah Seaman
John Spurlock, Jr.
John Sppurlock, Jr.
Wm. Short
David Short
John Small
John Sullivant
John Sumter
Wm. Stanley, Jr.
Thomas Richards
John Salmon
Geo. Reeves
James Standefer
Rowland Ben. Stimer
Amos Richardson
Ben Turman
John Smith
Rally Shelton
Matthew Small
Wm. Small
Joseph Sismonds
John Sergeant
Wm. Spurlock, Sr.
Jesse Spurlock
John Spurlock, Sr.
John Richardson
Ignatins Sims
Hezekiah Salmons
Richard Stanley
Gideon Smith
Wm. Stanley
John Stanley
Thomas Willingham, Sr.
Edward Polly
Geo. Pool
Jesse Law

Wm. Midkiff
John Murphy
Joseph Mayby
Lewis Morgan
John McKinsey
Thomas Morrow
Isac McDonald
Thomas Murrill
Elections Musick
Henry McGuffy
Thomas Nelson
Joseph Newman
Alex. McKeen
Alexander Pyle
James Stennet
Julius Scruggs
Daniel Smith
Richard Reel
John Reel
James Reel
Daniel Ross
John Ross
Moses Riddle
Geo. Rowland
Geo. Rowland, Jr.
Henry Sumpter
Edward Tatum
Robert Searsey
John Turner
Jesse Thesby
Israel Standefer
Jeremiah Strewsberry
John Royall
Abednigo Turner
Geo. Taylor
James Taylor
Wm. Tunstall
Henry Tate
Robert Tate
John Tarrance
Anthony Tittle
Geo. Tittle
John Tittle
Peter Vardenum
Nathaniel Yell
Wm. Vinson
Thomas Winningham
Abner Willingham
Amos Richardson
Elisha Walden
Eliphaz Shelton
Matthew Sims
Henry Smith

Elisha Solomon
Bartlett Sims
James Savant
Wm. Read
Geo. Sumpter
John Stamps
John Willinham
Wm. Swanson, Sr.
John Walker
John Watson
John Witt
Sylvanus Witt
Allen Ridley
Joel Walker
Jesse Williamson
John Witt
Joseph Willis
John Woodson
Morris Webb
Darrell Smith
Thomas Webb, Jr.
Nathan Swanson
Joseph Williams

Tolton Woody
John Woodall
Robert Woods
David Witt
James Young
Wm. Young
Wm. Ryan
Wm. Russell
Stephen Robinson
Richard Reynolds
John Rowland, Sr.
Ben Richardson
Merry Webb
Wm. Williams
John Swanson
Harris Wilson
John Wells
Daniel Willis
Geo. Waller
Wm. Witt
John Young
Archibald Young.

Personal property of John King sold on Leatherwood a century ago with name of purchaser and price of each article

Mary King, A. flax Wheel	$ 1.05
Charles Wingfield, A pot	1.35
John Francis Gregory, Five hogs	8.00
Michael Griggs, Four shoats, 2 choice	2.00
John Thomasson, A white sow and 5 shoats	4.00
Jacob L. King, A sow and 4 shoats	3.50
Fleming Gregory, One hilling hoe	1.00
Camillus King, I Cary Plow	1.25
Orthneal Minter, I cotton wheel	1.75
Jacob L. King, I Pigin	.25
Joseph E. Gravely, I loom	3.25
Charles Wingfield, 2 Iron wedges	.85
Thomas Eggleton, I fro	.50
John Finney, I yoke of oxen	30.00
John Finney, I ox cart	15.00
Jacob L. King, a tract of land	166.00
George King, I Negro, Bob	380.00
Jacob L. King, A Negro girl, Delphy,	375.00
Jacob L. King, A Negro girl, Catherine	200.00
Jacob L. King, I old woman	100.00
John Hoffman, 5 barrels of corn $2.50	12.50
Joseph K. Gravely, One horse	40.00
Daniel Pace, 3 sheep and lamb	3.00
Charles Wingfield, I house of tobacco	5.37
George King, I stack of top fodder	2.00
John Cheshire, I stack of blade fodder	3.00

George Gravely, Stack of oats 2.90
George Gregory, white cow 5.80
George King, a white yearling 1.35
Mary King, 1 large chest 3.00
Thomas Stultz, One folding table 1.30
Jacob L. King, a desk 4.00
John Finney, 1 cow-hide 1.30
Columbus King, 3 hogs 25.00
Thomas Eggleton, a pair of stiliards .... .71

NOTE. This is a partial list showing prices paid those days.

FIRST HENRY COUNTY COURT

(From the Virginia Magazine of History and Biography.)

The first court held for Henry County was in Jan. 1777, and composed of Edmund Lyne, Abraham Penn, Peter Saunders, and Geo. Waller, Justices.

Five commissioners were appointed to view the center of the county for the most covenient place thereat for fixing the courthouse.

Daniel Carla qualified as Capt. of Militia.

John Salmon qualified as Sheriff.

Matthew Small 2nd. Lieut. under Thomas Henderson took the oath. May—The commissioners report that the land of Henry Barksdale is the most convenient place for establishing the courthouse and the court concurred to the same.

Commissioners appointed to let the building a courthouse, Prison, Stocks and Pillory; said prison to be 20 ft. by 16 and double loggs 12 inches square, a chimney in the middle of brick or stone a fire place in each, room shingled roof, the joyst to be covered with loggs 12 inches square, a window in each room with iron grates, double doors with substantial locks. Also the courthouse 24 by 20 feet, with hewed or sawed logs, to 10 ft. pitch with boarded roof planked above and below, with a pair of steps and a Barr and benches with a window in each side and a door in each side.

Elizabeth Cooper came into court and made oath that John Bolling of Henry county, is the lawful heir of William Bolling, deceased, who went from the said county into the Continental service and there died.

Oct.—Hayner Morgan, Esqr., Produced commission from the Governor to practice law as an attorney and took the oath.

License granted Mordecai Hord to keep an ordinary at his house

License granted Brice Martin to keep an ordinary at this courthouse.

Abraham Penn appointed Lieut. Colonel in the room of Edmund Lyne, resigned.

James Lyon appointed Major in the room of Abraham Penn 1779, March—Eliphaz Shelton appointed Capt. in the room of James Lyon, Stephen Lyon, 1st Lieut., Wm. Halbert, 2nd Lieut. and David Rogers, Ensign.

License granted to John Marr to keep an ordinary at his house.

Peter Saunders is allowed 25 Pounds for necessaries found Mary Lawrence, wife of John Lawrence, who is in the Continental service. Thomas Smith produced a commission appointing him Capt. of the Militia in this county.

John Davis produced commission appointing him 2nd Lieut. in Thomas Smith's company.

Peter Harris produced a commission appointing him, Ensign, in Thomas Henderson's company.

Swinfield Hill is appointed Capt. of the militia in the room of Ed. Short.

Thomas Hasile is appointed Capt. in the room of Peter Vardeman, Thomas Jones 1st. Lieut. Jos. Jones 2nd. Lieut. and John Murphy Ensign.

COUNTY LEVY IS MADE

	Dr Tobacco.
To the Clerk his annual salary	1,248
" the Sheriff	1,248
" Ro. Williams as act'g Atto. for Com'wlth	1,248
" John Davis for one old Wolf's head	100
" The Clerk for attending 7 called Courts	1,400
" Do. for 2 Record Books for Clerk's office	1,600
" Do. for the press	1,000
" Do. for a copy of the list of Tythes	400
" James Lyon for one wolf's head	100
" Thomas Henderson for one wolf's head	100
" Do. for going after witnesses	734
" Sheriff for attending 5 called courts	1,000
" John Salmon per account	610

HISTORY OF HENRY COUNTY, VIRGINIA 313

" Henry Dillon, Jr. for guarding one day _____ 25
" John Crouch for guarding 2 days _____ 50
" John Dillon for guarding 3 days _____ 75
" Anthony Smith for guarding 1 day _____ 25
" John Briscoe for guarding 1 day _____ 25
" Geo. Waller for guarding 2 days _____ 50
" John Pursell for guarding 2 days _____ 50
" Wm. Dillon for guarding 1 day _____ 25
"" John Newman for guarding 1 day _____ 25
" Stanwix Hord for guarding 2 days _____ 50
" Wm. Graves for 3 Levies overpaid last year __ 48
" James Anthony for 3 Levies overpaid last year _ 48
" Daniel Ross for guarding 4 days _____ 100
" John Dickerson per account _____ 2,467
" Do. for 2nd book for Surveyor's office _____ 1,200
" Hezekiah Salmon for 8 days attendance _____ 200
" Geo. Hairston as per account _____ 3,153
" Hugh Woods for 3 young wolves' heads _____ 150
" same for 7 young wolves' heads _____ 350
" Thomas Hale for 1 Tythe overpaid last year __ 16
" James Poteat for 1 do. _____ 16
" Brice Martin for 1 Do. _____ 16
" Thomas Gof for 1 tythe overpaid last year __ 16
" John Pace for 7 days guarding John Gordon __ 175
" Josiah Carter for apprehending same _____ 100
" Daniel Richardson for damage done to Horse
    in conveying same to Public Jail _____ 600
" Jos. Bradberry for damage to saddle in same __ 60
" Burwell Reeves for one old wolf's head ____ 100
" Jos. Bradberry for 1 day's guard _____ 25
" Jonathan Davis for 1 day's guard _____ 25
" Samuel Patterson for 1 day's guard _____ 25
" Wm. Ryan for 1 day's guard _____ 25
" Wm. Rowland for 1 day's guard _____ 25
" Abraham Franklin for 1 day's guard _____ 25
" Brice Martin for maintaing prisoner 13 days __ 500
" Geo. Lawson for maintaining prisoner ten days __ 250
" Michael Rowland entertaining same 17 days _ 300
" Wm. McGraw guarding same 1 day _____ 25
" Josiah Carter guarding 2 days _____ 50
" Baines Carter for guarding same 5 days ____ 125
" Samuel Monday for guarding 2 days _____ 50
" John Barker for guarding 7 days _____ 175

" Hugh Woods for going after witnesses _____ 200
" A Deposition for the use of the county _____ 12,000
" The Sheriff 6 per cent for collecting 34,198 __ 2,051
By 1, 340 Tythables at 27 Lb. Tob. per poll _____ 36,249

Geo. Waller and John Salmon appointed to let the building of Prison, Stocks and Pillory.

License granted John and Baldwin Rowland to keep ordinary.

David Lanier appointed to furnish Elizabeth Cooper, wife of Thomas Cooper, who is in the Continental service with forty pounds worth of provisions, and that the same be certified to the Auditor of Public Accounts.

It appearing that Benjamin Hensley served as a Lieut. in the Va. Battalion in the year 1760, the same is certified to the Register of the Land Office.

Abraham Penn is appointed Escheator for this county. Patrick Henry, Hugh Innes, Archilaus Hughes, Robt. Hairston, Edmund Lyne, Abraham Penn, John Salmon, James Lyon, Robt. Woods, Jesse Heard, Jonathan Hanby, Peter Saunders, Wm. Tunstall, Geo. Waller, Frederick Reeves, Wm. Cook, Thomas Henderson, John Fontaine, Henry Lyne, John Dillard, John Marr and Wm. Letcher are recommended to his Excellency, the Governor as proper persons to serve in the Commission of the Peace for the county.

Abraham Penn, Esqr. appointed Burser for this county to receive all fines and forfeitures due to the commonwealth in this county.

1779 Oct.—Ordered that Alice Blair, wife of Joseph Blair, who is in the Continental service, be allowed 12 lbs. current money for her support.

Ordered that Robt. Holliday be allowed 13 lbs. of current money for necessaries found Robt. Hodges, whose sons are in the Continental service.

John Wells appointed Capt. in the room of Brice Martin's company in Leatherwood, Geo. Reynolds 1st. Lieut., Matthew Wells 2nd. Lieut., Reuben Nance, Ensign.

License is granted Brice Martin to keep an ordinary at this courthouse.

Henry Lyne and Thomas Thralkild appointed commissioners for the Grain tax.

License granted Josiah Shaw to keep an ordinary.

License granted to Mordecai Hord to keep an ordinary.

1780 March—Wm. Tunstall, Esqr., having resigned his office as county Lieut., Archilaus Hughes, Esq., Colo., is advanced to the said office and Abraham Penn, Esqr. Lt. Colo. to the office of Colo. and James Lyon Esqr. to the office of Lieut. Colo.

William Bartee made oath that he served as Sergeant under Capt. Wm. Byrd Esqr.

Matthew Small made oath that he served under Capt. Wm. Christian in the year 1760, who was under the command of Honorable Wm. Byrd, Noten Dickerson commissioned by the Governor as deputy surveyor qualified as such.

Samuel Walker allowed for 325 lbs. Beef and 1-2 Bush of Corn. Also 11 lbs. of Bacon for McCraw's Brigade of Wagons in the Continental service. Also 20 bus. of Corn and 20 lbs. of Bacon for Gen'l Sumter's Brigade of wagons under command of Col. Richard Hampton.

1782. Feb.—Edmund Edwards on certificate of Elisha Miller, Capt. in Continental service for 1 1-2 bus. Corn and forage for 4 horses.

Thomas Edwards, on certificate of Bukett Nicholls, Forage Matter to a brigade of wagons to Gen'l Greene for 2 bus. corn and 1-2 bu. sifted meal. Also 365 lbs. Beef 3 pecks of corn, 12 bundles of fodder and 12 Diets to the Commissioner of Provisions for this county.

William Edwards, on certificate of Geo. Carrington, for 10 lbs. Bacon for Lt. Col. Lee's Legion of Horse. Also forage for one horse one night of Doctor Elijah Gillet of the General Hospital.

Thomas Edwards allowed for 10 Diets to Capt. Cartmill on his return from the Southward also for 15 bundles of Fodder and 1-2 bus. of Corn.

Robert Mason allowed for 315 lbs. Beef also 2 Diets and forage for 2 horses to Zack Wosby of Col. Washington's Legion of Horse.

Robert Holliday for 20 lbs. Bacon to Col. Penn for use of militia of Henry county.

Anthony Smith allowed 4 pounds, 12. 6. specie for mending and repairing 27 Guns for use of State.

John Davis allowed 160 pounds Specie for a Wagon, Gun, 4 horses a saddle and 3 Bells, impressed for the use of Gen'l Greene's army. Also 48 pounds 2, o. Specie for 96 gallons and 1-4 of Brandy furnished Col. Otho

HISTORY OF HENRY COUNTY, VIRGINIA

Williams' light infantry, per certificate of Ben Andrews also .30 pounds specie for 32 gallons of Rum to William R. Davie's Com. G'l in Gen'l Greene's army. Also 9 pounds Specie for Horse impressed on the Cherokee Expedition commanded by Col. Christian.

Wm. Swanson allowed 1 pound 8, o. for use of Horse impressed 14 days in Continental service—Lieut. Jenkins.

Nathan Swanson 2 pounds Specie for use of Horse impressed in the Continental service—Capt. Conway.

John Woodall for 10 lbs. Bacon to Capt. Cowden.

John Loyd for 315 lbs. Beef to Commissioner of Provisions.

William Steward for 200 lbs. Beef, 2 bus. Corn, 11 Diets and pasturage for 45 head of cattle furnished same.

1782. March—Thomas Hewlett allowed for 4 1-2 Barrels Corn furnished Wm. Campbell, Sergeant to the General Hospital as Col. Peter Perkins—Dr. Brown.

Patrick Henry Esqr. allowed for 30 Bundles Fodder and 1 1-2 bus. corn to Maj. Hamton, Commanding Brigade of Wagons belonging to Gen'l Sumter. Also for 1 barrel corn furnished Lt. King for Dragon Horses belonging to Col. Washington's Legion. Also for 164 bus. of corn for the use of the Southern army under Gen'l Green and forage for 28 horses for one night.

Judith Carroll allowed for 14 1-2 lbs. Bacon, 6 bus. corn and 220 bundles fodder furnished Geo. Carrington Q. Master in Col. Lee's Legion of Horse. Also for 75 lbs. Bacon to the militia of the county on their march to join Gen'l Green March 1781.

Robert Woods allowed for 25 Diets and pasturage for 55 horses furnished Capt. Heard on his march to join Gen'l Sumner in N. C. Also for 35 Diets and forage for 34 horses to the said Heard on his return.

Robert Woods allowed for pasturage for 66 Beeves 15 days. Also 45 Diets and 36 forages for horses. Also for 160 lbs. fresh pork, 43 lbs. Bacon, and 3 bus. Oats furnished Hospital at Henry Ct. House March 1781.

Archibald Grayham on certificate of Jesse Heard Commissioner of Provisions for the county for 1, 600 lbs. Beef, 1 bu. corn and 12 Diets furnished.

Thomas Hewlett, on certificate of Robt. Wilson, that he furnished him 2 bus. Corn for 4 wagon horses and 2 riding ditto, employed in Continental service. Also 20 gallons and 1 pint of Whiskey and 50 lbs. Bacon for the use of the Southern General Hospital. William Campbell Serg't also 2 1-2 bus. corn for same.

George Waller allowed for 2 bus. corn and 1 peck of meal and 30 bundles fodder furnished Buckett Nicholls, belonging to Gen'l Greene's Brigade of Wagons. Also for bus. corn for use of Continental wagons.

Thomas Hewlett allowed for 4 bus. corn and 100 bundles fodder for use of teams and horses carrying sick to Hospital at Henry Ct. house belonging to Gen. Greene's army. Also for 2 bus. and a peck of corn and forage for horses one night, furnished Lieut. Reynolds on his march to Gen. Greene's army.

Marvell Nahl 18 1-2 bus. Corn and 15 bundles fodder for the Guard conveying the British Prisoners to Bedford county.

1780. August—Robert Tate allowed 45 pounds for carrying, grinding and bolting 7 barrels corn for the use of the militia ordered to the Southward.

Frederick Reeves resigned as Capt. and Tully Choice, Jr. appointed Capt., Wm. Yan 1st. Lieut., Wm. Choice 2nd. Lieut. and Thomas Prunty, Ensign.

John Wells resigned as Capt. and Peter Hairston appointed in his room, Geo. Reynolds 1st. Lieut., Matthew Wells 2nd. Lieut. and John Conway, Ensign.

1780. Sept.—Administration on estate of Wm. Letcher murdered by Tories—1st husband of the ancestress of Gen'l J. E. B. Stuart.

Austin Thomas resigned his office of Ensign.

Mary Hickey granted license to keep an ordinary.

The Court doth rate the following liquors, Diet Lodging. West India Rum per half pint 40. Dollars. Common rum 12 Dollars, Peach Brandy, 20 Do., Apple Brandy 12 Do., Whiskey 10 Do., Lodging 6 Do., Pasturage 6 Do.

1780. Oct Brice Martin licensed to keep an ordinary at Ct. house and Mordecai Hord to keep and ordinary at his house.

George Waller appointed Commissioner of the Taxes.

1781. March—By 1, 451 Tythables at 16 lbs. of Tobacco per poll 23, 220.

West India Rum per Jill 13 Dol., Common ditto 8, Good Peach Brandy per jill 12 Dol., Apple Brandy 8 Dol., Good Whiskey 8 Do., Dinner if hot 30 dol., if cold 20 dol.,

Corn per gallon 15 Dol., Oats 15 Ditto. Lodging for each person 8 Dol.

Pasturage for each horse 8 Dol., Stableage and fodder for each horse 8 Dol., and if fodder alone 2 Dol. per bundle; Cyder per quart 12 Dol.

Isaac McDonald licensed to keep an ordinary.

Thomas Smith appointed 1st. Lieut., Wm. Adams 2nd. Lieut. and John Miller, Ensign, under Capt. Haman Critz, Jr.

The court doth rate the following Liquors, Diet, Lodging, Pasturage, and Stablage.

	Lbs.	Ozs.
For Good West India Rum per gallon	36	0
Whiskey per Ditto	16	0
Dinner for each person if hot	1	10
Breakfast for ditto if hot	1	4
Corn per gallon	1	4
Oats the same	1	4
Lodging for each person		9
Common Rum per gallon	20	0
Brandy per gallon	25	0
Stableage for each horse		6
Pasturage		6
Fodder per Bundle		3

Geo. Waller, John Salmon, and Henry Lyne, appointed to let the building of the building of the courthouse to lowest bidder.

Ordered that the former sheriff pay to John Cox, Clerk, Ninety pounds to enable him to purchase Record Book.

Isaac McDonald made oath that he served as a soldier under Major John McNeel in the year 1762, who was under the command of Col. Adam Stephens.

Samuel Allen made oath that he served as a Capt. under Colo. Wise and Col Byrd. in 1760.

John Acuff made oath he served as a Sergeant under Capt. Robt. Munford in 1763, who was under command of Col. Wm. Byrd.

Marvel Nash made oath that Thomas Earls served as a Sergeant in Capt. Gists company in Col Byrd's regiment in 1760.

Marvel Nash made oath that he served as Sergeant under Capt. Gunn in Col. Byrd's regiment 1763.

Moses Going made oath that he served as a soldier under Capt. James Gunn in Col. Byrd's regiment 1760.

Francis Pony made oath that he served in Col Stephen's regiment 1762.

John Bloggs made oath that he served as a Capt. in Col. Adam Stephen's regiment 1762.

Edgecombe Guillaiame made oath that he served as soldier under Capt. Nathaniel Gist in Col. Adam Stephen's regiment 1762.

Joseph Webster made oath that he served as a soldier under Capt. James Gunn in Col. Byrd's regiment 1760.

Frederick Fitzgerald made oath that he served as soldier under Capt. Wm. Preston's Company of Rangers 1762.

Amos Evans made oath that he served as soldier under Capt. James Gunn in Col. Byrd's regiment 1760.

James McCutchin made oath that he served as soldier under Capt. John Blagge in Col. Byrd's regiment 1760.

Joseph Bradberry made oath that he served as soldier under Capt. John Lightfoot in Col. Byrd's regiment 1760.

By 1461 Tythables at 95 lbs. of Tobacco p. poll 138, 854.

1780. May—License is granted Reuben Payne to keep an ordinary.

John Dillard is appointed Commissioner of the tax in room of Geo. Waller Esqr. who is ordered into the service.

1780. June—George Waller Esqr. appointed Major in room of James Lyon Esqr.

John Fontaine Esqr. appointed Capt. in room of John Salmon, who hath resigned.

Henry Lyne Esqr. appointed Capt. came into court and resigned. Thomas Bedford Esqr. appointed 1st Lieut. under Brice Martin, John Barksdill 2nd. Lieut., John Redd, Ensign.

James Poteet appointed Capt. in room of Geo. Hairston, who hath resigned.

Geo. Hairston appointed Capt. in room of Geo. Waller who is appointed Major.

David Barton appointed 1st. Lieut., Daniel Ross 2nd. Lieut. and Gideon Smith under Owen Robel.

John Fontaine, Geo. Hairston, James Cowden, Owen Robel, James Poteet and Thomas Haile produced their Commissions as Capts. and took the oath.

Thomas Bedford, Joshua Barton and John Turner 1st. Lieuts.; John Barksdale 2nd. Lieut. and John Redd, Ensign, produced their commissions and took the oath.

July. 1780—Bailey Carter made oath that he served as soldier in Col. Adam Stephen's campaign 1762.

William Taylor made oath that he served as soldier under Thomas Fleming in Gen'l Forbers campaign 1758.

John Dillard appointed Capt. in room Capt. James Shelton, Geo. Taylor 1st. Lieut., Wm. Taylor 2nd. Licut. and James Spencer, Ensign.

John Rentfro appointed captain of the upper part of Capt. Haile's company. Thomas Jones 1ts. Lieut., Joshua Rentfro 2nd. Lieut. and Wm. Standefer, Ensign.

Joseph Jones is appointed 1st. Lieut., Luke Standefer 2nd. Lieut. and Wm. Manifee, Ensign under Capt. Thomas Haile.

Archalaus Hughes Esq. County Lieut. resigned and Abraham Penn, Col. is recommended in his room.

1782. Jan.—Robert Hairston produced a commission from his Excellency, Thomas Nelson, Jr. appointed him Sheriff of this county and took the oath and Geo. Hairston, Peter Hairston and Samuel Hairston qualified as his under sheriffs.

Michael Dillingham having taken the oath of Fidelity and producing a recommendation from the Baptist Society is licensed to solemnize marriage.

Isaac Donelson arrainged on a charge of High Treason and admitted bail.

1782. Feb.—Patrick Henry Esqr. produced a certificate from under, the hands of the Commissioner for 960 pounds of beef which is ordered to be certified. Also a certificate from under the hands of Lieut. Carter on his march to York in Sept. for one hog valued at 30 S. in specie and one bushel of corn and meal. Also a certificate from Peter Scales for 16 Diets furnished for 12 delinquents and 4 guards dated Sept. 1781.

Abraham Franklin produced proof that while he was in the States service he had a horse taken by an officer in Col. White's Com. of light Dragoons, worth 15 pounds in specie.

Matthew Wells, a certificate from Elijah King a Lieut. in Col. Washington's Dragoons, that he had impressed a horse into the service worth Fifty pounds in specie.

HISTORY OF HENRY COUNTY, VIRGINIA

John Wells, a certificate from Peter Hairston a Capt. that he impressed a horse when ordered out against an Insurrection of the Tories in Oct. 1780, worth 15 pounds in specie.

Reuben Tarrants from same, in said service a horse worth 12 pounds in specie.

Stephen Heard from Elijah King, Lieut. in Col Washington's light Dragoons, a horse 3-4 blooded and worth 130 pounds in specie.

John Short from Wm. Read, surgeon, a horse worth 20 pounds in specie.

Peter Gearhart from Col. Hugh Crockett of Botetourt county a mare for service in marching to the assistance of Gen'l Greene worth 20 pounds in specie.

Dennis O'Bryant that he furnished 300 pounds of nett beef.

Haman Critz, Sr. for 575 pounds nett beef also for 13 Diets and Forage for 8 horses also certificate from Geo. Hamilton Q. master to the assistance of Gen'l Greene for 17 and 1-4 lbs. Bacon also from Henry Lyne for 500 pounds nett beef also a certificate from John Latta a Commissary to Gen'l Sumpter's Brigade of Wagons for 20 pounds of Bacon.

Joseph Newman, a certificate from John Rowland, Wagon Master to Wm. McCraw, for 50 bundles of Fodder on his way from Charlotte to Peytonsburg. Peytonsburg was and is in Pittsylvania county.

Kinney McKinney from said Rowland for ten and a half bushels of corn and 10 pounds Bacon.

Henry Jones allowed for 4 barrels of corn and 27 pounds of Bacon furnished the Continental Hospital at C. I. Perkin's under direction of Dr. Brown also for 2-0 pounds of Beef.

Geo. Reynolds from Capt. Peter Hairston for 36 1-2 pounds Bacon while on the march to the assistance of Gen'l Greene.

Geo. Sandford 10 and 1-2 ditto for ditto.
Francis Cox 40 ditto for ditto.
Robert Pedigo 25 and 1-2 ditto for ditto.
John Conway 18 ditto and Bushel of corn for ditto.
Reuben Nance 12 ditto for ditto.
John Davis 17 ditto for ditto.
Mary Tarrants 32 and 1-2 ditto for ditto.

Peter Hairston for 900 pounds of nett Beef.
Isaac Donelson for 260 pounds ditto.
John Briscoe for 350 ditto.
Reuben Nance for 250 ditto.
Francis Cox allowed 146 lbs. of Meal and 46 lbs of Bacon, furnished Phillip Roth, mus'n to Col. Lee's legion of L. Dragoons, also 36 and 1-2 bushels of corn to same.
John Loyd allowed for 10 Diets furnished Alexr. Crawford on his march with the militia from the Battle of Guilford Courthouse Homeward.
William Stewart 45 bus. Corn furnished Hospital at Col. Perkins under direction of Dr. Brown also allowed for 8 Diets for same.
Henry Jones allowed Land 1-2 bus. of Corn meal furnished Alexander's company of Rockbridge county on their return from Gen'l Green in March 1781.
Robert Pedigo allowed for 47 lbs. of Bacon for Hospital at Henry Courthouse under Dr. Wm. Read.
Joseph Bouldin allowed for 21 bus. of Oats to McCraw's Brigade of wagons in Continental service. Also 7 Diets and 1 peck of corn and feeding 4 horses also for 175 pounds of beef.
1781 April—Michael Rowland licensed to keep an ordinary John Barksdale appointed 1st. Lieut.; John Redd 2nd. Lieut. and Christopher Owen Ensign in Capt. Brice Martin's Company.
George Waller Esqr. appointed to purchase and salt beef for use of the States is allowed 660 pounds current money for purchasing and curing 20 beeves. The court proceeded to laying a levy for the purchasing of a wagon, Team and for the use of the States and are of opinion that 20,000 pounds be collected from the respective Tythable persons in the county at 14 pounds 3 O. per poll. (6531). Over.
1781. June—Abraham Penn Produce a commission as Coroner of the County. Wm. Rentfro 2nd Lieut.; Luke Standefer 2nd Lieut.; Thomas Hill, Ensign in Capt. Thomas Haile's company.
Dinner 40 Dollars Breakfast 40, Good Rum per jill 15 Do., Brandy 15 Do., per jill.
1783. Jan. 23.—Daniel Carlin, One of the Gents named in the new Commission of the Peace took the oath of the Commonwealth of Va. the oath of a Justice of the

HISTORY OF HENRY COUNTY, VIRGINIA 323

Peace, the oath of a Justic in Chancery and a Justice of Oyer and Terminer.

William Ryan appointed Capt. of a company of militia in this county, Spencer Clark 1st. Lieut. and Samuel Bolling, Ensign.

William Choice appointed 1st. Lieut. to Capt. Tully Choice's company of militia and Burwell Reives, ensign.

1783. Feb. 27.—Thomas Dickinson allowed 10 1-2 bus, corn furnished the General Hospital at Col. Perkins on certificate of James McCubbins purchasing commissioner to the said Hospital.

William Stunstall Esqr. allowed 150 pounds and ten shillings money advanced by him to purchase Guns for militia of this county on certificate of James Shelton Capt. of the said militia.

John Loyd allowed 16 bus. Corn and 13 bundles fodder furnished General Hospital at Col. Perkins.

Stephen Lee allowed 200 lbs. Beef 6 Diets and 1-2 bu. Corn furnished commissioner of the Provision Law for said county.

Samuel Tarrant allowed 36 lbs. Bacon, 235 lbs. Indian Corn meal, 6 barrels and one peck of Corn and 36 ft. fodder for the use of Col. Lee's Partisan Legion furnished Geo. Carrington Q. M. P. to the said Legion.

Williams Sams allowed 20 lbs. pork furnished same.

John Barksdale allowed 79 days service as Steward to the Military Hospital at Henry Ct. house, Wm. Read State Surgeon.

Joseph Ellis 12 pounds 6 ounces for Gun impressed into the Military service.

Frederick Fulkerson 5 Diets to Montgomery Militia going home.

Daniel Reamey 16 lbs. Bacon to Geo. Carrington Q. M. P., Lee's Legion.

William Adams 375 lbs. Beef to Commissioner of Provision this county.

Mr. Parks 84 lbs. Pork to a party of Cavalry under command of Robt. Simons cornet to 1st. Reg. Light Dragoons.

William Roberts 600 bundles fodder to Col. Richard Hampton for Brigade of South Carolina wagons.

Jarrett Patterson 10 Barrels Corn for same.

Joseph Clark 60 bus. Corn for Col. Crockett's Troops.

Charles Foster 31 1-2 lbs. Bacon for Hospital at Ct. house.

Mark Rentfro 250 lbs. of Beef to Commissioner of Bedford county.

John Majors 3 pounds 10 ounces for Rifle Gun to Capt. Joseph Martin.

Samuel Coleman Morris 30 lbs. Bacon, 15 lbs. Pork and 1 barrel of corn to a brigade of S. C. wagons.

Jesse Witt 3 barrels Corn and 30 lbs. Bacon for same.

James Spencer 2 dozen sheaves oats for same.

Thomas Lowe 2 1-2 bus. Corn to Militia of Rockbridge on their return from the Southward also 2 -12 bus. Corn for wagons of Wm. McCraw A. D. Q. Gen'l at Peytonsburgh on their return from Charlotte.

The same 5 bundles fodder and 5 Diets to Samuel Moore F. M. to a Brigade of South Carolina wagons.

Also 37 pounds 10 ounces of paper currency for a hog, March 11th. 1781. also forage for 10 horses of the Guard to said Brigade of Wagons.

Stephen Lyon 2 bus. Salt to Lieut. Col. Lewis Burwell on certificate of Wm. Willis Q. M. 1781.

John Grisham 42 lbs. Bacon for So. Ca. Brigade Wagons.

William Poor 14 lbs. Bacon for S. C. Brigade Wagons.

James Roberts 40 lbs. Indian Meal and 33 lbs. of Bacon for Militia from Rockbridge commanded by Capt. James Gilmer from the Southward.

Leonard Vandgraft 4 bus. corn to Col. Airmont's Corps Light Horse and 15 bus. corn and 60 bundles fodder to Gen'l Sumpter's Brigade of Wagons.

James Rentfro 45 pounds Paper currency for a shot pouch for Militia May 26, 1781.

Wm. Mitchell 250 pounds paper currency for a Gun impressed June 1781.

William Coggins 1,000 pounds paper currency for a rifle Gun Impressed by Capt. Gen'l Hairston when ordered to join Gen'l Greene March 12, 1781.

Geo. Hamilton 325 pounds paper currency for a Rifle Gun—same—same May 20, 1781.

John Gibson 800 pounds paper currency for a Rifle Gun for same service by Capt. Hanby May 22, 1781.

William Russett 5 pounds 10 o. for a mare for use in the Cherokee Indian Expedition 1776.

John Journican 2 pounds 10 o. for smooth bored Gun for the militia when ordered out against the Indians.

William Roberts for one Hogg weight 80 lbs. to Capt. Robinson's Co. of Volunteers on their march to the southward.

Walter Dunn for 8 lbs. Bacon for Hospital at Ct. house also 11 barrels corn and 12 lbs. of Bacon for Lt. Col. Lee's Legion.

Elisha Wallen 2 pecks of meal and 20 lbs. Bacon to same also 17 lbs. Bacon to same.

Waters Dunn 28 lbs. Bacon to same.

Shadrack Turner for use of his horse and 9 diets to Capt. Robel's Camp Company ordered out against the Tories: also for 4 diets and 15 lbs. Fodder to Col. Crockett's Regiment.

James Standefer 5 dozen sheaves oats, 300 weight of hay and 6 bus. of corn to Brigade of Wagons on return from Charlotte to the northward.

Joseph Price 64 1-4 lbs. Bacon to Wm. Howard D. Commissioner of Buckingham county; also 325 pounds for a beef to John Bates Commissioner of said county 17 Nov. 1780.

James Standefer for rations for 4 men and 10 bundles of fodder for the Guard under Capt. James Tarrant on their return with British prisoners to Winchester.

Daniel Reamey 200 bundles fodder to Lee's Legion; also 24 lbs. Bacon for the militia to Wm. Blevins; also 287 lbs. Beef, 42 diets, 5 bundles fodder and one peck of corn to Commissioner of Provisions.

Geo. Waller and Henry Lyne appointed Commissioners for this county.

1783. March 29.—John Fontaine appointed to take a list of Souls, the List of Tythes and a List of taxable property in James T. Tarrant's and John Alexander's companies of militia.

David Lanier appointed for his own company.

John Dillard appointed to his company.

Archilaus Hughes to Haman Critz's company.

James Lyon to Shelton's and Cloud's companies.

Daniel Carlin to his own company.

William Tunstall to Samuel Tarrant's and Geo. Reyno's companies.

John Salmon to John Barksdale's and Jos. Cooper's companies.

Henry Lyne to John Cunningham's company.
Abraham Penn to Matthew Small's company.
John Rentfro to Thomas Hale's and his own company
Swinfield Hill to his own company.
Spencer Clark to Tully Choice's and Wm. Ryon's companies.
Jesse Heard to James Cawdin's and Thomas Smith's companies.
John Newman appointed to solemnize marriages.
James Lyon, Esqr. produced a commisson from the Governor appointing him Lieut. col. of the militia of the county and took usual oath.

MARRIAGE LICENSE BONDS FROM 1776 TO 1800

Alexander, Wm.-Jean Ferguson, Feb. 21, 1778.
Anderson, Robt.-Elizabeth Graves, Sept. 4, 1794.
Bassett, Burwell-Polly Hunter, Jan. 25, 1794.
Blakey, Churchill-Agnes Anthony, Aug. 2, 1780.
Brown, Isham-Mary Dilloner, July 19, 1793.
Bernar, Walter-Ruth Hill, April 6, 1782.
Briscoe, Truman-Catherine Dunn, Dec. 22, 1782.
Bledose, Peachy-Peggy George, July 12, 1780.
Bayles, Wm.-Tabitha Minnes, April 12, 1793.
Billeman, Wm.-Nilly Molen, Dec. 25, 1794.
Burgess, Davis-Lucy Pace, Jan. 26, 1794.
Burress, Jacob-Susannah Morris, Mar. 13, 1781.
Bailey, John-Lydia Wilson, Mar. 18, 1793.
Cannon, James-Patsy Wilson, Dec. 18, 1793.
Crouch, Joseph-Peggy Sanford, Feb. 20, 1778.
Cason, Edward-Lucy Edwards, April 27, 1793.
Colley, John-Sarah France, Oct. 17, 1789.
Cox, John-Leaner Bolling, Sept. 6, 1791.
Clark, John-Sally Standefer, Nov. 4, 1779.
Cunningham, Joe-Nancy Davis, July 16, 1793.
Cockram, Wm-Sally Edmondson, Aug. 5, 1780.
Compton, Ebenezer-Alcey Hopper, May 6, 1794.
Conway, John-Elizabeth Williams, Nov. 5, 1782.
Carter, Jos.-Nancy Manifee, June 24, 1778.
Chewning, John-Lettie Payne, April 26, 1778.
Cayton, Wm.-Rachel Oakes, Jan. 4, 1793.
Carter, Jos.-Mary Dillon, Jan. 16, 1794.
Cunningham, Wm.-Mary Pyrtle, Nov. 27, 1793.
Dillener, Henry-Lucy Murphy, July 19, 1793.

HISTORY OF HENRY COUNTY, VIRGINIA

Dooley, Thomas-Lucy Webb, April 13, 1779.
Dillon, Wm-Tabitha Witt, Dec. 19, 1792.
Dent, Shadrick-Mary Murphy, Nov. 16, 1783.
Dillon, Ben. Jr.,-Elizabeth Witty, Mar. 21, 1792.
Dillingham, Lott-Ann Dillingham, Mar, 2, 1792.
Dickinson, John-Isabell Woods, June 2, 1781.
Edmundson, Hump.-Frances Swanson, Nov. 22, 1779.
Elkins, David-Mary Pedigo, April 6, 1793.
Edwards, Wm.-Elizabeth Britain, Aug. 2, 1791.
Edwards, Owen-Judith Morton, Oct. 29, 1794.
Earles, Joshua-Elizabeth Lucas, June 18, 1792.
Farris, Thomas-Judith Quarles, Jan. 7, 1792.
Fuller, Britain-Nancy Jackson, Feb. 29, 1780.
Griffith, Wm.-Susannah Jones, July 25, 1782.
Griggs, John-Phoby Acholas, July 30, 1792.
Govan, Wm.-Sarah Griggs, Oct. 27, 1794.
Hailey, John-Lucy Ryan, July 28, 1794.
Hunt, James-Sarah Terry, May 25, 1780.
Hampton, Laban-Leany Stephens, Jan. 6, 1794.
Hamilton, Geo.-Agnes Cooper, April 18, 1783.
Hogans, Wm.-Nancy Dillard, Jan. 19, 1780.
Hawkins, Ben-Molly Taylor, Oct. 1, 1778.
Hopper, Wm.-Hecter Stephens, May 18, 1793.
Hardy, Charles-Rachel Parsley, Feb. 5, 1793.
Haley, Wm.-Nancy Jackson, Dec. 20, 1792.
Hannah, Alex.-Sarah Pelptory, Oct. 16, 1793.
Jones, Robt.-Sina Richards, June 20, 1785.
Joyce, Andrew-Betsy King, June 25, 1792.
Jamerson, Thomas-Hesy Huston, Dec. 2, 1794.
Kelly, John-Betty Bybee, Feb. 10, 1781.
Knox, Ben.-Jemima Gardner, Jan. 12, 1780.
King, Wm.-Nancy Mitchell, July 19, 1794.
Kirkham, Wm.-Elizabeth Blize, Dec. 15, 1792.
Lindsey, Henry-Elizabeth Smith, Nov. 26, 1791.
Letchworth, Ben.-Eleanor Adams, Oct. 24, 1792.
Lyon, Stephen-Elley Perkins, Dec. 11, 1782.
Lanier, Washington-Elizabeth Hicks, Nov. 15, 1784.
Moore, Shater-Ann Hooker, May 13, 1778.
Mitchell, Wm.-Martha Stoker, May 30, 1778.
McGuire, Allegania-Sarah Holliday, June 27, 1782.
Martin, Joseph-Susannah Graves, Feb. 24, 1784.
Martin, Joseph-Ruth Dillard, Aug. 30, 1793.
Melvin, Levi-Elizabeth Gooch, June 18, 1793.

Medley, John-Ann Carter, Oct. 30, 1797.
Melvin, Jarner-Katy Kannon, June 24, 1795.
Murphy, Gabriel-Ruth Peregoy, Nov. 7, 1794.
Matthews, Wm.-Elizabeth Hunter, June 30, 1794.
Mastin, Jacob-Elizabeth Melvin, July 12, 1792.
Mays, Liggin-Easter Daniel, July 2, 1792.
Nunn, Thomas-Jean Pace, Jan. 14, 1794.
Norris, Zebulon-Elizabeth Dillingham, Dec. 14, 1793.
Northcutt, Francis-Lucy Haley, May 26, 1794.
Norton, John-Sarah Penn, July 26, 1784.
Nichols, David-Clarey Rowland, Dec. 4, 1793.
O'Neal, Basil-Milly Briscoe, Jan. 17, 1780.
Pedigo, Robt. Jr.-Parsley, Jan. 3, 1792.
Pool, Geo.-Cloah Payne, Dec. 25, 1778.
Penn, Geo.-Patty Farriss, Dec. 6, 1784.
Patrick, James-Sarah Dunlop, Oct. 13, 1791.
Pearson, Meredith-Rhoda Delozier, May 10, 1794.
Philport, Samuel-Mary Hannah, Jan. 12, 1785.
Pyrtle, John-Polly Maupin, Feb. 5, 1793.
Parberry, James-Ann Graves, May 10, 1784.
Peck, David-Jean Martin, Aug. 26, 1779.
Philpott, Charles-Elizabeth Hubbard, Nov. 25, 1794.
Pitman, James-Martha Taylor, July 2, 1781.
Quarles, James-Elizabeth Pelphry, __ov. 22, 1791.
Reynolds, Geo.-Susannah Lansford, June 12, 1779.
Rowland, Michael-Elizabeth Hairston, June 20, 1778.
Rowland, Baldwin-Sarah Hairston, May 8, 1782.
Rowland, John, Jr.-Enis Sturgeon, July 23, 1780.
Richards, Shadrick-Susannah Hamilton, Oct. 28, 1779.
Rea, David-Frances East, July 22, 1794.
Richardson, John-Mary Ryan, Jan. 16,1779.
Rentfro, Mark-Naomi Standefer, April 22, 1779.
Ray, Joseph-Mary Ann Hayse, Nov. 10, 1793.
Standefer, Wm.-Jemima Jones, June 24, 1779.
Sandford, John-Judith Garner, Feb. 20, 1778.
Smith, Gideon-Mary Hairston, April 27, 1784.
Snidow, Phillip-Barabara Prilliman, Feb. 14, 1782.
Salmon, Thaddeus-Elizabeth Holmes, Mar. 26, 1794.
Shelton, Nathan-Mary Shelton, Sept. 16, 1794.
Steward, Wm.-Milly Eastes, June 17, 1792.
Stone, John-Mary Philpott, July 10, 1792.
Stanley, Joseph-Sarah Kitchen, June 15, 1785.
Stone, Wm.-Elizabeth Nunn, Sept. 14, 1793.

Sumpter, Wm.-Margaret Pyrtle, May 17, 1792.
Tankersley, Geo.-Elizabeth Garrison, Sept. 29, 1779.
Taylor, James-Elizabeth Williams, Dec. 29, 1794.
Threlkeld, Elijah-Elizabeth Cook, Nov. 14, 1781.
Thompson, Wm-Dolthien Stockton, Mar, 12, 1794.
Thomas, Augustine-Deborah Fulkerson, Dec. 1, 1778.
Wash, John-Nancy Frazier Gatewood, Aug. 2, 1779.
Wade, Moses-Fanny Ferguson, Sept. 29, 1779.
Woods, John-Lucy Hawkins, April 10, 1782.
Williamson, Robt.-Nancy Cox, Sept. 18, 1793.
Woods, Geo.-Fanny Mason, Feb. 17, 1778.
Wilson, Nathan-Susannah Stephens, May 19, 1793.
Ware, John-Margarett Lady, Sept. 6, 1780.
Woods, Hugh-Sarah Ann George, Aug. 5, 1779.

It is believed that this list does not include all the marriages in this county from 1776 to 1800 but thus far no other bonds have been found. Jan. 13, 1904.

LIST OF SUBSCRIBERS

1. D. M. Morris
2. Mrs. Richard T. Winston
3. Luther E. Wells
4. S. R. Hill
5. T. W. Graham
6. John H. Pedigo
7. Geo. A. Carter
8. John Lee Taylor
9. W. W. Hill, Sr.
10. Clyde B. Stanley
11. H. C. Clanton
12. Mary C. Childress
13. L. P. Mitchell
14. Ruth Callaway Pannill
15. D. A. Dyer
16. Mrs. J. H. Fulton
17. J. D. Bassett
18. K. L. Pannill
19. Loys White
20. Mrs. J. H. Spencer
21. Mrs. E. P. Amiss
22. J. J. Rangeley
23. Mrs. T. N. Barbour
24. Mrs. H. G. Mullins
25. Mrs. W. O. Howard
26. Harold C. Booker
27. Mrs. Kate Moore
28. Mr. and Mr. O. R. Gregory
29. G. A. Koger
30. J. Conrad Kearfott
31. Mrs. N. H. Hairston
32. John Wray
33. E. W. Nance
34. Mrs. R. T. Fagg
35. James P. Allen
36. Mrs. J. H. Schoolfield
37. J. P. Bassett
38. A. W. Miles
39. Mrs. J. W. Matthews
40. Mrs. Cynthia W. Royall
41. John R. Smith
42. Mrs. J. B. Lavinder
43. Elmer Bryan
44. J. M. Shackelford
45. Mrs. James Moore
46. Mrs. J. W. Jones
47. Louis G. Carter
48. D. L. Nance
49. David Campbell
50. J. C. Hamlett
51. Mrs. J. F. Farmer
52. Sallie J. Reamey
53. E. H. Wray
54. Kate Barrow
55. Geo. E. Davis
56. G. P. Franklin
57. A. D. Beckner
58. M. E. Stovall

HISTORY OF HENRY COUNTY, VIRGINIA

59. W. C. Shumate
60. J. W. Simmons
61. H. C. Gravely
62. Catherine Matthews
63. Judith Koger
64. Mrs. M. B. Hopper
65. Harry B. Stone
66. B. F. Barrow
67. Bessie Davis
68. Mrs. Sam Shelton
69. Jefferson Penn
70. Mrs. A. J. Lester
71. Mrs. W. B. Hawkins
72. Mamie R. Hundley
73. Mr. and Mrs. J. M. Shepherd
74. Anna G. Bouldin
75. B. B. Bassett
76. Hugh S. Kearfott
77. Mrs. W. B. Jett
78. Sue M. Hardie
79. Mrs. G. M. Dove
80. Judge Bassett
81. Mrs. J. W. Lyerly
82. P. R. Wray
83. Mrs. Whitney Shumate
84. E. T. Tyree
85. Mrs. N. T. Shumate
86. Kizzie Drewry Carter
87. W. J. Bassett
88. Gillie N. Koger
89. Mrs. John R. Aaron
90. W. S. Morris
91. J. R. Gregory
92. Mrs. Rora Clift
93. Jesse R. Taylor
94. Mrs. R. R. Lee
95. Walter S. Hodges
96. Mrs. J. W. Booker, Sr.
97. Elsie Shumate
98. T. C. Matthews
99. D. F. Davis
100. Mrs. M. L. Ford
101. R. E. Tuggle
102. Mrs. R. E. Stone
103. Mrs. Sallie C. Latimer
104. Mrs. John A. Shackelford
105. Mrs. W. T. Willis
106. Mrs. J. A. Scales
107. W. A. Shelton
108. Patty Holt
109. W. W. Bailey
110. Bettie S. Thomaas
111. Mrs. T. J. Patterson
112. L. H. Koger
113. Ed Waller
114. Mrs. Will Asbury
115. Miss Kate Robinson
116. Mr. and Mrs. T. A. F. Mitchell
117. Wirt Mitchell
118. Mrs. A. F. Harris
119. J. B. Allen
120. Glen G. Allen
121. A. B. Hopper
122. Mrs. W. A. Dove
123. T. G. Burch
124. J. B. DeShazo
125. O. D. Ford
126. H. A. Ford
127. Mrs. J. W. Booker, Jr.
128. L. H. Bailey
129. W. M. Wray
130. Virginia G. Pedigo
131. A. D. Jones
132. Mrs. Emory Hedgecock
133. Mrs. J. W. Stanley
134. Bunyon Vaughn
135. Paul Errett Allen
136. Lodowick Johnson Hill, Sr.
137. Mrs. W. F. Slaydon
138. Iantha Castilio
139. John R. Dillard
140. Mrs. A. A. Dillard
141. Mrs. J. H. Prather
142. J. R. Taylor
143. I. M. Groves, Jr.
144. Birdie Penn Lindsey
145. Frank P. Davis
146. J. F. Wilson
147. William Mitchell
148. Mollie H. Gravely
147. Mrs. Ada M. Avery
150. R. Rangely
151. Mrs. E. J. Pannill
152. Mr. Humphrey Traylor
153. Mrs. Mattie Northen
154. Capt. Geo. Northen
155. Janie Lavinder
156. Mrs. C. E. Crist
157 Mr. and Mrs. J. W. Hamilton
158. Mr. and Mrs. W. W. Hamilton

HISTORY OF HENRY COUNTY, VIRGINIA   331

159. Mrs. C. C. Bassett
160. Mrs. J. C. Hooker
161. Mrs. Weaver
162. W. W. Hill, Jr.
163. J. A. Brown
164. Mrs Daisey Weems
165. Everett Wray
166. Mrs. Janie Worth Martin Shriner
167. Mrs. M. S. Buchanan
168. Mrs. J. G. Penn
169. J. W. Hopper
170. Mrs. E. L. Connally
171. Miss Sally Eugenia Brown
172. Mrs. T. C. Jarrett
173. Mrs. T. P. Parish
174. Robert J. Fagg
175. Thomas M. Ford
176. R. L. Lewis
177. Gertrude Fusfeld
179. Terry W. Allen (2copies)
181. Mrs. G. D. Craig
182. Dr. H. Price.
183. J. S. Beck
184. J. H. Stanley
185. Mary L. Penn
186. Mrs. Lottie Turner Dodson
187. Mrs. R. P. Ray
188. Mrs. Nannie Ould
189. Mrs. Lottie Beaker
190. Mrs. L. Sloan
191. Mrs. Julian C. Lane
192. E. J. Davis
193. Mrs. Essie B. Farmer
194. Charles P. Ferrell
195. Mrs. Lucy Valentine
196. Mrs. Manie Hughes
197. Douglas Shackelford
198. Hon. Clarence Conner
199. John O. Coan
200. T. C. Coleman
201. J. D. Hodges
202. H. L. Franklin
203. W. W. Turner
204. Miss Kate Brown
205. Mrs. G. M. Finley
206. Mrs. Charles P. Smith
207. Mrs. S. D. English
208. Mrs. Andrew F. Tuttle
209. L. A. Willis
210. Miss K. E. Jones
211. Mrs. Geo. Jones

212. Swin Stanley
213. Mrs. E. K. Jones
215. D. J. Holcombe
214. Mrs. A. J. Weems (4 copies)
220. Dr. L. E. Johnson
221. Mrs. B. A. Cunningham
222. Mrs. Mattie Southgate
223. Miss Essie Jones
224. Mr. Adams
226. J. F. King
227. Thomas J. King
228. J. B. Dillon
229. G. F. Craig
231. E. T. Ramsey
232. Mrs. Ellen Allen
234. Mrs. Geo. M. Gibson, Jr.
235. Thomas K. Jones
236. G. W. DeShazo
237. Dr. F. P. Turner
238. Mrs. M. M. Mullins
239. Mrs. Walter Anglin
240. Mrs. J. B. Bassett
241. R. T Stone
242. G. E. Powell
243. R. B. Price
244. Miss Renetta Duffy
245. Mrs. W. J. Beard
246. Mrs. Victor Clay McAdoo
247. J. J. Finney
248. Mrs. Callie Mills
249. Dr. Dunbar Rowland
250. Mrs. Dunbar Rowland
251. Geo. Rangeley
252. Mrs. G. A. Brown
253. M. M. Coleman
254. W. J. Mitchell
255. W. C. Jones
256. Marshall Wingfield
257. Mr. Southgate Jones
258. John P. Hill
259. Miss Georgie T. Griggs
260. Maurice Hodges
261. Mrs. J. M. Barker
262. John S. DeShazo
263. J. W. Price
264. Mrs. C. E. Draper
265. Mrs. Henry House Littleton
266. Harry Dandridge
268. Miss Annie Dandridge
269. Sam Wall

270. Miss Nell Dandridge
271. Mrs. L. L. Wilborn
272. Miss Lightie Louisa Dandridge
273. Geo. Gilmer Dandridge
274. J. T. Penn
275. H. F. Hutchinson
276. T. S. Kyle
277. Ada D. Dalton
278. Mrs. Una Puckett
279. Mrs. A. B. Poindexter
280. Henry C. Pace
281. John E. Pace
282. Mrs. H. S. Richardson
283. Rev. C. A. Hamilton
284. C. A. Hamilton, Jr.
285. Mrs. J. S. Stone
286. Mrs. Emma Lavinder Gorham
287. Mrs. L. C. Claybrook
288. T. H. Morris
289. Fuller E. Callaway
290. J. W. Franklin
291. Miss Fannie Salmons
292. E. J. Sutherland
293. Mrs. C. J. Stanley
294. Mrs. Robbie Kyle Smith
295. Mr. Willis Clark
296. Jeff S. DeShazo
297. Mrs. C. T. Punham
298. H. H. Davis
299. Hon. B. A. Davis
300. Charlie Davis
301. Raymond Davis
302. Pannill Martin
303. Dr. L. G. Pedigo, Roanoke, Va.
304. Mrs. Tabitha Carter, Mayodan, N. C.
305. Edd Stanley
306. Mrs. Kate Allen

INDEX

AARON, Alice L 110 Christopher Columbus 110 Jacob 110 Jacob Davis 110 James F 110 Jesse Fillmore 110 Jessie Roberta 110 265 John Burwell 110 John Reid 110 265-266 Juda 110 Loula 110 Lucy L 110 Malina C 110 Malissa 211 Mrs Jessie 45 Mrs John R 330 Nicholas C 110 Sallie 110 Sarah Jane 110 Talitha J 110
ABEL, Rev 51
ABINGDON, Bowles 304 Fannie 111 259 Frances 100 John 304 Nannie 219 Sarah 222 William 111 Wm 259
ABINGTON, John 46
ACHOLAS, Phoby 327
ACKELAS, Phoebe 179
ACTON, James 304
ACUFF, John 318
ADAMS, Abraham 304 Eleanor 327 Elisha 294 Isaac 294 Jacob 13 294 304 Josiah 19 Luke 293 Miss 129 Mr 331 Peter 294 Richard 293 Sallie 222 Thomas Jr 294 William 323 Wm 294 304 318
ADKINS, Mark 304
ADKINSON, Joel 304
AIRMONT, Col 324
AKERS, Sallie 135
ALBRITTON, Robert 157 Tabitha Jane 157
ALEXANDER, 322 Jean 326 Jno Sr 304 John 14 294 304 325 R H 134 Roxy 210 Wm 304 326
ALFRED, The Great 146
ALFRIEND, Cassandra 41 225

ALLEN, 197 America 112 Anna 174 Anne Bailey 260 Beverley 111 Brooks 112 Celia 111 227 Charlotte 111 Coleman 111-112 157 Daniel 304 Darling 110-112 David 113-114 227 263 David Mullins 111 Dr 128 Eliza 221-222 227 Eliza Dabney 111-112 114 Ellen 111 331 Fannie 111-112 157 259 Fisher 14 Forest 112 114 Glen G 330 Henry 227 J B 330 James 19 110-112 James P 329 James Pines 113 John 128 157 John Mills 112-113 John Parks Bailey 112-113 John Pines 113 Joseph 19 Joseph Benson 112 Joseph S 111 Joseph Smith 111 113 Kate 332 Kate M 112 Lef 157 Lethridge 112 Logan 111 Martha 113 Martha Hairston 128 Mary 110 Meredith 110-112 Micajah 304 Minter 112 Nancy 111-112 O Coleman 157 O M 19 Obediah 112 Panes 113 Paul Errett 330 Pines 46 111-112 Pleasant 110 Rachel 111 Reuben 110 Rev Sgt 145 Robert 111 221 227 Robert Buxton 112 Sallie 227 Sallie Ann 111 263 Sally Ann 113 Samuel 304 318 Sarah 227 Sarah Ann 111 Sarah Smith 127 Spencer 112-113 Susan 111 Terry W 331 William 110-112 127 227 304 Wm 259
ALLEY, Erasmer 294
ALNDFORD, Eli 307
ALZIRA, Margarett 215
AMBROSE, J C 50

AMISS, J H 47 Mrs E P 329
ANDERSON, Armistead 304 Betsy Ann 198 Carrie 196 Charles 198 Elizabeth 114 326 Floria 267 Henrietta Alice 114-115 James 304 James Lewis 114-115 John 37 114 John Rice 114 Justina 114-115 Kate 115 Katherine Virginia 62 114 King 198 Lavillon 114 Len 97 Leonard 114 Leonard W 115 Lucy Frances 114-115 Mary 114 175 267 Mary Morton 114 Mrs Robt 173 Nancy 198 Nannie Madison 114 Pauline 114 Peter 14 Robert 198 267 Robert C 61 175 Robert Campbell 114-115 Robert Campbell Jr 114 Robt 191 294 326 Sadie 115 Samuel Amristead 114 Seward 198 Virginia 114
ANDES, G M 117 Mattie 117
ANDREWS, Ben 316
ANGLE, Bettie Brown 155 Carrie L 178 Charles J 178 Chas 155
ANGLIN, 158 203 Elizabeth 120 Joseph 14 Mrs Walter 331
ANNE, Daughter of Risley 214
ANSEN, Caroline F 173
ANSON, Alfred 50
ANTHONY, 42 Agnes 326 James 304 313 John 195 Joseph 293 304 Nannie 195
ANYON, Elizabeth 273
ARAGAN, John 13
ARCHER, Elizabeth 278 Gabriel 278 George 278 Judith 278 William S 35
ARMISTEAD, Annie 224 Justina 114 Mary 114 Sally 224 Samuel 114 224
ARMISTHEAD, Sarah 173
ARMS, Moses 13
ARMSTRONG, Francis 304 James 295 297 John R 19 Martin 67

ARNOLD, 266 Bethany 132 Cynthia 226 Edd 125 Elisha 12 226 Eliza 125 Franklin 226 Henry 304 Jacob 13 James 125 226 John 226 Julia 125 Lucy 226 Marshall 125 Nancy 226 Sallie 226 Sam 125 226 Susan 125 William 125
ARRINGTON, Daniel 155 Elizabeth Redd 155
ARTHUR, John 13
ASBURY, Bishop 101 279 Francis 42 Loulie C 185 Mrs Will 330 Will 185
ASCOUGH, Julia 290
ASHE, Thomas 192
ASHLEY, Thomas 304
ASHWORTH, Gus 37 J H 37
ASTOR, Nancy 133
ASTROP, Narcissus 261
ATHEY, Sarah Hay 228
ATKINS, David 13-14 304 John 14 John Francis 271 Lizzie 271 Lucinda 271 Noah 14 Sallie 275 Wm Stultz 271
ATKISSON, Jesse 298 Jesse Jr 298 Stephen 298
ATWELL, W H 47
AUGREEN, Philip 304
AUSTIN, Charles F 19 Mary 232
AVERETT, Edmond 288 J T 288 Lloyd 288 Martha Coleman 288 Thomas H 288
AVERY, Mrs Ada M 330
AYERS, Bettie Brown 155 Lum 155
AYLETTY, 132
AYRES, Hannah 251 Reid 251
BACON, Lord 83 Lord Of England 197 Nathaniel 122
BAGLEY, Sara 241
BAILEY, 46 Augusta 109 127 182 Augusta Parks 128-129 C C 254 Carr 304 Cecile 129 Chandler 304 Charles Cabaniss 102

INDEX

BAILEY (Cont.) Charles Cabiness 129 Charles Lewis 103 Charlotte 111 John 111 127 304 326 John B 128 L H 330 Lydia 326 Martha H 254 Martha Hairston 129 Martha Rowland 102 Mary 128-129 254 Mary Elizabeth 101-102 279 Parks 102-103 109 111 128-129 254 Patience 129 Robert Parks 129 Sam 109 182 Samuel 103 127-129 Sarah 237 Sarah Ann 111 Sarah Judith 127 182 Sarah Lewis 103 109 Sarah Smith 127 Tabitha 111 128 279 Thomas 304 Valerine 129 W W 330 William Adolphe 129 Wm 304
BAILY, Tabitha Churchill 99
BAKER, 46 Aquila 305 Betsy 166 Catherine 274 Daniel Webster 204 David 112 Dolly 83 204 Edmund 305 Fannie 204 Geo 47 166 Henry Clay 204 James 204 274 John 204 Joseph 304 Kate M 112 Katie 204 Leftrage 204 Leftridge 83 Lucinda 137 204 Lucy 204 Mack 59 Martha 166 187 Minnie 204 Polly 204 245 Ruth 204 Ruth P 274 William 204
BALDOCK, Betty 232 Mr 232
BALDWIN, D O 60
BALL, Anne 214 Elizabeth 161 John E 161
BALLARD, Lucy Duke 240 Mr 240
BALTIMORE, Lord 83 139 255
BANGELEY, J J 329
BANKS, Frances 240 Maria Bruce 240 William Bruce 242 Wm Bruce 240
BARBER, Carter 83 Nellie 83 Pitsy 83 Seth 83 Winnie 83
BARBOUR, Criss 19 Dick 19 Elizabeth 263 Frank 19 James 231 Joel 13 Mrs T N 329

BARBOUR (Cont.) Philip P 231 Sue 197 Thomas N 263
BARKER, Charles 304 Daisie 212 Hayes 212 J M 63 James 13 Joel 304 John 304 313 Michael 13 304 Mrs J M 331
BARKSDALE, Henry 304 311 John 281 304 320 322-323 325 Mary 281
BARNARD, Charles 305
BARNES, Alexander 14
BARNETT, Nathaniel 304
BARRAT, Francis 13 James 13
BARRETT, Waller 55
BARRETTT, Shadrack 13
BARROW, A F 19 Albert 126 Ann 125 Anne Nancy 172 B F 19 184 330 B F Sr 19 Ben F Nib 126 Benj F 258 Benjamin 125 164 Cassandra 125-126 Columbus 125 Corinne 118 Dora 126 Elizabeth 125 Elva 126 Ferdinand 19 125 Flournoy 19 George 125-126 Henry 126 Jennie 125 John A 125-126 Judith 126 Judith Parks 184 258 Julia 125 Kate 329 Katie 126 Mabel 126 Martha 206 Mary 125-126 Nannie 125-126 Nib 125 Orin W 126 Orrin 125 Orrin W 19 Pete S 118 Pete Tom 125-126 Robert 125 Susan 125-126 164 172 226 239 Tippey 125 Tom 126 Watt 125 William 125 172 206 226
BARTEE, William 14 315
BARTON, David 304 319 Joshua 320
BASETT, Burwell 122
BASHAM, Beulah 261
BASON, Betsy 211 Joseph 211
BASS, Horace A 207 Minnie 207
BASSETT, 51 A H 203 Ada 124 Addie 124 Alexander 125 Alexander Hunter 77 123-124

BASSETT (Cont.) Alice 124 Allan
121 Ann 125 Ann Pocahontas
266 Anna 124 Annie Maria 122
Beo Washington 122 Bettie
Carter 122 Bridget 122 Burwell
123 283 298 326 Burwell Jr 123
C C 124 331 Catherine 184
Columbia 123 Dink 124 Eliza
124 Elizabeth 122-123 Everett
124 Frances 122 Francis 121
Fulk 121 G W 123 Geo Hairston
123 Harden 124 Henry 124 J D
124 329 J P 329 Jane O 123
Joanna 122-123 John 122 124
John H 54 Joseph 124 138
Judith Frances Carter 122 Julia
123 Lord 120 Malinda 123 283
Mamie 124 Maria Jane 123
Martha 161 Martha A 123
Martha Hairston 123 Mary 77
123-125 203 235 Mary C 79
Mary Catherine 124 Mary
Dorsey 123 Mattie 124 Medora
124 Mrs J B 331 Nancy 124
Nathaniel 298 Osmond 120
Peter 121 Pocahontas 123-124
290 Polly 123 326 R B 330 Ralph
121 Ranseller 123 Richard 121
Roxie 124 Sallie 124 138 Samuel
124 Thomas 121 Virginia 123 W
J 123-124 330 W W 124 William
121 Wm 122 Wm Nathaniel 123
Woodson 123-124 235
BATES, John 325 W G 48
BATTIN, S J 47-48
BAUGHN, Aristophus 304
  Arristophus 14 Benry 304
  Hanna 236 Milliner 236 Reuben
  304
BAYARD, Thomas F 121
BAYLES, Tabitha 326 Wm 326
BAYS, Peter 13 305
BEAKER, Lottie 331
BEAL, Eliza 272 John 19 272 Julia
  272 Nancy 272 Nathan 12

BEAL (Cont.) Sam 19 Tom 272
  William 19
BEALE, John M 19 Marcus W 19
BEARD, Florence Ann 277 John Jr
  134 Medora Sabina 181 Mrs W J
  331 William J 277
BECK, J S 331 James 19
BECKHAM, B M 47
BECKNER, A D 49 329
BEDFORD, Thomas 319-320
BEEKER, Lottie 212 Mabel 212 S
  J 212
BEEL, Andrew 304 Michael 304
BELCHER, Jabe 19 John 19 171
  Susan 171 Thos 19
BELKNAP, Annie 287 Henry 287
BELL, G M 19 James 19 Tho 14
BELTON, Wm 19
BENNET, William 14
BENNETT, Ellen 214 Henry 214
BENNIE, 204
BENTON, 269 Nannie 269
BERNAR, Ruth 326 Walter 326
BETTS, 46 A D 80
BIBB, 46
BILL, Catherine 264 David S 264
  Lucy 264
BILLEMAN, Nilly 326 Wm 326
BILLINGS, James 13 P W 19
BINFORD, Dora 136 Hugh 136
BIRKS, Rowland 305
BISHOP, Fannie 275 Fanny 240
  Joseph 275 Lucy 159
BITCHELL, Edwin 219
BITTING, Col 221 Lewis 298
  Patsy 221
BLACK, Acquilla 13 Mr 101
BLACKWELL, Miss 220 243
BLAGGE, John 319
BLAIR, Alice 314 Annie 234
  Archibald 145 151 Elizabeth 145
  151 James 145 151 Joseph 304
  314 Magdalene 234 White 234
BLAKEY, Agnes 326 Churchill 304
  326

BLANCHETT, Peter 304
BLEDOSE, Peachy 326 Peggy 326
BLEDSOE, William 14
BLEVENS, Dillon 304 James Jr 304 John 304 Willoghby 304 Wm Jr 304
BLEVINS, Wm 325
BLIZE, Elizabeth 327
BLOGGS, John 319
BOAZ, S P 19
BOCK, R J 19
BOCOCK, Drury 289 James 289 Malinda 289 T M 19
BOHANAN, William 14
BOHANNAN, Wm 304
BOLIN, John 304
BOLING, Archibald 304 Christopher 304 Christopher Jr 304 Joseph 304
BOLLING, Anne 145 151 Elizabeth 145 151 Jane 151 John 145 151 311 Leaner 326 Mary 151 Robert 151 Samuel 323 William 311
BOLTON, James 304 Robt Sr 304 Thomas 304
BONDURANT, Dorothy 212 Harriet 212 J S 19 Mary 219
BONE, Annie 162
BONNER, Charles 304
BOOKER, Addie 75 Byrd 184 E H 19 E M 19 Edward 119-120 Edward Henry 184 Elizabeth 120 Ella Cook 120 Fletcher Clement 120 Geo W 44 George W 120 Harden Chapman 184 Harold 184 Harold C 329 J W 45 James Carter 184 Jesse Wooton 119 Jesse Wootton 120 John 75 119 John A 120 John Minor Botts 120 Judith 119 Judith Parks 184 Julia 119 Lena Alma 184 Leonard 119 Lowry 119 184 Lowry Sheffield 120 Margaret 119 Maria 120 Marshall E 120

BOOKER (Cont.) Martha 119 Mary Catherine 120 Mildred Ann 120 Miss 210 Mrs J W Jr 330 Mrs J W Sr 330 Phoebe 119 Rebecca 119 Richard 119 Richard A 120 Richard Jr 119 Ruth 120 Sallie 119-120 Samuel 34 Samuel Edward 120 Thomas J 120 Walter Shields 184 William 119
BOOL, Micajah 304
BOONE, Daniel 112 133 Jemima 132-133 Nathan 112
BOULDIN, 46 Ann 285 Anna G 330 Annie G 119 Joseph 322 Mary E 119 Miss 221 Obediah 47 285 Sallie Elizabeth 219 Thomas 119
BOUSMAN, A H 200 Harriett 136 Loula 200
BOWE, Anna 234
BOWEN, David 19
BOWLES, Eliza 284 G R 19 George 13 Mr 284
BOWLIN, John W 244 Nannie 244
BOWLING, John 14 Joseph 13 William 13
BOWMAN, Elizabeth 177 John 13
BOYD, Lizzie 232
BOYS, Miss 113
BRACKLEY, Joseph 14
BRADBERRY, Henry 304 Jos 313 Joseph 304 319 Lewis 14
BRADFIELD, James 104 Susan 65 106 Susan E 104 William Robert 65 105 Willie 106 Willie Florence 65
BRADLEY, Mr 217 Rebecca 217
BRAINBRIDGE, William 13
BRAMHAM, William 13
BRAMMER, John 14
BRANDT, Stella 185
BRANHAM, Barnabas 13 John 13
BRANKLEY, J C 75
BRASHEARS, Phillip 13

BRAYNE, Anne Butler 144
BREDEN, Wm 304
BRENGLE, Bettie 225 Maizie 225
  W D 225
BREWER, Matilda 252 Mr 217
  Nancy 217 William 202
BRISCO, Truman 304
BRISCOE, Catherine 326 John
  304 313 322 Louise 234 Milly
  328 Turman 326
BRITAIN, Elizabeth 327
BROCK, John 305 Sherwood 305 T
  F 19
BRODIE, Erie 239
BROOKS, Andrew 116 Maranda
  154 Mary 116
BROOS, Moses 14
BROWN, 51 Akers 37 Alice 118
  Ann Eliza 118 Anne Eliza 64
  Annie 118 Annie Eliza 117
  Augustine 304 Bettie Carter 122
  Bolin 177 Caroline 177 Corinne
  118 Cornelia 117 Doris 117 Dr
  316 321-322 Eliza Jane 116
  Elizabeth 117 Elizabeth E 116
  Etta 118 Frederick 116
  Frederick R 117-118 177
  Frederick Rives 64 George Akers
  117-118 223 Isham 326 J A 331
  Jack 116 James William 116-117
  Jane 116 177 John 116 John
  Andrew 118 263 John Andrew Jr
  118 John R 64 117-118 177 John
  S 65 John Spottswood 116 Kate
  65 118 331 Loula 118 200 Lucy
  116-117 Lucy Ashton 155 Lula
  117 Margaret 154 Mary 116 326
  Mary Elizabeth 118 Mattie 117
  May 118 Millard 116-117 Minnie
  118 223 Moss 118 Mrs G A 331
  N J 245 Nancy 116 229 Nannie
  Jane 118 263 Pattie 118 Pattie
  Hairston 263 Reuben Skelton
  116 Rives 117 Rosa 118 Ruben
  116 Sallie 177 Sally Eugenia 331

BROWN (Cont.) Sarah 116-118
  Susan 117 177 Tarleton 116
  Tarleton F 117 Thomas S 155
  Virginia 117 W A 118 Walter
  117 William 13 William A 177
  William Alexander 116-117
  William B 117 Willie 118
BROWNE, Dr 103 Hester 214
  Humphrey 214 Judith Walker
  122 Porteus 102 S J 47
BRUCE, Frances 240 James 240
  John 240 Robert 145 240 Robert
  King Of Scotland 188
BRYAN, Elmer 329 Josiah 305
  Mary 252
BRYANT, C B 19 Charles
  Benjamin 65 Col 66 Francis 284
  James 13 John 304 Malinda 65
  Mary 194 Rowland 65 Sadie 185
  Sallie 185 Stafford 284 Susan
  Rowland 284 Wm F 284
BUCHANAN, Henry C 265 Mary
  265 Mrs M S 54 331
BULGER, 201
BULLARD, Chester 51 Wm 247
BULLINGTON, Sis 272
BUNCH, Martin 293
BURCH, David 304 Girard 272 J B
  19 J G 19 J W 19 John 13
  Martin 304 Mary 272 Richard 19
  T G 330 W G 48
BURCHEL, Daniel 12
BURDET, Jarvis 304
BURGE, David 294 Etta 118
  Lakin 19 Wm 19 Woody 294
BURGESS, Davis 326 Dolly 204
  Emily 203 John 83 136 Lucy 326
  Martha 83 Victoria 136 W G 63
  Wm G 19
BURKE, 127
BURKS, John 305 Wm 305
BURNE, Charles Sr 304
BURNES, Charles Sr 304 Samuel
  304 Wm 304
BURNETT, Jese 13

INDEX

BURNS, Andrew 304 Michael 12
BURR, Aaron 35 237
BURRESS, Jacob 326 Susannah 326
BURRUS, Jacob 223 Susannah 223
BURTON, Ann 268 J W 19 W T 19
BURWELL, Joanna 122-123 Lewis 122 324
BUSH, Thomas 67
BYBEE, Betty 327
BYERLY, Annie 207 Samuel L 207
BYRD, Col 319 Jesse Thomas 219 Lucy Matt 219 S W 19 Samuel 304 Susan Ann 206 William 9 164 Wingfield 206 Wm 132 144 315 318
CABANISS, 103 Elizabeth 206
CABELL, 232 George C 64 J 131 Mary Elizabeth 133 Pocahontas 193 Wm 131
CABINESS, Annie Redd 267 Charles 128 Corrie 267 Elizabeth 267 Isabel 267 Jack 267 Mary 128-129 254 Recy B 267 Roy 267 Starling 267
CAHALL, Maria 125
CAHILL, A Holt 136 Ann 135-136 Ann Eliza 135 B M 19 B M Jr 136 Beatrice 136 Benjamin Marshall 136 Bessie W 136 Betsy Ann 136 Callie 285 Clementine 135 Dianah 134-135 Dora 136 Edgar 136 Eliza 135 Fannie 136 Florence 136 Gustavus B 136 Harriett 135 Jack 135 285 James Semple 136 Jane 135 Jennie Lily 136 Jesse 135 John 134 157 John Car 135 John Jr 135 John Taylor 136 John W 135 John William 136 Kate 136 Lelia 136 Lenora 136 Lettie 136 Lily 206 Lorenza Dow 136 Loula 136 Lucinda 135 Margaret 135 Maria 135 206

CAHILL (Cont.) Mariah 135 Marie 136 Marshall 135 Mary 135 206 Mary Jane 206 Maud 221 Nancy 135 Nathaniel 135 Obediah 135 Peregrine 135 Perry 19 135 Sallie 135 Susanna 157 Susannah 135 Tamesia 136 Taylor Z 135 Thomas 19 135-136 Thomas Sr 136 Victoria 136 William Price 136 Z T 19 Zachariah 136 Zachary Taylor 135
CALAWAY, Daniel 130 Marian 130 Richard 130
CALDWELL, Celestia 247 D F 134 Samuel 247
CALHOUN, 79 John C 129
CALLAN, Thomas 305
CALLAWAY, America 133 237 Bethany 132 Bethenia Ruth 237 Brantly 132 Elizabeth 131-133 Elizabeth M 134 Enoch 132 Flanders 131-133 Frances 131-132 Fuller E 132 Geo 132-133 Geo H 134 Geo Hairston 133 Hairston 133 Henry 130 Isaac 132 Jack 133 Jacob 132 James 131-132 134 Jemima 133 John 132-134 237 Joshua 132 Jubal 131 Mary Elizabeth 133 Polly Hairston 133 Richard 131-132 Ruth 238 Samuel H 134 Samuel Hairston 133 Sarah 131-132 Thomas 131-132 William 130 Wm 131-133
CALLOWAY, America 192 Geo 192 John 192 Mary 192 Ruth 192
CALLWAY, John 130
CALLWAYE, Wm 130
CALWEY, 130
CAMP, Martha 161
CAMPBELL, America 166 America Hairston 238 Bethenia 238-239 David 166 329

CAMPBELL (Cont.) Edwin
Ruthven 239 Erie 239 Evelyn
239 Fannie 285 Frances Pannill
239 J H 19 James 239 285
James P 166 John 305 Kate 166
Mary T 166 Mrs Norman 260
Norman 239 Pattie 166 Polly
166 Raymond 239 Robert 166
Ruth 239 Ruth Janet 238
William 317 William A 166 Wm
19 223 316 Wm Arthur 239 Wm
Pannill 238-239
CAMPER, Mary 279
CANDEM, Frances 232 Mr 232
CANNADAY, Annie 219 Mr 219
CANNADY, Bailey 244 Callie 244
John T 244 Lydia 244
CANNON, James 326 Patsy 326
CANTERBURY, Samuel 306
CANTWELL, Adam 304-305 John 305
CARDWELL, 278
CARLA, Daniel 311
CARLIN, Daniel 297 322 325
CARLTON, Daniel 294
CARPER, Emma 196 James 196
Jane Elizabeth 194 196 Lily 196
Moses 194 196 Robert Beverley 196
CARR, Ann Winston 107 281
Joseph 294 Miss 224
CARRINGTON, Geo 315-316 323
P 131 Paul 294
CARROL, John 13
CARROLL, John W 48 Judith 316
CARSON, Jennie 234 John
Hazzard 264 Margaret Allen 264
CARSTARPHEN, J E 161 Louisa B 161
CARTER, Ann 328 Annie Adelle
212 Apphia Fauntleroy 247
Bailey 305 320 Baines 313 Carey
19 E H 19 Edward 111 Elizabeth
184 Ellen 111 Geo 305 Geo A
329 J W Jr 184 James 256

CARTER (Cont.) James Harden
184 James J 19 Jesse 212 John
110 John W 119 165 John
Waddy 184 Jos 326 Joseph 19
Josiah 305 313 Judith 119 Kezia
165 Keziah Drewry 184 King
260 Kizzie 55 184 Kizzie Drewry
330 Lettie 136 Louis G 329
Louis Gordon 184 Louisa B 161
Lucy 287 Lula 53 Mary 326
Mary Lavinia 184 Mat 19 Mrs
John W 57 Nancy 326 Pres 101
Raynes 305 Rebecca 260 Robert
260 Ruth Redd 184 Sallie Ann
184 Susan Elizabeth 256 T J 19
Tabitha 332 Talitha Jane 110 W
L 161 William 68 287 Wm 294
CARTMILL, Capt 315
CARTWELL, John 13
CARTWRIGHT, 38
CARY, 152 Bridget 122 Miles 122
Wilson Miles 144
CASEY, Daniel 305
CASON, Edward 326 Lucy 326
CASTILIO, Iantha 330
CATHEY, Mary 149 Nannie 150
CAVE, Robert 305
CAVIN, Alexander 305
CAWDIN, James 326
CAYTON, Rachel 326 Wm 326
CHADWELL, David 305
CHAMBERLAIN, Mary 155 277
Matilda Hughes 155 William 155
CHAMBERS, Wm 305
CHAMPTON, James 19
CHANDLER, John 13 Joseph 305
Robert 305
CHANEY, Matilda 229 Mr 229
CHANNEL, Joseph 13
CHAPPEL, Jesse R 38
CHAPPELL, Lmarie 136
CHARLES, I 121 237 Ix King Of
France 213 James 305
CHEATHAM, Eleanor 217 H C 48

INDEX 341

CHEATHAM (Cont.) John C 19
  John D 19 Joseph 217 Rachael
  171 Susan 257 Tabitha 217
CHEEK, William 13
CHESHIRE, John 310 John W 19
CHEWNING, John 326 Lettie 326
CHILDERS, Patterson 12
CHILDRESS, Elizabeth 171 Mary
  Anne 140 Mary C 329 Maude
  140 Sidney P 140 Sidney P Jr
  140 Vincent Davis 140 William J
  171
CHILDS, Susanna 223
CHISM, Elijah 305 John 305
CHOICE, Cassandra 125 Gresham
  125 John 125 Tully 14 323 Tully
  Jr 305 317 Tully Sr 305 W 305
  William 323 Wm 317
CHRISTIAN, Col 92 316 W H 48
  Wm 315
CHURCHILL, Elizabeth 122 Mary
  82 199-200 Susan 181 Tabitha
  111
CLAIBORNE, Delia 123 John
  Hughes 123 Letitia 262 Virginia
  123
CLANTON, Bessie 138 Bessy 138
  Claudia 138 Columbia 138 Dolly
  138 Eliza 138 255 George 19 138
  H C 329 Hylton C 199 Hylton
  Claude 138 Jesse 138 206 208
  Jesse R 208 Kinnie 138 Lillie
  138 Lucille 138 Mary Ann 138
  Mary Bennie 138 199 Mary E
  138 Nancy Hylton 138 Nannie
  138 252 Nannie H 208 Polly 138
  Robert 138 Sallie 206 210 Sallie
  King 208 Washington 138
  William 255 Willie C 138 Wm
  138
CLARE, Gertrude Shipman 207
CLARK, Andrew 305 Ann 227
  Annie 136 264 Carnetta 136
  Cassandra 136 227 272 Cernetta
  272 Charles S 136

CLARK (Cont.) Elizabeth
  Cassandra 227 Ernest E 136
  George 298 Gideon 136 272
  Howell 227 Jacob 178 Jinsy 233
  Joe 136 272 John 227 326 John
  D 136 Joseph 323 Joseph E 136
  Letitia 272 Lettitia 136 Marion
  E 136 Martha 247 261 Mary 227
  Mr 247 N C 19 Nat 227
  Nathaniel 136 272 Nina G 136
  Patty 136 272 R A 19 Ruby 136
  Ruth 178 Sally 326 Sarah 136
  272 Spencer 323 326 T J 19 Tom
  136 272 W A 19 W F 302
  William 136 227 272 Willis 47
  332 Wm 50
CLARKSON, David 305
CLAY, 79 ---- 267 Mary 267
CLAYBORN, Mrs Libb 193
CLAYBROOK, Annie 118 Lewis C
  118 Mrs L C 332
CLAYTON, Elizabeth 231 Philip
  231 Samuel 231
CLEMENS, John 298
CLENDENNING, 202
CLEVELAND, Ben 223 Martha
  223 Wm 223
CLIFT, Mrs Rora 330
CLOPTON, Fanne 260
CLOUD, 325 Isaac 12 Joseph Jr
  305 Joseph Sr 305
COAN, Ann 198 Bettie 184 199-
  200 258 Billie 118 Bird 199-200
  George William 118 199-200
  John O 118 199-200 331 John O
  Jr 199-200 Loula 118 199-200
  Mary 118 Mary Ann 199-200
  Posey 199 Posey D 200
COATS, Jesse 14
COBBLER, Emma 280
COBBS, Thomas E 19
COBER, Thomas 305
COCKERHAN, Adner 305
COCKRAM, Sally 326 Wm 326
COE, Ann 155 Maj Gen 155

COFFER, Pink 221
COGGINS, William 324
COLAMEN, Ida 223
COLE, Abner 19 James 19 Martha 289 Sarah Miller 175
COLEMAN, Alice 137-138 All 137 Alvis 137 Azzie 137 Bruce 137-138 Burwell 137 Clyde 137 Emma Lou 218 Essie 138 Ethel 137 George 137 Harrison 137 Ida 137-138 James 137 John 137 Lottie 138 Loula 137 M M 331 Martha 139 Morgan A 137 Morton 137-138 Nannie 245 Pocahontas 137 Robert 137 Ruby 137 Ruth Angeline 137 Sallie 124 137-138 T C 331 Thomas C 137
COLES, Walton King 295
COLLEY, John 326 Sarah 326
COLLIER, 168 Charles 305 Jesse 305 Thomas 305 Wm 305
COLONNA, M S 47-48
COMER, C F 48
COMPTON, Alcey 326 Ebenezer 326
CONLEY, Enoch 305
CONNALLY, Mrs E L 331
CONNAUGHT, Duke Of 227
CONNER, Clarence 331
CONNOR, Miss 251
CONNOWAY, Ben 227 Dennis 227 Francis 227 Martha 227 Patsy 227 Sally 227
CONRAD, Antoinette 222 Julia 196
CONWAY, Capt 316 Elizabeth 157 326 John 317 321 326 Tabitha Jane 157
COOK, Ben Jr 305 Elizabeth 329 Jesse 14 Joseph 305 Mr 224 Sallie 119 Susan 224 Thomas 19 Wm 314
COOKE, Mrs Anthony Wayne 56
COOLEY, James 306

COOLY, James 305
COOPER, Agnes 327 Ashley 268 Austin 19 Elizabeth 268 311 314 Guss 19 James Fenimore 132 John 305 Jos 325 Joseph 305 Mollie 233 268 Nancy 112 Polly 268 282 Sallie 207 Sterling 19 Thomas 12 282 294 305 314 William 207
COPELAND, Richard 14 305
CORBIN, Benj 19
CORBITT, John 305
CORN, Jesse 12 Malinda 191 Mary 203 William 203
CORNWALL, 130
CORNWALLIS, Lord 81 96 108
COTTON, John 305 Savarus 305
COUSINS, Charles 278 John 278 Mary 278 Sarah 278
COWDEN, Capt 316 James 319
COWDIN, James 13
COWHERD, Selah 167
COWLER, John 305
COX, Annie Elizabeth 219 Darvin 19 Edmund 170 Eleanor 170 Forest 114 Francis 170 321-322 Frank 170 George 170 J H 19 Jabez 170 James 13 Jefferson 170 Joanna 171 John 13 58 171 247 293 298 305 318 326 John H 30 Joseph 170 Judith Elizabeth 171 Leaner 326 Lewis 170 Nancy 329 Peyton 170 Phoebe 119 Pinckney 219 Polly 170 Robert 298 Toliver 305 Will 114 William 13 Willis 170 Wm 19
COXE, J J 200
CRAGHEAD, Alexander 137 Angeline 137 Catherine 137 Charles 137 Emily 137 John 136-137 Lily 137 Lodowick 204 Loula 137 Loulie 185 Lucinda 137 204 222 Peter 306 Pocahontas 137 Robert 137 Ruth Angeline 137 Sallie 137 222

CRAGHEAD (Cont.) Sarah 136
Thomas 222 Thomas Lodowick
137 Townley 137 Virginia 137
CRAIG, Edward 219 Ella 219 G F
331 George D 220 Lucy 141 Mrs
G D 331 Nannie 220 269 Nannie
Elizabeth 218 Thomas 19
CRAWFORD, Alexr 322
CRAWLEY, James 13
CREASEY, Ben 19
CREWS, Jack 19
CRIDER, 46 J W 185
CRIST, C E 49 Charles Eugene
182 Dora 49 Medora 182 Mrs C
E 330 Virginia 182
CRITZ, Haman 148 325 Haman Jr
318 Haman Sr 321 Hamon 12
294 Mary 221 Mary Henrietta
211 Nancy 148 Peonia 259 Sallie
233
CROCKETT, Col 323 325 Hugh
321
CROMER, Mary 207
CROUCH, John 14 305 313 John
Jr 305 Joseph 326 Peggy 326
CROWDER, 46
CROWLEY, Elizabeth 295
CRUMB, Lucinda 201
CRUNK, John 299
CUMPTON, Anna Lou 150 Bessie
Lee 150 Dandridge 150 Mary
150 Walter G 150
CUNNINGHAM, Bettie A 195 Joe
326 John 12 305 326 Joseph 12
M C 195 Mary 326 Mrs B A 331
Nancy 326 Wm 326
CURSELLY, John 305
CURTIS, Mary 281
CUSTER, Elizabeth C 160 Zona
299
DABNEY, Sarah 223
DALTON, Ada 149 Ada D 332
Charlotte 222 Chas 149 David
161 Edgar Elliot 149 Elizabeth
198 222 Harry Lee 149

DALTON (Cont.) Hunter 149 Irene
149 James Hunter 148 Jane 198
John 198 Lou 198 Loula 236
Mary 153 198 222 Miss 237 Mr
222 Nancy 148 Nannie 196
Nannie Anderson 148-149 P W
149 Peter Washington 148 Polly
198 Puss 198 Rachel 160 Robert
198 Rufus 198 Sam C 19 Sarah
198 Susan 158 198 Walter 198
William 198 William Sr 236 Wm
305
DAME, Dr 165
DANDRIDGE, 100 Anne 145 151
Annie 147 252 331 Annie Maria
122 Beatrice 150 Bessie Lee 150
Bessie Less 146 Cathey
Spottswood 149 Clay 146-147
Dorothea 75 144 Edward 150
Emma Louise 146 150 Geo
Gilmer 332 George Gilmer 146
149-150 George Sameul 150
Harry 252 331 Harry C 147
James Spottswood 146 149-150
Jessie 150 Jimmie Ophelia 149
John 143 146-147 252 Lightie
Louisa 332 Lightie Louise 150
Martha 122 143 175 Martha
Washington 146 150 Mary 149-
150 Mary Jane 146 152 Mary
Pocahontas 149 Mary
Pochahontas 146 Mattie 147
149-150 Merle 150 Mildred
Hamner 150 Nancy 145 152
Nannie 149-150 Nannie
Anderson 146 148 Nathaniel 147
Nathaniel West 144 Nell 147
332 Pattie Washington 150
Robert Bolling 146-147 Robt B
252 Samuel Clark 150 Samuel
Hamner 146 150 Sarah 146-147
152 Susan 147 Susan Webster
252 Thomas 147 252 Thomas
West 146 Una 147 252 Unity
144 Walter Alexander 146 150

DANDRIDGE (Cont.) William 143-146 151 252 William Alexander 144 152 William Cathey 150 William R 147 Wm 149-150 Wm Alexander 150 Zelia Lightfoot 150
DANGERFIELD, Harig 155 Louie Frances 155
DANIEL, Easter 328 Edward 293 Geo 305 John Jr 306 John Sr 306 Pauline 114 Permelia 267
DARLINGTON, J M 44
DARNALL, H M 193 Louisa 193
DAVENPORT, Cassandra Ward 289 Nannie 222
DAVIE, William R 316
DAVIES, Samuel 165
DAVIS, 280 Anne 139-140 Anne Ursula 139-140 August 240 Azzie 137 B A 143 332 Baker 134 Ben 280 Benjamin 139-141 Benjamin S 142 Bessie 330 Bethenia Ruth Callaway 134 Betsy Anne 140-141 Bettie 139 269 Betty 134 231 Callaway Eaton 134 Charles 139 141 Charles Peter 139 Charles Peter Jr 140 Charlie W 277 Chas J 143 Chas W 140 D F 330 D S 142 David H 139 143 Doctor W 141 E J 331 E L 143 Earnest 240 Edith 239 Edmond 240 Edmond Pannill 238 Eleanor 139-140 Eli M 19 Elizabeth 139 143 Elizabeth M 134 Elizabeth Ruth 238 240 Ellye 140 Emily 139 240 Emioy Wade 139 Ernest 238 Ernestine 143 Evan 134 Evans 238 Evelyn 143 Everett J 143 Everett Jesse 141 Everett Jesse Jr 143 Everette Holland 140 Everette J 140 Fletcher A 140 Frank P 330 Frank Payne 140 Frank Payne Jr 140 Gen 195 Geo 238 Geo E 329

DAVIS (Cont.) Geo Evans 239 Geo Evans Jr 239 Geo W 19 George Thomas 141 Gillie Coleman 141 H H 332 Harry Holland 140 Hilda 240 Ida 140 Ida May 277 Jack 240 James 14 James P 142 James Spottswood 240 James W 19 Jane Hickey 139 215 Jesse 220 Jesse Guy 140 Jesse H 143 Jesse Heard 141 Joathan 139 John 13 269 305 312 315 321 John Benjamin 141 John H Jr 240 John Henry 134 238-239 John Henry Jr 238 John Mitchell 139-140 John Peter 139-140 Jonathan 313 Joseph 14 278 306 Joshua 139 Julia 140 Julian 140 Kate 134 139 Katherine 134 Katherine Langhorne 240 Laban J 139 143 Lena 140 Letitia 139 Lewellyn 140 Lillian 140 Lily 140 Lizzie 220 Lloyd Tilman 141 Lucy 141 Lucy Ann 83 Lula 141 Lydia 139 Mae Galloway 239 Margaret C 83 Margaret Carr 139 Martha 139 278 Martha Jane 277 Mary 134 139 141 238-239 Mary Elizabeth 139 Mary Frances 139-140 Mary Jane 139 Mary Sue 140 Maude Wall 140 Minnie 143 Moses 139 Nancy 139-141 326 Nathan 14 Nettie 139 Peggy 140-141 Peter 83 139 Peter Perkins 140 Pinkney G 83 Pinkney Gilmore 141 Polly 254-255 Rachel 139 Raymond 143 Robert Brown 139-140 Robt 19 Robt E 140 Rufus Franklin 141 Ruth 275 Sallie Elizabeth 140 Sarah 139 Sarah Elizabeth 140 Sarah Jane 139 Sarah Louise 169 Solomon 14 305 Susan 141 Thomas Holland 140 Thomas Holland Jr 140 Virginia 140

DAVIS (Cont.) Walter E 140
    Wilbur 48 William 141 231
    Winnie 140-141 Zela 277
DAVISON, Wm 305
DAWSON, Mrs J W 260
DEAN, Alice 228 Mr 228
DEBASSETT, Ralph 120
    Thurstine 120
DECOTTES, Kate 139
DEDREWRY, John 164
DEEMS, C F 250
DEESTE, 167
DEGRAFENRIED, Tabitha Jane 157
DEGRAFFENREID, John 206
    Tabby 206
DEITRICK, Helen 277
DEJARNETTE, Boler 287 Kesiah 287
DELAFONTAINE, Rev 174
DELAVINDER, 213 Richard 214
    William 214
DELAZIER, Edward 160 Frances 160
DELLINGHAM, William 14
DELOZIER, Rhoda 328
DELTHICK, William 214
DEMEDICIS, Catherine Queen Regent 213
DEMPSEY, Ann Eliza 227
    Dubartis 227 Fletcher 227
    Hamala 227 Marshall 227 Mary 227 Polly 227 Rufus 227 Sam 227 William 227
DENHAM, Charles 14
DENSON, James 306 Wm 306
DENT, Anne 139 Mary 327
    Shadrick 327
DEPITY, Mary 215
DEPRIEST, John 14
DEREMI, Abram 248 Count Raoul 248 Daniel 85 248 Elizabeth 85 194 Jean 85 Piere 248 Pierre 85 248 Samuel 85
DESHAZEAU, Clem 156

DESHAZEAU (Cont.) Edmund 156 John 156 Robin 156 William 156
DESHAZO, Annie D 158 Annie S 200 Bebe 158 Ben L 157 Bettie Rachael 236 C E 158 C N 158 Charles Henry 159 Chas I 157 Dameron F 159 Diana Garner 157 Dora 158 Edmund 156 159 Edwin Penn 159 Elizabeth E 157 Fannie 112 156-157 G B 157-158 G K 157 G W 331 Geo K 135 156 198 244 Geo W 158 George King 156-157 George Reid 19 George W 199 Gincy 205 H A 159 H F 158 Henrietta 199 Hilda 159 Homer A 159 236 Irene 158 J B 200 330 J Beverly 159 J E 47 159 J F 158 J S 158 J W 158 Jane 156 205 Jeff S 332 Job 158 John 156 John E 159 John S 331 John W 157 Larkin 19 157-159 198 Laurie 157 Lucy 159 M Florence 159 Martha 157 Mary 198 231 Mary E 157 Mary Hunter 159 Mary Virginia 158 Mattie 158 Minnie 158 Mrs T D 199 Nancy M 157 Nathaniel C 19 157 P L 158 Peter H 159 R A 158 R T 231 Richard 156-157 Richard T 19 Richard Tazwell 157 Robert Noble 159 Robin 156 158 Rosa 158 Rufus 158 S Lou 159 Sallie 156-158 Sallie A 244 Sallie Ann 177 Susan 158 198 Susanna 157 Susannah 135 T D 158 Tabitha Jane 156-157 Virginia 157 Virginia A 157 W Dalton 158 W T 157-158 William 12 112 156 205 300 William T 19 157 159 177 William T Sr 159 William Thomas 158 Wm A 157
DESLIN, Agnes 268
DEVALOIS, Margaret 213
DEWITT, Anderson 182
DEY, Bascom 48

DICKENSON, Thos 298
DICKERSON, Charles 13 E M 118
　Eliza 170 John 313 Moses 306
　Nancy 170 Noten 315 Pattie 118
　William 170
DICKINSON, Isabell 327 John 327
　Thomas 323
DICKS, James 306
DICKSON, Selina Christiana 232
　Thompson 305
DIEHL, Patricia S 13
DILLARD, 51 68 Adela Nash 155
　Adele 154 240 Adelle 156 Ann
　154-155 224 Ann Isabelle 153
　Annie 154-155 Archelaus
　Hughes 154 Archilous Rughes
　153 Bettie Brown 155 Bettie
　Redd 250 Beulah 245 Caroline
　155 Carrie 154 264 Carter L 155
　Charles Harden 156 Chas H 154
　Drury C 302 Elizabeth 152-154
　186 247 263 Elizabeth Redd 153
　155 Ethel C 155 Florence 155
　Geo 186 Geo L 28 George 152-
　154 268 George Lee 155 George
　Penn 153-154 H Dalton 155
　Hairston 155 Harry 154 264
　Helen 154 156 219 Herbert Nash
　155 Hughes 50 154-155 302
　Isabella 154 J R 183 240 James
　14 67 153 James Jr 152 James
　Madison 153-154 James Stephen
　152 Jane 174 Jane Athey 152-
　153 Jenney 154 John 9 67 69
　152 193 259 264 294 298 300
　314 319-320 325 John H 224
　John Henry 153 John Lea 153-
　155 John Lee 28 John R 43 155-
　156 330 John Redd 153-154
　John Wilson 155 Len 153 Lizzie
　174 Louie Frances 155 Lucy 152-
　154 264 Lucy Ashton 155 Lula
　154 Lydia Adela 155 Maranda
　154 Margaret 154 Martha Ann
　153-155 Martha Hughes 154-155

DILLARD (Cont.) Mary 67 152-153
　155 263 Mary Ann 152-153
　Mary C 155 Mary Dalton 154
　Matilda 153-154 Matilda
　Hughes 153 155 Mattie 155
　Miranda 154 Mrs A A 330 Mrs
　John R 45 Nancy 327 Nell 156
　Nellie 156 Nicholas 152 Obe 224
　Overton 174 Overton Redd 153-
　154 P F Sr 154 Pattie 152-153
　259 Percy 155 Peter 154 247 263
　Peter Francisco 153-154 Peter
　Francisco Jr 154 Peter H 43
　Peter Hairston 152-153 155
　Robert J 154 Robert Jordan 156
　Ruth 152 327 Sallie 154 224 268
　Sallie Hughes 171 Sally 152
　Sarah 152-154 Stephen 152
　Thomas 152 Tom 174 William
　154-156 William Terry 152
　Wilthem 154
DILLENER, Henry 326 Lucy 326
DILLER, Henry 306
DILLINGER, Jacob 305
DILLINGHAM, Ann 327 Elizabeth
　328 John 306 Joshua 298 Lott
　327 Michael 320 Moses 306
DILLON, Annie 220 Ben Jr 327
　Benjamin 305 Betsy 166 Carter
　305 Elijah 19 Elizabeth 327
　Henry 305 Henry H 19 Henry Jr
　313 J B 331 Jack 19 220 James
　19 Joe 220 John 305 313 Lizzie
　220 Mary 289 326 Mary Frances
　220 Matilda 246 Miss 284 Mrs J
　W 289 Nancy 166 Patsy 166 285
　Polly 166 Tabitha 327 Thad 19
　Tommy 166 William 246 Wm 19
　285 313 327
DILLONER, Mary 326
DIX, Eliza M 168 Lucy 168
　Thomas 168
DOBBS, John 305
DODD, Maria 147 Mattie 147
　Nathaniel 147

DODSON, B F 19 Charles 305 Jim 59 Lottie Turner 37 331 Mr 229 Nellie 229
DONEGAN, Eleanor 171 T E 58
DONELSON, Isaac 320 322
DONEVANT, Ruth Dillard 218
DONOTHAN, Nelson 13
DONOVANT, Catherine 186
DOOLEY, Lucy 327 Thomas 327
DOOLING, Thomas 305
DOOLINGS, Thomas 14
DOSS, E H 19
DOTSON, Charles 12 William 12
DOTTY, Moses 306 Thomas 305
DOUGHTEN, John 305
DOVE, Ashworth Sr 135 Eliza 206 Jane 135 Mrs G M 330 Mrs W A 330
DOVELL, Annie Ruth 212 F I 212
DOW, Lorenzo 35 Peggy 35
DOWNEY, Dorsey B 199 Dr 200 Elizabeth 199 Mary Dorsey 199 Mollie 199
DOYAL, John 13
DOYLE, Addie 261 Fred 261 Maggie Bouldin 261 S M 19 Same 261
DRAPER, Ann Eliza 135 E B 167 E H 19 Everett 167 Fletcher 280 Hass 167 John H 19 Keziah 167 Leslie 167 Lou Ella 280 Lucy 167 Lucy Frances 167 Mary 167 Mike 167 Mrs C E 331 Mrs John 193 Mrs William 29 Nancy Dent 139 Nannie Lee 280 P D 19 Polly 167 Robert 280 Thomas J 19 139 Tom 139 Truman 167 Vaughn 167 William 167 299 Wm 280
DREWRY, 247 A H 164-165 Deziah 165 F W 58 Flora 165 Henry Martin 165 Henry T 164 James 164 John 164 Kizzie 184 Madison R 165 Madison Redd 267 Martin 164 Mary 164 Mary Anderson 267 Milly 165

DREWRY (Cont.) Plummer 165 Sallie 164 Samuel 164 William 164
DUDLEY, Gustave B 118 Lula 117 Marion Mccrary 118 Priscilla Flint 118 Ruby 118 Sarah 118 Virginia Spottswood 118 William Brown 118
DUFFY, Renetta 331
DUGGER, Sallie 226
DUNAVANT, G W 19 T W 19
DUNBAR, Annie 187
DUNCAN, James 306 John 306 King Of Scotland 145 Maria 123 283
DUNHAM, Mrs C T 280
DUNKIRK, 122
DUNLAP, Eliza 194 Henry 305 Salina 194
DUNLOP, Sarah 328
DUNMORE, 91 Lord 84
DUNN, Catherine 326 Gatewood 305 Michael 306 Richard 305 Tarmesia 136 Walter 136 325 Waters 295 306 325 Waters Jr 305 William 14
DUPUY, A M 58 Anthony 47 Anthony M 301-302 Anthony Martin 163 Bartholomew 162 Harriet Amasia 163 Harriett Amasia 163 John Bartholomew 163 Magdalene 163 Margarett 163 Mary 163 Peter 163 Sarah Holman 163 Susane 163 Susanna 163 Susanne 163
DYER, 225 Agnes 162 Alice 161 Ann 160 255 Anne 161 Annie 162 Ballard 162 Ben 162 171 Benjamin 160-161 Cherokee 161 Choctaw 161 Coleman 160 Cora 161 D A 329 David 161 David A 161 David Dalton 123 160 162 David L 160 David P 160-161 Diana 162 Eleanor 160 Eliza 162 211 Elizabeth 161

DYER (Cont.) Elizabeth C 160
Elizabeth H 160 Ella 162 Eloise
161 Emma 161 Ezra 161 Fannie
161 Fanny 160 Fountain 160
Frances 160 Fredonia 161 Geo
83 162 George 12 160 George W
161 Grief 160 Harden H 29
Harriet 161 Henry Gustavus 161
Holt 162 Horace Levi 161 Hugh
49 160 162 Ida 161 Jabez 160-
161 James 160-162 Jefferson
160 Joel 160 John 123 162 John
S 161 Joseph 160-161 Joseph F
161 Julia 162 Kate 161-162
Leonidas C 161 Lizzie C 161
Lizzie Logan 161 Louisa B 160-
161 Lucy Jane 162 Luella 161
Lulu 161 Malinda 160 Margaret
160 254-255 Maria Louise 161
Martha 161 171 Martha A 123
Martha Eliza 161 Mary 160-161
254 Minnie 160-161 Missouri
160 Nancy 160-161 Nancy
Reynolds 160 162 Phoebe 160
Pocahontas 161 Polly 171
Rachael 160 Rachael M 161
Rachel 160 Rachel Elizabeth 255
Rebecca 160 255 Ruth 83
Sacville 160 Sallie 162 Sallie
Martha 160 Sarah 160-161 Sinai
161 Susan 160 162 Thomas 19
Tom 162 Trusten 161 Virginia
160-161 Willis 161 Zanie 160
EANES, B H 19 Edward 300
Emma 171 Henry Clay 171
James A 19 Lou 285 Mr 285
EARLES, Elizabeth 327 Joshua 327
EARLY, Elizabeth 131 133 Joab 192 Jubal 43 95 131 192 Jubal A 153 Ruth Stovall 192
EAST, Frances 328 John 14 294 Martin 19 Mary 178 Tho 293 Wm 306
EASTES, Milly 328

EATON, Betty 134 Elizabeth 134 Mr 134
ECHOLS, Florence 155
EDISON, Charles 37 Thomas A 37
EDMONDSON, Sally 326
EDMUND, Mandy 258
EDMUNDSON, Frances 327 Hump 327
EDWARD, III 146
EDWARDS, Alice 229 Edmund 315 Elizabeth 327 J L 19 John 13 Judith 327 Lucy 326 Mrs Allie 37 Owen 327 R W 19 Robt 19 T O 48 Thomas 13 315 W H 47 William 315 Wm 229 327
EGBERT, Saxon King Of England 145
EGGLESTON, Jane Abigail 167 M J 19
EGGLETON, Delilah 272 Eliza 272 Eliza Susan 167 Geo R 19 George 30 John 19 John H 272 Logan 19 Lucy 270 Mike 167 Nancy 270 Nathaniel 272 Newson 19 Patrick 30 Peyton W 272 Polly 167 Thomas 310-311 Wm S 272
ELIZABETH, Queen 164 287
ELKINS, David 327 James 293 306 Jesse 14 Mary 327 Nathaniel 306 William 13 Wm 306
ELLIOTT, William 13
ELLIS, John 298 Joseph 323
EMPRESS, Eugenia Of Paris 196
ENDICOTT, John 147
ENGLISH, Dorothy 174 Mrs S D 331 Robert 14
EPPERSON, Joseph 305
EPPES, 35
ESTES, Alstrop 305 Annie Lelia 169 Bell 168 Benjamin 167-168 Benjamin Jr 168 Betsy 169 230 Bettie Price 168 267 Bottom 306 Charles Watt 169 Dixie 168

ESTES (Cont.) E H 19 Edmund 167 Edward 168 Edward Harrison 168 Elisha 14 167-168 306 Eliza M 168 Elizabeth 167 Emma 168 Francis 169 G W G 40 77 George Washington Girard 169 Girard 169 James 305-306 James Dabney 168 267 James W G 169 Jesse 169 230 Jesse Edward 169 Joel 14 167 305 John 167 John Francis 169 Joseph 168 Lilla Elizabeth 169 Lucy 167-168 193 Mariah 169 Marion 168 Martha 167 Nancy 167 Nannie 168 Peggy 168 Sadie 169 Sarah 167 Sarah Louise 169 Selah 167 Thomas 167-168 Thrope 167 Triplet 167 Unie 168 William 167 William Alexander 169 William Dix 168 Wm 306
EVANS, Alice 236 Amos 319 Daniel 236 Dolly 236 Duke 236 Georgia 236 Madison 236 Polly 236 Yancey 236
EVOY, Howel 306
EWEL, Patrick 12
EWELL, Lmary 191
FAGG, Dr 197 Lucy 197 Mrs R T 329 Robert J 331
FAIR, Annie 261 C W 20 Thos M 261
FARGASON, George 14
FARMER, Abba 208 Essie B 331 Mrs J F 329
FARNS, Susan L 234
FARRELL, John 306
FARRIS, 268 Franky 223 Jacob 223 John 13 Judith 327 Mary 268 Thomas 327 Wm 306
FARRISH, 241 Frances 241
FARRISS, Patty 328
FEARS, Jesse 168 Lucy 168 Nancy 167 W A 60
FEE, William 14
FERGUSON, Fanny 329 Jean 326

FERGUSON (Cont.) Miss 246 Wm 306
FERRELL, Charles P 331
FERRIS, Polly 233
FERRISS, Charles 294 Jacob 293 Joshua 294
FIELDS, 235
FILLMORE, Millard 123
FINCH, Thomas 14 306 Wm 305
FINLEY, George M 118 May 118 Mrs G M 331
FINNEY, Amos 117 177 Ann 177 Annie 178 Annie Marshall 186 Babe 177 Betsy 117 177 Betsy Ann 136 177 Callie 178 Caroline 177 Carrie L 178 Dolly 177 Elizabeth 176-177 Frances 159 177 207 Franklin 177-178 George 177-178 J J 331 Jackson 177 Jacob 177 James 176 231 James L 177 Jane 177-178 John 159 176-177 207 310-311 John J 178 John Sr 177 231 Joshua 177 Louisa 177 Marshall 177-178 Martha 177 Mary 116 177-178 Mattie 178 Miss 217 Mollie 178 Nancy 176-177 Peter 176-177 Polly 177-178 231 Richard 176 Robert 177-178 Ruben 176 Ruth 178 Sallie 158-159 177 Sallie Ann 177 Sanford 177 Susan 117 177 231 Thomas 177 Wesley L 177 William 176-178 Zack 176-177 Zack Jr 177
FINNIE, William 176
FINNY, 176
FISCHER, Ella 248
FISH, Grace 185
FISHER, Alcin 171 Charles 134 Ruth 171
FITTS, Corrie 267
FITZGERALD, Frederick 319
FITZPATRICK, John E 242 Sarah Bagley Morton 242
FLEMING, Annie 216 Cora 215

FLEMING (Cont.) John 306
  Thomas 320
FLETCHER, 68
FLEUMAN, Thomas 12
FLING, John 306
FLOWER, John 252
FLOWERS, Thomas 306
FLOYD, W H 20
FLYNN, Fannie 136 Frank 158
  Mary 158
FOLDY, Geo 306
FOLEY, Bartlett 306 Luke 306
FOLLY, George 13
FONTAINE, Anne 175 Charles 175 Edward 175 Elizabeth 174 Genevieve 176 Gretchen 176 Jack 47 247 Jno R 302 John 12 14 174 314 319 325 John R 302 Justina 176 Kate 288 Marion 247 Martha 175 247 Mary Morton 114 Nancy Dabney 175 Nannie 247 Nathaniel Cole 175 Patrick 247 Patrick Henry 175-176 Peter 174 Polly`C 247 Robert 176 Sam 20 Samuel C 176 Samuel Cole 114 175 Sarah Ann 247 Sarah Miller 175 Unie 168 W Hale 20 Watson Hale 175 William 176 William Spotswood 175 William Winston 175
FORBER, Gen 320
FORBES, Ann 274 Caroline 285 Miss N A 266 Robert 285
FORD, Anna 174 Annie 174 Blanche 174 Cecil 174 Dorothy 174 Emma 203 Geo 174 H A 174 330 Henry 174 Hezekiah 173-174 J C 216 James 174 Jane 174 Jane Hickey 174 Janie 45 Jesse 174 John 174 Joseph 174 Lena 174 Lewis 174 Lizzie 174 Lucy 174 Maggie 36 Margaret Alzira 174 216 Mary Sherman 174 Mattie 174 Mrs M L 330 Mrs O D 58 O D 330 Obe Dillard 174

FORD (Cont.) Patricia 174 Pete 174 Sallie 174 Sam C 20 Samuel Calvin 173-174 Sarah 173-174 Thomas M 331 Tom 174 William 174 Willie 174
FORE, Samuel 306
FOREMAN, J M 161 Rachael M 161
FORSBERG, August 240 Hilda 240
FORTUNE, John 169 Mariah 169 Wm 294
FOSTER, Charles 233 306 324 Edd 198 Mark 306 Polly 233 Sarah 198
FOUNTAIN, Henry 175 Justina 175 Laura 281 Robert 175 Samuel Cole 175 Willie 175
FOUNTAINE, N C 20
FOWLKES, Bass 287 Elizabeth 287 Nathaniel 287 Polly 287
FOX, Samuel 14
FRALIN, Frank 177 Mary 177
FRANCE, 268 Annie 257 Daniel 294 Elizabeth 268 Gordon 256 Henry 256 James 256 John 294 Lucy 257 Peter 12 294 Sarah 326 Sarah Elizabeth 256 Susan 256
FRANCHER, Richard 305
FRANCISCO, James 35 Peter 35 123
FRANK, Miss 155
FRANKLIN, Abraham 306 313 320 Dick 290 G P 329 G T 20 Geo 290 H L 331 J L 20 J W 332 Laura 290 Lewis 12 290 Lily 290 Mary 290 Miss 285 Molly 290 Sol 181 Susan 181 Tyler 290 Virginia 290 W H 20
FRAZIER, P F 20 Peter 29
FREEMAN, Jess 20
FRENCH, John 46 Milton 101 Wm 298
FRENOR, James 306

FRITH, Miss 177
FRY, 51
FRYE, Allen 169 Annie L 169
  Brooksie 221 David M 169
  Elizabeth 169 Emma Hairston
  219 Franklin I 169 Henry A 169
  I J 169 I W 169 Isom 169 Jesse
  20 169 John C 169 John
  Harrison 219 Lusinia 169 Peter
  W 169 Rufus P 169 William 169
FULKERSON, Deborah 329
  Frederick 323
FULLER, Briatin 327 E Callaway
  332 F 50 Nancy 327
FULTON, Mrs J H 329
FUSFELD, Gertrude 331
GABRIEL, Ruth 328
GAINES, Alice 118 Edward 118
GAITHER, Sadie 115
GALLEAGER, 269 Elizabeth 269
GALLOWAY, Dr 239 Miss 239
GARDNER, Jemima 327 Wm 295
GARLAND, 269 Ann 232 Annie
  269 Peter 299
GARNER, Dianah 134 Judith 328
  Thomas 306
GARRET, Anna 236 James P 236
GARRETT, Alice 236 Alma 220
  Anna 220 Annie May 220 Bettie
  Rachael 199 236 Emma 236 F
  293 James P 220 John 306 Kate
  162 220 Lelia 199 236 Loula 236
  Mary 220 Mary Ann Eliza 236
  Paul 220 Peter G 220 Rachael
  220 Ruth 220 Sallie 245 Sue 46
  Susan 236 Susie 236 Thomas J
  236 William 220 William A 236
GARRISON, Elizabeth 329
GATES, Charles 305 James 306
  Samuel 306 W B 45 57 Wm 306
GATEWOOD, Nancy Frazier 329
GATHRIGHT, Arthur B 174 Mary
  Sherman 174
GEARHART, Peter 321
GEO, 3d 121 III 133

GEORGE, II King 200 III King of
  England 242
GEORGE Peggy 326 Sarah Ann
  329
GIBBONEY, Lucy K 207
GIBBONY, Lucy K 212
GIBSON, David 305 H 20 John 13
  324 Mrs Geo M Jr 331
GIDDINGS, Nap B 124
GILBERT, Humphrey 130 J H 20
  James 20
GILES, Edmund 171 Elizabeth
  171 Emma 171 Fairy 171 George
  171 Gustave A 171 Harry 171
  Joanna 171 John 134 Loula 110
  P H 20 Richard 171 Ruth 171 S
  S 20 Sallie 110 Susan 171
  Woody 171
GILLET, Elijah 315
GILLEY, Francis 305 Richard 13
GILLIAM, Deverix 12
GILLY, Elizabeth 272
GILMER, Geo 298 James 324
GILMORE, 50
GINCY, Jane 156
GIST, Nathaniel 319
GLASS, Armisted 272 Polly 272
GLEN, Harvey 158 Sallie 158
GLENN, Gov 222 Mary 195 Mollie
  261 Mrs J D 53 Sallie 222 Sarah
  H 56 T J 261 William 222
GODDARD, James 305
GODFREY, Joe P 18 40 42 95
GOF, Thomas 313
GOGGIN, 19
GOING, Moses 319 S William 12
GOOCH, Elizabeth 327 Tho 294
GOOD, John 306
GOODE, Mrs N S 141
GOODMAN, Joseph 306
GORDON, Jane 266 John 313
  Miss 233
GORHAM, Emma Lavinder 332
GORMAN, Armstead 116 Nancy
  116

GORRELL, J B 88
GOUGH, Andrew 306 Thomas 306
GOVAN, 152 Sarah 327 Wm 327
GOWING, David 306 John 306
GRAFTY, Belesworth 306
GRAHAM, Annie 217 Capt 238
  John 14 T W 329 W T 58
GRANT, Gen 109
GRANTHAM, Virginia 140
GRAVELEY, 47 Geo L 52 H C 108
  Hope 108 John 138 Mary 138
  Mrs Albert 55 Mrs L L 56 R P 49
GRAVELY, Albert S 173 Alice 171
  Alice Kennon 173 Ann 125 Anna
  171 Anne Nancy 172 Benjamin
  171 Benjamin Franklin 170
  Berta 172 Betsy 170 C B 171
  Caroline F 173 Chester Bullard
  172 Edmund 170-171 Edward
  Bonner 172 Eleanor 170 271
  Eliza 170-172 Elizabeth 170 195
  Ella 171 Emma 171 Emma
  Eugenia 172 Eugenie 171 Fount
  20 Frances 170 227 Francis 172
  Francis Cox 170 Francis
  Marshall 172 George 20 171 195
  301 311 George D 58 170 173
  George L 173 Goggin 20 271 H C
  330 Harriet 227 276 Hattie 229
  Helen 207 J E 20 Jabe 171 227
  271 Jabes 20 Jabez 170 Jackson
  171 Joe K 271 Joe Morton 171
  John 227 229 John King 207
  John W 170 271 Joseph 13 169-
  170 Joseph E 310 Joseph H 20
  Joseph Henry 172 Joseph
  Jackson 171 Joseph K 310
  Joseph Sr 171-172 Joseph W 171
  Judith 170 Judith Elizabeth 171
  Judy 227 Julia C 170 Julia
  Cassandra 172 Letitia 170-171
  173 Lewis 160 171-172 Lewis Jr
  171 Lilian 170 Lizzie 193 Lutie
  171 Marshall 227 Marshall
  Francis 172 Martha 160 171

GRAVELY (Cont.) Martha Annie
  172 Mary 160-161 170 172 270
  Mary Elizabeth 172 Mary
  Hughes 173 Mary Jane 171
  Matilda 171 Matilda Jane 172
  Mattie 172 263 May Bud 170
  Minnie 171 Minnie Walker 173
  Mollie H 330 Nancy 170 Nannie
  171 P B 20 Parmelia 271 Pattie
  171 Peyton 108 125 171 270-271
  Peyton B 172 Polly 171 Rachael
  171 Richard 229 Sadie 229 Sallie
  A 170 Sally 227 Sarah 171-172
  Spottsswood 171 Susan 170-171
  Susan Ellen 172 Thomas 20 W
  Frank 20 W S 193 William 171
  William Armistead 172 William
  H 173 Willis 125 172 Willis
  Lewis 172 Wm A 20
GRAVES, Ann 328 David 306
  Elizabeth 326 John Temple 101
  Obediah 14 Susanna 93
  Susannah 224 327 Tomas 93
  William 14 Wm 306 313 Wm Sr
  306
GRAY, John 13 Nancy 274 Samuel
  306 William 274
GRAYHAM, Archibald 316
GREEN, Gen 11-12 108 252 316
  322 Geo F 48 George 37 James
  306 Miss 129 Mrs C W 37 Wm
  306
GREENE, Gen 68 80 94 170 183
  189 227 241 243 282 315-317
  321 324 Sarah 272
GREENWADE, Fredonia 260
  Pabner 260
GREER, Aquila 306 Mary C 155
  Wm 305
GREGORY, Ann Dillard 264
  Cornelia 117 E J 284 Eliza
  James 185 Eron Pha 253
  Fleming 310 George 311 J R 45
  330 James 284 John Francis 211
  310 Joseph 20 284 Josie 284

GREGORY (Cont.) Lee Overman 264 Mary 284 Minnie 284 Minnie Walker 173 O R 47 54 78 185 329 Overton 37 Overton Hill 49 Overton R 284 R Lindsey 20 Susan 211 284 Tom 284 W H 48
GRIER, James 14
GRIFFIN, Thomas 20
GRIFFITH, Griffin 12 Susannah 327 Wm 327
GRIGGS, Adelaide 138 Alzira 70 Archie 180 Ben 181 Brice 179 Clay 181 Dolly 138 Edmond 138 Eliza 172 Emaline 207 212 Emeline 181 Frances 180-181 Francis 180 Franklin 138 179-180 272 Geo 270 Geo I 82 Geo Ira 180 George 179 George I 181 George K 181 207 212 George King 179-180 Greenberry T 45 Greenbury 138 Greenbury Thornton 179-180 Ida 181 Ira 179 206 Irie 270 J 301-302 J W 20 44 Jere W 212 Jeremiah 180 Jeremiah Michael 70 179 Jeremiah Sr 180 Jerre W 207 Jerry 58 Jerry W 180-181 Joe 181 270 John 179 181 327 Julia 138 Kate 181 Katy 181 270 Lee 179 Lewis 179 Lila 180 Lina 181 200 Margie 181 Mariah 179 270 Mary 138 May Bud 181 Michael 178-180 270 310 Miss George 58 Miss Georgie T 331 Moir 181 Mrs 50 Peter 59 179 Peter Franklin 270 Philip 179 Phoby 327 Phoebe 179 Robert 138 178 Rosa 181 Sallie 138 206 Sally 272 Sam 181 Samuel 138 Samuel J 180 Sarah 327 Susan 179-181 206 Susie 181 Tom 181 Wesley 41 179 206 225 270 William 20 179-181
GRIMES, Charlotte 77 100 105
GRIMMET, Robert 14
GRIMMIT, John 305 Robt 305
GRIMSLEY, Harry B 168 Lucy 168
GRINNET, Doziar 14
GRISHAM, John 324
GROGAN, Alice 211 Annie 236 B D 218 Emmett M 218 Ernest V 218 Frank 20 Geo 20 Hattie 211 J J 20 J W 20 Jennie L 218 Joseph 20 Lillian 218 Loula 199 Mary Hill 218 Mary L 218 Mollie 211 Ollie B 218 Robert 236 Robt P 218 Sallie 211 Virginia B 218 Virginia Dare 218 William D 218 Willie 211 Wm 20
GROGRAN, Ethel 200
GROVES, I M 49 I M Jr 54 330 Irvin 162 Mattie 162 Thomas 293
GUERRANT, Dora 126
GUILLAIAME, Edgecombe 319
GUILLIAMS, Edjecomb 306
GULIEL, William 130
GUNN, Capt 318 James 319
GUNNELL, Wm 20
GUSSETT, John 306
HAASE, H B 195 Maria Louisa 195
HAILE, 88 Thomas 14 319-320 322
HAILEY, John 327 Lucy 327
HAIRFIELD, James 20 John 20 Joseph 20
HAIRSTON, 198 Ada 192 Agnes 189 191 Agnes Ann 286 Alcey 192 Alcy 191 Alice 191 America 133 192 238 Andrew 188-189 Ann 191-192 Ann Marshall 192 Bethenia 68 133 Bethenia Letcher 134 Bettie Brown 155 Bettie Waller 192 Cabell 44 193 Capt Gen 324 Caroline 193 Constantine 191 Eliza 193 Elizabeth 56 153-154 189 191-192 243 250 252 328

HAIRSTON (Cont.) Elizabeth
  Hairston 286 Elizabeth P 194
  Elizabeth Perkins 193 Geo 47
  123 133 189-193 224 243 313
  319-320 Geo Jr 191 Geo Rusty
  171 Geo Sr 191 George 9 14 50
  68 80-81 188 244 297-298 302
  George Isham 262 Harden 192
  Hardyman 193 Henrietta 193
  Henry 191 J T W 20 J W T 193-
  194 Jack 205 John A 192 194
  John Adams 191 John H 192
  John Tyler 191 193 Judith 191-
  192 Keziah 192 Laura Hughes
  234 Lelia 193 Letitia 164 191-
  192 Lizzie 193 Louisa 191 193
  Lucy 193 Lydia 193 Malinda 191
  Margaret 189 Marshall 22 50
  102 192-194 276-277 Martha 189
  191 Mary 191-192 328 Matilda
  193 224 Mattie 193 Mrs Judge
  193 Mrs Marshall 167 Mrs N H
  56-57 329 Mrs Peter 56 N H 28
  44 193 Nannie 193 Nicholas 154
  191-192 Old Rusty 9 11 191 193
  224 Pattie 193 262 Percy 192
  Peter 13 20 67 187-189 191-193
  307 317 320-322 Peter Dillard
  193 Pocahontas 193 Powahatan
  193 Priscilla 189 Rob 192 Robert
  22 188 193 253 268 308 320 Robt
  189-191 286 314 Rusty 164 193
  Ruth 189 191 268 286 Ruth A
  192 Ruth Stovall 191-192 194
  253 Sallie 192 248 Sam 188 191
  Samuel 67 164 188-190 192-193
  286 307 320 Samuel Harden 192
  Sarah 154 189 191-192 253 328
  Susan 191 193 224-225 Susan A
  192 Susannah 189 Tyler 155 159
  193 248 Virginia 193 Watt 36
  193 Wm 193
HAISLIP, Frank 20
HALBERT, Wm 312
HALE, Ethel C 155 Joseph 14

HALE (Cont.) Lewis 307 Thomas
  313 326
HALEY, Jeff 270 Jim 270 John
  270 Leanna 270 Lucy 328 Nancy
  327 Polly 270 Tom 270 Wm 327
HALL, Ann 199 Isham 306 J H 20
  Jesse 13 307 John 306 Lanceford
  306-307 Marry Heard 306 Mrs
  Jesse 199 Nathan 307 Nathaniel
  50 Randolph 307 Robert 199
  Sam Sr 306 Thomas 306
HAMBLETON, Hans 14 Thomas
  14
HAMBY, Jonathan 12
HAMILTON, 47 Agnes 327 Alice
  M 181 Anne E 182 C A 64 185
  332 C A Jr 332 Charles Altley
  182 Charles Atley 73 181
  Charles Atley Jr 182 Dora 49
  Elizabeth 182 Ellen Frances 181
  Eugenia 181 Geo 321 324 327 J
  W 36-37 330 Janie 74 Jessie 182
  John 181 John Waddey 182 John
  Waddy Jr 182 M W 216 Martha
  Sophia 181 Martha Woodson 71
  73 185 Mary I 182 Medora 182
  Medora Sabina 181 Mrs Jno W
  53 Mrs W W 37 Nora Southall
  182 Oneta Augusta 182 Paul
  Price 181-182 Rose L 181
  Southall Weisiger 182 Sue
  Margaret 181 Susannah 328
  Thomas 307 Virginia Agnes 181
  W W 37 330 William Wirt 182
  Wm 181
HAMLET, Bedford 288 G 287
  Julia 119 Mary Grief 288 Nancy
  287
HAMLETT, Addie 75 Annie 75
  Cornelia M 75 Ellie 174 Geo T
  75 Henon 75 J C 75 329 James
  75 Jesse 75 Joe 174 John
  Thomas 75 Julia C 75 Julian 75
  Lena 174 Roy 75 Sarah 174
  Starling 75 Sydney 174 W J 301

HAMLETT (Cont.) Winnie 75 Wm
  Jesse 75 Wootton 75
HAMMOCK, Polly 223
HAMMOND, Joseph 307-308
HAMNER, Mary 149-150 Mary
  Jane 146 152 Nancy House 146
HAMPTON, Elizabeth 253 Laban
  327 Leany 327 Matilda Eliza
  235 Richard 315 323
HAMTON, Maj 316
HANBRICK, Nimrod 306
HANBY, Capt 324 John 13
  Jonathan 307 314
HANCOCK, Peter 20 Thomas 306
HANDY, John 307
HANKINS, Miss 170 Mrs Wm 278
HANNAH, Alex 327 George 300
  Mary 328 Sarah 327
HARBER, Adojah 306 David 306
HARBOUR, Abner 307 Elisha 306
  Joel 307 Thomas 306
HARDEMAN, Louisa 191
HARDEN, 81 190
HARDIE, Elijah 20 Elizabeth
  Matilda 228 Ella 228 Henry 228
  Joe 20 John A 228 Sue M 330
  Susan 228 Thrashley 20
HARDIN, Elections 307
HARDMAN, Charles 308 John 306
  Uriah 306 Wm 306
HARDY, Ann 125 Charles 327
  Elizabeth 83 Rachel 327
HARISTON, George 12 Lelia 237
  Marshall 192 Watt 237
HARMON, Martha 289 S S F 289
HARNOM, 202
HARPER, Frances 226
HARRELL, Josiah 256 Rachel 256
  Sarah Ann 256 Wm 307
HARRIS, Elizabeth 278 G L 20
  Henry 20 306 Hezekiah 13 John
  20 Moses 307 Mrs A F 330 Mrs
  John 260 Paul 20 Peter 307 312
  Robt 307 Spencer F 113 Thomas
  14

HARRISBY, Thomas 13
HARRISON, Benjamin 123 162
  Elizabeth 123 Lovicy S 230 Mary
  164 Randolph 93 Wm Henry 123
HART, Charles M 277 George
  Richard 277 Lucy Ellen 277
HARVEY, Nancy 160
HASILE, Thomas 312
HATCHER, Archibald 13 Mary
  259 Robt 20 W H 20
HATHAWAY, Ann 130
HAWKINS, Ben 327 Lucy 286 329
  Molly 327 Mrs W B 330
HAY, Wm 306
HAYGOOD, Annie 220 Nancy 217
HAYMORE, Charlotte 232 Mr 50
  R A 232
HAYNES, Geo 307 Hal H 216
  Henry 307 Henry Sr 307 M
  Katherine 216 Wm 307
HAYS, John 298 Mary 192 Pink
  228 Susan 228 William 14 Wm
  298
HAYSE, Mary Ann 328
HEARD, Eliza 143 Jesse 314 316
  326 John 307 Lily 140 Mary 139
  Minnie 143 Nancy 140 Obediah
  143 Stephen 321 William 140
  Wm 139 307
HEDGECOCK, Mrs Emory 330
HEFFERFINGER, John 20
HEGGIE, Ginnie 222 Mr 222
HELDERNESS, 103
HELM, Geo T 20
HENDERSON, Elizabeth 132
  Fanny 132 John 306 Mary I 182
  Samuel 67 132 Thomas 13 308
  311-312 314 W A 20
HENDREN, 46
HENICK, Miss 172
HENLY, John 298
HENNESSEY, George Thomas
  277 Gracie May 277 Michael
  Richard 277
HENNING, 268

HENRY, 5th 121 I King 130 II King 146 II King of France 213 III King 146 IV King of France 213
HENRY Dorothea 75 Martha 175 Patrick 9 15-16 34 55 75 92 96 98 103-104 133 145 156 165 168 175-176 314 316 320 Sarah 75 Thomas 306
HENSLEY, Ben 13 Benjamin 314 Henry 13 Hickman 13
HERBERT, Lydia Adela 155
HERD, Stephen 13
HEREFORD, Bullard 20 Fell 20 Joseph 20 216
HERNDON, John 243 Mary 243 Susanna 227
HEWLETT, Thomas 316-317
HIBBERT, Charles 13
HIBBERTS, Charles 44 308
HICKEY, John 306 Mary 317
HICKS, Betsy 271 Eleanor 140 Elizabeth 327 John 271 Lucy 271 Melindy 271 Nancy 271 Nelly 271 Sister 106 Tom 271 William 271
HILL, 43 46 Ambrosia 187 Annie 178 187 Annie Marshall 186 Betsy 221 Bettie 37 47 184 Burke 186 Catherine 137 186 258 Catherine Ann 183 Catherine Bassett 185 Catherine Matilda 183-184 D W 186 Daivd 186 David 183-184 David Parks 183-184 E J 284 E W 186 Edith 284 Edith Parks 185 Eliza 184 Eliza James 184-185 Elizabeth 153 183 185 263 Elizabeth Saunders 183-184 186 Ella 47 77 79 Ernest 187 Ethel Maud 186 Fannie 187 Frances Ruth 184-185 Francis 185 284 286 G W 186-187 Grace 185 Harry M 186 Helen 187 Hester Ann 183-184 I Y 127 182 Ida 187 Isaac 306

HILL (Cont.) J P 186 John P 331 John Parks 183-184 John Payne 187 John W 184 John Waddy 79 183-186 258 John Waddy Jr 183 Joseph 284 Joseph Wilson 185 Judith 185 258 Judith P A 293 Judith Parks 79 183 186 Judith Parks America 184 Katherine 186-187 Kittie 187 Kittie Ann 273 Kitty 185 L M 185 Leonard 184 Lodowick Johnson Sr 330 Loula 137 185 Loulie 185 Lucinda 186 Lucy 47 137 183-184 288 Lucy J 186 Lucy M 185 Lucy Matilda 184-185 Lucy Wootton 184 M M 186 M W 216 Mabel C 187 Martha 186 Martha Woodson 71 184-185 Mary 217 Mary C 79 185 Mary Catherine 77 124 184-185 204 Mary Lucinda 186 Mary M 187 Matilda 187 Matilda Winston 183 228 Miss 41 Miss J P A 294 Mollie Finney 186 Mrs 59 78 Nancy Langhorne 185 Overton 137 Overton Gregory 185 Peter Marshall 186 Robt 137 Ruby Lee 187 Russell 187 Ruth 326 Ruth Angeline 185 S R 54 78 284 329 Sadie 185 Sallie 183-185 263 284 Sallie Parks 183 186 Sally Parks 111 Sam 137 Samuel C 183 228 Samuel Robt 183-185 Sarah Alexander 184-185 Sarah Judith 127 182 Sarrah Cotton 286 Stella 185 Susan 187 Swinfield 14 312 326 T J 186-187 T Jefferson 187 Thomas 183 322 Thomas L 185 Thomas Lodowick 137 Thomas S 186 218 W D 20 186 W D Sr 187 W W 40 47 71 77 124 185 204 W W Jr 331 W W Sr 329 William 137 153 183 263 William D 178 William David 186 William Wirt 79 Willie 187

HILL (Cont.)Wirt 185 Wm Nathan 185 Wm Wirt 183-185
HILLL, Matilda Winston 183
HINES, J K 101 Mollie 219 Mr 219
HINTON, David 307 James 307 Samuel 308 Wm Robt 306
HOBSON, Monroe 20
HODGES, 46 Alice 166 D F 80 H K 20 Hilda Woodson 204 Hiram K 166 Ida 166 J D 166 331 Josiah 307 Mary T 166 Maurice 204 331 Miss 194 Pattie 166 Robt 314 Walter 166 Walter S 330 William 13 166 Wm Jr 307
HODGSON, A N 118 Pattie 118
HODNETT, Essie 138
HOFFMAN, John 310
HOGANS, Nancy 327 Wm 327
HOLCOMB, Araminta 195 John H 195
HOLCOMBE, D J 331
HOLDEN, John 307 Marion 168
HOLLAND, Amelia 197 Anna 222 Elmer 277 John 140 John William 277 Mary France 139 Mary Frances 140 Mat 222 Mattie 222 Sarah 140
HOLLANDSWORTH, Fount 20 James 20 John 20 William 20
HOLLIDAY, Robert 315 Robt 314 Sarah 327
HOLLINSWORTH, Bart 20 Thomas 12 307 Wm 306
HOLLODAY, Jeremiah 14 John 14
HOLMAN, Mary Elizabeth 172 Sallie A 170 William Allen 172
HOLMES, Elizabeth 328
HOLT, Ambrose 307 Francis 308 Gov 241 John Manass 269 John W 269 Lawrence 264 Lucy 264 Lucy Jane 162 Mary Ann 269 Mr 290 Patty 330 Richard 305 Thomas 307
HOOF, Samuel 13
HOOKER, Ann 327 Annie 156

HOOKER (Cont.) J C 331 J Murry 156 John T 301
HOOPER, Theresa 196 Virginia 196 Wm 196
HOPPER, A B 330 Alcey 326 Allen 124 Anna 124 Eliza 124 Hecter 327 J W 331 James 124 Mamie 124 Moran 124 Mrs M B 330 William 12 Wm 327
HORD, Mordecai 295 308 312 314 317 Stanwix 313
HORSELY, G W 20 J W 20
HORSLY, George 34
HOSKINS, 86
HOUSTON, Martha 280 Nancy 168 Sally 194 Sam 168 194
HOWARD, J Earnest 118 Laura 260 Mrs W O 329 Rhoda E 260 Ruby 118 Wm 325
HOWCHIN, Mrs 205
HOWELL, Daniel 307 J W 48 John 13
HOYLE, Dossie 60
HUBBARD, Ben 13 306 Elizabeth 328 Eusebuis 307 Miss 266
HUDDLESTONE, Wm 20
HUDSON, Peter 306 Thomas 13
HUDSPETH, Bessie 241
HUGHES, Archalaus 320 Archelans 153 Archelaus 224 308 Archilaus 314-315 325 Elizabeth 167 Manie 331 Mary 153 170 Matilda 153 Nancy 111 224 268 Polly 224 Reuben 224 Sally 224
HUIE, James 134
HUMBERT, Priscilla Flint 118
HUMPHREYS, Dora 237 Ira 237 Morris 14
HUMPHRIES, George W 256 John 256 Martha 256
HUNDLEY, Anthony 215 Ben 162 Ella 162 H B 20 J L 20 J W 20 Jane Hickey 215 Lottie 138 Lucy 117 M E 117 Mamie R 330

HUNDLEY (Cont.) Mammie 162
  Mary Edna 212 Mary Jane 206
  Mattie 162 Pattie 277
  Pocahontas 124 Roxie 124 W B
  212 William 206
HUNNICUTT, Augustine 308
HUNT, Isabella 231 James 327
  Joseph 307 Lizzie C 161 Mary 67
  Sarah 327
HUNTER, 46 Alexander 189 191
  293 Anne 139 Caroline 245
  Elizabeth 328 Fannie 222 James
  148 Martha 189 191 Mary 123
  Polly 123 326
HURD, H C 20 Jesse 307 John 13
  Loula 220 Mary Letitia 215 Mr
  215 Thomas 13
HURT, Joseph 13
HUSTON, Hesy 327
HUTCHINSON, H F 332 Paul 307
  Philip 307 Wm 307
HUTT, Samuel 307
HYATT, Lulu 217
HYLTON, George W 206 208
  Jeremiah 138 Mary 198 Mary
  Ann 138 Nancy Jane 260 Sallie
  J 206 Susan E 206 208
  Valentine 198
INDIAN, Chief Powhatan 150
  Dragon Canoe 92 Pocahontas
  151 Princess Pocahontas 150
INGLES, Mrs B H 56 Mrs C H 193
INGRAM, C W 20 J D 20 J L 20 J
  T 20 Mary 203 Miss 204
INNES, Hugh 314
INNIS, Hugh Jr 298
ISHAM, John 306
ISON, Clark 306 James 306 John
  306 Jonatahn 305 Wm 305
IVEY, Howell 14
IVIE, Elisha 305 Martha Eliza 161
  Sallie 211
IVY, Mattie 172
JACKSON, 85 224 Andrew 133
  Elizabeth 182 Maj 86 Nancy 327

JACKSON (Cont.) Stonewall 262
JAMERSON, Annie 255 Bettie 255
  Dick 269 Dollie 255 Edd
  Salmons 255 Fannie 255 Geo C
  255 Geo W 255 George H 37
  Harry 255 Henry Clay 255 Hesy
  327 J W 255 John 14 Kemper
  255 Lou 255 Sallie 269 Sam 255
  Samuel 14 Thomas 255 305 327
  Thomas J 20 Tom 255 Will
  Salmons 255 Wm 305
JAMES, Ann 194 Annie M 195
  Catherine 137 Ii 188 Jamey 306
  John 137 195 Jules 195 Rorer
  194 Spencer 137
JAMISON, Thomas 293
JAMMERSON, Gerge H 255
JANNEY, Hails 265 Maggie 265
JARRED, Mrs 110
JARRETT, A J 20 A L 20 Charlie
  269 Devereau 85 H F 20 Henry
  166 187 J H 20 John 269 294
  Martha 166 187 Mary 269 Mrs T
  C 331 Nannie 269 Peter 20
  Robert 269 Rosaline 269 Sallie
  269 Susan 187
JARVIS, Alex 307
JAY, Annie 214 Henry 214
JEFFERSON, Mr 35 75 Sarah 116
  Thomas 131 133 145 273
JEFFRESS, Jane 288
JENKINS, John 20 308 Lewis 308
  Lieut 316
JENKS, John 214 Judith 214
JENNINGS, Sm'l 298
JERUSALEM, Crusader King Of
  104
JETT, Mrs W B 330 W B 48-49 78-
  79
JOHN, King 146
JOHNS, Mary 237 243
JOHNSON, David 20 Edward 283
  James 12 307 Joseph 196 L E
  331 Moble 14 Theresa 196 Wm
  308

INDEX

JOHNSTON, James 300-301
JONAKIN, John 308
JONES, 181 A D 330 A M 20
　Abraham 14 Abram 83 Abram
　Gabriel 196 Abrose Jefferson
　194 Adolphus Dorsett 195
　Alexander 13 Alexander C 197
　Alexander Conrad 196 Alonza
　Thomas 83 Alonzo Thomas 84
　Ambrose 305 Ambrose Jefferson
　83 210 Amelia 197 Ann 198-199
　210 Anna 198-199 220 Annie
　195 Annie S 199-200 Arminta
　195 Armistead 125 Babe 84
　Bartlett 194-196 Ben 44 157 Ben
　S 199 Benj 298 Benj S 199
　Benjamin 12 84-85 194 197 249
　300 Benjamin Churchill 195
　Benjamin Rush 194 196
　Benjamin Seward 20 198
　Benjamin Tazewell 84 Benjamin
　Tazewell 83 Bessie 200 Bessie
　Gray 84 Betsy 198 Bettie 199
　Bettie A 195 Bettie Rachael 199
　236 Beverly 85 194 196 Carrie
　196 Cassandra 125 Charles 83
　194-195 197-198 205-206
　Charles W 84 Charlie Coan 198
　200 Chas W 20 Constantine 194
　Cornelia 84 Daisy 199 Daisy
　King 200 David 20 84 194
　Decatur 195 Dolly 83 Dorsey 195
　Eleanor Conrad 197 Elisha 195
　Eliza 194 Elizabeth 83 85 170
　194-195 249 Ella 197 Ella Mary
　196 Emmie 195 Erasmus Dowen
　195 Erastus Beverly 196-197
　Essie 331 Estelle 198-199 Ethel
　200 Frances Adair 197 Gabriel
　Remi 194 Gabriel Remime 196
　Geo 240 305 Geo O 46 199 271
　George 44 George Byron 199-200
　George King 198-199 210 George
　O 200 George Osborne 20 82 199
　George Washington 86 194

JONES (Cont.) Gertrude 199-200
　Green 20 83 Harriet 161 195
　Henrietta 193 198-199 Henry
　321-322 Hervey Louise 197 Ida
　197 Isaac 14 Isabel 194 Isabella
　154 Jack 161 Jackson 83 James
　83 194 196 James Benjamin 196
　199-200 Jane 198 Jane
　Elizabeth 194 196 Jemima 328
　John 14 44 194 294 306 John
　Brengle 199 John C 36 198-200
　220 262 John G 20 John Jr 308
　John Kean 195 John Litten 307
　John Sr 308 John William 198-
　199 Jos 312 Joseph 139 306 320
　Joseph Mosby 83-84 Joseph P 83
　Joshua 194 Julia 196-197 Julia
　P 196 Kate 195 197 Kate E 196
　Keen 195 Lelia 198-199 236 Lina
　200 Loula 199 Lucien G 196
　Lucy Ann 83 Lucy Charles 240
　Luien 197 Margaret C 83
　Margaret Carr 139 Maria 240
　Maria Louisa 195 Martha 194
　196 Martin 194 Mary 82-83 118
　157 195-196 198-199 210 240
　Mary Ann 198 200 Mary
　Baldwin 84 Mary Bennie 138
　198-199 Mary Cedatur 194 Mary
　Churchill 199 Mary Elizabeth
　118 Mary Flair 195 Mary
　Frances 196 Mary Louisa 216
　Mary Theresa 194 Mattie 195
　Miss K E 331 Mollie 198-199
　Mrs 86 Mrs Alphis 199 Mrs E K
　331 Mrs Geo 331 Mrs J W 329
　Nancy 198 Nannie 83 195-196
　198 Nannie Witcher 195 Nathan
　13 Nathaniel 199 Nathaniel L
　198 Nellie 83 Nora 195 Pamela
　194-195 Paul 199 Pitsy 83 Polly
　197-198 205 Rami 195 Robert
　308 Robert H 197 Robert Henry
　196 Robert L 198-199 Robt 327
　Ruth 83 Ruth Tazewell 84

JONES (Cont.) Salina 194 Sallie
  83 197-199 Sallie L 84 Sally 194
  Sanford 194 Sina 327 Southgate
  331 Squire King 43 Stuart 240
  Sue 197 Susannah 327 Theresa
  196 Thomas 13 194-195 305 312
  320 Thomas D 195 Thomas G
  199 Thomas K 331 Thomas King
  199-200 Thos J 199 Virginia 194
  196 Virginia E 196-197 W C 331
  W Clyde 199 W L 20 William 83
  298 William B 198-199 William
  Henry 195 William Joseph 84
  Willie Ben 236 Winnie 83
  Witcher 195 Wm 306
JORDAN, Hezekiah 307 Martha
  Hughes 155 Robert 155
JOURNICAN, John 325
JOYCE, Alexander 14 Alfred 20
  Alice 236 Andrew 327 Betsy 327
  Frank 236 Miss 124 Mr 235
  Nancy 235
JOYNER, 46 Sally 73
KALLAM, Anna 236 Luther W 236
KANE, Rebecca 235
KANNON, Katy 328
KEAN, Elizabeth 195 Harriet 195
KEARFOTT, C P 36 50 Clarence B
  88 Clarence P 88 Genevieve 176
  Hugh S 330 Hugh Smith 88 J
  Conrad 88 329 Mary Lu 56 Mary
  Lucretia 88 Mrs C P 56 Mrs H S
  53 Mrs J C 53 Rebecca 88 Robert
  Ryland 88
KEARTLEY, ---- 243 Anne 243
KEEN, Elisha 307 Miss 195
KEESEE, Mr 74 Mrs 74 Olivia
  Simmons 56
KELLEY, Fannie 204
KELLY, Arnabas 307 Betty 327
  Emily Ball 139 Emily Wade 139
  Ernest 36 Ernest Lywood 139
  James Webb 139 Jane Davis 140
  John 14 327 Mary Davis 139
  Sarah Jane 139

KEMPER, 179
KENDRICK, Barnabas 308 John
  Jr 308 Thomas 308
KENNERLY, Christine 233
KENNON, Dr 151 Mary 151
KENT, Elizabeth 246
KESEE, Bettie 249
KEY, Mary 281
KEZEE, Bettie 95
KIMSEY, Benj Sr 308
KINDRICK, John 20 308
KING, Abba 208 Alice 207 Ann
  135 198 210 Anna 135 206 222
  Anna Adelle 212 Annie 207
  Annie Adelle 212 Annie Ruth
  212 Annie Scales 208 Benjamin
  208 Benjamin S 210 210
  Benjamin S Jr 210 Benjamin
  Seward 209 Benjamin Sr 212
  Berta 211 Betsy 197 210 327
  Bettie 210 Beulah 222 Bnejamin
  Jr 212 Bulah 212 Caleb 212 212
  Camillus 138 205-207 310
  Cephas 205-206 Charity 205
  Charles 222 Charles R 207
  Charlie 212 Clare L 208
  Clarence 252 Columbia 138
  Columbus 125 135 138 207-208
  311 Columbus Sr 206 Corinne
  208 D F 20 Daisie 212 Dolly 210
  Dorothy 212 281 Earnest 212
  Edgar 212 Edward Burdett 211
  Edward Starling 208 Elijah 320-
  321 Eliza 162 206 208 211-212
  Eliza Jane 222 Elizabeth 87 125
  205-206 210-212 Elsie 211 Elza
  Caroline 252 Emaline 207 212
  Emeline 181 206 Emmerline E
  210 Estelle G 207 212 Etsy 211
  Fannie 205 208 222 Florence
  Ann 277 Frances 159 177 205
  207 Frank 110 211-212 222
  Franklin 87 162 210-211 Geo
  224 Geo C 244 George 9 12 38
  156 197 204 207-209 310-311

KING (Cont.) George Perry 135
206 George Shelton 210 212 222
George W 205-206 George W Jr
205 Gertrude 252 Gertrude C
208 Gertrude Shipman 207
Gincy 205 Gracie May 277
Harriett 212 Hattie 211 Helen
207-208 237 252 Henry 209
Herbert 208 Herman 211 Ida
211 Irene 212 Isaac 207 J C 231
252 J F 331 Jack 207 210 Jacob
207-208 Jacob L 310-311 Jacob
Love 205 James 212 222 307
James N 208 James R 207 Jane
156 197 207 246 Jennie Lily 136
Jeremiah C 206 208 Jesse 210
Jesse C 211 Jesse Critz 86 Jesse
O 211 Joe 22 210 Joe B 20 John
12 46 86-87 197-198 202 204-207
209-210 252 302 310 John C 208
208 John Lewis 135 206 John M
206-207 210 212 John O 119 210
John O Jr 277 John Seward 210-
211 John Tyler 210-211 John W
135 Joseph 209-210 307 Joseph
Bolin 20 Joseph Bouldin 210-211
Joseph Seward 87 210-211
Joseph W 211 Judith 209
Katherine 208 Katie 211 Kinnie
138 Laura L 212 Lelia 212 Lewis
Graves 205-207 210 212 Lewis
Graves Jr 206-207 210 212 Lily
206 222 Lottie 212 Lou 208
Louisa 207 Lt 316 Lucy E 212
Lucy Elizabeth 207 Lucy K 207
212 Madame 60 Maggie 211
Malinda Carr 110 Malissa 211
Mamie 208 237 252 Margarett
208 Marhiah 135 Maria 125 206
Martha 119 205-206 210-211 275
Mary 123 137 177 202-203 205-
207 209-210 231 310-311 Mary
Edna 212 Mary Elizabeth 207-
208 Mary Henrietta 211 Mary J
135 Mary Jane 135 206

KING (Cont.) Mary Lily 212 Mary
Lodosky 211 Mattie 208 222
Minnie 207 212 222 Miss 170
Mollie 208 211 Myrtle 208 212
Nancy 197 206 252 327 Nannie
211 236 Nannie H 206 208
Nannie Witcher 195 Nathaniel
307 Pearl 208 Polly 197 205 210
R R 195 Richard 208 Robert L
211 Robt Carter 49 Roxy 210-
211 Ruth 210 Sallie 205-207 210
210-211 252 Sallie J 206 Sallie
Lou 135 206 Sallie R 208 Sarah
E 212 Sarah Elizabeth 222
Saunders 209 Starling 207
Stephen 14 Susan 135 179 197
205-207 210-211 Susan Ann 206
Susan E 206 208 Susannah 224
T B 208 Tabby 206 Thenie 205
Theodore 208 Thomas 224 252
Thomas G 135 Thomas H 20
205-206 Thomas J 20 206-207
331 Thomas Jesse 135-136 206
Thornton 208 Tyler 20 William
179 206-211 211 222 William
Brengle 211 William E 205 212
Willie 208 Willie Townes 277
Wm 327 Xenia 244
KINNEY, Benj Sr 307 James 307
KIRBY, David 307 Jesse 307
Joseph 308 Lilly 229 Richard
307
KIRKHAM, Elizabeth 327 Wm 327
KITCHEN, John 14 Sarah 328
KIZIAH, Sadwick 14
KNOX, Ben 327 Jemima 327
KOEHLER, Mr 55
KOGER, Abraham 202-203 Betsy
202-203 Bettie 203 Billy 202-203
Bland S 204 Caroline 203
Carson 204 Catherine 202 274
Columbus 205 Daniel King 203
Edd 203 Eliza 203 Emily 203
203 203 Emly 204 Emma 203-
204 Emma M 204 Fannie 205

KOGER (Cont.) G A 329 Geo A 204
George 203 George W 205 Gillie
204 204 Gillie C 203 231 Gillie N
45 330 Henry 123 137 201-203
209 231 294 Henry Jr 203 Hill
203 J L 20 Jacob 12 200-202
James 203 Jane 205 Joe Henry
203 John 141 202-205 231 305
John Bucket 203 John Harden
203 John Jr 203 John M 204
John S 203 Joseph 200-203
Judith 204 330 Jute 203 Kate O
204 Katie 204 Kit Carson 204
Kittie 203-204 L H 330 Lee 203
Lucinda 201 203 Lute H 204 M
M 185 Margarett 203 Marion
204 Martha A 203 Martha V 204
Mary 77 123 125 201-203 205
209 231 Mary Annie 204 Mary C
204 Mary Catherin 185 Mary
Catherine 204 Michael 201
Middleton 203 Minor Botts 204
204 217 Minor Botts Jr 204
Mollie 222 Moses Marion 203-
204 204 Nicholas 200-201 305
Perry 203 Peter 200-201 Pink 20
203 Polly 202 Sallie 202-203
Susan 141 203 205 Tabb 205
Thenie 205 Thomas 203 205
Victoria 203-204 Virginia 204
217 W L 20 William 203 Wm 20
Wm M 204 Woodson 203
Woodson Hill 204
KOPER, Kora Koma 204
KRATZ, Rebecca 88
KYLE, Elizabeth 195 James 195
Robert 195 T S 332
LADY, Margarett 329
LAFAYETTE, 156 Gen 134
LAGARRONDE, Miss 163
LAKE, Wm 307
LAMKIN, Jos 20
LAMPING, Mrs W C 260
LANCASTER, J F 275-276
LAND, John 307 Joseph 20

LAND (Cont.) Thomas 308 Wm 20
LANE, Dutton 263 John 308 Mrs
Julian C 331 Sarah 263
LANGHORNE, Henry 133
Maurice 34
LANIER, 14 David 12 314 325
Elizabeth 327 John 294 Thomas
W 276 Washington 327
LANKFORD, Benjamin 294
LANSFORD, Susannah 328
LARMAND, John 302
LASH, Jacob 196
LASTROPES, Cecile 129
LATER, Capt 241
LATIMER, Bessie May 184 Cora
Alyce 184 James Carter 184
Louisa Hamilton 184 Mrs Sallie
C 330 Sallie Ann 184 Wm A 184
LATTA, John 321
LAUGHTON, J R 48
LAVENDER, 213
LAVILLON, Susanne 163
LAVINDER, 47 212-213 Alice
Greyson 216 Alice P 170 Anne
214 Annie 214 216 Chilton 215
D H 216 Elias 214 Elizabeth 214
Ellen 214 Emily 215 Emma 284
Emma Jane 215 Frances 215
Greyson 241 Henry G 36 Henry
Geo 216 Hester 214 J B 36 49 64
J P 20 James 215 Jane H 57
Jane Hickey 71 139 215 Janie 37
49 330 Janie Hichkey 216 Jesse
139 215 Jesse Ben 20 216 John
214-215 John Peter 83 216
Joseph 215 Judith 214
Katherine 216 Laura 216 M
Katherine 216 M W 216 Maggie
36 Margaret Alzira 174 215-216
Margarett 214-215 Martha
Woodson 71 185 Mary 37 214-
215 Mary Catherine 71 216
Mary Lou 83 Mary Louisa 216
Mary Peters 216 Miss 285 Mr 72
Mrs J B 329 Mrs M W 182

LAVINDER (Cont.) Nancy 215
Nathaniel 214 Richard 214 S H
185 Sam Henry 215-216 Samuel
Henry 71 Sarah 214 Thomas
214-215 Thornton 215 William
214-215
LAW, Fairy 171 Green 20 Henry
13 307 Jesse 309 Nathaniel 308
Wm 308
LAWRENCE, John 312 Mary 312
Peter F 20 Sallie 269 Wm 269
LAWSON, David 294 307 Geo 308
313 Jacob 294 John 307 Wm
307-308
LEAK, Thomas 14 294
LEAKE, J B 20 Nannie 168 P F 20
Rebecca 119
LEATH, Anna 233 Frances 233
LEE, 232 Adele 154 Annie 223
Annie Page 126 Charles 126 177
Col 316 322-323 Harden W 20
John 265 John S 274 Lottie 241
Louisa 177 Lt Col 315 325 Lula
Watkins 126 Mary Anderson 265
Mattie 265 Miss 45 Mrs R R 330
Nannie 126 Philip Ludwell 132
R E 133 168 Rob R 223 Robert
265 Robert R 126 Robt E 154
Stephen 323 Susan 239 Susie
239 W H F 177 239 W P 20
Willie F H 126 Willie L 126 Wm
Henry 158 250
LEFEVRE, Madame 165
LEIGH, William 176
LESEAU, Mary 83
LESSIEUR, Geo 307
LESTER, Ainslee J 197 Elizabeth
87 H C 163 Henry C 116-117
John C 20 Loula 220 Lucy 116-
117 M J 20 Mary 197 210 Mary
Martin 56 Mrs A J 330 Osborne
20 Polly 271 Wm A 20
LETCHER, Bethenia 133 237 243
Capt 81 190 Elizabeth 237 243-
244 Widow 190 William 68 244

LETCHER (Cont.) Wm 237 243
314 317
LETCHWORTH, Ben 327 Eleanor
327
LEWIS, Emma 204 Gen 295 Hilda
Woodson 204 James P 165 John
201 204 Kate 136 Mary 110
Milly 165 R L 331
LIGHTFOOT, John 319
LIGHTLY, Nellie 49
LIGHTSEY, Josie Lee 267
LIGON, Henry 287 Martha 287
LINDSAY, J D 298 Jacob 298
LINDSEY, Birdie Penn 330
Elizabeth 327 Henry 327 Lizzie
264 Richard W 264
LITTLETON, Mrs Henry House
331 O 47
LIVINGSTON, John 308
LOCKE, Geo 134
LOCKHART, Thomas 12
LOESCH, Jacob 196
LOFTIS, Robert 236 Susie 236
LOGGINS, Samuel 307
LOGIN, Wm 307
LONDON, Lord Bishop Of 151
LONG, John 307 William 14
LONGS, Wm 308
LONGSTREET, 283
LOUIS, Iv King Of France 163
LOVE, Mary 177 205-206
LOVELACE, J W 20
LOVELL, Markham 293 Martha
265 Mrs J W 136 Nina G 136
LOVING, Sallie 261
LOWE, Thomas 324
LOWRY, Frances 119 Margaret
119 William 119
LOYD, John 316 322-323
LUCAS, Elizabeth 327 Sarah 91
223
LURAY, John 307
LURAYA, Lucas 307
LUTTREL, Samuel 14
LUTTRELL, 203

LYELL, Elizabeth 194
LYERLY, Mrs J W 330
LYLE, Alexander 307 Bartlett 20
  271 J H 20 Jeff 271 Joe Henry
  271 Ruth Anna 271 Thena 271
LYNCH, Charles 131
LYND, John 308
LYNE, E 295 Edmund 307 311-312
  314 Henry 266 295 298 314 318-
  319 321 325-326 Susanna 266
  William 266
LYON, Elley 327 James 307 312
  314-315 319 325-326 Joel 307
  Stephen 312 324 327
MACBETH, 145
MACMURROUGH, 127
MADCLAF, Thomas 308
MADISON, 223 Mary 114
MAGRUDER, Blizzard 298
MAHONE, Mr 232 Sarah 232
MAHOOD, Alex 220 Kathleen 220
MAJORS, John 324
MALLORY, Sarah 242
MANIFEE, Nancy 326 Wm 320
MANNING, Samuel 21
MANNINGS, Henry 14
MARKHAM, Elizabeth 225
MARKS, Walter 307
MARKSDILL, John 319
MARR, John 282 312 314
MARSHALL, Abigail M 226
  Alfriend 226 Ambrosia 187 Ann
  44 194 Anne Nancy 172 Ben 225
  Benjamin 226 Cassandra 41
  225-226 Celia 222 Dennis 18 40-
  41 98 125 171 225-226 272
  Dennis Sr 226 Edmond S 226
  Elizabeth 225 Elizabeth
  Cassandra 227 Fannie 187
  Frances 170 227 Frances Harper
  98 272 Frances M 226 Giles 226
  Hugh 226 James 21 John 41 98
  225-226 Julia E 226 Lewis 225-
  226 Martha 171 Martha J 226
  Mary Ann 226 Mary B 226

MARSHALL (Cont.) Melissa L 226
  Mrs Benj 205 Mrs J T 57 Nancy
  225 227 Nancy M 226 Patsy 226-
  227 Peyton S 226 Polly 226-227
  Reuben D 226 Ruth Stovall 194
  Sallie 226-227 Sally 225-226
  Sam 41 225-226 271 Sarah L
  226 Susan 125 172 225 Susan B
  226 Thomas 172 225 William
  222 225 William H 226
MARTIN, Alexander 224 Alice 207
  Ann 224 Annie 224 Annie
  Wilson 260 Archie 224 Bailey
  161 Bethenia 240 Betsy 92
  Bettie 225 Brice 13 223 308 312-
  314 317 319 322 Brice Jr 223-
  224 Cecelia 224 Eliza 224-225
  Elizabeth 223 Ella 197 224
  Franky 223 Geo 224 Gov 169
  230 Isabelle 153 James O 195
  James O Jr 197 James S 260
  Jane 224 Jarratt 13 Jean 328
  Jesse 224 Jos 293 297 Joseph 9
  91 96-97 153 174 197 205 223-
  225 234 324 327 Lester A 212
  Lewis 224 Loula 225 257 Lucy
  197 Margaret 197 Margarett 163
  Martha 223 Mary 171 195 197
  Mary B 161 Mary Lily 212
  Matilda 193 223-224 Minnie 228
  Mr 240 Nancy 224 Oregon 21
  Pannill 332 Patrick 171 Patrick
  Henry 224 Polly 223-224 Rorer
  James 197 Ruth 327 Sadie 169
  Sallie 154 224 Sally 224 Sam 22
  224 Samuel 225 Sarah 91 174
  223 Suanna 223 Susan 193 197
  205-206 224-225 Susanna 93
  Susannah 223-224 327 Susie 197
  Thenia 224 Thomas J 21
  Thomas W 224 William 225 257
  Wm 47 193 223-224
MARY, 175 Queen of Scots 164
MASON, Albert 161 Fanny 329
  James 21 Lee 21

MASON (Cont.) Mary Campbell 218 Robert 315 Sarah 161
MASSEY, Phillip 14
MASTIN, Elizabeth 328 Jacob 328
MATHELEY, G W 21
MATHESON, Ida 197
MATHEWS, Calvin 228 Ida 138 John Hill 228 Lucy Catherine 228 Minnie 118 Sampson 201 Susan 228 Tandy 228 Thomas Calvin 138
MATLOCK, David 309 James 309
MATTHEWS, 51 Ann Eliza 218 Annie 222-223 Antoinette 222 Betsy 221 Bettie 222 Botts 204 Bristol 307 Caleb 221-222 Calvin 221 Catherine 204 330 Celia 204 221-222 Charlotte 222 Dave 198 David 21 221-222 Edward 221-222 Eliza 212 221-222 227 Eliza Dabney 112 Eliza Jane 212 221-222 Elizabeth 198 222 237 328 Frank 222 George 222 Ginnie 222 Ida 223 J H 58 James 112 221-222 227 James W 204 John 222 John H 137 John Hill 90 218 221 260 Len 237 Leonard 222 Loula 222 Lucy 221 223 Marcella 221 Mary 221-222 Mary L 204 Minnie 223 Mollie 222 Mrs J W 329 Nannie 222 Patsy 221 Pink 221 Robert 90 221-222 Robt M 204 Sadie E 204 Sallie 137 222 Sarah 222 Sarah Elizabeth 222 Susan Louisa 260 T C 58 330 Tandy 221 Tandy Jr 221 Thomas 222 Thomas C 91 Thomas Calvin 221 223 Walter 222 Warren 204 William 221-222 Wm 328
MATTOCKS, Virginia 137
MAUPIN, Polly 328
MAVITY, Wm 307
MAY, Rachel 111
MAYBERRY, Joshua 309

MAYBY, Joseph 309
MAYS, Abraham 309 David 14 309 Easter 328 Henry 309 Jane Athey 153 Liggin 328 Sherod 309 Stephen 307
MCADOO, Mrs Victor Clay 331 Nannie Witcher 195 Victor 195
MCALEXANDER, Wm 307
MCBRIDE, Patrick 309
MCBRYDE, Robt 21
MCCABE, Abner 172 Annie Whitten 229 Francis 172 J P 50 197 Jane 224 Mr 224 Susan Ellen 172 Susie 197
MCCAIN, Ham 14
MCCLINTOC, Mmiss 185
MCCORKLE, Kate 134 Katherine 134 May 134
MCCOY, Wm 308
MCCRAW, 315 322 Elizabeth 282 Jacob 12 282 309 Wm 282 309 321 324
MCCUBBINS, James 323
MCCULLOCK, Fannie 205 James 205
MCCUTCHIN, James 319
MCDONALD, ---- 278 Elizabeth 278 Isaac 318 Isac 309
MCFADDEN, Mary 258
MCGEE, John 294
MCGHEE, Nancy 139 William 13
MCGRAW, Wm 313
MCGUFFY, Henry 309
MCGUIRE, Allegania 327 Anderson 14 Sarah 327
MCINNEY, Benjamin 294
MCINTOSH, Daniel M 115 Lucy Frances 115
MCKEEN, Alex 309 Hance 309 Hugh 309 Thomas 307
MCKINNEY, Kinney 321
MCKINSEY, John 309
MCKIVER, Jennie 220
MCLARAY, J G 21
MCLAURY, John 134 Kate 134

MCLAURY (Cont.) Katherine 134
MCMELLON, Joseph 21 S H 21
  Thomas 21
MCMICHAEL, Annie D 158 W P
  158
MCMILLION, James 167 Joe 167
  Lucy Frances 167 Mike 167 Mrs
  R F 167
MCNEEL, John 318
MCQUEERY, John 307
MEADE, Sarah 44
MEADOWS, Bettie 199 D T 21
MEANS, Alexander 103
MEDLEY, Ann 328 John 328
MEDLOCK, John Jr 308 John Sr
  307
MEEKS, J T 21 Thomas 21
MELVIN, Elizabeth 327-328
  Jarner 328 Katy 328 Levi 327
MENIFEE, John 307 Wm 307
MENN, Mag 234
MENZIES, John 195 Pamela 195
MEREDITH, Bradley 307 James
  298 307 James Sr 307 Lucy 167
  Samuel 307 Wm 307
MERIDITH, William 67
MERRYMAN, J B 21 J L 21 James
  21
METTS, John A 21
MICHAEL, Virginia 57
MIDDLETON, Elizabeth 286
MIDKIFF, Wm 309
MILEHAM, Dudley 13 Jordan 13
MILES, A W 329 John 14
  Margaret 232 Miss 218 Mr 232 S
  J 21
MILLER, Elisha 315 J D 208 John
  34 318 Lucy 168 Martha 168
  Nancy 168 Nancy Dabney 175
  Sallie R 208
MILLINER, Katie 211
MILLS, Callie 178 331 Col 237
  Frances 237 Francis 21 J P 21
  John 294 Margarett 203 Polk
  178 Rich 21 Susan 100 111

MILLS (Cont.) W F 46 Wm F 111
  298
MINNES, Tabitha 326
MINOR, J H 302
MINTER, Annie 246 Betty 270
  Cynthia 270 James 21 Jane
  Abigail 167 Jim 270 Joe 270
  John 270 293 307 Joseph 21
  Martha 270 Miss 179 Mr 141
  Mrs J C 246 Nancy 270 Obediah
  157 Orthneal 310 Otniel 270
  Peggy 141 Richard 270 Silas 21
  167 270 Susan 270 William 270
  William S 21
MITCHELL, Anna 199 219-220
  236 Annie 219-221 269 Belva
  219-220 236 Benjamin Franklin
  219 Bessie 220 Betsy 231 Bettie
  219 272 Brooksie 221 Buck 219
  235 Dora 221 269 285 E R 21
  256 Edd 220 Eddie 269 Edward
  R 220 Edwin 219 Eliza 219-220
  Elizabeth 217 220-221 269
  Elizabeth Napier 139 Fletcher
  219 Florence 221 269 Frances
  220 269 Frances Ruth 185
  Franklin 47 Geo L 272 George
  220-221 269 Harry 221 269 285
  Hughes 221 269 James 221 269
  Jennie 220 John 139 231 Joseph
  269 Joseph T 220 Josiah T 302
  Jubal 220 Jubal Early 269 Kate
  166 Katherine 219 236 Kettie
  219 L P 329 Landis 220 Landis
  P 269 Laura 219 Loula 220 Lucy
  183-184 220 Lula 236 Martha
  220 327 Martha Ann 256 Mary
  219-220 Mary Churchill 200
  Mary Frances 220 Mary Jane
  139 Maud 221 Mildred 285
  Mollie 219 Nancy 327 Nancy
  Grayer 269 Nannie 219-220 235
  269 Pattie 288 Peter 13 Quince
  Stovall 269 Richard 219 296
  Robert 219 Sallie Ann 220-221

MITCHELL (Cont.) Sarah 219-220
Susan 177 T A F 185 330
Thomas 236 Thomas Bondurant
219 Trotter 220 269 Virginia 219
W J 331 Wade 220-221 269
William 219 236 269 330
William D 199 220 William J
200 220 Willie 220 269 Wirt 330
Wm 294 324 327
MITT, Eliza Jane 212 222
MOIR, Judge 181 Marion Mccrary
118
MOLEN, Nilly 326
MONDAY, Samuel 313
MONTAGU, Duke of 144
MONTAGUE, A J 63 Mary 200
MOORE, A L 21 Abraham 13 Ann
327 Annie 136 B D 187
Benjamin 253 Berry 294 Berry
Scott 187 Biddy 235 Cindy 235 D
M 211 Eleanor 170 Eron Byrd
253 Eron Pha 253 Garrett 307
Hilda D 187 James 46 Katherine
187 Lemuel 253 Mag 234 Mary
E 187 Mary Lodosky 211
Matilda 187 Mrs James 329 Mrs
Jim 235 Mrs Kate 329 Mrs T S
136 Rodsham 307 Ruth Rowland
253 Samuel 324 Shater 327
Thomas 21 William 13 170
MOORMAN, Charles 252 Lucy 153
MOREFIELD, Miss 232
MOREHEAD, Joseph 195 Kate
195
MORELAND, Sarah 139
MORGAN, Emily 137 Hayner 311
Haynes Jr 298 John 137 Lewis
309 Mary 110
MORIS, Addison 217
MORRIS, 51 Anderson 266 Ann
217 Ann Eliza 218 Ann Winston
283 Annie 222 Annie Elizabeth
219 Annie Lou 218 Ben 216-217
Bernard 218 Bessie Haymaker
218 Booker 217 D M 329

MORRIS (Cont.) Daisy 219
Dandridge W 283 Dandridge
Wade 217 David H 218 Dewy
218 E A 289 Edgar 218-219
Eleanor 217 Eliza 184 217
Elizabeth 217 220 Ellen Morton
218-219 Emma Hairston 219
Emma Hariston 218 Emma Lou
218 Geo Emerson 218 Grace 218
Grace Forest 219 Gregory 217
Hairston 219 Helen 156 217 219
Henry Sanders 218 J T 89
James Harrison 218 James M
222 James Madison 217-218
James Walter 219 Jennie 217
John 216-217 285 John T 21 218
John Thomas Hill 218 John W
220 Joseph 216-217 298
Katherine Leak 218 Kellie Reed
266 Logan 217 Lucy Matt 219
Lulu 217 M E 217 Maggie 211
218-219 Mamie J 219 Martha
Louisa 218 Mary 178 217 Mary
A 218 Mary Campbell 218 Mary
Dorsey 123 Mary Emeline 89
256 Mary Evelyn 218 Mrs Ben
285 Mrs N A 266 Nancy 216-217
Nannie Elizabeth 218 Patsy 217
Pocahontas 219 Reamey 217
Rebecca 216-217 Richard
Hairston 218 Robert Ernest 218
Robert Saunders 218 Robt
Vaughn 218 Ruth Dillard 218
Sallie Elizabeth 219 Samuel A
218 Samuel Coleman 216 324
Samuel Madison 218 Sarah E
218 Susan 217 Susannah 326 T
H 332 Tabitha 217 Thomas 156
219 Thomas Hill 218 Virginia
204 217 219 285 Virginia Dare
218 W S 330 W W 21 38 128 256
Walter C 218 William 216-217
219 285 William W 89 218 Wm
21 Woodson 44 123
MORRISON, Bushrod 21

MORRISON (Cont.) Martha Annie
  172 Royall Washington 172
  Sarah 172 Thomas 307
MORROW, Thomas 309
MORTON, Ann 237 Anne 242
  Hezekiah 114 Jeremiah 242
  Judith 327 Lucy 167 Mary 114
  175 Sarah 242
MOSBY, Kate Merrimac 45
MOSELEY, Miss 192
MOSLEY, Thomas 307
MOTTIS, Mary Hill 218
MOVAE, Diana 162
MULLIN, 43
MULLINS, Alice 228-229 Ambrose
  13 307 America Augusta 228
  Anna 228 Annie Whitten 229
  Burwell 227-228 Celia 111 227-
  228 Con 229 David 12 111 227
  David Hill 228 Elizabeth
  Matilda 228 Ellen 229 H G 28
  Hattie 228-229 Henry 221 Henry
  G 90 183 Henry Green 227-229
  Henry Hill 228 Jack 228 James
  228-229 Jesse 228 Jimmy 59
  John 13 227 307 Kettie 99 Lucy
  221 Lucy Catherine 228 265
  Marion 229 Mary 228 Matilda
  Winston 183 228 Minnie 228
  Minnie Martin 56 Mrs H G 56
  329 Mrs M M 99 331 Nancy 164
  228 Nat 164 Nathaniel 227-228
  Nellie 229 Patrick Henry 228
  Peter 228-229 Preston Martin
  229 S J 28 97 246 Sadie 229
  Sallie 228 Samuel Jesse 228-229
  Sarah Hay 228 Susan 228
  Susanna 227 Virginia 228-229
  William 14 Willie 228 Winston
  59 228 Wm 307
MUNFORD, Robt 318
MURPHEY, Archie 13
MURPHY, Gebriel 328 John 309
  312 Lucy 326 Mary 327
MURRELL, Jeffrey 307
MURRILL, Thomas 309
MURRY, J Ogden 149
MUSE, Miss 177
MUSICK, Elections 309
MYERS, Charles F 45
NAHL, Marvell 317
NANCE, Allen 229 Amy 229
  Barton Garrett 230 Bud 229
  Clement 230 D L 329 E W 329
  Edmund 230 Emmett Warren
  230 Isaac 229 Joham 230 John
  13 230 Joseph 230 Lovicy S 230
  Martha 167 Mary 229 Mary Ann
  226 Nancy 229-230 Payton 230
  Polly 230 Reuben 229-230 293
  314 321-322 Ruben 226 230 270
  Sally 229-230 Sofronby 230
  Stephen 230 Suhanna 230
  Tabitha 230 Tabitha Jane 157
  William 229 William E 230
NANCY, Mrs Peyton 205
NAPIER, Ann 231 Betsy 169 230-
  231 Bettie 139 Betty 231 Boothe
  230 Champion 169 230-231
  Frances 230-231 Geo 178 George
  231 George Jr 231 Gillie 204
  Gillie C 203 231 James 230 John
  230 Mary 157 231 Moses 231
  Nannie 230 Polly 178 230-231
  Robert 230 Ruth 231 Sinai 231
  Susan 177 231 Tarleton 203 230-
  231 Tom 231 Valentine 230
NASH, Lydia Adela 155 Marvel
  318 Thomas 155
NATTHEWS, Mary C 204
NAVARRE, Henry Of 213
NEAL, Anna Adele 212 Peggy 168
NEAVILLE, John 307
NEBLETTE, A V 245 Sudie 245
NELSON, Elijah Richard 219 Mr
  228 Pocahontas 219 Thomas 189
  309 Thomas Jr 320
NEVEN, Valerine 129
NEVIL, George 13
NEWBOLD, Mary 250-251

NEWBOLD (Cont.) William 250
   Wm 251
NEWMAN, Daniel 308 James 308
   John 313 326 Joseph 309 321
   Samuel 58
NIBLET, Mary 205
NICHOLDS, Bettie 288
   Greenberry 146 Sarah 146-147
   152
NICHOLLS, Buckett 317 Bukett
   315
NICHOLS, 243 America 263 Annie
   Miller 286 Bettie 263 Clarey 328
   David 328 Greenbury 263 John
   Fontaine 263 286 Sallie 263
   Sarah 263 Thomas 263 William
   263
NICKOLDS, John 68
NISSEN, Cora Pannill 240 Mr 240
NOE, John Jr 309 John Sr 307
   Samuel 308
NOEL, Dr 251 Mary 251 Sarah
   167
NORFLEET, Mattie 149
NORMAN, Alfred 46 Isabel 194
   James B 302 Lucy W 302 Mary
   284 Ruth 104 Sallie 199 William
   H 199
NORMANDY, William Of 126
NORRIS, Elizabeth 328 Zebulon
   328
NORTHCUTT, Francis 328 Lucy
   328
NORTHEN, Geo 330 George
   Traylor 280 Martha 280 Mattie
   330 Thomas H 280
NORTHERN, Ruth 280
NORTON, John 293 328 Sarah
   328
NOWLIN, Frances 243 Samuel
   243
NUNN, Elizabeth 328 Jean 328
   Joseph 308 Thomas 308 328 Wm
   Riley 49
O'BRYAN, Dennis 308

O'BRYANT, Dennis 321
O'NEAL, Basil 328 Milly 328
OAKES, James K 110 Rachel 326
   Sarah Jane 110
OAKLEY, Ben 308 C S 200 Callie
   285 Gertrude 200 Hughes 162
   Jack 285 James 308 Sallie 162
ODELL, George 21
OGLESBY, Katherine 208
OGLETHORPE, 144
OLIVER, N G 21
ORR, Mrs J C 279
OSCANT, Jesse 293
OULD, A H 211 Nanie 331 Nannie
   211
OVERTON, Miss 221
OWEN, Christopher 322
OWENS, Howard 217 Lucy 287
   Susan 217
OXFORD, William 143
PACE, 249 Allie 246 Ann 271
   Ballard P 271 Callie 245
   Caroline 245 Cassandra 246
   Charles P 245 Christine 246
   Corinne 245 Daniel 207 246 271
   310 Emma 246 George 246
   German 245 Green 245 Grief
   245 H C 21 Henry 271 Henry C
   246 332 James Baker 245 273
   Jane 207 246 Jean 328 Jimmie
   271 Joel 293 John 245 308 313
   John E 332 John T 246 Joseph
   246 Judith C 245 Julia 271 Kate
   245 Kitty Ann 245 Lafayette 246
   Leatha Ann 246 Lily 246 Lucy
   245-246 326 Lucy Elizabeth 273
   Mariah 179 Martha Tolly 246
   Mary Tabitha 271 Matilda 246
   Nannie Eleanor 246 Nellie 246
   Newsum 12 Pace 271 Polly 245
   Raymond 246 Reed 245 Sallie
   157 Sally 271 Sam Green 273
   Samuel Green 245 Sarina 271
   Spottswood 245 273 William 245
   271 Wm 293

HISTORY OF HENRY COUNTY, VA

PACKARD, Patricia 174
PACKWOOD, Richard 307 Samuel 12 308
PAGE, 152 Thomas Nelson 240
PAINELL, 241
PAINTER, Margarett 208
PALMER, John M 261
PANELL, Walter 244
PANIL, 244 John 241
PANNELL, 241
PANNILL, 46 238 Adele 240 Adelle 156 Alice 238 Alice Christina 241 America 166 America Hairston 238-239 Amy 239 Ann 237-238 Anne 240 242-243 Augusta 240 Augustus Hunter 240-241 Bessie 241 Bethenia 68 243 Bethenia Letcher 238-240 Bethenia Ruth 237 239 Bethenia Ruth Callaway 134 Betheniah Ruth 238 Cora 240 D H 216 David 68 237 242-243 David H 241 David Harry 241 David P 240 Edmond Johns 238-239 Eliza 238-239 Eliza Reamey 56 Elizabeth 238 240 242 Frances 237 241-243 G 302 Geo 47 134 237 Geo Edmond 239 George 238 243 Gordon 240 Greyson 241 Hardin 238 Jack 21 238 Jeb Stuart 238-239 Jeremiah 243 John 240 242 Joseph 237 241-243 260 K L 329 Kate 238 Katherine Langhorne 238-239 Lottie 241 Loula 238 Loulie 238 Lucy Moir 241 Lutie 238 Magdalene 238 Maria Bruce 240 Mariah Waller 238-239 Mary 134 237-238 243 Mary Elizabeth 239 Mary Lavinder 241 Mildred 238 Morton 237-238 243 Mrs D H 53 Mrs E J 45 330 Peter Shelton 238 Robt 241 Ruth Callaway 238 329 Sallie R 263 Sallie Reamey 238-239

PANNILL (Cont.) Samuel 237 242-243 Samuel Banks 241 Samuel Roberts 240 Sara 241 Sarah 237 241-242 Sarah Ann Catherine 238 Sarah Bagley Morton 242 Sarah Martin 260 Stuart 242 Susan 224 Thenia 224 Thomas 237 241 William 21 241-243 William Hairston 238 William L 156 Willie 238 Wm 237-238 Wm Banks 240-241
PARBERRY, Ann 328 James 328
PARCELL, Peter 21 Robert 21
PARISH, Lucy 223 Mrs T P 331 T P 223
PARKER, William 208
PARKS, Augusta 109 127 182 David 128 Judith 258 Mr 323 Sallie 263
PARR, John Jr 298 John Sr 307 Nancy 233
PARROTT, Faith 53 55 108 Faith Thomas 56 Mr 44
PARSELL, Moses 308
PARSLEY, 328 Abraham 307 John 308 Rachel 327 Richard 14 Thomas 14 308
PARTOR, Jonathan 308
PATRICK, James 328 Sarah 328
PATTERSON, D M 21 Elizabeth 169 George W 21 Giles 21 Grandaughter 104 James 46 300 Jarrat 21 Jarrett 323 John 21 M Bradfield 107 Mrs T J 330 Samuel 313 Thomas 21
PAUL, Wm 298
PAYNE, Abraham 14 293 Cloah 328 Green B 21 John 307 Lettie 326 Lucinda 186 Miss 243 R C 21 Reuben 319 Robert 299
PEAKE, David 14
PEARSON, Joseph 13 Meredith 328 Rhoda 328
PEAY, Sam 21
PECK, David 328 Jean 328

PEDIGO, Edd 171 Emma 171
Emma Eugenia 172 Frank 171
George D 171 Georgia 171
Henry 43 J F 171 John H 329 L
G 332 Letitia 139 Lewis G 171
Martha 171 Mary 171 327 Miss
179 Rachael 171 Robert 321-322
Robt Jr 328 Sallie Hughes 171
Sallie L 84 Thomas 171 Virginia
45 53 56 Virginia G 330
PEGRAM, Franes 278 George 278
PELFREY, John 308
PELL, Geo P 158 Mary Virginia
158
PELPHRY, Elizabeth 328
PELPTORY, Sarah 327
PEMBERTON, Scolis 252
PENDELTON, Elizabeth Rachel
231
PENDLETON, 264 Alexander
Garland 232 Ann 232 Benjamin
231 Betty 232 Birdie 264
Caroline 231 Charlotte 232
Edmund 231 Frances 232 Glen
Alexander 232 Henry 231 Isaac
231 Isabella 231 Isobelle 231
James 232 John 231 Lizzie 232
Margaret 232 Mary 231-232 281
Nathaniel 231 Philip 231 Polly
232 Reuben 232 Richard 232
Sarah 232 Selina Christiana 232
Taylor 232 William 232
PENN, 47 Abraham 67 189 311-
312 314-315 320 326 Abram 11-
12 92 94 107 148 232-234 268
Abram Jr 233 America Augusta
228 Anna 233-234 Annie 234
264 Baraham 322 Bethenia
Ruth 238-239 Birdie 264
Caroline 155 Carrie 264 Charles
264 Christine 233 Earnest G 234
Edmund 21 233 Edwin G 234
Eliza 193 Fancy 154 Frances
232-233 Frank 264 Gab 298
Gabriel 132 232-234 Geo 328

PENN (Cont.) Geo Jackson 238-
239 George 232-233 Greenville
233-234 Gussie 229 Hardy 264
Hattie M 234 Horatio 233
Hunter 229 J T 332 James 228-
229 233 Jefferson 264 330
Jennie 234 Jinsy 233 John 94
132 John Edmund 234 John
Harrison 234 John T 234 Joseph
G 21 234 260 Katherine 232
Laura Hairston 56 Laura
Hughes 234 Lilly 229 Lizzie 264
Louise 234 Lucinda 233 Luvenia
233 Magdalene 234 Martha 233
Martha Ann 155 Martin 238-239
Mary L 331 Mary Tatum 234
Matilda 50 228 Matilda Hughes
154 Moses 232 Mrs Champe 49
Mrs E G 58 Mrs J G 331 Nancy
233 Patty 328 Philip 232 234
Phillip 233 Polly 233 Priscilla
Jane 234 Robert Edmond 238
Robert Leath 234 Robt 239
Rufus 264 Ruth 94 233-234 268
Ruth Stovall 260 Sallie 233
Sallie L 234 Sarah 132 328
Shelton 154 Spencer 264 Susan
L 234 Susie 239 Susie Letitiia
234 Thomas 233 Thomas Green
64 Ugh C 234 Walter 264 Walter
H 155 William 232 William F
234 William Leath 234 Wm J
155
PENNILEN, Geo 294
PENNY, Elizabeth 211 George 211
PENTECOST, Miss 173
PERCY, Henry 146
PEREGOY, Ruth 328
PERISON, Richard 308
PERKINS, 81 Alice 191 Bigbee 237
C I 321 Col 322-323 Elizabeth
237 243 Elley 327 Martha 175
Matilda 223 Nicholas 190 Peter
316
PERREGOY, Joseph 13 13

PERRY, 34 Anna 199 M F 21 199
PERRYMAN, John 308 Mumford 12 Robert 308
PERWIT, David Jr 308 John 308
PERWITT, David 308 David Jr 308 Elijah 308
PETERS, Alice 216 Alice P 170 Dr 216 Electra 263 George D 170 H G 170 Henry D 170 Herbert 216 Herbert G 263 Mary 170 Robert 170
PETTIGREW, Mrs Todd M 260
PETTIT, Christine 246 Robt 21 William 246
PEYTON, Judith 209 Will 37 Wythe 44
PHARIS, 47 Jno H 49 John H 38 Reamey 217
PHILIPS, Julia C 75 W C 75
PHILLIP, Geo Sr 307
PHILLIPS, 46 Charles 80 John 294
PHILPORT, Mary 328 Samuel 328
PHILPOTT, A B 141 B W L 21 Ben 170 Betsy 138 170 Bettie 269 C W 21 Charles 12 123 293 328 Columbus 135 David 120 135 Elizabeth 328 Garret 138 Joe 293 John 21 307 John Edd 269 Maggie 245 Maria 120 Mary 161 328 Mary Dorsey 123 Mattie 178 Miss 218 255 Nancy 135 Nannie 265 Nat 21 Polly 230 Sallie 203 Sinai 231 Thomas 21
PICKETT, 283
PILLOW, Col 223
PIPER, Joseph 13
PITMAN, James 328 Martha 328 Willie Florence 65
PLASTER, Micael 307
PLUMMER, Sallie 164
POCAHONTAS, 145
POINDEXTER, A B 136 Lelia 136 Miss 231 Mrs A B 332
POLK, Thos 134

POLLY, Edward 309
POMEROY, Janie 260
PONY, Francis 319
POOL, Cloah 328 Geo 309 328 George 14
POOLE, Kettie 99
POOR, Willim 324
PORTER, ---- 278 Martha 278
POSEY, Humphrey 308
POTEAT, James 67 313 Mary M 187 Royer 187
POTEET, James 13 308 319
POTSON, Richard 13
POTTER, Ben 307 Thomas 308 William 300
POWEL, Sarah 136
POWELL, Ben F 21 Frank B 110 G E 47 79 331 Lucy Evelyn 110 Robert 308
POWERS, Mary Ann 269
POYTHRESS, Jane 151
PRATER, Ninon 13
PRATHER, Jesse H 169 Lilla Elizabeth 169 Mrs J H 330
PRATHEY, James 12
PRATLEY, James 14
PRATOR, Archibald 308
PRATT, Alice 138 G C 138 Jonathan 13 Joseph 294 Liliy 222 Richard 21 Thomas 21
PRESTON, 101 247 Ballard 54 Col 92 Jim 73 Miss 169 Mrs Ballard 23 Mrs P R 56 Sarah 117 Wm 319
PRIBBLE, J L 80 185
PRICE, 237 Ada 237 Addie 124 Alice 236 Allen 235 Allen G 236 Anna 236 Anna Lee 237 Annie 236 Beaver Island John 237 Bert Allen 237 Biddy 235 Charles H 208 Charlie 236 Cindy 235 Daniel 217 Dean 261 Dolly 235-236 Dora 237 Drury 235 Duke 235 Elizabeth 222 237 Fannie 208 Frank 235 Geo L 261 H 331

INDEX

PRICE (Cont.) Hanna 235-236
  Harriet 235 Harvey V 208 237
  Hattie 237 Helen 208 237 J M
  44 J W 331 James 135 235 Joe
  Henry 235 John 12 29 124 219
  235 John A 124 John H 237
  John W 208 236 Joseph 325
  Katherine 219 235-236 Lelia 193
  237 Lou 198 Loula 185 236
  Loulie 236 Mamie 208 237
  Marion 217 Mary 124 135 219
  235 Mary Ann Eliza 235-236
  Matilda Eliza 235 Medora
  Sabina 181 Minerva 236 Miss
  260 Nancy 235 Nannie 198 208
  235-236 Patsy 217 Pleas 235
  Polly 235 Preston 235-236 R B
  331 R P 44 Rachel 235 Rebecca
  235 Reece 234-235 Robert 237
  Robert P 236 Robt P 198 235
  Sallie 235 Sam 217 Samuel 236
  Sterling 124 Steve 236 Thomas
  P 135 Tom 235 Whit 235
  William 135 235 Wm 308
PRILLAMAN, Benjamin 244-245
  Bernice 245 Beulah 245 Callie
  244 Christopher 244 Cliff 244
  Clifford 245 Daniel 244 Dicie
  244 Drusilla 244 Eliza Susan
  167 Ellen 245 F M 244 Gabriel
  244 Geo 167 245 George 244
  Hassie 167 Hortense 244-245
  Jacob 244-245 Jim 167 John 245
  Lafe 167 Letcher 244-245 Loula
  244-245 Lydia 244 Maggie 245
  Martha 244 Mary 167 Nannie
  244-245 272 Nick 167 P M 244
  Pete 167 Robert 167 Ruth 167
  Sallie 245 Shields 244-245 Sudie
  244-245 Theodora 167 Vance
  167 Xeonia 244
PRILLIMAN, Barbara 328 Daniel
  308 F M 21 Mrs 231
PRINCE, Nell 156
PROCTOR, W R 48

PRUIT, David 14
PRUNTY, Ann 177 Betsy 117
  Elizabeth 176 James 14 308
  Jane 116 177 Jesse 116 Jesse Sr
  177 John 124 Julia 124 Keziah
  167 Mary 116 Nancy 177 Robert
  177 Thomas 177 308 317
  William 21
PRYATT, Ebenezer 14
PRYTLE, John 13
PUCKETT, Miss 75 Mrs Una 332
PULLEN, Ardena 109 Sarah
  Lewis 109 Sarah Lewis Bailey
  129
PULLIAM, George 222 Mamie 222
  Nancy 145 152 William 302
PUNHAM, Mrs C T 332
PURCELL, Ann 246 Annie 246
  Arthur 246 C R 21 Charles
  Rufus 246 Dallas 246 Elizabeth
  Ann 246 Geo Dallas 246 James
  O 246 Martha F 246 Mary S 246
  Mildred 238 Mildred V 246
  Minnie 246 Nannie 246 Peter
  246 Thomas Hill 246
PURCHAS, 151
PURDLE, 107 Ann 135
PURDY, Anderson 270 Chester
  270 Cynthy 270 Geo 270 James
  21 Jim 270 Joseph 21 Miss 222
PUREFOY, Frances 119
PURSELL, John 13 313 Richard
  309
PUSSY, Robert 308
PUTNAM, Mrs Allen 280
PUTZEL, 47 Sarah Louise 283
  Sigmund 302
PUTZELL, Sarah 283
PYLE, Alexander 309
PYRTLE, John 328 Margaret 329
  Mary 326 Polly 328
QUARLES, Elizabeth 328 Francis
  308 James 328 Judith 327
QUILLEN, Robt 294
RALEIGH, Walter 130

RALLS, Maria 267
RAMEY, Mary Ann 249
RAMSEY, Betsy Anne 141 Daniel 309 E T 331 Hailey W 141 J W 124 John 309 John H 21 Mary 124 141 Tandy 141 Thomas 141 Winnie 141 Woody 171 Wootson 141
RANDEL, John 294
RANDOLPH, 35 John 279 Martha 278 Thomas Mann 34 176
RANGELEY, Ada 251 Alice 251-252 Annette 252 Annie 251 Carrie 251 Clarence 251 Eliza 252 Eliza Caroline 251-252 Emily 240 252 Emma 251 Frank 251 Fred 251 Geo 331 George 252 Hannah 251 Hattie 251 Henry 251 Ida 251 James 250-252 John 21 147 251 Joseph 251 Lily 251 Maggie 251 Mary 147 250-251 Nancy 138 252 Nannie 252 Nellie 251 Raynie 252 Samuel 251 Sarah 251 Susan 147 Susan Webster 251-252 W H 252 Walter 251 Will 138 William 251-252 Willie 251 Wm H 251
RANGELY, Eliza 208 R 330
RANSON, Mrs T A 56
RATCLIFF, John 308 Richard 308 Silas 308
RATFORD, John 13
RAY, Andrew 308 Berta 211 James 308 Joseph 328 Mary Ann 328 Mrs R P 331 Rufus P 211 Virginia 182
REA, Ben 294 David 328 Frances 328 James 14 John 13 308 Wm 294 Wm Collins 293
READ, Cecelia 224 Charlotte 232 Frances 232 Francis 232 Jacob 308 Janet 232 John 232 Josie 232 Lizzie 239 Louise 232 Manson 232 Mariah Waller 239 Martha 233 Mary 232

READ (Cont.) Robert A 232 Taylor Pendleton 239 Virginia Dare Thurman Virginia Dare 232 Wm 310 321-323 Wm Brumfield 239
REAMEY, 47 247 Alice 249 Annie 250 Bettie 95 249 Bettie Redd 250 Daisy 219 Daisy Martin 250 Daniel 45 108 309 323 325 Daniel Jr 249 Daniel Webster 249-250 Eliza 238-239 249 Elizabeth 85 154 250 Elizabeth Perkins 193 Florence 249 Frank G 250 George 249 Henry 249 Henry Clay 249 Jack 249 James W 250 Jasper 249 John 154 193 249-250 John Starling 249 Kate 249 Lucy 249-250 Lyne Starling 250 Mary Ann 108 249-250 Mattie 48 249 Mrs 267 Overton 248 250 Overton Redd 249 P R 34 45 302 Pattie Ruth 250 Peter 193 249-250 Peter R 43 95 263 Peter Randolph 238 Pettie 248 Sallie 45 95 238 249 Sallie J 329 Sam 250 Sanford 58 Starling 249 Sue Starling 250 Susan 249 Susan Starling 108 Walter 249
REDD, Annie 247-248 267 Apphia Fauntleroy 247 Carr 247 Celestia 247 Edmund B 248 Edmund Burwell 247 Edmund Madison 247-248 Elizabeth 153 247 263 Ella 247-248 Flora 165 H C 302 Hill M 302 J G 302 James Madison 165 247 James S 247 John 12 96 153 165 247 249 261 263 267 319-320 322 John G 47 John O 301 Keziah 247 L W 302 Lucy 248 288 Lucy Dabney 247 Maj 288 Marion 247 Martha 247 261 Mary 96 247 Mrs James S 193 Nannie 247 Overton 247 Pattie 248 Polly C 247 Ruth 23 165 Ruth Penn 247 Sallie 247 Sarah Ann 247 Spottswood 288

REDD (Cont.) W S 21 248 Waller 58 247 Wm Spottswood 247
REDFERN, 269 Dora 269
REED, 202 Ferguson 155 J C 47 Mary 155
REEL, James 309 John 309 Richard 309
REEVES, Burwell 313 Frederick 314 317 Geo 309
REIVES, Burwell 323
REMIE, Daniel 248-249 Elizabeth 249 John 249
RENNOE, John 308
RENTFRO, James 324 John 14 308 320 326 Joshua 12 Mark 324 328 Naomi 328 Wm 308 322
RETZACK, Anne E 182
REYNO, Geo 325
REYNOLDS, Bartlett 14 294 Geo 314 317 321 328 Richard 13 310 Sarah 160 Susannah 202 328 Wm 294
RICE, Joseph 14 Leroy 21
RICH, 46
RICHARDS, Joseph 14 Shadrick 328 Sina 327 Susannah 328 Thomas 309
RICHARDSON, Abner 271 Amos 309 Ann 136 Annie 248 Arthur B 176 Beatrice 136 Ben 310 Betsy 271 Daniel 14 313 Elijah 171 Eliza 171 271 Eugene 115 Frank 21 271 Geo 271 George L 21 Henrietta Alice 115 Henry 21 Hettie 115 Horace Leonard 115 Jesse 98 136 Jesse Martin 97 Joe 271 John 14 21 271 309 328 Joseph 21 171 Junstina 176 Katherine Virginia 115 Louise 115 Lowery 115 Lucinda 271 Mary 328 Mary Jane 171 Mrs H S 332 Nancy 271 Nelly 271 Robert Anderson 115 Sam 21 Thomas G 21
RICKMAN, Peter 308

RIDDLE, Judith 170 Moses 309
RIDLEY, Allen 310
RIERSON, Josie 284
RILEY, Ben F 21
RISCHER, R 248
RISLEY, of Risley 214
RIVERS, John 14
RIVES, Robert 242 Sarah 116 William C 242
ROACH, W E 50
ROBEL, Capt 325 Owen 319
ROBERT, Bruce King of Scotland 145
ROBERTS, Alice 236 Augusta 240 James 14 324 Jeff 236 Minerva 236 Thomas 308 William 14 298 323 325
ROBERTSON, Anna Laura 272 Bettie 255 Ella 224 Jane 286 John 13 274 300 Laura 212 Miss 167 Mr 224 R R 260 S T 272 Virginia Magdalene 260 Wyndham 152
ROBEY, Virginia 267
ROBINS, J W S 48-49 Lena 49
ROBINSON, Annie 195 Capt 325 John Sr 308 Kate 330 Maj 34 Stephen 310 Susan 170
RODERY, Bell 168
RODGERS, Milly 237
ROGERS, David 308 312 Geo 308 Mary Frances 196 Peleg 13
ROLFE, Henry 151 Jane 151 John 150 Pocahontas 150 Thomas 151
ROMAN, John 294 Peter 294 Robt 294
ROSCOE, Delia 123 Wm 123
ROSENTHAL, Edward 55
ROSS, Daniel 309 313 319 Dicie 244 Ellen 245 Gen 81 190 John 309 Lee 244 Thomas J 21
ROT, Phillip 322
ROTZ, Christian 308
ROUBIES, Owen 308
ROWLAND, Andrew 252-253

ROWLAND (Cont.) Baldwin 104
189 191 252-254 314 328
Benjamin 253 Clarey 328 Creed
T 252 Dunbar 252 331 Elizabeth
104 189 191 252-253 328
Elizabeth Hampton 102 254
Enis 328 Eron Pha 253 Geo 309
Geo Jr 309 John 11 252-253 314
321 John Jr 252 328 John Sr 310
Judith 254 Kate Mason 254
Martha Hairston 129 Martha
Hampton 254 Mary 252 Matilda
252 Michael 13 189 191 252-253
308 313 322 328 Mike 294 Mrs
Dunbar 331 Robert 254 Ruth
104 254 Samuel 254 Sarah 189
191 253 328 Scolis 252 Thomas
252 William Brewer 252 Wm
313
ROWZIE, 46
ROYAL, Lizzie 232 239 W W 48
ROYALL, Cynthis W 329 John 309
RUBLE, Owen 14
RUCKER, Eliza Jane 116 Frances
232 Gideon 308 Joseph 116 Miss
224 Mr 232
RUFFNER, 44 Dr 180
RUNNELLS, Maj 294
RUSSELL, Wm 310
RUSSETT, William 324
RYAN, Lucy 327 Mary 328 Nathan
14 Philip 308 William 296 323
Wm 310 313
RYON, Wm 326
SALISBURY, Ambrose 214
Margarett 214
SALMON, Elizabeth 328 Hezekiah
298 313 John 295 298 309 311-
312 314 318-319 325 Nancy
Reynolds 162 Rowland 308
Thaddeus 328 W J 302
SALMONS, Bethenia 255 Betsy
Holt 254 Dollie 255 Dolly 138
Edmund 138 Eliza 138 255
Elizabeth 254-255 Fannie 332

SALMONS (Cont.) Geo 138
Hezekiah 254-255 309 James
254 Jesse 138 John 12 138 254
289 294 John Jr 254-255 Lou
138 255 Margaret 160 254
Martha 255 Mary 160 Nancy
Reynolds 160 Pea Ridge John
255 Polly 254-255 Rebecca Ann
255 Susan 255 Thaddeus 254-
255 Virginia 255 289 W J 290
Wm J 255
SAMS, James 308 Williams 323
SANDERS, 47 J R 48
SANDFORD, Geo 321 John 328
Judith 328
SANFORD, Peggy 326
SAUNDERS, Elizabeth 183 193
263 Fleming 298 Judith 191-192
254 Mrs 288 Mrs Flem 193 Peter
311-312 314
SAVANT, James 310
SCALE, Peter 320
SCALES, Daisy 261 Joe 261 John
Pinckney 261 Judith 261 Mary
O 260 Mrs J A 330 Sue 261
SCHLOTTLAND, Bros 38
SCHOOLFIELD, 46 Annie 257
Emaline Anne 256 Henry
Asmond 256 James E 48 James
Edward 256-257 James Lorenzo
256 John Harrell 256 Joseph 256
Laura Virginia 256 Lucy 257 M
E 217 Martha 220 256 Mary
Emeline 89 256 Mrs J H 329
Professor 100 Robert Addison
256-257 Sarah Ann 256 Sarah
Elizabeth 256 Susan 256 W M
47 William Henry 256 William
Miranda 256 Wm M 89
SCHRODER, Cornelia M 75 W H
75
SCOTT, 191 Wm 294
SCROGGINS, Humphrey 13
Thomas 13
SCRUGGS, Julius 309 Lee 21

SCRUGGS (Cont.) Riley 21
SEAMAN, Zachariah 309
SEAMORE, Lelia 212 Mary 222
  Thomas 222
SEARSEY, Robert 309
SEAWELL, Elizabeth 193
  Hairston 193 John 193 Louisa
  193 Mollie 193
SEAY, B H 21
SEGER, William 214
SELF, Mary 83 Silas M 21 Silas N
  83 W J 21
SELLERS, John 88
SELMOUR, Samuel 308
SEMPLE, 209 Baylor 249 George
  249 James 249 Kate 249
  Kathleen Eggleston 249 Lucy
  249 Mary Lavinder 49 Mary
  Peters 216 Mrs R B 37 57-58
  Muscoe 249 R B 37 Reamey 249
  Richard B 216 249 Susie 249
SERGEANT, John 309
SEWARD, Lena 140 Mary 209
SEWELL, Joseph 14
SHACKELFORD, Douglas 331
  Everett Bassett 290 Harriet 235
  J M 224 329 John A 264
  Margaret 264 Mrs John A 330
  Mrs W G 290
SHACKFORD, J W 48
SHACKLEFORD, W G 45 Wm 12
SHARP, Robert 298
SHAW, Josiah 12 314
SHEFFIELD, 51 Annie Coan 258
  Bettie 200 258 Catherine 258
  Catherine Matilda 184 Duke
  John 257 Elizabeth 258 Frances
  Jane America W 257 Henry 257
  James M 257 James R 258 Jesse
  257 John A 257 John T 258 John
  W 258-259 John Waddy 258
  Joseph 257 Judith 126 Judith
  Parks 184 Kate 258 Len 44
  Leonard 200 257-258 288 Loula
  225 257 Lucy 257 Lucy O 257

SHEFFIELD (Cont.) Lucy Owen
  288 Lucy Parks 258 Lucy
  Wootten 258-259 Mamie 258
  Mandy 258 Martha 119 Martha
  Ann 257 Mary 258 Nancy 257
  Nicholas 257 Sam G 225 Samuel
  G 257 Susan C 257 Susan E 259
  Thomas 257 W A 184 William
  126 257 William A 119 258-259
  William E 258
SHELBY, 188
SHELTON, 325 A N 21 Addie 261
  Adeline 261 Alcie Bobinreith 260
  Alfred 259 Anne Bailey 260
  Annie 261 Annie Wilson 260 Ben
  261 Beulah 261 Byrd 260
  Chester 261 Daisy 261 Dean 261
  Elephaz 13 Eliphaz 298 309 312
  Fanne 260 Fannie 111 259
  Fanny 261 Fredonia 260 Geo
  259 261 Geo Hunt 260 George 21
  George James 260 Henderson 21
  Hezekiah 294 James 12 21 111
  259 294 320 323 James
  Buchanan 260 James Lamar 260
  James Lamertine 260 James
  Taylor 261 Janie 260 Joe 261
  John 259 John Watkins 260
  Joseph 259 261 Judith 259 261
  Kittie Wootton 289 Laura 260
  Loula 222 Lucy 261 275 Lula
  260 Magdalene 50 164 238
  Magdalene Dupuy 260 Maggie
  261 Martha 261 Martha K 289
  Mary 259 328 Mary Elizabeth
  260 Mollie 261 Mrs Sam 330
  Nancy 111 259 Nancy Jane 260
  Narcissus 261 Nathan 259-260
  328 P H Sr 21 Pattie 153 259
  Peonia 259 Peter 153 164 222
  238 259 294 Peter Fowler 260
  Pines Henderson 111 259-260
  Polly 111 233 259 Rally 309
  Rebecca 260 Rhoda E 260 Ruth
  234 259 Ruth Stovall 260 Sallie

SHELTON (Cont.) 261 Sarah 75
 238 Sarah Martin 260 Susan
 203 259 Susan Louisa 260
 Thomas Marvin 260 Thomas
 Meade 260 Vann R 289 Virginia
 Magdalene 260 W A 330 William
 259 285 William P 261 Wm 294
 298 Wm A 260 Wm Henderson
 260 Wm Nathan 261
SHEPHERD, Adela Nash 155 J M
 330 J Moorman 185 Kent 155
 Kitty 185 Mary C 185
SHERMAN, Gen 22
SHERRILL, Sarah 171
SHORES, Richard 308
SHORT, David 309 Ed 312 John
 321 Wm 309
SHRINER, Janie Worth Martin
 331
SHROPHIRE, Wm 308
SHULTZ, Bessie Gray 84 Edwin M
 84
SHUMATE, Annie May 280 Betty
 239 Elsie 330 Joseph 239 Louise
 239 Martha 285 Martha Tolly
 246 Mary Jane 285 Miss 219
 Mrs N T 330 Mrs Whitney 330
 Norman Taliafeno 239 Russell
 285 Ruth Janet 239 Sam 21
 Samuel 12 W C 285 330 Wesley
 285
SIMMONS, Elizabeth Morgan 56 J
 W 330 John 308
SIMMS, J Marion 196 Theresa 196
SIMONS, Robt 323
SIMPSON, ---- 269 Annie 269
 Eliza 222 Hannibal 222
SIMS, Augustin 14 Bartlett 310
 Ignatins 309 Matthew 13 309
SISMONDS, Joseph 309
SKIDMORE, Isaac 14
SKULFEEL, 255 Aaron 256
 Benjamin 256 David 256 Enoch
 256 Jane 256 John 256 Rachel
 256 Samuel 256 Sidney 256

SLAUGHTER, Betsy 203 Sallie
 164
SLAWRON, Margaret 197
SLAYDON, Mrs W F 330
SLOAN, Mrs L 331
SMALL, John 309 Matthew 309
 311 315 326 Thomas 13 Wm 309
SMEAD, Mary Lavinia 184
SMITH, Alice Laura 110 Andrew
 Jackson 217 Annie 217 Anthony
 313 315 Barzellai 235 Beulah
 222 Charles P 118 Charles
 Purnell 262 Daniel 12 284 309
 Darrell 310 David 21 Dolly 177
 Edith 250 Edward 13 Electra 44
 262-263 Eliza 217 284 Elizabeth
 262-263 327 Elsie 211 Emily 217
 Frank 21 284 Gideon 309 319
 328 Grace Forest 219 Harry 111
 Harry Dillard 219 Henry 13 128
 298 309 Hugh 50 Ivey 56 J M 45
 118 J R 49 J T 217 James 110
 249-250 James M 21 247 302
 James M Sr 193 James Moss
 261-263 James Moss Jr 262
 James R 21 217 James Sr 47
 Jane 198 Janette 217 Jas M 302
 Jno R 57 John 12 21 177 222 249
 278 298 308-309 John R 329
 John Redd 239 262-263 Joshua
 18 40 43-44 Josiah 14 Judge 99
 Katherine 238 Laura 73 212
 Letitia 262 Lucy Bell 249 Lyne
 Starling 249 Maggie 219 Martha
 217 247 261 Mary 126 207 236
 328 Mattie 172 263 Mildred 281
 Miss Roy 56 Mort 73 Mrs Cabell
 55 Mrs Charles P 331 Mrs H C
 56 Mrs O C 56-57 Mrs Robbie
 Kyle 332 Munford 294 N Emory
 28 98 Nancy 284 Nannie Jane
 118 262 Nath'l 298 Nathaniel
 294 Nettie 139 O C 21 Patsy
 Pannill 239 Pattie 118 193 268
 Pattie Hairston 262-263

SMITH (Cont.) Pomp 49 Randall
308 Richard 238 Robert 284
Sallie 235 Sallie R 263 Sallie
Reamey 239 Sarah 227 284
Sarah Ann 111 Snow 268 Susan
217 231 284 Tabitha 111 217
Thomas 13 312 318 326 Tommy
284 Vincen 217 Virginia 157 W
C 263 W S 21 Walker 157 198
Watt Wade 219 Will 262 William
12 284 Wm 298 Wm Sr 308
Zachariah 308
SMITHSON, Miss 219
SMYTHE, J F D 10
SNEAD, Junius 134
SNEED, John 13
SNIDOW, Barbara 328 Phillip 328
SOLOMON, Elisha 310
SOUTHALL, Betsy 164
SOUTHGATE, Mattie 195 331
SPARROW, Belva 220 Jeff 220
Kathleen 220 Rose 220
SPENCER, 51 America 186 263
Ann Dillard 264 Annie 263-264
Billy 111 186 Blanche 264 David
Harrison 263 George Overton
263 Gerge Overton 264 Harrison
154 186 Hass 264 James 294
320 324 James Harrison 263-264
John 153 263 John D 264 Lizzie
263-264 Lucy 154 263-264
Maggie 263 265 Margaret Allen
264 Martha C 161 Mary 154 263
265 Mary Hold 264 Mary Waller
264 Mattie 263 265 Moses 12
153 Mrs J H 329 Nancy 124
Nathaniel 161 Peter 263 Rev 51
Robert Lee 263-264 Ruth 153
Sallie 227 263 Sallie Ann 111
Sallie Parks 186 Sally Ann 113
263 Sally Parks 111 Tobe 264
Wm David 263 Wm Clark 264
SPOTSWOOD, Gov 75
SPOTTSWOOD, Alexander 144-
145 Anne Butler 144

SPOTTSWOOD (Cont.) Dorothea
144 Gov 144 175
SPURLOCK, Jesse 309 John Jr
309 John Sr 309 Wm Sr 309
STACY, Elizabeth Rice 299 John
299
STALINGS, Jacob 13
STAMPS, John 310
STANDEFER, Israel 309 James
309 325 Jemima 328 Luke 320
322 Naomi 328 Sally 326 Wm
320 328
STANFORD, Maggie 261 W A 261
STANLEY, Abigail 265 Addie 266
Ann Pocahontas 266 Berta Ann
265 Berta Anna 265 Berta Annie
266 Bethenia 239 Burwell 21
Callie Matt 266 Charlie J 239
Clyde B 329 Crockett 265-266
Cynthy Ann 265 Edd 332
Gertrude 239 Helen Booth 266 J
H 331 James Jefferson 266 Jane
265 Jessie Roberta 110 265 John
14 309 John Walker 265-266
Joseph 328 Kellie Reed 266 Lucy
Matt 265 Martha 265 Mrs C J
332 Mrs J W 330 Nannie 265
Nellie Bee 266 Richard 309
Robert Hille 265 Robt Hillie 265
Royal 239 Samuel William 265
Sarah 328 Susan Matilda 265
Swin 331 Swin David 266
Thomas Bahnson 265-266
William Green 265 Wm 309 Wm
Jr 309
STAPLE, Ruth Penn 247
STAPLES, Caroline 177 Columbia
123 Dr 148 Geo 221 Jane O 123
John 268 281 298 Keziah 192
247 Lucinda 233 Martha 268
Mary 221 Mrs George 288 Polly
281 Ruth 165 Sam 123 Samuel
43 233 268 298 Sarah 192
Waller 192 Walter 43
STARING, Thomas 247

STARLING, Agnes 268 Alvis
    Daniel 267 Annie 247 267 Annie
    Preston 268 Ballard 267 Ballard
    Preston 268 Bettie Price 168 267
    E T 302 Edmund 268 Edmund
    Thomas 267 Elizabeth 267
    Floria 267 Hallie Brown 268
    Jane 266 Jane G 267 Jervin
    Daniel 267 John R 267 Josie Lee
    267 Leonard Anderson 267 Lyne
    267 Maria 267 Mary Anderson
    267 Miss 165 224 Overton 267
    Pattie 268 Permelia 267 Robert
    Anderson 267 Roderick 266
    Sallie Miller 267 Sally 266
    Susan 249 Susanna 266-267
    Thomas 266 Virginia 267
    William 266-267
STEGALL, William 21
STENNET, James 309
STEPHEN, Adam 319-320
STEPHENS, Adam 318 Dudley 13
    Harper 260 Hecter 327 Joshua
    13 Leany 327 Miss Woods 56
    Susannah 329
STEPTOE, Frances 132 Frances
    Callaway 133 James 132 James
    Callaway 133 Philip 132
STEVENS, Gen 68
STEWARD, Milly 328 William 316
    Wm 328
STEWART, George 13 William 13-
    14 322
STIGGLEMAN, Dr 229
STIMER, Rowland Ben 309
STOB, Jarrett 21
STOCKSTON, Richard 293
STOCKTON, 207 Charity 205
    Charles 125 Dolthien 329
    Edward 125 John 125 Mary 125
    Miss 284 Molly 125 Peter 125
    Sallie 206 Sarah Virginia 271
    Susan 125 Virginia 125 William
    125
STOKER, Martha 327

STOKES, Benton H 21 John 308
    John Jr 298
STONE, A J 21 Alvah 126 Annette
    252 Bessie Haymaker 218 C M
    218 Cassandra 126 Clack 126
    Daniel 186 301 Dink 124 Dr 201
    Edd 126 Elizabeth 328 Francis
    198 Harry 126 Harry B 330 J D
    21 J L 21 J O 21 James 21
    Jeremiah 298 John 328 Mamie
    126 Mary 201 328 Mrs 299 Mrs
    J S 332 Mrs R E 330 Nancy 124
    Nannie 126 Page 126 Polly 298
    Puss 198 R T 331 Reid 21 124
    Rev 51 Wm 328
STONEMAN, 54 284 Gen 22-23
STOVALL, Albert 268 Alexander
    269 Ann 268 Annie 269 B 298
    Bartholomew 268 Bettie 269
    Bonnie 269 Brett 268 Callie 269
    Christopher 269 Elizabeth 268
    Florence 221 269 Frances 220
    269 Francis 269 Geo 189 George
    152 268 J T 21 Jack 269 James
    94 233 245 268 James Read 269
    Jennie 269 John 245 John
    Manassa 269 Joseph 268-269
    Landis 269 Lucy Friend 269 M E
    329 Martha 268 Mary Green 269
    Mary Isabel 268 Melvina 269
    Miss 284 Mollie 233 268 Nancy
    268 Nancy Grayer 269 Pleasant
    A 268 Polly 268 Quince 268-269
    Read 268-269 Reed 245 Ruth 94
    189 191 233 268 286 Sallie 268-
    269 Sarah 152 Thomas 268 Tom
    269 Tone 269 Tony 245 Virginia
    269 W T 21 William Morris 269
STRANGE, James 13
STRATTON, Benjamin 12
STREET, Joseph 13
STREWSBERRY, Jeremiah 309
STRONG, Agnes 162
STROTHER, Bessie 200 Frances
    Banks 242 Sarah 242

STROTHER (Cont.) Susanah 242
  William Davney 242
STUART, Alexander 43 101 240
  Archibald 68 101 240 244
  Columbia 240 Elizabeth 240 244
  Henry Carter 240 J E B 43 68 81
  101 190 192-193 241 317 James
  Edward Banks 240 Sallie 222
STULTZ, A M 21 Abner 270 Abner
  Dennis 272 Achilles 272 Achilles
  M 270 Adam 269-270 Alice 271
  Amelia 270 Amy 270-271
  Anderson 270-271 Anna 206
  271-272 B L 21 Beechy 272 Ben
  21 270-271 Betsy 270-271 Betty
  272 Bob 272 Brice 270-271 284
  Calvin 271 Cassandra 136 270
  272 Clarissa 270 Daniel 271
  Davis 272 Delilah 270 272 Edd
  271 Eliza 271 Eliza Ann 272
  Emma 272 Frances 226 Frances
  Harper 98 272 Frances M 226
  Francis 271 Frank 272 G H 21
  Geo 271 Geo H 270 272 Georgia
  171 271 Girard 272 Henry 271-
  272 Ida 272 Isabella 272 J W 21
  Jack 211 272 James Achilles 272
  Jane 271 Janie 272 Jesse Davis
  272 Jim 272 Joe 270-271 Joe
  Abner 272 Joe King 272 John
  271 Johnson W 21 270 272
  Joseph 246 Jubal Early 271
  Judy 270 Julia 270 272 Katie
  272 Katy 270 Leatha Ann 246
  Lethy 270 Lou 272 Louisa 270
  Lucinda 270-271 Lucy 270 Lula
  272 Malinda 271 Martha Ann
  270 Martha Jane 270 Mary 269
  Mary Lou 272 Mattie 211 272
  Millard Filmore 271 Miss 179
  Miss Zeph 271 Mr 226 Nancy
  270 284 Nancy Missouri 272
  Nellie 270 272 Nelly 271 O M 21
  Orthniel 272 Othniel M 270
  Parmelia 271 Patsy 270

STULTZ (Cont.) Peter Hairston
  272 Peyton W 21 270 Polly 270-
  272 Roxy 211 Ruben Nance 272
  Rufus Janifer 271 Sallie Melissa
  272 Sally 270-272 Sam Johnson
  272 Sarah Virginia 271 Sarina
  270-271 Saunders 270 Shields
  272 Silas 21 Susan 270 Susan
  Frances 272 Synthy 270 T C 21
  Tamsy 271 284 Thena 271
  Thenia 270 Thomas 21 206 311
  Thomas Benjamin 272 Thomas J
  136 270-271 Thomas Leftwich
  270 Tom 272 Tyler 270 V L 21
  Virginia 272 Walter 272 Will
  272 William David 227 William
  Davis 98 270 272 William
  Marshall 272 Zephania 270
  Zephaniah 271
STUNSTALL, William 323
STURGEON, Enis 328
SULLIVAN, Beverly N 197 H L
  197 Virginia E 197
SULLIVANT, John 309
SULLY, 55
SUMMERDALE, Charles 13
SUMNER, Gen 316
SUMPTER, Gen 321 324 Geo 310
  Henry 309 Margaret 329 Wm
  329
SUMTER, Gen 315-316 John 309
SUTHERLAND, E J 332
SUTHERLIN, 278
SWANSON, Frances 327 John 310
  Miss 177 Nathan 310 316 Wm
  316 Wm Sr 310
SWILWANT, S Daniel 12
TANKERSLEY, Elizabeth 329 Geo
  329
TARRANCE, John 309
TARRANT, James 13 325 S 13
  Samuel 323 325
TARRANTS, Mary 321 Reuben
  321
TATE, Henry 13 309 Mrs R C 193

TATE (Cont.) Nathaniel 13 308
Robert 13 309 317
TATUM, Alice 236 Edw 298
Edward 12 294 309 Priscilla
Jane 234
TAYLOR, Adeline 261 274 Alfred
21 Alice 124 Ann 274 Betsy 270
Blagrove 273 Botts 274 Caroline
231 Catherine Ann 183 Col 84
Daniel 211 Daniel G 274 Daniel
Gray 275 Elizabeth 273 329
Elizabeth Ruth 240 Ella 275
Fannie 275 Fanny 240 Frances
Pannill 240 Geo 309 320 Geo W
275 George 273 299 George Sr
274 George W 274 Henry 275
Irene 212 J B 276 J C 111 J F Jr
21 J Judson 275 J P H 204 J W
B 274 Jack 273-274 James 273
309 329 James L 274 Janet 232
Jesse 275 Jesse Ben 212 Jesse R
330 Jessie Read 232 Joe 275
John 14 231 273 John Davis 240
John L 274-275 John Lee 329
John S 275 John Spotttswood
240 Jos I 276 Josiah 273 Josiah
F 274-275 Judith Ann 273 Kate
274 Katherine 232 Kittie Ann
273-274 L C 21 Lily 275 Lucy
245 274-275 Lucy Elizabeth 273
Maggie 275 Martha 211 275 328
Mary 155 231 274 Minnie 222
Mollie 275 Molly 327 Mrs J R 58
Mrs Richard 53 Nancy 274
Nannie 275 Pendleton 232 R
Reid 275 Rachael 299 Read 232
Reuben 273-276 Richard 242
Rosa 158 Ruth 204 275 Ruth P
274 Sallie 275 Sam 158 Sam
Frank 275 Samuel 273 Samuel
C 274-275 Sarah 242 274
Spotswood 273 Spottswood 274
Sunshine 212 Susan 162
Tabitha 111 Tom 275 Tom G 276
Uncle Billy 273 W A 40 46 183

TAYLOR (Cont.) W C 276 W F B
240 William 320 William A 273
William F B 273 275 Wm
Clayborne 240 Zachary 242
TEAFORD, Maria Jane 123
Thomas J 123
TEAGUE, H S 49
TECH, Hattie 237 Mr 237
TEMPLETON, Oneta Augusta 182
TERRY, George 231 Jake 21 Mary
Elizabeth 208 Misses 205 Ruth
231 Sarah 327 Silas Wright 172
William Parker 208
TERRYS, Misses 45
THESBY, Jesse 309
THIESEN, Mrs R J 280
THOMAS, 247 Augustine 308 329
Austin 317 Bettie S 330
Blackburn 139 C Y 172 301-302
Charles 308 Christopher 249
Christopher Y 108 Cynthy Ann
265 Deborah 329 Elizabeth 184
258 Faith 55 108 249 Frank 249
Frank W 108 Hope 108 249
Isabella 231 J A 47 James 265
James H 59 Jane 178 249 John
249 Julia C 170 Kate 108 249 L
S 49 L Starling 249 Lucie 249
Lucinda 203 Lyne Starling 108
258 Mary Ann 108 249-250
Matilda 172 Mrs Starling 37
Richard 231 Starling 184 Susie
49 108 Willie 269
THOMASSON, Arnold 160 G H
206 J R 21 Jane 286 John 310
John D 286 John S 21 Joseph
135 Lucinda 135 M 21 Maggie
286 Margaret 135 Mike 21
Phoebe 160 R W 21 S G 21 Sallie
Lou 206 W O 21
THOMPSON, Dolthien 329 Nellie
290 William 14 Wm 329
THORNTON, Dandridge 150 J W
150 Jane 207 Margaret 150
Martha Washington 150

INDEX

THORNTON (Cont.) Mary 150
Pattie Dandridge 150 Polly 138
THORP, Wm 308
THORPE, Selah 167
THRALKILD, Thomas 314
THRASHER, Annie Adelle 212 M 212
THRELKELD, Elijah 329
Elizabeth 329
THURMAN, Mrs 110 Sarah 256
TILLSTON, Francis 13
TILLY, Elizabeth 131 133
TINCH, Wm 308
TINSLEY, Miss 231
TINSON, Thomas 13
TITTLE, Anthony 309 Geo 309
John 309 Peter 13
TOOMBS, Edmon 293
TORRENTS, James 67
TOWLER, Anna 171
TOWNES, Ben Marshall 277
Benjamin Hairston 277
Catherine 276 Charlie Davis 277
Daniel Coleman 276 Daniel
Marshall 276 Edward 276
Edwin 277 Elizabeth 277
Florence Ann 277 Frances 276
Frank Davis 277 Frederick
William 269 George 276 George
Edward 277 George J 277
Harriet 276 Harvey 277 Helen
277 Ida 140 Ida May 277 J
Edward 276 Jabe 276 James
276-277 John Stephens 276 John
Willie 277 Kate 276 Lucy Ellen
277 Martha 276 Martha Jane
277 Mary 276-277 Melvina 269
Nathaniel 276 Nettie Willie 276
Pattie 277 Rebecca 276 Robert
276 Ruth 277 Sallie 276 Sarah
276 Stephen Coleman 276
Stephen Halcot 276 Stobie 277
Thomas J 276 William 276
Wilmoth 276 Zela 277
TRAVIS, John 46

TRAYLER, E R 101
TRAYLOR, 43 Albert Washington
129 Alfred 101 Celia 228
Edward 278 Elizabeth 278
Elizabeth Rowland 104 280
Frances 280 Frederick 278
George 278-279 Hill Mullins 228
Humphrey 278 330 Humphrey
Jr 278 J C 42 46-47 65 102 113
129 183 254 280 J H 102 129
280 James 278 Jere 280 Jerry
279 Joel 279 John 278 John C
128 218 John Cousins 99 279
John H 103 107 254 John
Humphrey 99 279 Jon H 228
Joseph 278 Judith 278 Lucy 279
Marjory 278 Martha 278-280
Mary 129 254 Mary Bailey 106
Mary Elizabeth 101-102 279
Matilda 228 Mattie 106 Patience
129 Robert 107 278-279 Robert
B 228 Robert Lee 130 Sarah 100
278 Susan 65 100-101 106 279
Susan E 104 T Patterson 129
Tabitha 106 128 279 Tabitha
Churchill 99 Thomas Humphrey
279-280 William 278
TREADWAY, Berta 172
TRENT, Charlie 220 Dolly 210
Eliza 220 George W 21 210 J D
21 James 210 James W 220
John 34 John B 288 John Tyler
210 King Benjamin 210 Kittie
288-289 Lillian 140 Martha 289
Marthy 210 Mary V 210 Mattie
S 289 Mollie 220 Pattie 288 Poet
G 44 Rachel 235 Ranseleer 36
Robert 220 Roxy 210 Sarah 220
Susan 236 Thomas F 21 Van R
289 Virginia 289 William 210
220
TROGDON, Joe L 136 Loula 136
TROTTER, Lucy 220
TROTTIE, Sarah Elizabeth 222
TROUT, Miss 136

TUGGLE, 47 Bessie 49 53 57-58 R
  E 330
TULLY, 326
TUNSTALL, Will 295 William 297
  325 Wm 309 314-315
TURMAN, Ben 309
TURNBULL, Lily 196
TURNER, Abednigo 309 Andrew
  244 Anna Laura 272 Annie May
  280 Ben 280 Bettie 272 C M 21
  C Roy 245 C S 54 245 Celestia
  280 Chas S 245 272 Clementine
  135 Conway 245 Douglas 245
  Drusilla 244 E B 142 E Homer
  280 Edward 251 Edwin 245
  Elizabeth 139 272 Elkanah 210
  Elkanah B 301 Ella 126 197
  Emma 280 F P 331 F Paul 171
  Geo W 272 Green 280 H C 21
  Harry 251 Howard 245 Irvin 126
  Isaiah 272 J H 21 J Platt 212
  James 135 Jesse H 126 Jessie
  182 John 309 320 John W 21
  Josiah 12 Lelia 126 Letitia 285
  Lillie 251 Lottie 126 Lou Ella
  280 Mable 245 Mallie Simmons
  280 Martha 244 Mary 126 203
  280 Meshack 244 Minnie C 245
  Morton 245 Murray 251 Myrtle
  212 N P 272 Nancy 139 Nannie
  245 272 Nannie Lee 280 Nat 21
  Nellie 251 Ninon 272 Noel 251
  Orrin 126 Robert E 280 Salie A
  244 Sallie 135 Sarah 251 272
  Shadrack 325 Sis 272
  Spottswood J 272 Susan 171 285
  Thomas Ira 280 Vera 245 W W
  331 Walter 126 Watt 126
  William 12 Willie Lee 280 Wm
  280 308 Wm H H 21
TUTTLE, Andrew F 200 Daisy
  King 200 Mrs Andrew F 331
TYLER, J Hoge 63 John 191
  Judith 214 Thomas 214
TYREE, E T 330

UNRUH, J G 48
VALENTINE, Lucy 331
VANDGRAFT, Leonard 324
VANWAGENER, Mrs 257
VARDEMAN, Peter 312
VARDENUM, Peter 309
VASS, John 231 Miss 257 Rachael
  231
VAUGHAN, Addie 266
VAUGHN, Annie Lou 218 Bunyon
  330
VERDEL, John A 299
VERNON, Adm 144
VIA, Alice 251 James 203 Kittie
  203 Polly 204
VIAL, Ann Eliza 118 Anne Eliza
  64
VINSON, Wm 309
WADE, Anderson 22 44 50 302
  Ballenger 298 Ballinger 207
  Chester 127-128 Emily 139
  Fanny 329 Henry 22 James A 22
  John 139 Jonadab 298 Mary 44
  Miss 216 Moses 329 Richard 298
  Sarah 111
WALDEN, Elisha 309
WALDIN, Joseph 13
WALES, C M 51
WALKER, Alice 228 Ann 177
  Arnold 140 Blanche 174 Eleanor
  170 Ellye 140 J A 22 170 J B 248
  Joel 310 John 310 Kate 115
  Lucy Catherine 228 265 Martha
  161 Minnie 284 Pattie 248
  Robert 228 265 Samuel 315
  Samuel S 118 Susan Matilda
  228 265 Virginia Spottswood 118
WALL, Catrina 222 Celia 222
  Charlie 222 Elizabeth Roseboro
  148 Granville 222 Hunter 222
  James 222 John 222 Mollie 222
  Mr 230 Muncey 222 Nannie 222
  Nannie Spottswood 148 Robert
  Edward 148 Sam 331 Samuel
  148 Sarah 148 Thomas 148

WALL (Cont.) Walter 222 Zachary
222
WALLEN, Elisha 325
WALLER, 47 Albert R 282 Ann
217 Ann W 282 Ann Winston
107 281 283 Annie 281
Benjamin 281 Carr 223 Dorothy
Jemina 281 Ed 330 Edmund 123
281-283 Eliza Finley 283
Elizabeth 223 281-282 Ella
Finley 282 Geo 247 298 310-311
313-314 318-319 325 Geo Jr 293
George 12 65 96 107 281-284 317
322 George E 22 George Jr 281
Granville 104 James Anthony
282 James Mourning 281 Jean
284 John 280-281 John Stephens
282 Judith A M 282 Laura 281
Leonard 281 Lewis S 282
Malinda 65 123 283 Margaret
282 Maria 123 282-283 Mary 96
247 263 281 Mary Eliza 282
Mary Mccauley 284 Mildred 281
Mrs S L 56 Nancy 281-282
Narcissus Jane 283 Patsy 282
Penelope 282 Polly 281-282
Richard 281 Sallie 95 238 249
281-282 Samuel G 282 Samuel
Sigmund 284 Sarah 223 282
Sarah Louise 283 Stephen 281
Thomas 281-282 Thos 223
William 281 William D 282
William Edmund 281 William
Lewis 284 Winston 282
WALTER, King Of Great Britain
295
WALTERS, Mary 172 Miss 281
WALTON, Jeremiha 287 Simeon
287 Tabitha 287
WANE, Samuel 13
WARD, Betsy 92 Jane 177 John
177 Nancy 92
WARE, John 329 Margarett 329
WARREN, Ambrose 14 Columbus
S 22 Henry 13 J S 22 Mary 277

WARREN (Cont.) Mrs Henry 246
Nannie 246
WASH, John 329 Nancy Frazier
329
WASHBURN, Janette 217
Shadrack 217
WASHINGTON, 11-12 76 86 104
156 162 249 Charles 122 Col
315-316 320-321 Frances 122
Gen 85 Geo 132 214 Geo
Augustine 122 George 10 176
Henry 103 Martha 122 143 Mrs
George 175 Samuel 132
WATKINS, Ann 154 Benjamin 163
Betsy 164 H S 22 Hairston 22
Harriett Amasia 163 Horsley 22
Jenny 154 John 125 163 228 260
274 Letitia 164 192 Louisa 193
Magdalene 163-164 Magdalene
Dupuy 260 Mary 163 Minnie 158
Miss 224 Nancy 164 228 Peter
W 164 193 Ptolemy Lefebre 163
Richard 154 Sam 158 Sarah
Holman 163 Stephen 13 Stephen
Dupuy 163 Susan 125 164
Susanna 163 Thomas 163-164
192 Wesley 22 William 154 Wm
22
WATSON, John 310 Martha
Hughes 155 Mary 269 Miss 147
P P 155 Robert 294 Robt 12
Thomas 13 Virginia 269
WATT, Sarah 154 William P 154
WATTLINGTON, Ella 247 John
247
WATTS, A 84 C E 47 Cornelia 84
WAYNE, Gen 156
WAYT, John 247 Mary 247 Sallie
197
WEAVER, Adolphus 285 Caroline
285 Mrs 331 Samuel 14
WEBB, 203 Betsy 198 Lucy 327
Merry 310 Morris 310 Sill 198
Thomas Jr 310
WEBSTER, 79 Daniel 251

WEBSTER (Cont.) Joseph 319
Mary 147 Miss 251-252 Reuben 12
WEEMS, Daisey 331 Daisy W 109
Mrs A J 331
WEISIGER, Nora Southall 182
WELCH, Thomas 14
WELLS, 46 Ann 285 Archie 246
Baker 261 285 Burwell 285
Callie 285 Caroline 285 Cora 215 David 285 Emma 284 Emma Jane 215 Fannie 285 Frank 269 284 Frank M 215 Geo 285 Harry 215 Isham 294 James 22 Jennie 269 John 22 37 261 285 310 314 317 321 Judith 170 Kittie 187 Letitia 285 Lou 285 Lucy 274 Luther E 329 Margaret 284 Martha 261 285 Mary Jane 285 Matilda 261 285 Matthew 314 317 320 Minnie 246 Mrs W D 119 Nannie 83 Norvell 284 Patsy 166 285 Robert 285 Rowland 284 Sallie 284 Sarah 284 Starling 166 285 Susan 285 Tamsy 271 284 Taylor 285 Thomas 187 285 Victoria 285 Virginia 219 285 W B 22 W H 22 Wm 22
WELTY, Gretchen 176
WERE, Miss 251
WESLEY, John 42 Susannah 100
WEST, John 144-145 175 Mary 83 Thomas 83 Unity 144 William 35
WESTERE, Henry 214 Sarah 214
WHEELER, 22
WHEELWRIGHT, Gertrude C 208 W H 208
WHITE, Ada 124 Col 320 Dr 84 Loys 329 N M 124
WHITECOTTON, Axton 12
WHITESIDES, Mr 85
WHITLOCK, Eliza 211
WHITTLE, 42 Francis Mcniece 43 Kennon 264 Lewis Neale 43

WHITTLE (Cont.) Mary Holt 264
Mrs K C 53 Ruth 165 S G 43 90 Stafford G 165 Stephen Decatur 43
WHITTRITT, James 293
WICKHAM, John 35
WIGGINGTON, C N 22
WILBORN, Bessie 149 Durward 149 James W 149 Marcus 149 Mary Pocahontas 149 Mrs L L 332 Willie 149
WILKES, John 14
WILKINSON, 269 Mary 269 Mary Flair 195
WILLIAM, King 144 164 Prince Of Orange 188 The Conqueror 120 146 164 252
WILLIAMS, 201 Alice 171 Alice Kennon 173 Ardena 109 C C 109 Catherine 276 Daisy W 109 Elam 281 Eliza 224 Elizabeth 326 329 Florence 136 Freda 165 H S 173 Hattie 44 Joseph 67 310 L T 48 Lewis 154 Lucy 154 Martin 225 Miss 279 Mrs H S 56 N W 298 Otho 316 Plummer 165 Ro 312 Sallie 281 Samuel 224-225 Susan 173 Virginia 117 193 Wm 310
WILLIAMSON, Amy 229 Blanche 264 Chas 160 Emmett 114 James N 264 Jesse 310 Julia 162 Nancy 329 Nannie Madison 114 Robt 329
WILLINGHAM, Abner 309 John 14 Thomas Sr 309
WILLINHAM, John 310
WILLIS, Daniel 310 Ebba 285 Geo 285 Joseph 310 L A 331 Luther 285 Mrs W T 330 Polly 210 Robert 285 Tom 285 Victoria 285 Virginia 285 W T 285 Wm 324
WILLS, Francis 180 Susan 205 Thenie 205
WILMONTT, Pleasant 302

INDEX

WILMUT, Caroline 155 Charles 155
WILSON, 86 Agnes J P 191 Albert 22 Catherine 264 Daniel A 34 Harris 310 J F 330 John 294 John Jr 13 John Sr 13 Lydia 326 Mary 196 Mattie 155 Miss 163 260 Nathan 329 Patsy 326 Peter 189 191 Robt 316 Ruth 189 191 Susannah 329 W C 22 W W 22 Woodrow 65
WIMBISH, Miss 242
WINGFIELD, Ann 177 227 Betsy 177 Charles 310 Charles M 227 Ellen Morton 219 Francis 227 H 22 Jane 177 227 271 John Wm 219 Julia 227 Louisa 227 Marshall 293-294 331 Mary 227 272 Miss 269 Sallie 227 Sally 227 Walter 227 William 227
WINGUFIELD, Martha 255 Mat 255
WINN, Andrew 22 Henry J 22 Mamie J 219 Robert B 219 T L 22
WINNINGHAM, Thomas 309
WINSTON, Celestia 280 Edm'd 294 Elizabeth 96 174 Martha 168 Mr 168 Mrs Richard T 329 Nora 195 Sarah 75
WINSUREID, Mrs Alvin 260
WIRT, 103 Mildred 298 William 298
WISE, 152 Colo 318 Lucy 152
WITHERS, Amy 270 Josie 232 Lucy 184 259 Mary 267 R E 117 173 232 Susan 173
WITHERSPOON, James 196 Mary 196
WITT, David 310 Jesse 14 294 324 John 310 Miss 166 Sylvanus 310 Tabitha 327 Wm 310
WITTEN, Cecil 174 Mr 232 Mrs A D 45 Polly 232
WITTY, Elizabeth 327

WOLSEY, 129
WOMACK, C T 48 Dr 49 Lena 49
WOOD, Mary 228 Virginia 228
WOODALL, John 310 316
WOODLEY, Kate 238 Sara Ann Catherine 238 Wm T 238
WOODS, Agnes 189 191 Agnes Ann 286 Annie Miller 286 Charles Carroll 286 Elizabeth 192 Elizabeth Hairston 286 Fanny 329 Francis 286 Geo 329 Hugh 313-314 329 Isabell 327 Jno 286 John 14 189 191 329 Josiah 14 286 Lucy 286 329 Robert 310 316 Robt 286 314 Sarah Ann 329 Sarrah Cotton 286
WOODSON, John 310 Maria 147
WOODWARD, E O 60
WOODY, Tolton 310
WOOTTEN, Bettie 263 Henry Clay 263 John Francis 247 John Taylor 247 Lucy 257 Lucy Dabney 247 Martha 247 Mary 247
WOOTTON, Annie 286 Bettie 288 Edward Knight 287 Frank Taylor 75 Henry Clay 288 Jack 288 Jane 288 Jeremiah 287 Jesse 50 287-288 John Francis 288 John Taylor 288 Kate 288 Kesiah 287 Kittie 288-289 Lucy 287 Lucy Owen 288 Martha 287 Martha Coleman 288 Mary Grief 288 Miles 287 Nancy 287 Nicholas 287 Overton 288 Polly 287 Richard 287 Robert 286 Samuel 287 Samuel Grief 288 Spottswood 288 Tabitha 287 Taylor 288 Thomas 287 Thomas I 46 Tobe 288 William 287-288
WOSBY, Zack 315
WRAY, Adam 289 Ann Eliza 218 Cassandra Ward 289 Sir Christopher VII 289 Coan 22

WRAY (Cont.) E A 289 E H 329 Ernest Hunter 289 Everett 331 Everett Bassett 290 Frank M 289 H L 22 Irma Virginia 289 James Iredell 289 James R 218 289 Jno L 289 John 329 Julia 290 Malinda 289 Martha 289 Mary 289 Molly 289-290 Mrs J I 290 Nellie 290 P C 289-290 P R 124 330 Peter R 289 Pinkey C 22 Pinkney C 289 Pocahontas 45 124 290 Rebecca 289-290 Virginia 289 W M 330 William 289-290 Wm S 289.
WRIGHT, Della 238 Elizabeth 238 Flora 165 John A 165 Matilda 228 Mr 228 238 Vera 238 W P 47
WROLFE, Rebecca 151 Thomas 151
WYATT, Douglas 161 Mary 260

WYATT (Cont.) Miss 136 Nancy J 161 Nannie Eleanor 246 Silas 22 V E 22 W T 22
WYTHE, Thomas 144
YAGER, John L 123 Pocahontas 123
YAN, Wm 317
YANCEY, William L 253
YARBER, Mary 280 Richard 280
YATES, A D 245 Loula 245
YELL, Nathaniel 309
YOUNG, Archibald 310 James 310 John 310 Tamesia 136 Wm 310
ZENTMEYER, Hattie M 234 Mrs E P 193 Mrs M L 56 P L 234 S Lou 159
ZIEGLER, Emily 203 John 203
ZIGGLER, Charles 198 Eliza 198 Jane 198 John 198 Mary 198

uct-compliance

www.ingramcontent.com/pod-product-compliance
Lightning Source LLC
Chambersburg PA
CBHW050326230426
43663CB00010B/1752